INDIAN LITERATURE IN CHINA

INDIAN LITERATURE IN CHINA
AND THE FAR EAST

By

PROBHAT K. MUKHERJI

GYAN

ISBN : 978-81-212-1644-9(HB)

First Published, 1931

Published, 2018

Published by

Gyan Publishing House
5, Ansari Road
Daryaganj, New Delhi-110002
Phone: 011-47034999, 9811692060
www.gyanbooks.com
E-mail: books@gyanbooks.com

Printed at: G. Print Process, Delhi.

To

Sri Rabindranath Tagore

"কত অজানারে জানাইলে তুমি
কত ঘরে দিলে ঠাঁই
দূরকে করিলে নিকট বন্ধু
পরকে করিলে ভাই।"

হে কবি তুমি দ্রষ্টা, তুমি মনীষী, তুমি স্রষ্টা,
কল্পনায় যাহা দেখিয়াছিলে,
ধ্যানে যাহা পাইয়াছিলে,
কর্ম্ম তাহা রূপ পাইয়াছে
বিশ্বভারতীর এই সৃষ্টিতে।
ধ্যান তোমার মূর্ত্তি পাইয়াছে
শান্তিনিকেতনের কর্ম্মে
কল্পনা প্রাণ পাইয়াছে
শ্রীনিকেতনের সৌন্দর্য্যে।

আত্মবিস্মৃত ভারতে তুমি প্রাচ্যের সঙ্গে তাহার
আত্মার নিবিড় সম্বন্ধকে পুনর্প্রতিষ্ঠিত করিলে ;
আত্মশক্তিতে আস্থাহীন জাতিকে বিশ্বের নিকট
গৌরবান্বিত করিয়া নূতন প্রাণশক্তি সঞ্চারিত করিলে।
প্রাচ্যের সঙ্গে অতীত ভারতের সেই
যোগসূত্রের ইতিহাসকে তোমারই নিকট উপস্থিত
করিলাম। আজিকার এই পূণ্য দিনের উৎসব প্রাতে
"প্রভাতের পরে দক্ষিণ করে
রবির আশীর্ব্বাদ"
বর্ষিত হউক।

প্রভাত
শান্তিনিকেতন
রবীন্দ্র জয়ন্তী
২৫ বৈশাখ
১৩৩৮

CONTENTS

PREFACE

The history of Indian Literature abroad is practically the history of the spread of Indian religions outside India. Earliest literature is religious literature.

The term 'Indian' has been used by western scholars to cover Sanskrit, Pali and Prakrit; some have even included the vernaculars of India. I have used the term 'Indian' in that comprehensive sense ; for the translations that appeared outside India were made not only from the classical languages, but from the old Bengali, Dardaic languages, central Asian dialects and even Elu.

The term 'Literature' used in the title of the book needs also a word of explanation. Pure literature does not seem to have gone to China: at least, there is no record of such works. The bulk of literature, that went outside India with the monks, was Buddhist. The majority of these books are unknown in India, because the originals are lost. It is well-known to the students of Buddhism that Pali and Prakrit were not the only vehicles of expression: Sanskrit came to be used largely as the literary language by the Mahayanists and even many sections of the Hinayanists used the same language. Several thousands of books were written in Sanskrit ; but these are almost all lost except those preserved in Nepal and one or two found here and there in India.

The history of this vast Buddhist literature written in Sanskrit, is generally cmitted from the orthodox history of Sanskrit literature and when dealt, only the extant books are described. Here is the first attempt at compiling the entire history of Buddhist Sanskrit literature as they are preserved in Chinese translation, whether the original is extant or extinct. There is little pretension to originality in the work ; the researches done by French, Japanese, English and Indian authors, have been largely utilized so far available in the Visvabharati Library and Calcutta Libraries.

The word Hindu has been used in this book in a sense not

ordinarily used by historians. There has been much confusion on the interpretation of the word 'Hindu.' It is generally believed that Hinduism is *a* religion : but it is well-known that till now no satisfactory definition has been advanced, which has been acceptable to all shades of beliefs. Opinions differ as to who is a 'Hindu and who is not. But there is no confusion of its meaning when we use it in the sense of Culture. Religion requires definition and dogma and Hinduism fails to fulfil it ; whereas the term 'Hindu culture' would cover a larger sphere and would include people and cult, which would otherwise fall outside the ken of definition. The heterodox Hindu who is not willing to believe in the socalled 'Hindu Dharma'—a term unknown in ancient books —would still like to be called a Hindu, because he admits the inheritance of Hindu culture.

Buddhism is not Hinduism—although Buddha has been made into an *avatara* by the Hindus, and many images and temples of the Buddha have been appropriated by the Hindus to their own advantage. But none can deny that Buddhism is the product of the spiritual realisation of one of the ancient sages of India, who flourished in the post-upanishadic era. Therefore we claim the Buddhist culture as the Hindu culture and the spread of Buddhist culture in China and other parts of Eastern Asia means the spread of the best that was in Hinduism.

It must be borne in mind by our readers that with the Chinese, the study of Sanskrit and Buddhism was not undertaken as an academic refinement or for an economic gain, but was studied with the intense sincereity of a devotee. Thousand of pilgrims from different parts of Asia came to India and the channels of communication of those days were neither attractive nor pleasant for such undertaking.

The study of Buddhism changed the life of millions : they explained the old texts with new interpretation. Thus a vast rich indegenous literature grew in Chinese. It gave rise to new thought movements and several sects grew in the East. Buddhism is still a dynamic force in China and Japan and the creative genius of the peeple is manifested by the rich literary production of the present age.

A word about the Chinese translation. Generally the translation was made with the help of interpreters, who had imperfect knowledge of the Buddhist terminology ; the translator himself, for his want of good knowledge of Chinese, could hardly detect the imperfect expressions used by the interpreters. It took them several centuries to develop a Buddhist vocabulary. The Chinese translations are not so literal as the Tibetan. Of course there are literal Chinese translations of Sanskrit texts ; but they are unreadable and a good Chinese scholar would hardly read them. The Chinese love literature and their literateur are very particular about the style. That is why, I believe, we find a book with several translations done at different periods. When the translation was undertaken at the instance of an emperor several boards were formed to superintend the work ; some to see the correctness of the interpretation of the Sanskrit text, some to see the use of correct ideoms and some to look to the literary finish of the whole. This, it must be admitted, is the best method of rendering one language into another, when the two are so different as Sanskrit from Chinese.

This book originally appeared in the Indian Historical Quaterly and subsequently taken reprint of the same and published in the Calcutta Oriental Series by my friend Dr. Narendranath Law. With his kind permission the book was made over to the Greater India Society, the publisher of the book. I must admit that the book would not have come out in its present shape, but for Dr. Kalidas Nag. I am greatly indebted to Prof. Sylvain Levi of Paris, Dr. G. Tucci of Rome and Dr. P. Bagchi of Calcutta. The valuable help that I obtained from them cannot de expressed in words. I am much indebted to my young friend Batakrishna Ghosh, who is now in Germany, for the great help he gave me in producing the book. To Pandit Vidhusekhar Bhattacharya, Principal Vidyabhavana, Visvabharati, I owe a good deal. He has been a 'never failing friend' to me and to so many others devoted to Chinese and Tibetan studies.

The book has been dedicated to *pujaniya* Rabindranath Tagore. It is not much known that it was Rabindranath who brought Prof. S. Levi from France to Santiniketan and inaugurated Chinese and Tibetan studies in the Visvabharati. It was he who in the modern times, went to China, to revive the ancient bond of union between these 'oldest' of civilizations after centuries of break of cultural contact.

The Greater India Society which is doing so many useful work in this line, is the outcome of that spirit which was kindled in the young scholars of Bengal specially those of the Calcutta University.

The last but not the least is the acknowledgement with thanks and gratitude of the handsome donation given by Mr. Yugolkrishna Birala, whose charity is wellknown in India for the printing of the book. Sincere thanks are due to Srijut Padamraj Jain for helping us in finding the financial help mentioned above.

Book-production is an art; but no book has so severaly fallen short of the standard as this book of mine. The book is full of minor mistakes, which should not have occurred, if the proof were carefully looked through. No critic need point out these to me; for I am fully alive to these and am really sorry for it. I have amply quoted, adapted and translated from the writings of sinologues, to whom I offer my sincere thanks.

Santiniketon
11 Sravan 1338
(27 July 1931) } Probhat K. Mukherji

Indian Literature in China and the Far East

CHINA

I. Earliest Contact

China is known to her inhabitants as *Chung-Kuo* [1] or 'the middle Kingdom,' and the inhabitants speak of themselves as the people of Han' in the North and as 'the people of T'ang' in the South. But in Europe they have been distinguished by different appellations. China is referred to as *Sinai* (*Sinae*) and *Seres*[2] by the Greek (and Latin) writers[3] and as *Cathay* by medieval European travellers. In modern times the country is known as *China* and

Origin of the word *China*

---

1. In ancient times the people called themselves commonly *Li-min* "Black-Haired Folk" and their country, *Chung-kuo*, the middle Kingdom, from the patriotic belief of the Chinese that their land is "the hub of the Universe." Other favourite names are *Hua-kuo* (the flowery kingdom) possibly from the name of the oldest of the sacred mountains in Shensi, *Chung-Hua* (the central flower), and *Szu-hai-nei* (within the four seas). The name for China generally used under the Republic is *Chung-Hua-Min-kuo*, literally, 'Middle Flower, people country' *i.e.* The Republic of the Middle Flower', Gowon—*An Outline History of China* 1, p. 10.

2. The *Periplus* reads :

"After this region under the very north, the sea outside ending in a land called this there is a very great inland city called Thinae, from which raw silk and silk yarn and silk cloth are brought on foot through Bactria to Baraygaza, andlare also exported to Damirica (Tamilakam-Draviḍa or Tamil country) by the way of river Ganges. But the land of This [Ts'in] is not easy of access; a few men come from there and seldom. The country lies under the Lesser Bear, and is said to border on the farthest parts of Pontus and the Caspian Sea, next to which lies Lake Maeotis ; all of which empty into the ocean."—Translated by W. H. Schoff—1912, p. 48.

3. G. Cœdès *Textes d'auteurs grecs et latins relatifs a l'Extreme-Orient*... Paris 1910, Intro. p xxiv. "Le pays des Sinai correspond ainsi au Tonkin et à la partie meridionale de la Chine, et la capitale des Sinai situé au nord-est de Kattigara est manifestement l'ancienne capitale Lo-yang, aujourdhui Ho-nan-fou."

the people as Chinese throughout the western world, except in Russia, where they use the medieval designation in the form *Khitai.*

The word *China* is probably derived from *Ts'in* the name of a dynasty, which ruled over China from B. C. 249 to A. D. 220. [1] Yule suggests that the name of *Sin*, *Chin*, *Sinai* (*Sinae*) etc. reached the West by the southern sea-route, and the name *Seres* by the nothern land-route of Asia [2]. He further says that the name China "probably came to Europe through the Arabs [3], who made the China of *the farther East* into *Sīn*, and perhaps sometimes into *Thīn*. Hence the *Thinai* of the author of the *Periplus of the Erythrean sea*,[4] whose appears to be the first extant work in which this name has been employed in this form; hence also the *Sinae* and *Thinae* of Ptolemy" (*ibid*) [5].

Sanskrit literature abounds with references to China (Cīna चीन) ; but as the chronology of Indian books is very difficult

---

1. But this point is not yet settled. B. Laufer rejects this theory of the dynastic origin of the name *China* ; he is of opinion that the word 'China' was imported into China and later identified with Ts'in. The word according to him is of Malaya origin, see *T'oung Pao*, 1912, p. 719-726. But Pelliot holds the older view, which is corroborated by a Central Asian inscription of the second centnry A.D. where the word *Tsin-jen* or man of Ts'in occurs. See L'origine du nom de 'Chine', *T'oung Pao*, 1912, p. 727-742, also *BEFE-O*, 1904. p. 33-36.

2. *Enc. Brit.* (11th Ed), vol. VI. p. 188: But compare : *Ar-si* written as *An-si* in Chinese : possibly *Sin*=*Ser*.

3. "In the form of Tchina the name was carried, it is said, by Malaya traders to India and other lands in the West." Gowen *loc-cit.* p. 9

4. The word *Seres* is said to be derived from the ancient form of the Chinese word *ssi* which means silk. The ancient Chinese form of *ssi*, which evidently had a *r* at the end, became in Korean *Sir*, in Mongolian *Sirkek*. Hence the Greek *Ser*, Latin *Sericum* from which English *Silk* is also derived. From this word the name *Seres* was applied to the peoples through whose lands the product came: by which must be understood not the Chinese alone, but all the intermediary Turkish and Turanian tribes, See Schoff. *ibid.* Note p. 266.

5. Some late Greek writers use *Tzinista* which seems to be a corrupt form of Sanskrit *Cīnasthāna.*

to fix, we cannot definitely say how early the Hindus came to know of China. The *Mahābhārata* mentions the name several times [1], so does Kālidāsa in his works [2]; Kauṭilya [3] knew China; Caraka, Varāhamihira also mention the Cīna people among the peoples inhabiting north-west India. One of the earliest references in Indian literature other than Sanskrit is met with in the Pāli *Milinda-Pañho* [4], a well-known ancient work of the 1st. cent. A.D. In the Chinese translation of the *Sūtrlaṁkāra*, a work ascribed to Aśvaghoṣa, *Ta-Tsin* is mentioned [5]. Some of the Tāntrik texts speak of *Cīnācāra* and *Mahā-cīna* and Tibet is very often mentioned in Tāntrika literature. However on account of the uncertainty of Indian chronology we cannot fix any particular date of the earliest references to China: but we might be allowed to pronounce definitely that it was hardly beyond the beginning of the Christian era.

Cīna in Sanskrit works

But the knowledge of the Chinese about India is more definite. In Chinese the general term used for India is *T'ien-Chu*: but the old names were *Shen-tu* or *Sien* (or *Hsien*)-*tu*. The earliest use of *Shen-tu* was made by the Chinese envoy Chang-k'ien (B. C. 123) (see below). It is the opinion of Chinese writers, adopted and repeated by western scholars, that the *Shin-tu* of Chang-K'ien was India. It has been held that all the other

Chinese names for *India*

1. See Sorenssen—*Index to the Mahābhārata* pp. 175-176. In *Mbht.* the *Cīnas* are referred to as a people sprung from Vaṣiṣṭha's cow. They are mentioned with the *Kirātas* and *Bālhī(ka)*, *Yavanas* and *Kambojas*. The *Cīnas* brought presents at the *Rājasūya* sacrifice of Yudhiṣṭhira. On the way from Himālaya to king Subāhu the Pāṇḍavas crossed the country of the *Cīnas*.

2. *Cīnāṁśuka* is met with in Kālidāsa's Śakuntalā and Kumārasambhava; *Cīna* is also met with in the Raghuvaṁśam.

3. Kauṭilya—*Arthaśāstra* Book II. chap II. *Cīnasī* some kind of apparel is mentioned.

4. *Milinda-Pañho* (IV. 1. 46) Cīna-visaye Cīna-rājā...p 121 also *SBE* vol. 35. p. 182.

5. Aśvaghoṣa—Sūtrālaṁkāra, traduit en francais sur la version chinoise de Kumārajīva par Ed. Huber...Paris, 1908, story 90. The merchant of Takṣaśilā, who is enriched in the country of *Ta-tsin*, p. 461; but here *Ta-tsin* signifies the Roman Empire.

designations for India in Chinese books such as *Hien-tu*, *Kan-tu*, *Kuan* (*Yuan*)-*tu*, *T'ien-chu*, *T'ien-tu* and *Yin-tu* are only phonetic corruptions of *Shen-tu*[1]. Hiuen Tsang pretends to give the correct pronunciation as *Yin-tu*. The learned Chinese traveller explains *Yin-tu* as Indu, which in Sanskrit means 'moon.' But this is a clear instance of wrong etymology learnedly explained. The most usual name for India is however *T'ien-chu* and *Chung-T'ien*.

Earliest Sino-Indian contact

The earliest story of Sino-Indian contact is connected with the Emperor Hiao-Wu (140-80 B. C.) of the early Han Dynasty. We read that about B. C. 121 an image of some deity was secured in Central Asia and brought to China. It is said to have been brought by a victorious general from a Hun chieftain, who was in the habit of worshipping it. This image was indeed one of Buddha.[2] It should be observed that during this period the Chinese began to come in contact with the Central Asian peoples. Recent archaeological discoveries in Central Asia further corroborate the same, and we learn that an Indian colony with Buddhists population was in existence even in the second century B. C.[3].

In the Annals of the Early Hans, India[4] is mentioned by name for the first time as *Shen-tu*. In the year 125 B. C. a Chinese ambassador named Chang-k'ien[5] returned from Central Asia and brought information about western countries such as *Ta-yuan* (Ferganah), *Ngan-si* (Parthia), *Ta-hia* (Bactria) etc. Among other things he said that when he was in the country of *Ta-hia* he saw

---

1. Watters *On Yuan-Chwang*; vol. I. p. 131-141, where the origin of the Chinese names for India has been discussed in detail.

2. Giles. *Confucianism and its rivals*—Hibbert Lectures.. p. 165-10.

3. Chavannes—*Les documents Chinois decouverts par Sir. A. Stein*; 1913. Introduction. Also, Charles Elliot—*Hinduism and Buddhism* vol. III...

4. 'India' is a Latin word derived from the Greek Indos or India used for the people. The Greeks seem to have got it from the Persians ; in old Persian *Hendu*, *Hindu* (Skt. Sindhu) means India.

5. Chang-ki'en was sent by Emperor Hiao. Wu (140-80 B.C.) to the Yuch-chi and was taken pris oner by the Hiung-nu. He was abroad from 139 to 127 B. C. Cordier—*Melanges d'histoire et la geographie Orientales*. vol. II. p. 14.

bamboo staves from the Chinese provinces of Yun-nan and Sse-Chaan. On asking as to the place of thoir origin he was told that they were brought from southern China through the rich and powerful country of *Shen-tu* [1].

In the *Annals of the Liang dynesty*, we are told that during the time of Emperor Ho (89-105 A. D.) of the Han Dynasty several embassies from India came to China through Central Asia. Afterwards under Huan-ti (147-167 A. D.) the embassies from India came by the southern seas. (Pelliot—*Le Funan*, *BEFEO*, 1903, p. 27).

Wei-lio refers to Buddha.

The first historical reference to the introduction of Buddhism is met with in an historical work called *Wei-lio* written between A.D. 239 and 265. It gives a history of the Western countries of China and furnishes a brief account of Buddha's birth and states that in the year 2 B. C., an ambassador sent by the Emperor Ai to the court of the Yüeh-chi prince, was taught orally some sacred texts (i. e., Buddhist Sūtras) by the order of the king [2]. Later Han Annals also inform us that the Prince of Chu was a Buddhist and that there were *Śramaṇas* (monks) and *Upāsakas* (lay disciples) in his territory [3].

Emperor Ming-ti (A. D. 58-75)

The starting point of Sino-Indian intercourse is generally put at A. D. 64 [4]. The legendary chronicles tell us that the Emperor Ming (A. D. 58-75) of the Eastern Han dynasty (B. C. 20-221 A. D.) once dreamt that a golden man came flying into the palace, and the Emperor then enquired of his courtiers the meaning of that dream, one of them immediately informed him that it was the sage of the west, called Buddha *Fo* or *Fo-to* (*F'o-Bhyuwat* in

---

1. P. Bagchi—*Le canon Bouddhique en Chine*, Paris, 1927. Intro. p. viii. also Edkins—*Chinese Buddhism*--pp. 88-89.
2. Chavannes—Les pays d'occident d'après le Wei-lio *T'oung Pao* 1905, p. 519 ff. Chavannes has translated the Chinese text with copious notes which should be studied by all students of Central Asian history. Fr. Hirth has quoted extensively from this Chinese text in his work—*China and the Roman Orient*.
3. Elliot, *Hinduism and Buddhism* vol. III p. 245.
4. Chavannes, *op-cit. T'oung Pao* 1905, p. 546.

early Chinese, used to render the Indian word *Buddha* or *Buddh.*) Ming-ti was so much impressed by the dream that he sent an embassy consisting of Ts'ai-Yin, Ts'in-King, Wang-Tsuan and others to India to bring Buddhist scriptures and priests. The party returned in A. D. 64 with two Indian monks named in Chinese Kia-yeh Mo-t'ang and Chu Fa-lan (Kāśyapa Mātaṅga and Dharmaratna).

Thirteen accounts of this legend have been dealt with at length by Maspero ; Pelliot speaks of a few more [1]. According to these accounts the envoys returned with the monks to Loyang, where they were installed in a monastery called *Pai-ma-sse* or *the White Horse Monastery*, from the fact that these Hindu monks came to China riding white horses or with scriptures and images on the back of white horses. The event of Ming-ti's dream (if it is to be accepted as an historical fact) and the consequent return of the envoy have been variously dated by Chinese writers in the years ranging from 61 to 75 A.D. The return of the mission is generally put at A.D. 64.

But there have been attempts on the part of pious Chinese Buddhists to stretch the history of Buddhism in China to a hoary antiquity. The Taoists who were a very powerful sect in China were averse to the introduction of the new faith from a foreign land, which greatly wounded their national pride. They launched propaganda against the Buddhists and tried to belittle Buddha in the eyes of the Chinese. They concocted fanciful stories about Buddha to show that Buddha was junior to Lao-tzu. The Buddhist enthusiasts retaliated by fabricating similar stories about Lao-tzu. A Chinese

Taoists and Buddhists

work called *Hua Hu-King* which describes the conversion into Buddhism of a foreign people generally called in the Chinese texts: *hu* i. e. barbarian, has been long lost. But this book has been quoted by the Taoists to prove the antiquity of Lao-tzu [2]. Sectarian historians wrote works or quoted from

1. *BEFE-O* 1906 p. 394 f IV.
2. Pelliot—Les Mo-ni et le Houa-Hou king *BEFE-O*, 1903. p 318 ff. It has been said that Lao-tzu went to (Ki-pin) Kashmir but could not see

works which they alleged to be ancient books to show the antiquity of Buddha and the introduction of Buddhism into China. Giles refers to such a Chinese Buddhist writer of 11th century A. D. who has quoted a few semi-historical texts. We are told that in the year 216 B. C. a Buddhist priest Shih Li-fang and others arrived at the Chinese capital bringing with them, for the first time, Sūtras written in Sanskrit. A later work states more definitely that the company consisted of eighteen priests. In a work of the sixth century A. D. it is stated that "those books had long been circulated far and wide, but disappeared with the advent of the Ts'in dynasty." It is further told that books were burned by the order of Shih Huang-ti [1], the first great Emperor of China, of the Han dynasty to stamp out the opposition of the literati [2].

Vague rumours of 'a divine teacher in the west' had probably crossed the deserts of Central Asia and penetrated into China, and Ming-ti, who might have heard of such tales from his courtiers, sent an envoy to which we have already referred.

Unreliable antiquity

But anyhow the whole story of this early Sino-Indian contact should be taken critically and with reservation and too much importance should not be attached to it.

The earliest Chinese work on Buddhism is the *Sūtra of the 42 Sections*, attributed to the first Indian missionaries Kāśyapa Mātaṅga and Dharmaratna, referred to in the legend of Ming-ti's dream. Maspero who studied the Chinese text of the Sūtra in the three existing recensidns as well as all the Chinese literature relating to it, has completely demolished the traditional history of Ming-ti's embassy to India for Buddhist books. Although he does not believe in the story of the embassy and the legend of the dream, he could not brush aside the authenticity of Mātaṅga's translation. He says: "*The Sūtra of 42 Articles* passes for the earliest Buddhist work in Chinese,

Buddha, and he was very sorry. Lao-tzu admits that Buddha is his master, see Chavannes, Les Pays d'Occident d'apres le Wei-lio. *T'oung Pao*, 1905. p 537 f. IV.

1. Shih Huang-Ti, B. C. 259-210. See Giles, *Chinese Biog D'ict* No 1712.
2. Giles, *Confucianism and its rivals, loc. cit.*

and it is attributed to Mātaṅga and Chu Fa-tan. There is no reason to doubt the authenticity of this attribution ; in any case the book is very ancient ; a phrase of an article from this book is cited in the memoir presented by Siang-Kiai, and the title is mentioned by Meu-Tseu (see below). At that epoch it was considered to be an important work, for it was re-translated in the middle of the third century by Che-K'ien"[1]

Chinese translations: Kia-yeh Mo-tang.

Kāśyapa Mātaṅga, according to the legend, was a native of Central India ; he was a great adept in the Hīnayāna literature. It is said that he had gone to Southern India to preach the *Dharma.* His companion Dharmaratna was also a native of Central India and a man well-known for erudition. There remains to us from these two men a single pamphlet, and Chinese titles of four lost works[2].

Their literary work.

Mātaṅga and Dharmaratna "did not translate Indian treatises in their entirety, 'but set forth briefly the fundamental doctrines of Buddhism." They gave in the *Sūtra of the 42 Sections*, (1) a summary of the legends concerning the birth and infancy of Buddha ; (2) a summary of his teachings ; (3) a short statement of Buddhist principles ; (4) a summary of a discourse by Buddha on the purity of life required by the monks ; (5) a summary of the rules of asceticism to be followed by aspirants to perfections[3].

'Sūtra of the 42 sections.'

This *Sūtra* is interesting to us at least for two reasons : firstly, it throws some light on the development of Buddhism in India from the passing of Gautama Śākyamuni to the first century A. D.,

1. H Maspero—Le Songe et l'ambassade de l'Empereur Ming. (*BEFE-O* 1910, pp. 95-130). Hackmann, who has translated the work recently in *Acta Orientalia,* Vol. V, part iii, 1927, p. 197-237 and has studied the Sūtra thoroughly, does not reject the story as a 'pious legend' ('quelques legendes pieuses de la fin du IIe siecle' of Maspero); he says : Es scheint mir, dass das Urteil nicht so negativ auszufallen wie Maspero meint. Ibid. p. 198

2. See *BEFEO* 1910 p.115, Quoted from *Kao-seng- chuan.*

3. (Wieger—*History of the Religious Bsliefs and Philosophical opinions in China :* Translated from the French by E. C. Werner. Hsien-Hsien, China, 1927, p.343. Henceforward cited as Wieger).

when this work is said to have been introduced into China. Secondly, it allows us to see what the first Buddhist preachers thought best to introduce as the most essential doctrines of Buddhist faith in a land where K'ung-Fu-Tzu (Confucius) and Lao-Tzu were revered. This work does not seem to have existed in the original Sanskrit; but the intelligent translator extracted passages from different Buddhist canonical works.[1]

Summary of the work

This Sūtra is the first Indian work that was translated into the Chinese language and a careful study of this work will be of great value. A few quotations from this work will illustrate the nature of the work:

"The Buddha said, 'He who has left his family to follow the Law, is called (Sha-men) śramaṇa. He observes two hundred and fifty rules. According to the effort made and the purity acquired, four stages can be attained.

"The highest stage, that of the *arhan* (a-lo-han), confers the power of flying in the air and of transforming one's self at will. The second stage is that of the *anāgamin* (a-nan-han).[2]

"After death, the soul of the *anāgamin* ascends to one of the nineteen heavens, where it will attain the stage of *arhan*. The third stage is that of the *sakṛdāgamin* (ssu-to-han). After his death the *sakṛdāgamin* will ascend to one of the heavens, be born again and become an *arhan* on the earth during its first terrestrial life. The fourth stage is that of the *srotāpanna* (hsu-to-heng), who will become an *arhan* after seven deaths and seven re-births.

"The śramaṇa does not shave, renounces all property, begs his food from day to day, passes the night under a tree and never

1 Suzuki thinks that the book was compiled in the model of Confucian *Analects*, in which each chapter begins with the saying "The Master said", while in the Sanskrit work it is "The Buddha said." See *Sermons of a Buddhist Abbot, Chicago, 1908.* But in Sanskrit books this method is not unknown.

2 For explanation see Mc Govern, *Introduction to Mahayana Buddhism*, London 1922, p. 100.

two nights under the same. And all that, in order to extinguish affection and desire, which bind and infatuate human beings.

"Good conduct, according to the Law, requires that the ten rules should be observed." Then the ten rules are laid down. About *pāpa* and *puṇya* the author says : "Every committed fault, which man approves of and does not condemn, becomes a sin, which is carried to his debt. Multiplied sins are added, one to the other, as drops of water form the ocean. Whoever would progress, must force himself to wipe out his sins, day by day, by good actions." About the attitude towards the evil-doer, it is said, "One must consider that the wrong-doer is ignorant, not malevolent, and do good to him." "The great law," the Buddha said, "is universal affection, compassion for all, consistently to do good to others, to rejoice in it and praise it ; thus one shares the merits of others." Five things are declared difficult to attain : (1) It is difficult for the poor to practise charity ; (2) it is difficult for the rich and strong to observe the *Dharma* ; (3) it is difficult to disregard life and go to meet certain death ; (4) it is only a favoured few that get acquainted with a Buddhist Sutra ; (5) it is difficult to see with one's own eyes a living Buddha.

Another passage speaks of the impermanency of the world, and in another, monks are warned against meeting women. In brief, this short treatise gives one at once a complete idea of Buddhism, which was a need of the hour in a distant land like China.[1]

1 Bibliography of 'Sūtra of the 42 Sections'

This Chinese book has undergone many editions and revisions. Che K'ien is said to have made a second translation of this work in the middle of the third century A. D. In the Kyoto Edition of the Tripiṭaka, five commentaries, all by Chinese authors, are preserved (Bagchi, *op. cit.* p. 6). The Chinese version of the text was greatly modified since the T'ang dynasty.

The *Sūtra of the 42 Sections* was translated into *Tibetan* by Dkah-bcha Subhagan Sreyadhvaja, Dkah-bcha Dhyānarishtam Vyāsa. It was translated into the *Manchu* language by the order of the 'High One guarded by Heaven.' It was rendered into the language of Sog (*Mongolian*) by the learned professor Prajñodaya Vyāsa.

The Tibetan version of Mātaṅga's work has been thrice translated into three European languages :

(1) A. Schiefner, Das buddhistische Sūtra der Zweiundvierzig Sätze, aus dem Tibetischen übersetzt. *Bull. Acad. Imp.* St. Petersberg. IX. 1852. 65-78.

Kāśyapa Mātaṅga did not translate many works and he 'concealed his good understanding from the people,' but Dharma-ratna (ChuFa-lan[1]) was more zealous in his literary activities and five translations, all lost, are attributed to him. From the Chinese titles, various conjectures have been made as to the original works in Indian language. It has been suggested by some that his *Fo-pen-hing-king* was the translation of the *Buddha-Carita*, while others hold it to be the *Lalita-Vistara*; but both the theories are sharply criticized and denied by many. His other works too are hopelessly lost and various have been the opinions of scholars as to their original forms. It is not necessary in our broad survey of the history of Indian literature in China to go into the details of these discussions, the basis of which is very uncertain.[2]

---

(2) Leon Feer, Le sūtra en Quarante-deux articles : Textes Chinois, Tibetain, Mongol, Manchu autographies, Paris, 1868.

(3) W. W. Rockhill, The Sūtra in Forty-two Sections from the Tibetan, *Proceedings of the American Oriental Society*, Oct. 1880; also see *Ind. Ant.* 1882, pp. 295-296.

There is a French translation of the Mongol version : Gabet et Huc, Les Quarante-deux points d'enseignements etc., traduit du Mongol, *Journal Asiatique* 1848, pp. 535-557.

From the Chinese of Mātaṅga several translations in modern European languages have been made:

(1) De Guignes, *Sūtra en 42 articles* (Histoire des Huns, 2[e] part, Tome 1, pp. 227-233).

(2) Ch. de Harlez, Les Quarante-deux Leçons de Bouddha ou le *king* des XLII sections, Texte Chinois avec traduction et notes, 1899.

(3) S. Beal, *Catena of Chinese Buddhist Literature*, pp. 188—203.

(4) Soyen Shaku, *Sermons of a Buddhist Abbot*, Suzuki's translation, pp. 3-24, Open Court, Chicago, 1906.

(5) L. Wieger, *Religious Beliefs and Philosophical Opinions in China*, pp. 345-350. See also the French original.

(6) Hackmann, Die Textgestalt des Sūtra der 42 Abschnitte, *Acta Orientalia*, 1927, pp. 197—237. Critical study of the text with a German translation.

1 Chu Fa-lan: *Tien-chu* in Chinese means *India*; generally *Chu* is used to denote the Indian origin of the translators. *Fa* in Chinese means *Dharma*, but *lan* is a transliteration of *raññа* or *ratna*. See *T'oung Pao*, 1919, p. 344; also Bagchi, p. 5. In Tibetan the word Chu Fa-lan has been read as a transliteration of Gobharana or Bharana. But this is purely a 'sound' philology. See *JASB*, 1882.

2 Bagchi, *op. cit.* pp. 7-8.

The pioneer work of Mātaṅga and Dharmaratna does not seem to have had any far-reaching influence in China. They were probably not known beyond the walls of the *Pai-ma-sse*, if it had at all been built at the time we are speaking of. We should not, however, exaggerate the importance of their work, for the earliest catalogue of Tao-an (see below) does not mention the *Sūtra of 42 Sections*; neither are the works of Dharmaratna mentionec in it.

The value of the literary works of the pioneers is doubtful

But it should be noted that Tao-an compiled the catalogue in South China, and there is nothing surprising if a work translated in the North escaped his notice.

II. China's Contact With Central Asia

The real contact of China with the west, i.e. with Central Asia, began about seventy years after the first alleged mission of the Indian monks. China had already come in touch with the Iranian countries of the west, towards the end of the second century B. C., when Chang K'ien came back to China in 126 B. C. with informations about the adjoining countries of Central Asia after concluding an alliance with the great Yueh-chi tribes against the Hiung-nu. In 114 B. C. the first çaravan left China for the western countries [1].

Parthia—a Budhist country

Parthia or the ancient Persia, had at this period come to the forefront of the political history of Central and Western Asia. Parthia was known to the Chinese as An-si from the name of a dynasty called Arsacidan, ruling over Parthia in the first century B. C. The characters for An-si in ancient Chinese pronunciation seem to have had the sound *Ar-śak (or *An-śak). Parthia [2] was at this time taking an important part in the international commerce of Asia. Chinese silk passed to the Roman market through Parthia.[3] The Chinese people soon came to know

1 Cordier, *op. cit.* p. XII. refers to Richtofen'. *China*, Vol. I. pp. 455 and 475.

2 See Smith. *Early History of India*, p. 234 (4th ed.).

3 "They [the Romans] traffic by sea with *An-si* (Parthia) and *Tien-chu* (India), the profit of which trade is tenfold ... Their kings always desired to send embassies to China, but the *An-si* (Parthians) wished to carry on trade with them in Chinese silks, and it is for this reason that they were cut off from communication. This lasted till the ninth year of the Yen-hsi period during the Emperor Huan-ti's reign (= A. D. 166) when the King of *Ta-ts'in* (Rome) An-tun (Marcus Aurelius Antoninus) sent an embassy which, from the frontier of Jih-nan (Annam) offered ivory, rhinoceros horns and tortoise shell. From that date (A. D. 166) dates the (direct) intercourse with this country." This is from the Annals of the Han Dynasty of China, Chap. 88, Section *Hou-Han-Shu*, partly written during the 5th century A. D. and embracing the period A. D. 25 to 220 Hirth has translated the whole text in his *China and the Roman Empire*. This is the first detailed account of the Roman Empire (Roman Syria and its capital Antioch) based on the report of the Chinese ambassador Kan-Ying, A. D. 97.

about this great western power which touched the western boundary of the territory of the Parthians, and the shrewd Chinese business people at once conceived the idea of establishing direct contact with the Roman world. But the road to the west passed through deserts and steppes, inhabited by a fierce people known in Chinese history as the Hiung-nu, identified with the Huns of ancient history. The conquests of the two great Chinese generals Pan-Chao (97 A. D.) [1] and his worthy son Pan-Yong (124 A. D.) in Central Asia, removed the marauding Huns from the caravan route to the west, and thus established a direct relation with the Iranian countries and the Greco-Roman world. An active trade relation between China and Parthia was formed at this stage. But the relation between China and the western countries was not long confined to the exchange of commodities of merchandise only, but soon it expressed itself through a nobler form of relationship, namely intellectual brotherhood, which finally brought China into a closer bond of alliance with the cultural and spiritual world of India. [2] Regular missionary activities of the Buddhists began in China from the middle of the second century A. D. Many of these monks were not of Indian origin, but Buddhist monks of Central Asia. The most renowned of the earliest batch of missionaries in China was a monk from Parthia, An Shi-Kao. Shi-Kao was an Arsacidan (An-si) prince who renounced the world, giving up his kingdom to his uncle to become a Buddhist monk. Attempts have been made to identify Shi-Kao with certain Arsacidan Princes, but the result does not seem to be very conclusive. [3] Shi-Kao seems to be the Chinese translation of a religious name (probably in Sanskrit)

Trade with West

Central Asian conquests by Pan-Chao & Pan-Yong

Shi-Kao of Parthia (An-Shi)

---

1 Giles, *Chinese Biographical Dict.* No. 1598 ; for details see Ed. Chavannes, Trois généraux Chinois de la dynastie des Han Orientaux, *T'oung Pao,* 1906, pp. 210- 269 : translation of the Chinese annals *Heou Han Chou,* Chap. LXXVII.

2 Dr. P. Bagchi, Some early Buddhist missionaries of Persia, *Calcutta Review,* July, 1927.

3 Wieger *op. cit.* p. 353 ; also Bagchi, p. 8.

adopted by the Buddhist monk; possibly it was *Lokottama*. Shi-Kao came to China in 148 A. D. and settled in the Pai-ma-sse or White Horse monastery to resuscitate the old traditions left by the noble pioneers.

Shi-Kao translated 179 Sūtras

During the twenty-two years of his life in China at the Loyang monastery, Shi-Kao devoted himself to the spread of Buddhist literature in China. He is alleged to have translated 179 Sūtras or pamphlets into the Chinese language. What the original of these works were, is very difficult to ascertain; these might have been in Sanskrit or some Prakrit dialect or even some Central Asian language. All the translations of Shi-Kao are not preserved. One of the most important Chinese catalogues of Buddhist books, the *K'ai-yuan-lu*, compiled in the year 730 A. D., mentions the name of 95 books and says that of these only 54 are preserved. In Nanjio's *Catalogue*, 55 works are mentioned (Nanjio, App. II. 3). Dr. Bagchi in his *Le Canon Bouddhique* gives however the names of all the 179 Sūtras.

The works translated by Shi-Kao at Loyang reveal the character of the needs felt by those early workers. Buddhism was not sufficiently known to the Chinese people at that time, and therefore, the pioneers wanted to give briefly the principal elements of Buddhist theology and philosophy to the followers of this new faith. A large part of Shi-Kao's works are extracts from the Āgamas,[1] with which we shall have occasion to deal at length. Anesaki, identifies 21 Sūtras of Shi-Kao with the existing Chinese texts of the Āgamas [2]. But from an intensive study of the works attributed to him it seems that quite a large number are apocryphal and of a later date.

---

1 3 Sūtras from the Dīrgha Āgama (Dīgha Nikāya), 9 Sūtras from the Madhyama Āgama (Majjhima Nikāya), 6 Sūtras from the Saṁyukta Āgama (Samyutta Nikāya), 4 or 6 or 14 Sūtras from the Ekottara Āgama (Aṅguttara Nikāya). For details see under Saṅghadeva and others.

2 Anesaki, Four Buddhist Āgamas in Chinese, *Transactions of the Asiatic Society of Japan*, 1904.

The works of Shi-Kao, if they are all his, reveal quite a discreminating character. He made a selection suitable for the Chinese from the literature of the Buddhists which was already quite extensive in Northern India by the second century A. D. His sūtras are "without distinction of schools, without doctrinal partiality." "The form in which his works have come down to us, is also interesting, for it shows the method that the first translators, little conversant with so difficult a written language as Chinese, adopted to accomplish their task."

Characteristics of Shi-Kao's works

"It is clear that the Parthian preacher first translated it himself word for word, a scribe putting the translation in (Chinese) characters ; then he explained it to a scholar, who first annotated it, and then wrote it out in his own way, if the content was considered worth while"[1]

The translated text attributed to An Shi-Kao can be divided into two parts, Hīnayānistic and Mahāyānistic; the first more for the use of the laity and the second more for the use of monks. The principal subjects treated are: the Buddhist cosmology, its heavens and hells; the moral duty, the wheel of re-births; the endless chain of evils and sorrow; the cause of that chain being lust and desire, salvation is possible only through the Buddhist faith; the necessity of salvation, and the observation of the precepts; the peace enjoyed by those who have understood that there is neither self nor others; that everything is impermanent, a vain dream (*ibid.* p. 353). In brief, the elementary principles—theological and philosophical—of Buddhism were all laid down in the works introduced by Shi-Kao; but as already mentioned, there is a strong suspicion that the books attributed to Shi-Kao are not all his own.

What Shi-Kao taught

Shi-Kao is not merely remembered as a great translator, but is recognised as the head of the school of translators at Loyang

1 Wieger, *op. cit.* p. 353.

which soon became the centre of Hindu thought and culture in China. The band of workers, who worked with or after the Parthian monk, were all inspired by him, and therefore, some of them should be mentioned briefly.

Followers of Shi-kao at Loyang

Lokakṣema [1] (Chi-lu-kia-chan) a Śaka (Yueh-chi) [2] of Central Asia came to China a year or two after An Shi-kao and lived in the Loyang monastery helping Shi-kao in his translation work.

Lokakṣema, a Yueh-chi monk

After his death, Lokakṣema continued Shi-kao's work assisted by two Chinese monks. The number of works translated by this Śaka monk was 23. It will not be possible to describe all the works attributed to this monk, but only a few may be just mentioned.

It was Lokakṣema who is responsible for the first Chinese translation of a recension of the Prajñāpāramitā (Pan-joopo-lo-mi) known as the Daśasāhasrikā P. P. (Nanjio, 5). No original of it is known to be existing, although other recensions exist. The existence of a Prajñāpāramitā text in Chinese translation in the second century A.D. ensures the early growth of Mahāyāna in India. As we shall deal with this Prajñā literature in details, we should leave this matter here. The effect of the translation of the Prajñāpāramitā into Chinese does not seem to be of any lasting value, and the responsibility of popularising this literature rested with an abler scholar, Kumārajīva, a century and half hence.

Prajñāpāramitā in Chinese, 2nd cent. A.D.

The next translator, who seems to have come from India

---

1 The name has been restored by Dr. Bagchi, *loc. cit.* Tibetan historians have mistakingly read this Chinese transliteration as Chilukākṣa. See *JASB,* 1882. Nanjio, App. II. 3.

2 The national name Yueh-chi is simply written in a contracted form in Chinese as Chi, just as to indicate Hindu nationality we find the contracted expression Chu instead of T'ien-chu.

3

proper, was Chu Fo-cho[1]. Chu is prefixed to Hindu names and Fo-cho is the Chinese for Bodhisattva, so that 'Chu Fo-cho' means Hindu or Indian Bodhisattva. Fo-cho was a contemporary of Shi-kao and Lokakṣema and collaborator with the latter in his work of translation. His own works in Chinese are lost. It seems that one of his translations was a book on Prajñā.

Chu Fo-cho or 'Bodhisattva.'

The rest of the translators of the Han dynasty were men of Central Asia. An Hiuen[2], like the great Parthian royal monk Shi-kao, was a man of Parthia. He came to Loyang in A.D. 181, as a merchant, and was made 'the Head officer of the cavalry' for some service rendered to the Emperor Ling. He was not a monk, but evidently was an ardent lay follower of Buddhism. In collaboration with a Chinese scholar he translated Ugra paripṛcchā, a work of superb excellence, which was afterwards twice translated into Chinese. This paripṛcchā, which belongs to the Ratnakuṭa group of Mahāyāna works, was an important treatise, and Śāntideva in his Śikṣā-samuccaya, quotes it about twenty times. The topics discussed in it are self-abnegation, duty to a wife, mindfulness, the dole, clothing, preparation of mind, indifference to worldly conditions, life in the forest and purity.[3]

Ugra paripṛcchā quoted in Śikṣā-samuccaya

An Hiuen's other work is the Āgamokta-dvādaśa-nidāna-sūtra (Nanjio, 1339), which is a treatise on the twelve causes or nidānas, explained according to the Āgamas of the Sarvāstivādins. The whole basis of Śākyamuni's teaching, it may be mentioned incidentally, is the theory of Pratitya-samutpāda or the chain of causes and effects. This theory of causation, introduced by An Hiuen for the first time into China, must have greatly facilitated the proper understanding of the elements of Buddhist psychology.

1 Nanjio, App. II. 5 ; also Bagchi, p. 44 : *BEFEO*, 1910, p. 228.
2 Nanjio, App. II. 4; Bagchi, p. 47.
3 Bendall and Rouse, English translation of *Śikṣā-samuccaya* (Indian Texts Series).

An Hiuen's Chinese collaborator was Yen Fo-tiao [1]. It is said of him that he had studied the original language of Buddhism, and could recite the entire Prātimokṣa, without the help of a Chinese translation. This was no doubt a high standard of efficiency in those days. He further wrote a work on Vinaya for the guidance of the Chinese monks.

The catalogues of Nei-tien-lu and T'u-chi ascribe to him 7 distinct works in 9 or 10 fasc.; but the K'ai-yuen-lu mentions 5 works in 8 fasc. and states that 4 works in 7 fasc. were lost already in A. D. 730. But to-day only one work has come down to us. It is a sūtra of the Bodhisattva's inner practice of the six Pāramitās; that is, salvation could be attained by practising Dāna or charity, Kṣānti or forgiveness, Vīrya or strength, Dhyāna or meditation and Prajñā or wisdom.

Chi Yao 184-189 A. D.

The Śaka or Yueh-chi monk Chi Yao [2] is said to have come from some Central Asian settlement in 184 A. D. and he worked till 189 A. D. According to Nei-t'ien-lu and T'u-chi during this short period of six years this Śaka monk translated eleven sūtras in 12 or 13 fasc.; but the K'ai-yuen-lu mentions only 10 in 11 fasc. and states that five works in 6 fasc. were already lost by 730 A. D. Two of his extant translations are from the Saṁyukta Āgama. One is a sūtra on the eight characters of a bad horse compared with those of a bad man, and the other a sūtra on the three characteristic marks of a good horse (Nanjio, 661, 662).

The rest of the Han translators and workers in the spread of Buddhist culture in China will be briefly enumerated. Two of these were Hindus Chu Ta-li or Mahābala [3] and Tan-kuo [4] or Dharmaphala. Two others were Buddhists of Sogdiana, K'ang Kiu [5] and K'ang Mong-siang [6]. Sogdiana is modern Samarkhand

1 Nanjio, App. II. 9; Bagchi *loc. cit* p. 48, *BEFEO*, 1910, p. 228-229, *T'oung Pao*, XIX, 44-45.
2 Nanjio, App. II. 7; Bagchi, *loc cit* p. 50.
3 Nanjio, App. II. 11; Bagchi, p. 55.
4 Nanjio, App. II. 12; Bagchi, p. 56.
5 Nanjio, App. II 8; Bagchi, p. 52.
6 Nanjio, App. II 12; Bagchi, p. 53.

and is known in ancient Sanskrit literature as Śulika (See Central Asia). K'ang Mong-siang is reputed to be the translator of six works, most of which are lost. His 'Nidānācarya sūtra' (Nanjio, 733), is a collection of ten short sūtras, each relating a nidāna or event happening to Buddha, such as his headache, pain in his back, Devadatta's throwing a stone at him, a brahmana's abuse, his eating the horse-barley, penance and other topics.

Han Translators all Central Asian monks

Mong-siang further helped the Hindu pandit Dharmaphala to translate a Sanskrit text which the latter had brought from Kapilavastu.[1] The text contained a legendary life of the Buddha and is said to have been an extract from the Dīrgha Āgama, one of the sūtra works of the Sarvāstivādins.

The total number of works translated during the Han period was about 434; of these 227 were by the workers mentioned above; of about 207 the translators' names are lost. This fact amply testifies to the great intellectual keenness of the first batch of Hindu and Serindian Buddhist monks.

434 Sūtras translated

The Buddhist propaganda in this period consisted chiefly in translations of the scriptures and in miracle-working. The works of art and architecture in a new style, introduced by the Hindu monks aided by elaborate rituals and music, were sources of great attraction to the masses of the Chinese. It is said that the White Horse monastery of Loyang was decorated with mural paintings representing Buddha and his monks; "but the worship of Buddha's relics and the miracles worked by them are mentioned oftener than the works of art. The relics (sarīra, Chin., sho-li) were represented by pearls of mysterious origin, and the miracles ascribed to them were mostly the rising of variegated mists from them. Little is heard of works of charity."[2]

---

1 Chinese, Kia-po-lo-wei, a Praktria form of Kapilawai.

2 Quoted and adapted; Anesaki, Buddhist Mission, ERE, vol. 8.

III Buddhism In The Three Kingdoms

The latter Han dynasty came to an end in A.D. 220, and was followed by the interesting and romantic epoch known as the Three Kingdoms or San Kuo (A.D. 221-265). The period derives its name from the fact that at this time the empire was divided into three separate kingdoms. The first was the kingdom of Wei, which comprised the central and the northern provinces and had as its capital, the old capital of Loyang The second was the kingdom of Wu consisting of provinces south of the river Yang-tse with the capital of Nanking in the south. The third was the kingdom of Shu which included the western part of the empire with the capital at Cheng-tu. The king of Shu claimed descent from the emperors of the Han dynasty and was considered the rightful sovereign of China. This dynasty is known in Chinese Annals as the Minor Han dynasty, and is recognised as the lawful line during this period of confusion, when the Three Kingdoms struggled for supremacy. [1]

Three Kingdoms of Wei, Wu, Shu

The whole of the ancient Chinese empire, which, it must be remembered, consisted only of a portion of present-day China, became disunited at this period ; chaos, confusion and contest continued down to the close of sixth century. The fate of the Buddhist missionaries was always influenced by the vicissitudes of the ruling dynasties ; centres of Hindu culture and Buddhist activities always were identical with the residences of the dynasties and the missionaries either worked under their patronage, or were expelled by the rulers, who preferred Taoism or Confucianism to Buddhism. [2]

Loyang continued to be the capital of the Wei dynasty (220-265 A.D.) ; and the work of the Buddhist missionaries in the peaceful White Horse monastery of the city continued. The waves of political unrest that passed over the empire after the fall of the great Hans, although hampered the progress of Hindu culture, could not however stop the influx of Buddhist missionaries during the

1 See Liung Bing, Outlines of Chinese History, Shanghai, 1914.
2 Anesaki, Buddhist Mission, ERE, vol, 8, p. 701,

Wei rule. During a period of about half a century, only five translators are mentioned in the Wei Annals.

Dharmakāla's first Vinaya work in Chinese

Till the early third century, the Buddhist works that were translated consisted mainly of sūtras of Āgama literature; no important book on Vinaya or discipline had yet been made known to the Chinese Buddhists. The early translators had only spoken of śīla or morality and were contented with a mere sowing of the seed. The name of Dharmakāla [1] is associated with the first Vinaya work in Chinese. Dharmakāla was a native of Central India and came of a very rich family. In his childhood and youth he studied the Vedas the Vedāṅgas and other brahmanical works usually read by a brahmana. It is said that one day while he was entering a Buddhist monastery he came across a work called (Dharmottara) Abhidharma-hṛdaya-sūtra which he was unable to comprehend. At his request a monk explained to him the meaning of the treatise and thus new avenues of philosophical insight were opened before him. [2] He left India and came to China in A.D. 222, where he worked for many years. In A.D. 250 Dharmakāla translated the Prātimokṣa of the Mahā-sāṅghika school, to which he himself probably belonged. But monastic life had not yet come to be appreciated among the Chinese Buddhists, because it was opposed to the traditional ethics of China. The book is now lost, and the study of Vinaya was not seriously taken up before two centuries.

Monastic life is against Chinese genius

K'ang Seng-k'ai (Saṅghavarman)

Contemporaneous with Dharmakāla was the monk K'ang Seng-k'ai, [3] who came to China in A. D. 252. From his Chinese name K'ang Seng-k'ai it seems that he was not an Indian but a Sogdian (K'ang). Of his translations

---

1 Nanjio, App. II. 13; Bagchi, pp. 73-76. Tan-k'o-(mo)-kia-lo, in Chinese transliteration; Fa-Shih or lit. 'Law-time' in translation.

2 Bagchi, p. 74.

3 Saṅghavarman, Nanjio, App. II. 14; Bagchi, p. 76. Seng is the first character of *Seng-kie,* the transliteration of Sanskrit *Saṅgha,* and *K'ai* means 'armour' or varman.

two exist. One is the Ugra paripṛcchā (Nanjio, 23.19) and the other is Aparimitāyuḥ sūtra (Nanjio, 27). Both of these are re-translations. The Ugra-paripṛcchā had already been translated by An Hiuen. His Aparimitāyuḥ sūtra is the fourth translation of the Sūtra. This Sūtra is connected with an important movement in China and Japan, called the Pure land (Sukhāvatī) and we shall discuss the question in detail in another chapter (See below., Bodhiruci). The translation of Saṅghavarman is good and is praised by the Chinese. He was further responsible for a translation of a Vinaya Karma-vācā, according to the Dharmagupta school (Nanjio, 1163). There is however an old tradition of the introduction of the Dharmagupta Vinaya in the year 168 A. D., but this is doubted by some scholars. [1]

The Karma-vācā of the Dharmagupta school was further rendered into Chinese by another monk of this age named Tan-wu-ti or Dharmasatya. [2] Tan-wu-ti was a Parthian monk born in a noble family, who came to Loyang in 254 A. D. and translated the work in the next year. We do not know anything of Po Yen [3] who is mentioned in Chinese works as a śramaṇa of the western countries but really was a Kuchean monk. He translated six works between A. D. 256-260; but of these only one has survived, namely, Surataparipṛcchā (Nanjio, 43.). He was also the translator of a version of the Sukhāvatī vyūha the fully restored title of which is 'Amita-Buddha-samyak-sambuddha-sūtra.' According to T'u-chi there were two versions of the Sukhāvatī-vyūha, made by him; but one of them is not given by the K'ai-yuen lu.

254 A. D. Dharmasatya & Po Yen

An Fa-hien or Dharmabhadra was a Parthian, who came to China during this period, but whose exact date is not known. He translated two works. [4] One was an abridged translation of the

1 See Bagchi, p. 78; also Chavannes, *T'oung Pao*, 1908, p. 423; Levi & Chavannes *J. As.* 1916 p. 44; but Pelliot rejects it. *T'oung Pao* XIX, p. 346.

2 Tan-wu-ti; translated Fa-shih 'Law-truth;' Nanjio, App. II. 15; Bagchi, p. 78.

3 Nanjio, App. II. 16; Bagchi, p. 79.

4 Nanjio, App. II. 17; Bagchi, p. 81.

Dharmadhātuvarga of the Avataṁska called Ramaka sūtra (c. f. Nanjio, 106) and the other was the Mahāparinirvāṇa sūtra; both have perished. According to the catalogues Nei-tien-lu, T'u-chi and K'ai-yuen-lu 12 works were translated from the Sanskrit by the five translators of the Wei dynasty (A. D. 220-265). In A. D. 730 when the K'ai-yuen-lu was compiled, only 4 works in 5 fasc. were in existence, and 8 works in 15 fasc. had been lost. But Nanjio has 3 more works; one of them, is however mentioned under the Wei dynasty in the older catalogues (Nanjio, p. 387).

While Buddhism was being preached from the monastery of Loyang by Indian and Serindian monks in northern China, southern China was equally actively busy in assimilating and propagating Hindu culture, which she received from another source by a different route.

IV BUDDHIST LITERATURE IN SOUTHERN CHINA

North and South China

Southern China is clearly distinguishable from the North; this is traceable to the very root of Chinese history. Although we are not concerned with the socio-political history of China, still we must not fail to note this inherent difference between the North and the South in our study. Southern China received Buddhism and developed it, independently of the North. There was an intermittent traffic between Gangetic India and Sse-chuan since the first century A. D., and it is not unlikely that southern China came to know of India and Buddhism through this channel about the same time as the northern China came to know of it through Central Asia.

Maritime connection between China and India.

Besides this intermittent traffic there seems to have been some maritime connection between southern China, and India and Indonesia. The Sanskrit inscription of Vocan [1] in Champa (Annam) show clearly that the connection with India dates as early as the second century A. D., if not earlier. The Romans, when they reached the Persian Gulf, conceived the idea of reaching India and China by water. Roman merchants of some parts of the Roman Empire visited India and came by sea to Kattigara (Cochin China) about the beginning of the second century A. D.; in A. D. 166, one of them landed at Kiao-chu which is the present Tong-king. (see above, Chap. II).

Later arrivals are recorded in the third century A. D. The Indian ocean was not an unknown sea to the Hindu merchants and marines and Brahmana and Buddhist missionaries always availed themselves of their ships carrying merchandise. Southern China, therefore seems to have been very early influenced by the Buddhist monks who either sailed from Indonesian Hindu colonies or direct from the motherland. The Buddhist culture of the South China

1 L. Finot, Notes d' Epigraphie, *BEFEO.* 1904, pp. 227ff.

also bears a distinct stamp of South India, which we shall have occasion to observe in the sequel.

Meu-tseu, father of Buddhist polemic writings A. D. 165-170.

The earliest distinct influence of Buddhism in South China is traceable to Meu-tseu, who was born in the last quarter of the second century. Born in South China probably between 165-170 A. D., Meu-tseu lived in Tong-king, where he came to be acquainted with Buddhism. Educated as a thorough Chinese scholar, he was well-versed in the literature of Kung-fu-tzu and Lao-tzu. Judging Confucianism to be insufficient, he exerted himself to get Buddhism accepted in China. He thought that Confucianism should be the state religion and Buddhism that of the masses—the two thus helping each other. Meu-tseu wrote thirty-seven sets of questions and answers in defence of his new faith, Buddhism. These questions may be divided into two groups :[1] those from the Confucianist side, asserting that Buddha's ascetic religion was against humanity and[2] those from the Taoist point of view, asserting that immortality (or rather physical longevity) was attainable only by Taoist practices, and not by Buddhist teaching.[1]

Meu-tseu defended his new faith with abundant quotations from Kung-fu-tzu and Lao-tzu, but the doctrines with which he confronted the attacks were really Buddhistic.[2]

Thesis of his essay

In his pamphlet Meu-tseu begins by relating fairly accurately and without too much of the marvellous, the story of the life of Buddha. Born in India, says the Chinese scholar, in the centre of the earth, he preached a doctrine to save all beings. When he left the world he left behind him a society which applied itself to the salvation of all. Meu-tseu holds that the teaching of Buddha is not contrary to the ancient sages of China, summarised by Kung-fu-tzu. The aim of the two doctrines is different. The same man can practise both. It is not necessary to reject Buddhism *a priori*, because Kung-fu-tzu

1 Weiger, *op. cit.*
2 *ERE*, Vol. 8. Missions by Anesaki.

did not know it. A good book in addition to those of Kung-fu-tzu, is so much the better. A reasonable man takes the good wherever he finds it, and learns from him who teaches it [1].

Thus Meu-tseu goes on answering the arguments of the literati of China who were generally staunch Confucianists and dreadfully inimical towards the new faith. He quoted extensively from their old classics, whereupon said a literatus, "If the Buddhists have so many and such good arguments, why do you not then quote them? Why do you quote the *Annals* and the *Odes?*" "It is because," replied Meu-tseu, "the oxen love only the bellowings of their kind, and mosquitoes the song of their species: that is all you understand." [2].

This is the beginning of apologetic literature in Chinese Buddhism, most brilliantly defended by a Chinese scholar.

Wu dynasty in Kien-ye (Nanking) 220-280 A. D.

Meu-tseu was not the only Chinese in southern China to receive the message of Buddha. As already told, Buddhism penetrated into the South by the sea route and was able to implant itself there. After the collapse of the Han rule in China, the Wu dynasty (A. D. 220-280) began to rule in Kien-ye, the ancient name of modern Nanking (Southern City, as opposed to Peking, Northern City). The Wu dynasty was ruling in the South contemporaneously with the Wei dynasty of Loyang, of whom we have already spoken.

The relation both political and spiritual between China and Indonesia was becoming intimate. Suen-k'iuen, the Wu Emperor (222-251 A. D.) wanted to establish some political relation with Funan and sent K'ang-t'ai and Chou-ying. The ambassadors wrote an account of their travels, which is lost; but interesting passages have been preserved in the Annals of the Liang. In Funan the Chinese envoys met an Indian named Chen-song and asked

1 Wieger, op. cit. p. 370.

2 For the detailed and critical study of Meu-tseu see Pelliot, *T'oung Pao* XIX, 1920.

him about the customs of India. The reply of the Hindu ambassador is preserved in the same Annals. The description of the kingdom does not give anything of particular interest and therefore we omit the details.[1]

This international relation between China and Indonesia rested on politics and commerce, but it soon paved the way for deeper relations and monks from Funan and India went to China to preach the religion of the Buddha.

During the six decades in which the Wu ruled in the South, we have names of five translators, who rendered Indian books into the Chinese language. Of these Chi Chien[2] was the greatest personality in the church of Kien-ye (Nanking) during the Wu dynasty. He was a Yueh-chi or Śaka upāsaka, who had come to China towards the end of the Han dynasty and received instruction under Lokakṣema. After the dismemberment of the Hans, he took refuse in the southern kingdom of Wu, where he was appointed a tutor by the King for teaching the heir-apparent. He was greatly honoured in the court and his name is mentioned in the annals of the period. Suen-k'iuen, the first Wu Emperor, honoured the Śaka pandit with the title of Po-shi or 'the learned man.' Chi Chien being a man of Central Asia knew many of the foreign scripts and understood the languages of six kingdoms. Probably, he knew Sanskrit well and was thus able to translate as many as one hundred and twenty-nine different texts into Chinese. In his translation he was helped by a group of workers, among whom was the illustrious histriographer, poet and musician Wei-yao.[3] During his thirty years residence in China (223-253 A. D.), he worked wonders in the literary field. But unfortunately most of his books are lost, and of his vast literary productions only forty-nine works are extant.

Chi Chien, a Yueh-chi monk, translates 129 works.

1 Lévi, *Mélanges de Harlez*, pp. 176-185 : also Bijanraj Chatterji, *Indian Influence in Cambodia*, Calcutta, 1928, p. 18.

2 Nanjio, App. II. 18 : Bagchi, pp. 282-310 ; also Chavannes, *T'oung Pao*, X. 1909, p. 200.

3 Giles, *Chinese Biog. Dict.* No. 2297.

Chi Chien's works principally belong to the Sūtra literature and a few distinctly bear traces of Vinaya example. Thus A-nan-sseu-che-king (Nanjio, 696) is a sūtra of this nature. It advises people to support monks and feed animals; to help the poor with a compassionate heart; to abstain from eating meat and to observe the five precepts and lastly to honour the śramaṇas. In Aṣṭaguru sūtra (Nanjio, 710) eight topics are dealt with, such as killing, stealing, adultery, disease and death. But the most important work that was rendered into Chinese by Chi Chien, which has won him a permanent place in Chinese literature, is the translation of the Avadāna śataka [1] (Nanjio, 1324), a work existing in the original Sanskrit. The learned editor in his preface has shown clearly the relation between the various avadānas, of which there were several—some lost, some preserved, either in Chinese and Tibetan or only in Tibetan such as the Karma śataka. [2]

His principal works.

Translation of Avadāna śataka.

It will not be out of place to explain the characteristics of the Avadāna literature, which forms such an important branch of the Buddhist literature in Chinese. The avadāna type is closely related to jātaka. In both of them we find edifying tales with the purpose of inculcating moral precepts as taught by the Saddharma revealed by the Buddhas; both are preferably employed for preaching purposes. They agree also with respect to the character of the precepts, inasmuch as the main tendency of both is, on the one hand, to show the irresistible and all-pervading power of Karman, determining for each creature the course of his existences within the immense and boundless circle of never-resting Saṁsāra, and on the other, to impress on the minds of the audience the individual power of every creature, and to gather, by performing good actions, stores of *suklaṁ karma* which shall have precious results. *paratra*, in

Avadāna & Jātaka.

1 The Sanskrit version has been edited by Dr. J. S. Spejer. Bibiliotheca Bouddhica, St. Petersburg, 1902-1909.

2 Leon Feer, *J. As.* 1901.

time to come. The difference between avadāna and jātaka... consists in this that in a jātaka the Bodhisattva must be one of the *dramatis personæ* but not in the avadāna. Yet, a great number of our avadānas, contain the personal stories of the Boddhisattva. Every jātaka, may, therefore, be called an avadāna, but the reverse is not true[1].

Main contents of the Avadāna śataka.

The Chinese translation of the Avadāna śataka is divided like the original into ten sections, each of them presenting a particular aspect. The first and the third sections deal with prophecies, vyākaraṇāni of future Buddhahood and Pratyeka-Buddhahood; the second and fourth contain mainly avadānas of the Buddha in former existences; the characters of the two vargas are different. The fifth is devoted to stories about pretas, several of them identical with tales treated or hinted at in the Petavatthu. The sixth deals with pudgalas, who, owing to the merit of some pious action, attained heaven. In the three following vargas the heroes become arhats. In the seventh Śākyamuni is born at Kapilāvastu; the last varga is chiefly occupied with the evil consequences of bad actions in former existences, which are a cause of the sufferings of holy persons even in their last existence. The last avadāna brings the main story up to the days of Aśoka and Upagupta.[2]

Translation of *Mātangī Sūtra*

Chi Chien translated some of the well-known Sanskrit texts, which had already appeared in Chinese before, but which seem to have been unknown at that time in the South where Chi Chien did his translation work. Among such works one should be mentioned here, which Chi Chien translated in collaboration with an Indian monk named Chu Liu-yen. This treatise is the *Mātangī sūtra* There have been four translations of this sūtra, the first was that by An Shih-kao, the second by an unknown person during the reign of the Eastern Tsin dynasty (Nanjio, 644, 645). Both these

1 Spejer, Preface to *Avadānaśataka, op. cit.* p. IV
2 *Ibid.* pp. XIV, XV.

translations are incomplete or rather abridged versions of the sūtra. Chi Chien's translation was a complete one and therefore it deserves a detailed study. Another complete translation was prepared by Chu Fa-hu at the time of the Western Tsin dynasty (A. D. 265-316).

This is a famous story first summarised by Burnouf in his *Introduction* [1], from the Sanskrit text, which is preserved in the *Divyāvadāna.* The story is so interesting, and some of the social ideals enunciated in India in the first century A. D., are so radical and modern in spirit, that a summary of the story is given below :

Summary of the story

The Lord Buddha was once sojourning in Śrāvastī ; his great disciple Ānanda used daily to go to the city to collect alms. One day while returning from the city he felt thirsty and seeing a girl raising water, asked her for a drink. The girl was a caṇḍālī, Prakṛti by name. She felt distressed and told Ānanda that she was caṇḍālī by caste. "Sister", said Ānanda, "I don't ask you about your family and caste ; if you have any water left, give it to me and I will drink." He is duly served with water ; but the caṇḍālī girl (mātaṅgī) falls in love with the handsome monk. Ānanda went away never suspecting that he had roused the passion of the mātaṅginī. Prakṛti besought her mother, who was proficient in charms and incantations, to bewitch Ānanda by her art. The charm is effective enough and Ānanda comes into the house of the caṇḍāla, when suddenly Ānanda realises his awkward position and supplicates the Buddha in his distress. The Lord at once delivers him by uttering counter charms. Ānanda leaves the caṇḍāla's house ; but Prakṛti was not to be disheartened by this failure. She followed Ānanda wherever he would go for his alms. This caused a great scandal in Śrāvastī and the Buddha sent for this girl, consoled her and by his charming personality brought her to such an attitude of mind, that she became a bhikṣuṇī. She

1. Burnouf, *Introduction du Bouddhisme* (Ed. 1876, p. 183; first ed, p. 203).

not only had her hair shaven but took the nun's cowl, and delved deep into the profundity of the Buddha's religion.

This conversion of the caṇḍālī girl created a great sensation, and the whole city including the king Prasenajit, came to the Buddha remonstrating against his conduct. Thereupon the Buddha narrated the story of Triśaṅku and his son Śārdūlakarṇa. Triśaṅku was a caṇḍāla chief. He was a great scholar and had studied all the scriptures of the brahmanas. His son was equally versed in scriptures. Now Triśaṅku wanted his son to marry the daughter of the Brahmana Puṣkarasāri, who however, rejected the caṇḍāla chief's offer with supreme contempt. But Triśāṅku challenged the Brahmana in a learned dispute and demonstrated that between members of the various castes there exists no such natural difference as between divers species of animals and plants. By arguments he silenced the arrogant Brahmana, who thereupon gave his daughter in marriage to the caṇḍāla chief's son, notwithstanding the opposition of his disciples and caste people. The Brahmana's daughter, said the Lord at the end, was in the former birth, no other than mātaṅgī Prakṛti, Triśaṅku was the Buddha himself and Ānanda was Śārdūla-karṇa.[1]

Story of Triśaṅku and Puṣkarasāri

Chi Chien's translation of the *Mātaṅgī sūtra* is in seven chapters and it follows the Sanskrit narrative as described above[2].

It is not necessary to describe his other works, which are doubtless important, but as many of them were retranslated by abler men, they will be dealt with below. According to some authorities, a second translation of the *Sūtra of the forty-two sections*, rendered into Chinese originally by Kaśyapa Mātaṅga, was made by Chi Chien; but

1 See Nariman, *Sanskrit Buddhism*, Bombay, pp. 56; also Rajendralala Mitra, *Buddhist Literature of Nepal* pp. 223-226. Henceforward quoted as Nariman and Rajendralala. This discussion which took place between the Brāhmaṇa Puṣkarasāri and the caṇḍāla Triśaṅku reminds one of the Vajrasūci, alleged to be of Aśveghoṣa, which is a polemic against caste system and supremacy of the Vedas (See below).

2 Cowell, *Divyāvadāna*, App. I., vide the notes on Chinese versions supplied by B. Nanjio, which are however not found in details in his Catalogue.

it had been lost before A. D. 730. It is stated in an ancient work that this translation differed a little from that made by Mātaṅga and the meaning of the words were more correct and the composition perspicuous (Nanjio, 388). Some of his important works are the Daśasāhasrikā p.p., Sukhāvatī vyūha, Vimalakīrti nirdeśa, Vatsa sūtra, Śālistambha sūtra, Brahmajāla sūtra etc.

Vighna (Wei-k'i-nan) A. D. 224.

In 224 A. D., came to China, probably by the sea-route, an Indian monk named Vighna [1] accompanied by another compatriot named Liu-yen. Vighna was born in India in a family of a yājñika brahmana and many legends are connected with his conversion to Buddhism. After traversing many countries he at last reached China with a copy of the *Dhammapada* which he probably secured in Ceylon, on his way to China. This he translated into Chinese with the help of his Indian friend. The original book consisted of 26 chapters; but after the translation was finished, 13 new chapters or *vargas* were added in China making up the whole in 39 chapters of 752 verses. The Pali *Dhammapada*, it may be noted, consisted of 26 chapters; this work is too well-known to be described in detail. In comparing the two versions, the Chinese and the Pali, we find that they agree from the 9th to 35th chapter (except the 33rd), so far as the title of chapters are concerned, though the Chinese has 79 verses more than the Pali. But this Chinese translation has eight additional chapters in the beginning, four at the end, and one in the thirty-third [2].

Translates the Dhammapada

1 Nanjio, App. II. 19; Bagchi, p. 301; also Lévi, *J. As.*, 1913, pp. 206 ff.

2 Chapters of the Fa-chiu-ching [1 anitya, 2 śikṣa, 3 bahuśruta, 4 śraddhā, 5 śīla, 6 bhāvanā 7 prema, 8 vākya (eight additional chapters in Chin. not found in Pali Dhp.)] 9 yuga or yamaka (Pali 1), 10 pramāda (2), 11 citta (3), 12 puṣpa (4). 13 bāla (5), 14 paṇḍita (6), 15 arhanta (7), 16 sahasra. (8), 17 pāpa (9), 18 daṇḍa (10), 19 jarā (11), 20 ātma (12), 21 loka (13), 22 Buddha (14), 23 sukha (15), 24 priya (16), 25 krodha (17), 26 mala (18), 27 Dharma (19), 28 mārga (20), 29 prakīrṇa (21), 30 Naraka (22), 31 nāga (23), 32 tṛṣṇa (24), [33 sambhoga, (additional in Chin.)] 34 śramaṇa (25) 35 brāhmaṇa (26), [36 Nirvāṇa, 37 saṁsāra, 38 Bodhisattva, 39 saubhāgya (four additional in Chin. not found in Pali Dhp.)]

It has been definitely told in the preface to the Fa-chiu-ching (Dhammapada-sūtra) that the 13 new chapters were added in China. The titles of the chapters of the Fa-chiu-ching entirely agree with those of the extant Pali version and even in many instances verses agree. It can be suggested with fair amount of certainty that the original of the Chinese was Pali, which Vighna secured in Ceylon on his way to China. It is quite likely that Vighna, who was a man of N. India and a Sanskritist, was unfamiliar with the Pali text. Vighna's translation was imperfect and it therefore could not be popular with the Chinese. A few years later a selection of a hundred verses with suitable and short introductory parables was made by a Chinese monk (see below) [1].

The Indian companion of Vighna, Liu-yen seemed to have acquired more knowledge of the Chinese language and was thus able to translate four sūtras (A. D. 230), of which three are found in the present collection of the Tripiṭaka [2].

K'ang Seng-huei, a man of Central Asia, also came to China by the southern route. Seng-huei was a Sogdian or *Śūlika* whose family had been living in India. His father was a merchant of

K'ang Seng-huei a Sogdian monk

Kiao-che or modern Tonkin in S.-E. China, where he had business. Seng-huei, was born in Tonkin and was probably Chinese by education. When he was ten years old his parents died and the funeral ceremonies made such a deep impression on his mind that he left home and became a monk. Seng-huei became a great scholar and made extensive studies in the Chinese classics ; he made a large collection of astronomical and non-canonical texts. He was an earnest Buddhist and went to China in the hope of converting the people (247 A. D.). Suen-k'iuan, the Wu emperor, gave him permission for building the monastery of Kien-chu, which was also known as Fo-to-li or the Buddha-grāma. Suen-hao, the successor of Suen-

1 S. Beal, *The Dhammapada* translated from the Chinese, (Trübner's Oriental Series). The whole *Dhammapada-Udānavarga* question has been dealt with in a chapter in author's *Indian Literature in Central Asia.* (In press)

2 Nanjio, App. II. 20 Bagchi, pp. 302-303.

k'iuan was not favourably disposed towards Buddhism and Seng-huei was challenged by his officer Chang-yu in a discussion ; but the learning of the Sogdian monk was too deep to be gauged by the official representative of the king and the latter was defeated. Thereupon the king changed his mind and began to respect Buddhism. Seng-huei died in 280 A. D. [1].

Fourteen books are credited to this Sogdian translator ; but only five have survived the neglect of time and two of them have received the most careful attention of European scholars. These works are Saṭpāramitā sannipāta sūtra (Nanjio, 143) and Saṁyukta avadāna sūtra (Nanjio, 1359) which have been completely translated by Chavannes in his *Cinq cents contes* [2].

Translates Saṭpāramitā sannipāta sūtra and Saṁyukta avadāna

These are all avadāna and jātaka stories and by way of illustration the names of a few only may be mentioned to show the nature of the work : story of Sarvada, Ṛsinanda, Dīrghāyuṣ, sūtra of king Po-ye, story of the king of Vārāṇasi, sūtra of Rājarṣi Mūrdhvan, story of sparrow-king etc. The stories of Saṁyukta avadāna are short.

One story however got wide appreciation in China and it is found in both these works of Seng-huei as well as among the translated works of Kumārjīva (404-413 A. D.) and Hwui-chiao (A. D. 445). This is the famous story of Kalmāṣapāda. The text of the Saṁyukta avadāna is almost literally translated below :

Story of Kalmāśpāda

"Once in remote ages there was a brahmana, who begged a king to give him something. The king was about to go out hunting, and therefore made the brahmana wait till his return to the palace. Stalking his game and getting separated from his followers, the king entered a deep valley, where he met with a rākṣasa waiting to devour him. The king said, 'Listen, this morning I have met with a brahmana, to whom

1 Nanjio, App. II. 21 ; Bagchi, pp. 304-307 ; also Chavannes, *T'oung Pao*, 1910. pp. 199-212.

2 Tome I, Avadāna Nos. 89-155, pp. 347-428, comprise *Saṁyukta avadāna*.

I have promised something on my return. I shall first give him alms and then come back here as thy victim.' The rākṣasa said, 'I wish to devour now. Will thou certainly come here again ?' The king answered, 'Were I not true to my word, I should have forgotten the brahmana.' The rākṣasa allowed him to go free. So the king returned to his palace, gave liberal alms to the brahmana, and delivered over his kingdom to his successor. Then he came back again to the rākṣasa, who was deeply moved by his truthfulness, paid great homage to him and gave up the intention of devouring him."

Another version of this story is also found in the other translation of Seng-huei viz, Satapāramitā sannipāta. There the king is Phu-ming or Samantaprabhāsa ; the story is narrated in detail. The brahmana who met Phu-ming preached the Buddhist doctrine of impermanence in four stanzas, which have been quoted by subsequent writers [1]

Another story from the Liu-tsi-ching or Sannipāta sūtra of Seng-huei evoked wide interest throughout proper India and Greater India amongst her writers and artists. This is the famous story of the 'Elephant with six tusks' or *Sad-danta jātaka.* The story is told here briefly.

Story of *ṣaḍ-danta* in literature and art

This marvellous animal was none other than one of the innumerable past incarnations of the Buddha ; the jātaka says that the elephant lived happily in the company of his troop of subjects in a hidden valley of the Himālayas. However, the second wife, wrongly believing herself slighted for love of the first, gives herself up to death in the access of jealous fury, making a vow to avenge herself upon her husband one day for his supposed want of affection. In the course of her succeeding existences she becomes a queen of Benares and possesses the power of remembering her previous birth. She obtains from the king permission to despatch against her former husband the most skilful hunter in the country, with orders to kill him and

1 K. Watanabe, The story of Kalmāṣapāda and its evolution in India literature, *Journal of the Pali Text Society*, 1909, pp. 236-310.

bring back his tusks as a proof of the success of his mission. The man does, in fact, succeed at great risk of his life in striking the noble elephant with a deadly arrow. But the soul of the Bodhisattva is inaccessible to any evil passion ; not content with sparing his murderer, he voluntarily makes a present of the tusks, whereof the man had come to rob him. When the hunter finally brings back to the queen this mournful trophy, she feels her heart break at the sight of it. Such is the touching story, reduced to its essential and most generally reported features, for it is known under multiple forms.*

During the fifty-eight years of the reign of the Wu dynasty according to Nei-tien-lu and T'u-chi 259 treatises were translated from the Indian languages into Chinese by these five pandits. But in A. D. 730 there were sixty-one works in 92 fasc. The K'ai-yuen-lu mentions one hundred and eighty-nine works in 417 fasc. In A. D. 730 there were only sixty-one works in 92 fasc in existence, and one hundred and twenty-eight works in 325 fasc. had long been lost. Of this large number of works only fifty-six are found in the Chinese Tripiṭaka ; the rest are all lost, lost to

---

* Bibliography of *Saḍdanta Jātaka*

(1) It is known in Pali ; see Fausoboll's edition of Jātaka, vol. VI. No. 514.

(2) Sanskrit account in the *Kalpadruma avadāna* analysed by Leon feer, *Journal Asitique*, 1895, No. 1., Also Rajendralal, pp. 301-303.

(3) *Liu-tu-tsi-ching* or *Saṭpāramitā sannipāta sūtra* (Nanjio, 143) described above.

(4) *Tsa-pao tsang-ching* (Nanjio, 1329), by Chi Chia-ye of the Northern Wei Dynasty, A. D. 386-534 ; 8 fasc : there are 121 Avadāna stories.

(5) *Sūtrālaṁkāra* alleged to Aśvaghosa preserved in Chinese ; translated into French by Ed. Huber. Story No. 69, pp. 403ff.

(6) *Ta-che-tu-lun* or *Mahā-Prajñāpāramitā sūtraśāstra* of Nāgārjuna (Nanjio, 1169).

These are the six literary versions of this story preserved in Chinese and Sanskrit. In art it has also been represented ; (1) on a madallion from Barhut ; (2) another from Amarāvatī ; (3) a lintel from Sanchi ; (4), a fragment of a frieze from Gāndhāra ; (5, 6), Two frescoes from the Ajanta. M. Foucher, the great French archaeologist has discussed the whole subject in his article 'Chronologie des versions du Sad-danta jātaka' in *Melanges Sylvain Levi* ; also *The Beginning of the Buddhist Art* by A. Foucher, translated into English by L. A. Thomas and F. W. Thomas (1917), where the translation of the above article with illustrations occur, pp. 185-205.

India, lost to China and we have nothig left to us except the titles of these works.

Besides the translations of the well-known translators of the Wu dynasty, one hundred and ten distinct works (in 287 fasc) of unknown authorship are mentioned in T'u-chi, one of the early catalogues of the Buddhist Tripiṭaka. According to K'ai-yuen-lu eighty-seven of these works are authentic and the rest have no canonical authority. In 730 there were only four works in 6 fasc. in existence but today only three are preserved: (1) *Abhidharmāmṛta śāstra* by venerable Ghoṣa in two chapters (Nanjio, 1278); (2) Sūtra of the patronymics and names of the parents of the seven Buddha (Nanjio, 626); this is a translation of the 45th chapter of the *Ekottara āgama.* (3) *Saṁyukta-āgama* is in one chapter; this is an adridged translation having only twenty-five sūtras of the Saṁyukta-āgama, which we shall discuss at length in future (Nanjio, 547.)[1]

Works of unknown authorship.

---

1. Anesaki, Four Sanskrit Āgamas in Chinese. *Transactions of the Japan Asiatic Society,* 1908.

V. Beginning of Sino-Indian Contact

The *San-Kuo* or the Three Kingdoms of Wu, Wei and Shu decayed in course of time, and the dynasty known in Chinese Annals as Western Tsin (265-316 A. D.) rose in their place. The Tsin emperors for a short period reunited the dismembered empire and assumed the pretentious imperial titles. This is really the beginning of a period which finally separated North and South China for several centuries. In the North the period of unrest due to Tartar invasion began, while the South, away from the scenes of political troubles, developed its art and literature in a rather peaceful atmosphere.

Rise of Western Tsin

The Western Tsin dynasty eked out a very precarious imperial authority for half a century (A. D. 265-316) in Chang-an, which had till then kept up the fire of Hindu culture burning in its monasteries. The Buddhist monasteries attracted Indian monks from abroad and offered shelter to the Chinese Buddhists. During this half a century fifteen scholars worked at the translation of Buddhist literature and rendered four hundred and forty-four works into the Chinese language; sixty-three works were translated by unknown writers. It must be said to the credit of the workers of this period that during five decades they translated more than five hundred works.

Fifteen monks translated 444 Indian works

Dharmarakṣa's[1] name tops the list of the translators of this age. He is the translator of some of the most important Buddhist works and the total number of his works amounted to two hundered and eleven. This person was a Yueh-chi, who had assumed a Hindu name. It may be mentioned here incidentally that the practice of assuming Hindu names was very common among Central Asian, Chinese, Korean and Japanese Buddhists. Dharmarakṣa's

Dharmarakṣa, A. D. 266-313

1 Nanjio, App. II. 23; Bagchi, p. 83; transliteration, Chu Tan-mo-lo-ch'a; Chin. translation Fa-hu, lit. 'law-perception'.

parents had been living in the Tun-huang district in the province of Kan-su and the child grew up in a Chinese atmosphere. When he was eight years old he left home and became a śramaṇa under the influence of an Indian Buddhist monk. The young Śaka monk was highly intelligent and learned the scripture very quickly. He travelled abroad with a foreign monk, presumably an Indian, for several years collecting numerous manuscripts on Buddhist literature. During his travel *he learned thirty-six languages* and must have visited India where he collected some manuscripts. He came back and settled at Chang-an in A. D. 284, the centre of Buddhist propaganda and culture. He founded a monastery in the city, where disciples numbering several thousands gathered round the monk to listen to his erudite discourses on Buddhism. Dharmarakṣa worked at Chang-an from A. D. 284 to 313. He not only translated a large number of works but became the father of a school which produced a galaxy of translators, workers and missionaries in the cause of the religion of India. He himself worked and was able to inspire a band of workers, of whom Nie Cheng-yuen and his son Nie Tao-chen, Ch'ang-she, Ming-ch'ang, Fa-jui, T'an-suei, Wen-long and others helped him a good deal.[1] The political troubles of the North however compelled him and his disciples to leave Chang-an and procede towards Chang-chan (Shantung province) where he died in his 78th year in 317 or 318 A. D.

Translated 211 works into Chinese

It will not be possible to give a list of all the works of this great writer, or even to describe the most important among them. Of his two hundred and eleven works today only ninty exist in the Chinese Tripiṭaka ; a few important texts may be mentioned here in order to understand the man and appreciate his work.

The Prajñāpāramitā literature, as we shall find in the course of our study, comprised several treatises of different sizes and recensions. Dharmarakṣa translated in 286 A. D. the Pañcaviṁśati sāhasrikā prajñāpāramitā (Nanjio, 4), which formed the second

Translated a Prajñāpāramitā text

1 Bagchi, p. 85.

section of the *Prajñā* literature. Dharmarakṣa's translation was incomplete as it consisted of 10 fasc. and 21 chapters, while the complete Sanskrit work is in 76 chapters. A century and a quarter later a complete and brilliant translation was made by Kumārajīva, of whom we shall learn more.

His Daśabhūmika sūtra

Dharmarakṣa's translation of the Daśabhūmika sūtra (Nanjio, 110), which is a part of the great Avataṁsaka literature, was done in A. D. 297. It is a treatise on the ten stages which a person must pass through before he can attain Buddhahood. These stages are technically called *Bhūmis* and the subject will be discussed in another part of this work.

Sadharmapuṇḍarīka and *Avalokita* cult

Dharmarakṣa was highly intelligent and more than any other of his contemporaries, he understood what suited the popular genius of the Chinese people. The first text on the cult of Amita Buddha had been introduced into China in the days of An Shi-kao ; we shall hear more of this cult below. Dharmarakṣa added to it the cult of Avalokiteśvara by translating the great Saddharmapuṇḍarīka (Nanjio, 138). He endeavoured to set in relief the catechism of Amitābha, the Bodhisattva (*pu-sa*) Avalokiteśvara, whose name, translated into Chinese, became *Kuan-yin*, 'the one who perceives sounds'. Of course this is a wrong translation of the Sanskrit word which has been arbitrarily taken as *avalokita* and *svara*. From the translation of the Saddharmapuṇḍarīka dates the vogue in China of the worship of Kuan-yin, the purest and the gentlest of the Bodhisattvas.

Dharmarakṣa preached eloquently : "No matter what misfortune a man may be afflicted with, if he invokes Kuan-shih-yin, the latter will immediately listen to his appeal and deliver him from the distress. Whoever invokes him, is saved from fire, water, and the attacks of brigands or demons. If a condemned person invokes him, the sword which should decapitate him will break on his neck. The prisoner who invokes him will be delivered from his shackles and irons. If, in a party of travellers or merchants, there is a devotee who invokes Kuan-shih-yin, the whole caravan will come out of all dangers unscathed. Many words are not necessary to move Kuan-shih-yin. It is sufficient only to cry in misfortune, from the bottom of the heart, "Oh Kuan shih-yin, I bow to thee," and one will be immediately succoured.

Faith in Kuan-shih-yin

Whoever invokes him, finds himself delivered from evil thoughts, from spasms of hate, from unintelligence and callousness. Every woman who has recourse to him to obtain a child, will see her demand fulfilled. All men ought to pray incessantly to so powerful and so benevolent a *pu-sa*. His happiness is to work for the deliverance of all beings. He assumes for that end the most diverse forms, appearing as Buddha, Bodhisattva, Brahmā, Indra, Vaiśravaṇa, Vajrapāṇi, king, brahmana, monk, an ordinary man, woman, nun or with the features of a child. In a word, he will appear in that form in which, he knows, he will be listened to. Invoke him then, and you will no longer have any cause of fear." Here ends the exhortation in prose, which is repeated in verse still more emphatically. [1] Dharmarakṣa's Saddharmapuṇḍarīka therefore must be considered to be an important work in Chinese.

Another important Sanskrit text which greatly changed the religious conceptions of the Chinese Buddhists rendered into their language by Dharmarakṣa was the celebrated Ullambana sūtra (Nanjio, 303).

Ullambana sūtra and the worship of the dead

The story of the Ullambana sūtra is briefly this: Maudgalyāyana (Chin. Mu-lien), a disciple of the Buddha, had obtained the power of visiting the *pretaloka* or the netherworld, where he found his mother emaciated to bone. Mu-lien offered her food, but the food turned into burning charcoal and she could not eat. Mu-lien was greatly touched at the sight and returned to seek counsel of the Buddha. The Buddha advised him to take refuge in the saṅgha and said that only the saṅgha could deliver his mother from *pretaloka*; for this purpose however rich presents of food, drink and clothing should be made to the saṅgha. The

1 Wieger, *op. cit.*, p. 409.

Buddha concluded his discourse saying, "Good men and good women, every true disciple of the Buddha ought to remember with gratitude what his parents formerly did for him. He owes gratitude to his ancestors to the seventh generation. In proof of his gratitude, he would do well to offer for their deliverance, *Ullambana*, on the fifteenth day of the seventh moon. Every true disciple of the Buddha ought to do that." Since his time when Dharmarakṣa popularised this idea of ancestor worship, this particular ritual has been greatly modified; but the fifteenth day of the seventh lunation has remained in China the day of the festival in honour of the dead.[1]

Dharmarakṣa was the translator of many important Buddhist Sanskrit works of which a few may be mentioned here. *Lalita-Vistara* (Nanjio, 161) the well-known biography of the Buddha, described in a later chapter of this work, was for the first time rendered into the Chinese by Dharmarakṣa in collaboration with that illustrious band of Chinese workers which helped him all along (A. D. 308). The work in its Chinese title means 'Samantaprabhāsa sūtra'; its another title was *Vaipulya nidāna sūtra.*

Translation of *Lalita-Vistara*

Besides this a large number of paripṛcchās and some very important sūtras from the Avataṁsaka and Mahāsannipāta group were rendered into Chinese by him. Dharmarakṣa was fortunate in having been able to gathor round him an earnest batch of workers to help him in the translation of Buddhist texts into Chinese, some of whom we shall meet in the course of our study.

The next great translator and missionary was An Fa-kin,[2] who translated five treatises from Sanskrit into Chinese. Fa-kin was a Parthian, who came to China in A. D. 281 and worked till the reign of emperor Huei in 306 A. D. Of his extant works only one deserves special notice. It is his translation of the *Aśokāvadāna* (Nanjio, 1459). This is a collection of stories in which the central figure

Fa-kin the Parthian's *Aśokāvadāna*. A. D 281-306

1 Wieger, *op. cit.*, pp. 412 ff.

2 Nanjio, App. II. 25; Bagchi, 115.

is Aśoka. In Chinese there are however two versions of these stories; one introduced at this period by Fa-kin from Central Asia and the other brought by Saṅghabhara of Funan (Cambodia) two centuries later by the southern sea-route. Fa-kin's translation of *A-yu-wang-ching* or *Aśoka-rāja-sūtra*, has been rendered into French by Przyluski. In Chinese Buddhist literature as well as in the extant Sanskrit literature various legends bearing on Aśoka are met with. Przyluski has most searchingly gone into the stories as they are preserved in the Chinese versions of the *Aśokāvadāna*, the Chinese Saṁyuktāgama, the Divyāvadāna and the Sūtrālaṁkāra.

Przyluski's *Le Legende de l'empereur Aśoka*

It is clear that various stories, some of which must have originated before the Christian era, were moulded in the avadāna form by some unknown writers in past times. Thus there are two distinct groups of stories in the work, viz., the stories centering round Aśoka, and stories centering round his teacher Upagupta. These stories, at a later age but before the third century A. D., were grouped into one work and known as the *Aśokāvadāna*. This work, of which we have the Chinese version, belongs to the Mūlasarvāstivāda school which originated at Mathura.[1]

The work gives an account of the early life of Aśoka and his conversion to Buddhism and narrates tales and anecdotes related to him by the monk Upagupta with a view to illustrate the teachings of the Buddha. The name of the author is not given anywhere in the text; but the stories are narrated by one Jaya in the grove of Kalandaka in Rājagṛha. The first chapter gives the genealogy of Aśoka, beginning with Bimbisāra of Magadha, a contemporary of Buddha. Here the story of Aśoka's youth and his coronation is told in details.[1] The chapter two describes how Aśoka met Upagupta and narrates his devotion to Buddhism, the

1 See below, under Yi-tsing. It may be mentioned here incidentally that Przyluski holds that there were two Vinayas of the Sarvāstivādins, one of Mathura with Avadānas or Jātakas, one of Kashmir without them; the whole of the Divyvāadāna may be derived from the first of these Vinayas. *Le Legende de l'empereur Aśoka*, Paris, 1923, pp. viii, 214; also Lévi, *Toung Pao*, viii. 105-22; *J.As.* 1914, ii. 494: Keith, *Sanskrit Literature*, 1928, p. 64.

story of Tiṣyarakṣitā and the Bodhi tree, his meeting with Piṇḍola Bharadvāja etc. The story of Aśoka's younger brother Siu-ta-to (Chinese) or Vigatāśoka is narrated in the third chapter. The next chapter describes the sad story of Kuṇāla, the beloved son of Aśoka. The chapter five gives the story of Aśoka's death and the successors to his empire. Much historical information is contained in this chapter. The sixth chapter may be termed the beginning of the second part of the work. It narrates how the Buddha had prophesied about Upagupta. It describes the last journey and death of the Buddha and narrates the details of the first council of Rājagṛha. The nirvāṇa of Mahākāśyapa, Śānavāsa's entrance into thes aṅgha, Ānanda's nirvāṇa, Madhyāntika's nirvāṇa, the foundation of a monastery on the urumuṇḍa by Śānavāsa, Upagupta's appeal, his conquest of Māra, his propaganda and Śānavāsa's nirvāṇa are described in the seventh chapter. In the eighth the stories about the pupils of Upagupta, Dhitaka's appeal, Upagupta's nirvāṇa are delineated. The Buddha's prophecy about the disappearance of his teaching is narrated in the next and in the tenth or the last chapter twelve short stories are told. [1]

Apart from the above facts this avadāna furnishes us with a clue to many legends of Aśoka, and has been responsible to a great extent in establishing the relations among the avadānas. The study made by Przyluski has, therefore, been of great value to the history of Indian literature in general. This one work of Fa-kin made him famous in China, and his translation has been of immense value to us in modern times.

Another important avadāna was rendered into Chinese by Shih Fa-li, [2] a contemporary of Fa-kin. Of the author we know nothing except the fact that while living at Loyang he translated in collaboration with Fa-chiu four works in 12 fasc. during the reign of Huei-ti (290-316 A. D.). Of his translations the Dharmapadāvadāna sūtra (Nanjio, 1353) is well-known to us

Fa-li's comm. on Dhammapada

1 Przyluski, *op. cit.*
2 Nanjio, App. II. 29 ; Bagchi, 133

through the English translation of Beal. We have seen above that Wei-chi-nan or Vighna brought a copy of the Pali Dhammapada from India and translated it about 224 A. D. But owing to his defective translation the book did not receive much attention from the Chinese Buddhists. Fa-li, therefore, made a selection of about a hundred verses and supplemented each verse with a short avadāna or story connected with the verse, that is, the circumstances under which the Buddha narrated the story, summing up its teaching in a verse. The book, therefore, for its concise character and illustrative stories must have fulfilled the purpose of Vighna, who introduced it into China. Fa-li's other works are Lokadhātu sūtra (Nanjio, 551), Mahāvaipulya-Tathāgata-garbha sūtra (lost) and Sarvaguṇa-puṇyakṣetra sūtra (Nanjio, 383).

Shih Fa-li's collaborator Shih Fa-chiu continued his friend's work after his death during the reign of Huei-ti and translated one hundred and thirty-three texts into Chinese. All these texts are small and unimportant sūtras from larger texts, mainly the āgamas. Nanjio however mentions only twenty-three of his works which are extant, the rest are lost. [1] The meaning of Shih Fa-chin is ācārya Dharmaśikha.

Others translators mostly Non-Indians

The other translators of this period are Kālaruci [2] who came to Canton in A. D. 281, Chu Shih-hing, Mokṣala, Chu Shu-lan, Nie Tao Chen, [3] Po Fa-tsu [4], Wei She-tu [5], Che Min-tu [6], Che Fa-tu [7] and Jo-lo-yen or Nārāyaṇa. [8]

The name of Chu Shih-hing is not mentioned by Nanjio in his catalogue, as he was not a translator of any Sanskrit book.

1 Nanjio, App. II. 30 ; Bagchi, 136-147.
2 Nanjio, App. II, 24. In Chin. Kiang-liang leu-che is a transliteration. Bagchi, 114.
3 Nanjio, App. II, 32 ; Bagchi 124.
4 Nanjio, App. II ; Bagchi p. 129.
5 Bagchi 134.
6 Bagchi 135.
7 Nanjio, App. II, 34 ; Bagchi 147
8 Nanjio, App. II, 34 ; Bagchi 148.

But his share in the work of the diffusion of Buddhist literature in China was so immense that we cannot afford to neglect him.

Shih-hing was born in the province of Ying-ch'uan (modern Hiu-cheu). He became a śramaṇera while young and embraced the life of a monk. He began to study the sacred books of Buddhism at Loyang, but found great difficulty in the interpretation of Tao-hing-ching. He thereupon made up his mind to proceed to the western countries, i. e. Central Asia and probably India, in search of a learned teacher and the original texts. After having visited many provinces in China, Shih-hing came to Khotan, which was a great centre of Sanskrit culture in those days. There he was able to get a copy of the Sanskrit Pañcaviṁśatisāhasrikā prajñā-pāramitā. But when he wanted to send the manuscript to China through his disciple Fu-ju-tan (Puṇyadhana), the monks of Khotan, who belonged to the Hīnayāna branch, demanded that particular care should be taken to have it properly interpreted, and that there should be no confusion between this and and the Brāhmaṇic texts. Shih-hing promised to do so and obtained permission from the king of Khotan to send the texts to China. Puṇyadhana brought them to China, where they were deposited in the temple of Shuei-nan-sse in Honan. These were the texts which were translated by Mokṣala and Chu Shu-lan in A. D. 291.[1]

Mokṣala[2] is a restored name. In Chinese it is mentioned as Wu-lo-ch'a (Wu-ch'a-lo) pi-kiu, i. e. Mokṣala Bhikṣu. It has been suggested that Mokṣala was an Indian monk but really he was a Serindian. At Loyang he worked in collaboration with Chu Shu-lan and translated the Pañcaviṁśatisāhasrikā prajñāpāramitā (Nanjio, 2), the manuscript of which had been brought to China by Puṇyadhana in A. D. 291 as mentioned above.

Mokṣala's colleague Shu-lan seems to have been an Indian. His name has been restored as Śukla-ratna. It is distinctly stated in his biography that his family came from India, and that his

1 Bagchi, 117-119

2 Nanjio, App. II. 26 ; Bagchi, pp. 119 f. ; our Courant, *Catalogue des livres Chinois*, vol. V, p. 251.

grandfather's name was Rudra (Lu-to), a man well-known for his learning. It is also stated that he held a high position in the court of an Indian prince, and a civil war in the country drove him and his son Dharmaśiras (Ta-mo-she-lo) out of the state and they came to China and settled down in Honan, where Shu-lan was born. Shu-lan was an intelligent boy and he learned Sanskrit from his uncle, who had come with his parents. But in his youth he became addicted to hunting and drinking, and it was through the intervention and the influence of his mother that he got rid of his evil habits and finally devoted himself to Buddhist studies. He became a disciple of Fa-hu (Dharmarakṣa) and his knowledge of Sanskrit and Chinese was well utilised in the translation of Buddhist works. He helped Mokṣala in translating the Pañcaviṁśatisāhasrikā and himself translated two other works (A. D. 291) which have unfortunately perished.[1]

Besides Mokṣala and Shu-lan, there was a number of brilliant translators, who were mostly inspired by Fa-hu (Dharmarakṣa), and a brief account of some of them will certainly be interesting.

Nie Cheng-yuan, a Chinese upāsaka (lay brother) who had learned Sanskrit, helped Dharmarakṣa in his translations. After the death of the latter, Cheng-yuan corrected some of those works and prepared better translations ; he worked at Loyang in the reign of Huei-ti (A. D. 209-306).[2]

His son Nie Tao-chen, who had acquired a perfect knowledge of Sanskrit was also an assistant of Dharmarakṣa. He translated fifty-four sūtras, most of which were small tracts, into Chinese, of which only four exist to this day.[3]

Po Fa-tsu was another outstanding figure of this age. He became a monk at an early age and learned the sacred literature. He studied Vaipulya śāstra in all its details and understood its meaning perfectly.

1 Bagchi, 120-22.

2 Bagchi, 122-24; Nanjio, App. II, 31 ; Maspero, BEFEO, 1910, p. 223.

3 These are : (1) Mañjuśrī parinirvāṇa sūtra (Nanjio, 508), (2) 'Sūtra on the original actions of the Bodhisattvas who are seeking the state of Buddha' (Nanjio, 107), (3) Vimaladatta paripṛcchā (Nanjio, 23.33), (4) Abhiniṣkramaṇa sūtra (Nanjio, 509). Nanjio, App. II. 32 ; Bagchi, 129-128 :

At Chang-an he built a monastery for the study of sacred texts and the practice of religion and became himself its ācārya. His erudtion and personality drew round him a large number of disciples. The governor of Chang-an respected Fa-tsu as his master; Fa-tsu also wielded great influeuce in the western province, and he was held in deep veneration by numerous young people and scholars. The civil war which took place towards the end of the Tsin dynasty, compelled Fa-tsu to leave the city. He went to Kan-su province and settled in Long-yu. There he was requested by the governor of the province to quit his monastic life and betake himself to lay living, which however the noble monk declined to do. This greatly enraged the official who took the earliest opportunity to wreak vengence on him. Po Fa-tsu was arrested and killed.

Po Fa-tsu, a martyr

His death created a great sensation. The barbarians of Long-shan, numbering several thousands, came to the city to take him to their western country. Now, when they heard that Fa-tsu was dead, they became furious and another civil war began. After a great effort and a good deal of skilful negotiation the barbarians were satisfied. The martyrdom of Po Fa-tsu left a deep mark on the mind of the people.

Fa-tsu is well known for his successful discussion with Wang-feu the Taoist monk, who compiled the Lao-tsu Hua-hu-ching, to vilify the Buddhist religion. He translated twenty-three works from Sanskrit, of which only five exist to this day.[1]

The Western Tsin Dynasty (A. D. 265-316), under the benign rule of which the Buddhist church greatly developed in Northern China, came to an end in A. D. 316. Signs of disintegration had been evident in the latter part of the reign of this dynasty. The North was never secure from the ravages of the Tartars and Huns. "In 310 Liu-yuan, Khan of the Huns and king of Han, engaged in a contest for the empire and become the absolute master of all the land north of the Huang-ho or the Blue river. The two ancient capitals Chang-an

Political condition of North China

1 Bagchi, 129-133.

and Lo-yang were occupied in 316 and the two generals of Liu-yuan, after the death of the successor of the latter, partitioned the Han kingdom which took the name of Chao. Liu-yao reigned at Chang-an and Shi-lei at Siang-kuo (Chuan-to-fu in Chih-li province). The domination of these foreign dynasties in North China became particularly propitious to the propagation of Buddhism." It was at the court of this king that a monk named Fo-t'u-teng (Buddhadāna) came from a western country. Fo-t'u-teng was probably a monk of Kuchean origin, who had gone twice to Kipin (Kashmir) for the purpose of studying Buddhism. All the authorities describe him as a great magician and his biography is full of such miraculous stories. He came to Lo-yang in A. D. 310; but after the occupation of the city by the Huns, he was presented to the king Shi-lei who felt a great respect for this Buddhist monk on account of his infallible predictions and always sought his counsel. Fo-t'u-teng gained greater influence on Shi-hu, the successor of Shi-lei, who, to repay his services, promulgated in 335 A. D. the first edict of tolerance accorded to Buddhism in China. The edict of Shi-hu runs thus :

Fo-t'u-teng gets an edict in favour of the Buddhists

"The Buddha is a deity of the foreign country; he is not worthy of the offerings of the Sons of Heaven and the Chinese. I, who was born in the frontier country, had the good luck of becoming ruler of China. As for sacrifices, I should keep up the custom of my nation. The Buddha being a barbarian deity, it is proper that I sacrifice to him. Ah! the laws, which since antiquity eternally serve as model! If one thing is perfect and without defect, why to spend one's time with what was done in the ancient dynasties? The people of Chao are barbarians; I pardon their sacrilege that they love to serve the Buddha. They are fully authorised to enter the religion."

Fo-t'u-teng lived at Ye (Chang-to-fu in Honan province), where King Shi-hu had transferred his capital, till the extermination of the dynasty in 349 A. D. During his sojourn at Ye, Fo-t'u-teng with the Indian monk Fo-tiao and the Shaman Shi-yu and Tao-kai of Tun-huang, made this place an important centre of Buddhist studies. It is here that Tao-an began to study sacred literature with Fo-t'u-teng and founded a flourishing community. It is not till the political trouble which broke out in 349, that Tao-an and his disciples left Ye. [1]

---

1 Translated from Bagchi's Intro. pp. XV-XVII. For the legendary life of Fo-t'u-teng see also Wieger, as translated from *Annals of Tsin*, Chapetr 95, p 413-416; also *ERE.* vol. 8, 'Mission' by Anesaki.

V. China's Direct Intercourse With India

Numerous Tartar principalities rose in North China after the downfall of the Western Tsin dynasty (A. D. 265-316). The North was rent up by barbarous hordes from the steppes, who overran the kingdom. None of these Tartar princes was acknowledged as the emperor of China. The hereditary honour of the emperor was however claimed by the Eastern Tsin dynasty that rose to great eminence in South China at Khien-ye (Nanking) in A. D. 317 and reigned till A. D. 420. All the emperors of the Eastern Tsin dynasty were well-disposed towards Buddhism and Hiao-wu-ti, the ninth sovereign of this line, was the first Chinese emperor to embrace Buddhism.

No Emperor in North China

Nanking was already a centre of Hindu culture and Buddhist propaganda during the rule of the Wu dynasty (A. D. 222-280). During the inetrvening period of thirty-seven years, from the fall of the Wu dynasty (A. D. 280) to the rise of that of Eastern Tsin (A. D. 317), the lamp of faith went on burning as brightly as ever in the zealous hearts of the followers of Buddhism. When the Tsin dynasty came into power, the Buddhists felt that a new era would dawn in China; learned monks both from India and Central Asia began to flock into the capital. Seventeen translators are mentioned who flourished during the century of their rule. We must not forget that at this period monks were coming also to North China, with which we shall deal in the next chapter.

Eastern Tsin of Nanking (A. D. 317-420)

Po Śrīmitra,[1] who is mentioned as a monk of the western country, seems to be a man of Kucha, an important centre of Hindu culture in those days. Śrīmitra was the heir-apparent to a king, but gave up his kingdom to his younger brother to become a monk. He came to Northern China sometime between 307-312 A.D., when the Western Tsins were

Monk Śrīmitra of Kucha

1 Nanjio, App. II. 36; Bagchi, 319; Po Shih-li-mi-to-lo; in Chinese translation, Chi-Yu, 'lucky friend.'

in their last gasp of life on account of the exhausting struggle with the Chao. The political turmoil in the country made it impossible for him to live there and prosecute his Buddhistic studies. He therefore left the North and came to Nanking.

Śrīmitra was a Tantric Buddhist and is considered to be the pioneer of Tantrism in China. He put great stress on the correct pronunciation of the religious texts and was responsible for the translation a few dhāraṇīs. What a dhāraṇī is and how it came to be in use among the Buddhists, has been discussed in another volume by the author.[1] Śrīmitra has left two versions of a dhāraṇī called Mahāmāyurī vidyā-rājñī (Nanjio, 309, 310). This is a peculiar work which later on formed a part of the Pañca-rakṣā dhāraṇī, and is described in detail in the Tibetan section: of this work. It is nothing but a collection of mantras for neutralising the effect of snake-bite. The story says that once upon a time when the Buddha was in the Jetavana at Śrāvasti, Ānanda reported that a bhikṣu had been bitten by a black serpent and was on the point of death ; at this the lord revealed the mantras of the Mahāmāyurī. The mantras are said to have been originally known to a king of the Peacocks, who dwelt on the southern side of the Himalayas.[2]

Tantrism said to be introduced into China by Śrīmitra

This period of Buddhist literary activity dealt, as we shall see, mainly with the Āgama literature. Dharmaratna[3] translated one hundred and ten works from Sanskrit, of which the majority belonged to Āgama. The author colected separate sūtras of the Madhyama, Dīrgha, Saṁyukta and Ekottara āgamas. This Dharmaratna is mentioned as a man of the western countries and seems to have been an Indian. The details of his life-history are unknown except that he carried on his translation works in the monastery of Sie-chen-si in Yang-tu during the reign of Hiao-wu-ti between 381

Dharmaratna translates 110 works, mostly Sūtras of Āgama

1 See Author's *Indian Literature in Tibet.*

2 Rajendralal, *op. cit.*, p. 173 ;

3 In Chinese Chu Tan-wu-lan, Nanjio, App. II. 38, where it is transcribed as Dharmarakṣa ; See Bagchi, p. 322 ; also Pelliot, *T'oung pao*, XIX, p. 345.

and 395 A. D. Of his hundred and ten works only twenty-three are preserved in the Chinese Tripiṭaka, the rest having perished before A. D. 730, when the K'ai-yuen-lu was compiled. His translations which were mainly āgamic, were supplanted by the better and more comprehensive translations of Saṅghaveda and Dharmanandī ; that seems to be the cause of the disappearance of a large number of his works.

It was at this period that the Āgamas were translated from Sanskrit into Chinese by several Indian monks residing in the North as well as in the South of China. The earliest was the translation of the Madhyama āgama by Dharmanandī, of whom we shall presently speak. Saṅghadeva was another monk who was responsible for the complete Chinese version of some of the Āgamas. Saṅghadeva [1] was a profound scholar and zealous preacher. He had studied the Tripiṭaka and had made a special study of the Abhidharma. Saṅghadeva was a man of Kashmir and arrived at Chang-an by the Central Asian route in A. D. 383 during the reign of the later Tsin dynasty (387-417).

Gautama Saṅghadeva, A. D. 383-398

A few years before his arrival in Chang-an an Indian monk named Dharmanandī had come to that place and translated the Sanskrit Ekottara āgama into Chinese. But the translation was not well executed. The North at that time was suffering from political upheavals and there was hardly any patronage from the rulers. There was no learned monk who could verify and correct the translation made by Dharmanandī. The great Tao-an was dead. But a friend of that great Buddhist scholar named Shamen Fa-ho invited Saṅghadeva to Loyang to verify the translation of Dharmanandī with the original. Saṅghadeva lived there for four or five years explaining Scriptures and at the same time learning the Chinese language. During his sojourn in Loyang he translated the great Sarvāstivāda works, Abhidharma-jñānaprasthāna śāstra, Abhidharma Vibhāṣā

Revises the translation of Ekottara and Madhyama āgama

1 Nanjio, App. II. 39 ; Bagchi, 335, 161. Gautama Saṅghadeva, *Chin.* Chü-tang Seng-chie-ti-p'o. Saṅghadeva is translated as Chung-tien 'Company-god'.

and Abhidharma hṛdaya śāstra. Finding that Buddhism was decaying in North China, he left Loyang in 391 A.D., crossed the Yang-tse and came to the South. In the South at that time was living a pious Chinese monk named Huei-yuan [1] who had founded the famous monastery at Lu-shan. Huei-yuan was a man of profound learning and intelligence and as soon as he heard of the arival of Saṅghadeva in South China, he sent a cordial invitation to the Indian monk and requested him to live in the monastry of Lu-shan. Saṅghadeva accepted his hospitality and lived in the monastery for a few years where he translated two minor works.

In 397 he moved still farther south and came to Kienye (Nanking), where he translated the Madhyama āgama (Nanjio, 542), the Ekottara āgama (now lost) and a few works of the Abhidharma. His profound learning created a deep impression in the minds of the official circle of the capital. A high official named Wang-suen, who was a devout Buddhist, erected a monastery for Saṅghadeva, where he was surrounded by a number of disciples, eager to listen to his lectures. He used to explain to them the subtleties of Buddhist philosophy from the Abhidharma texts [2] and translated some of the very best works on Sarvāstivāda. It may be remarked incidentally that it was the monks of the Sarvāstivāda who first systematized the philosophy of Buddhism and to Saṅghadeva goes the credit of first introducing it into China. He was the pioneer in bringing out in Chinese the first translation of the most important Abhidharma work, Kātyāyanīputra's Jñānaprasthāna-śāstra [3] and also the Mahāvibhāṣā or the great commentary on the same, which however is lost. The former he translated in co-operation with the learned monk Chu Fo-nien, to whom we shall return below.

The Abhidharma or Śāstra, as it is also called, of the Sarvāsti-

---

1 Giles, *Chin. Biog. Dict.*, No. 882.

2 Bagchi, 335-37.

3 Nanjio, 127 : *Chin.* A-pi-ta-mo pa-chien-tu-lun or Abhidharma aṣṭakhaṇḍa-śāstra.

vādins, cannot be found to-day in the original Sanskrit, and translations of them are preserved only in Chinese. The Sarvāstivādins had seven supplementary canonical works attached to the Jñānaprasthāna. Hiuen-tsang translated the whole canonical literature of the Sarvāstivādin abhidharma and they have been described in details in chap. XIV. Saṅghadeva translated also a few more works of Abhidharma, such as the Tridharmakakāyaśāstra (Nanjio, 1271) and the Abhidharma-hṛdaya śāstra (Nanjio, 1288). Thus Saṅghadeva fulfilled the mission for which he was invited by preaching Abhidharma among the Chinese and translating Abhidharma texts into the Chinese language.

The next great and illustrious Indian was Buddhabhadra[1] who is responsible for the translation of the Avataṁsaka Sūtras and a few other treatises. Buddhabhadra [2] was born in Kapilavastu, in the royal family of Amṛtodana, the uncle of Śākyamuni. He became a śramaṇera at a very early age and when he was seventeen he surpassed all his friends in studies. Later on he specialized in the study of Vinaya, while staying in Kashmir. At that time the Chinese monk Che-yen, the companion of Fa-hien (see below), came to Kashmir and met Buddhabhadra who was prevailed upon to go to China to preach the Law of Buddha.

Buddhabhadra, A. D. 398-421

Che-yen and Buddhabhadra went eastwards from Kashmir, traversed the whole of India and came to Tonkin by sea, whence they again embarked for China. In China he met the great Kuchean monk Kumārajīva, with whom he had a religious controversy and established his superior wisdom and erudition over Kumārajīva. Since then the learned monk always sought the help of Buddhabhadra, whenever he found any difficulty with the texts. The great Chinese traveller Fa-hien helped Buddhabhadra in translating a few works.

Buddhabhadra was a man of independent spirit who never cared to visit the emperor or seek his patronage. He had therefore

1. Nanjio, App. II. 92 ; Bagchi, 341 ; *Chin.* Fo-to-po-to-lo.
2 Nanjio, App. II. 42 ; Bagchi, 341

difficulties with the monks of Chang-an and was finally compelled to leave the capital. But he was invited by Huei-yuani in his newly founded monastery at Lushan where he worked at translations. The number of works translated by Buddhabhadra is not very large but the volume and importance of his works was enormous. His principal work is Buddha-Avataṁsaka sūtra (Nanjio, 88) in 60 fasc., which was responsible for the founding of a new sect three centuries hence, when a new and an enlarged translation was made by Śikṣānanda, a monk of Khotan (see below).

The Avataṁsaka sūtra

The Buddha is the alleged author of the Avantaṁsaka sūtra; he is said to have delivered it as soon as he obtained Buddhatva at Gayā. He declared, "Alas, Alas, all living beings do not know or see on account of their ignorance, the fact that they possess the same wisdom and virtues as the Tathāgatas. I will show them the 'Holy Path' which shall enable them to become entirely free from false notions and attachment, and shall make them realise that they possess in themselves the boundless wisdom which is, by no means, different from that of the Buddhas.[1]

The Avataṁsaka school calls this sūtra the Mūla-dharmacakra, and other sūtras Śākhā-dharmacakra; the Saddharmapuṇḍarīka is considered as one from 'the branches to the root'. The three are called Tri-dharmacakra.

The general principles and notions of the Mahāyāna system are accepted by the Avataṁsaka school. Besides this it has its own philosophy and world-conception. The work played such an important rôle in the religious life of China and is still of such an importance to a large section of the Japanese Buddhists, that a detailed analysis of the work will be useful.

What the Avataṁsaka teaches

The Buddha as the central figure occupies the most important position throughout the discourse. It is a peculiar feature of this work that the attending Bodhisattvas and not the Buddha himself

1 Translated from Chinese by Sogen, Yamakami, *Buddhist Philosophical Systems*, p. 288.

deliver sermons. The part played by the Buddha is just to show off his splendour, and this is the most important point in understanding the Avatamsaka. The Buddha here is not the historical Buddha, but one absorbed in the *Sāgaramudrā Samādhi*, which means that the Buddha keeps the mind serene and tranparent as ocean, in the surface of which everything is reflected in its true shape ; the world thus appearing to the Buddha is not a world of the senses, but one of light and spirit. The world is called the Dharmadhātu, that is, a world of pure beings, or simply spiritual world. The world becomes radiant with light when it is contemplated by the Buddha in the samādhi, for the light issues from his body, in fact from every pore of his skin, illuminating the ten quarters of the universe and covering all time—past, present and future. The Buddha himself is reflected in every object on which his light falls. His gaze turns towards the east and all the holy lands of the Buddhas and Bodhisattvas with their innumerable attendants in the quarter are manifested ; when it is directed to the west or south or north, the same miracle happens. This applies not only to space but to time as well.

Inter-penetration or Inter-mutuality the essence of the teaching.

"In every particle of dust there are present Buddhas innumerable,
Revealing innumerable worlds of indescribable sublimity,
And they are perceived in one thought,
And all the Kalpas past, present and future are also manifested in one thought."
"All the Buddha-lands and all the Buddhas themselves,
Are manifested in my own being freely and without hindrance
And even at the point of a single hair a Buddha-land is perceivable."

Inter-penetration or Inter-mutuality sums up the doctrine of the Avatamasaka ; each object is not only itself but every other object, and that all things are mutually conditioning to such an extent that the withdrawal of one of them means the disturbance of the whole system, which is to say the world grows imperfect to that extent. The world is, therefore, a world of inter-penetration, intermutuality, inter-relation, which is considered as the highest form of Mahāyāna.

So long as this insight is not attained, the world remains sense-bound and misery follows beings at every step. This the Buddha pities, and with his overflowing love (karuṇā), he embraces the world and all creatures in it : his activity, which is called the 'Deeds of Samantabhadra', never ceases until every being is delivered ; he will go to Hell even, in order to get the suffering souls out of it. The Bodhisattva follows the example of the Buddha, for he strictly observes the six pāramitās which constitute the essence of Buddhahood. The Bodhisattva practising these caryās attains Buddhahood after ages. They have also conceived the ten stages in the spiritual life of a Bodhisattva, known as Daśabhūmi. The theory of Daśabhūmi is common to all Mahāyānists and it forms a part of the Avataṁsaka translation by Buddhabhadra [1].

The complete Sanskrit original of the Avataṁsaka does not seem to be existing. But it has been contended by Pelliot, Takakusu and others that that the Sanskrit Gaṇḍavyūha, a work preserved in Sanskrit, forms a part of the lost sūtra [2].

In spite of the intellectual appreciation of the Buddhist view of life by the Chinese, the idea of Saṅgha, and the discipline of the church was neither followed seriously, nor understood properly. Therefore Vinaya was a neglected subject among the Chinese Buddhists. This led, as we shall see, Fa-hien to proceed to India to study the working of the church organisation. He brought a number of works on Vinaya. Buddhabhadra in collaboration of Fa-hien translated the large treatise on the Mahāsāṅghika vinaya in 46 fasc., and 18 sections. It may be mentioned here that in 250 A. D., Dharmakāla had translated the Prātimokṣa of the Mahāsāṅghikas but it was lost. Therefore Buddhabhadra's translation must have

Vinaya works translated by Buddhabhadra and Fa-hien

1 Chapter 22 of Nanjio, 87 ; Chapter 26 of Nanjio, 88. There is a Tibetan translation of Avataṁsaka in 45 chapters, *Asiatic Researches*, 1836 p. 401 etc ; *Annals du Musee Guimet*, Vol. XI, p. 288. The whole text above about Avataṁsaka is taken from the articles in *The Eastern Buddhist*, 1921, Nos. 1. 2, 3 ; 1922, No. 4, Otani University, Otani, Japan.

2 Pelliot, Notes á propos d'un catalogue du Kanjur, *Journal Asiatique*, 1914, pp. 118-121 ; a minute and a comperative study of Buddhabhadra's and Śikṣānanda's translations with the Tibetan translation and the *Gaṇḍa-vyūha* may establish this fact and the inter-relation among these texts may be known.

removed a long-felt want in China. The Buddhists of India had different Vinayas for different schools. The origin of separate Vinayas is said to have been based on the following declaration of the Buddha. He is said to have declared that everything which is consonant with good sense, or generally speaking with the particular circumstances of the case, is also in conformity with truth and ought to be taken as a guide, as being the rule of Buddha's teaching." [1]

Rise of different vinayas in India

This led to different interpretations of one and the same fact by different people, and sects began to form from flimsy differences of opinion. The Mahāsāṅghika sect is one of the earliest sects which developed a vinaya of its own. After the death of the Buddha, the elderly people or the sthaviras naturally ruled the church; but in time the more liberal and go-ahead party or the younger element in the church, who were numerically strong, felt uneasy at the conservative attitude of the elderly people. The eternal struggle between the old and the young resulted in a schism, and the democratic party of the Buddhist Saṅgha formed themselves into a community called the Mahāsāṅghikas, the members of a large saṅgha. The Sthaviravādins retained the primitive form of orthodoxy. The Mahāsāṅghikas were more heretical, bolder in speculation, and in aims and ideals more comprehensive. Therefore the introduction of the vinaya of this school into China by Buddhabhadra was of singular importance. It may be suggested here that the Mahāyāna probably rose out of the Mahāsāṅghika sect and in matters regarding the Buddhalogy the views of the Mahāyāna are foreshadowed in those of the Mahāsāṅghikas.

The Mahāsāṅghika vinaya introduced into China

The school of the Mahāsāṅghikas was once strong in Northern India, where the first schism took place after the quarrel with the Vajjian monks. The stronghold of the Mahāsāṅghikas probably shifted after this and they settled in Ceylon, where the Sthaviravādins were equally strong. It was from Ceylon that Fa-hien got a copy

1 Quoted from Wassilief by Dutt, *Spread of Buddhism*, Calcutta, 1926.

of the vinaya of this school, which BuddhabKadra translated in collaboration with him.[1]

Buddhabbadra's other works of importance are Buddhadhyāna-samādhisāgara-sūtra (Nanjio, 430), Dharmatrātadhyāna-sūtra (Nanjio, 1341), Mahāvaipulyatathāgatagarbha-sūtra (lost), Mañjuśrīpraṇidhāna-sūtra (Nanjio, 1336) and Anantamukha-sādhakadhāraṇī (Nanjio, 356).

Fa-hien, 399-414.

The pioneer path-finder to India

Fa-hien was, as we have seen, responsible for bringing to China a large number of Indian original works, which were translated during the reign of the Tsin dynasty. With him began a period of intercourse between China and India, the importance of which we cannot fully appreciate in the present age of internationalism. Till the end of the fourth century A.D., the Chinese had no direct contact with Indians although they met in China and Central Asia Parthian, Saka and Kuchean Buddhists and sometimes Buddhist preachers from India. But no Chinese monk before Fa-hien had ever left China for India. The year 399 A. D., the last year of the fourth century, was the red-letter year in the history of Eastern Asia, when the first batch of Chinese youths wended their way towards India, that centre of culture and illumination of the then civilized Asia. The pioneer of this new movement was Fa-hien, who left China in A.D. 399 and returned in A. D. 414 after a sojourn of fifteen years in foreign lands. The life of this monk is important for our purpose.

His life and travels

Fa-hien was born in the district of modern Shan-si. In his early childhood he was put in a monastery by his parents. When his parents died, he took ordination formally and at once made himself distinguished amongst the monks by his spirit of faith and zeal for discipline or rules of vinaya. vinaya was very imperfectly known and followed in the Chinese monasteries, as no one had any first-hand knowledge of the actual working of a monastery. Fa-hien keenly felt this deficiency and resolved

1 Bagchi, p. 343.

to go to India to learn the vinaya. He left Chang-an in A. D. 399, crossed the Gobi desert and had to wait at Turfan for the opportunity of joining a caravan. He then arrived at Khotan after crossing the Taklamakan desert by a painful march of thirty-five days. Khotan was, since the first century, a Buddhist country. It is said that a single convent had more than three-thousand monks. It is here that Fa-hien observed the discipline of a monastery. The orderly behaviour of the monks, so different from the Chinese monks, was a revelation to Fa-hien, who had only seen the monks loafing about for their daily meal.

From Khotan the Chinese pilgrim went to Kashmir in fifty-four stages and then following the course of the Indus to the Punjab. He passed through the northern states of India visiting the convents and holy places. He studied the vinaya rules of various communities, copied their rules and read their books in the Vihāra libraries. Finally he descended down the Ganges to its mouth and studied in Bengal for a few years. From Tāmralipti, the port of Bengal, he embarked on a ship and came to Ceylon, the stronghold of Sthaviravādin and Mahāsāṅghika Buddhists, where he carried on his studies for several years. Here he collected a large number of manuscripts.

After fifteen years of travel and keen observation he embarked on a trading Hindu merchantman, which sailed for the East. The ship was caught by a terrific storm and the Hindu merchants wanted to throw away his Buddhist manuscripts which they thought were responsible for the pending disaster. The storm however subsided and his valuable treasures were spared. He stopped at Java for five months, when he got on another Hindu trading vessel proceeding to China. The ship touched at Shantung. The governor of the place gave Fa-hien a hearty welcome and had him brought to Nanking, the capital of the Eastern Tsin dynasty. Fa-hien devoted the rest of his life to the promotion of monastic discipline in the monasteries of South China. He died at the age of 86 [1].

1 Wieger, *op. cit.* pp. 418-419.

Fa-hien's translations are not many. He translated six works, of which three are long lost. Of his extant works the Mahāparinirvāṇa-sūtra (Nanjio, 118) in 6 chapters is the most important. His other two works are the Parinirvāṇa-sūtra (Nanjio, 120) in 2 chapters and the Saṁyuktapiṭaka-sūtra (Nanjio, 676). But Fa-hien has not been immortal for these translations; his Li-yu-tien-shu-ki-shuan, (Nanjio, 1476) in which he records his travels in the Buddhist kingdoms, has immortalized him in China. In this work he has described the flourishing condition of Buddhism in Ceylon and Central Asia, among the Uigurs and the tribes residing near the Caspian Sea and in Afghanisthan. About his travels and dangerous expedition through Central Asia, Giles remarks, "in the glow of which the journeys of St. Paul melt into insignificance.[1] At the end of his book on travels, Fa-hien is said to have remarked the following about his own work :

His literary works

"When I look back on what I have gone through, my heart is involuntarily moved, and the perspiration flows forth. That I encountered danger and trod the most perilous places, without thinking of, or sparing, myself, was because I had a definite aim, and thought of nothing but to do my best in my simplicity and straightforwardness. Thus it was that I exposed my life where death seemed inevitable, if I might accomplish but a ten-thousandth part of what I hoped."[2]

Fa-hien is a man of North China. His earlier years were spent in the North; but his literary activity was connected with the Tsin dynasty of the South and has therefore been described here.

Besides these important translators and missionaries, a number of minor workers flourished during this dynasty. Vimalākṣa,[3]

1 Introduction, *Travels of Fa-Hien*, Cambridge 1923.
2 Legge, *Travels of Fa-hien*, p. 117.
3 Nanjio, App. II, 44; Bagchi, 338.

of whom we shall speak in the next chapter, is one of the important vinaya translators; Jitamitra[1], who came to China during the reign of An-ti (391-418), is said to have translated twenty-five works, but of which only two remain; Nandi[2], who seems to be of Indian origin, translated three works in the reign of Kong-ti (A.D. 419). Dharmapriya[3] and Kālodaka[4] are described as monks who came from foreign lands. Dharmabala or Chu Fa-li[5] seems to be an Indian monk. Che Song-kong[6], Che T'ui kong[7], Che Fa-yong[8] were Chinese translators. K'ang Tao-ho[9] was a Sogdian monk as also was K'ang Fa-suen.[10]

Other writers of the age

Besides these known translators there were many unknown ones whose works are mentioned in old catalogues and some are even preserved to this day. According to some old catalogues, fifty-three works in 57 fasciculi were translated by unknown translators, of which all but one have perished, and according to another, there are thirty-eight more, of which all but two are extant. Nanjio has put two more names under this dynasty, so that there are altogether ninety-three works from the pens of unknown translators. Among these there are some very important works, which have been thoroughly studied in the West, such as Na-Sien Ching or Nāgasena-sūtra (Nanjio 1358), which is a version of the Milinda-pañho.[11]

In Pali the Milinda-pañho is a well-known work.[12] It

1 Nanjio, App. II. 46; Bagchi, 349.
2 Nanjio, App. II. 47; Bagchi, 352.
3 Nanjio, App. II, 43; Bagchi, 340.
4 Nanjio, App. II. 40; Bagchi, 335.
5 Nanjio, App. II. 48; Bagchi. 353.
6 Nanjio, App. II. 49: Bagchi, 353.
7 Nanjio, App. II, 50; Bagchi, 354.
8 Nanjio, App. II. 51; Bagchi, 354.
9 Nanjio, App. II, 41; Bagchi. 334.
10 Bagchi, p. 322.
11 Kāśyapa parivarta (Nanjio 58)
12 Pali Text Edited by V. Trenckner, London, 1880; Rhys Davids, *Questions of King Milinda*, *S.B.E.* xxxv (1890), xxxvi (1894); O. Schrader, *Die Fragen des Koenigs Menandros*, Berlin, 1907; A. Gueth, *Die Fragen des Milindo*, Leipzig, 1919, vol. I. Finot, *Les questions de Milinda*, Les classiques d' orient, Bossard, 1923, (Abridged); Vidhuśekhara Bhaṭṭācārya, *Bengali* translation with the Pali text in Bengali script.

consists of the discussion of a number of points of Buddhist doctrine treated in the form of conversations between king Milinda and Ṅāgasena thera. King Milinda plays a very subordinate part, he simply puts the questions or 'dilemmas', but the solutions, which are the really important part of the work, are put in the mouth of Nāgasena. Nāgasena here is the most important person and the Chinese version is rightly called Na-sien pi-k'iou ching or Nāgasena-bhikṣu-sūtra.

Nāgasena-sūtra and Milinda-pañho

In Chinese there have been three versions of the Nāgasena-sūtra. The earliest was translated in the third century A. D. and consisted of four fasc. But it perished in the fifth century.

The second version was done during the reign of the Eastern Tsin dynasty, the dynasty we are dealing with. This version is anonymous. It was probably translated from a dialect of India, perhaps Pali. There is no evidence that the original was Sanskrit. The third translation was done by Guṇabhadra between 435 and 455 A.D., but it is lost (see below). There are two recensions of this Chinese work ; the longer one, having 22,657 or 22,651 characters, is about twice as long as the shorter, consisting of 13,752 Chinese characters. But this is due to mistake on the part of either the scribe or the printer, and the two recensions may be considered as really one, the difference in bulk being due merely to repetitions.

The Chinese version of Nāgasena-bhikṣu-sūtra has been completely translated into French by Demiéville[1] ; it is not a large work and is less than one sixth the bulk of the Pali[2] Milinda-pañho. It is evident that the texts of these two versions are derived from a common source, now lost, of which the Pali version is an expanded form. Demiéville has also compared the Pali and the Chinese versions.[3]

1 Paul Demiéville, Les Versions Chinois du Milindapañho, *BEFEO*, 1924, pp. 75-180.

2 Eng. translation of the Pali text consists of 580 pages ; the French translation, if we omit the long notes, would not be more than 90 pages.

3 In Pali there are seven books, whereas in Chinese the number of chapters is 124. Of the first book of Pali, the chapter 2 agrees roughly with ch. xxv

The Chinese Nāgasena-sūtra begins with an introductory story of the former births of Milinda and Nāgasena, in which the latter was an elephant and the former a brahmana. Then it goes on narrating how Nāgasena became a Sramaṇera, received śila and tried to be an arhat. After having attained arhatship, he makes a preaching tour and his fame spreads all over India. Thus a brief life history of Nāgasena is met with at the beginning. Milan (Milinda) on the other hand, as the story runs, studies sūtras and heretical literature and in time becomes a king. He asks publicly if there is anyone who can discuss the doctrine of Buddha with him. The ministers tell him that in the North there are śramaṇas who are wise and learned. One of his courtiers introduces a śramaṇa named Āyuṣpāla (Ya-ho-la). Milinda begins his discussion with the comparative merit of homeless life and the life of a layman and the final result or nirvāṇa. As the śramaṇa answers that both produce one and the same result, the king further puts the question why then he (Āyuṣpāla) has become a śramaṇa, if a śramaṇa has no advantage over an upāsaka so far as the final result is concerned. Thus Āyuṣpala is silenced after one or two questions. Milinda's minister this time introduces Na-sien (Nāgasena), who was familiar with the twelve divisions of the sacred books and the ninety-six systems of heretics.[1]

When the two meet, the real '*Questions of Milinda*' begins ; in Chinese this introduction occupies about nine folios. The remaining 50 folios contain philosophical discussions proper which more or less agree with and Books II, III and IV of the Pali version.

---

of Chinese, 9 with xxvi, 10 with xxiv, xxvii, 23-24 with xi-xii, 25 with xii-xiii, 27 with xiv, 29 with xv, 30-32 with xvii-xviii, 34-35 with xix, 36 with xx, 37 with xxvii, 37-38 with xxviii, 39 with xxix, 40 with xxx, 41 with xxxi, 42 with xxxii-xxxiii, 43-44 with xxxiv. The first part of the *Milinda-pañho* is not the important portion of the work. The Books ii, iii, iv of the Pāli version correspond to the Chinese chapters xxxvi to cxxiv to a great extent: only the chapters II, 1, 2, II, 3, 12-13, III, 6, 8-9, of the Pali version are wanting in Chinese. The Pali books iv, v, vi, vii, have no corresponding parts in Chinese. In Rhys Davids' translation of the Pali text, the last four books form one volume of 375 pages (vol. 2]; *S.B.E* xxxvi).

1 J. Takakusu, Chinese translations of the Milindapañha, *TRAS.*, 1896, pp. 1-21.

It has been well established that the king Mi-lan or Milinda is the Greek king Menander who conquered part of India in the 1st cent. B. C. In the Chinese Nāgasena-sūtra we simply find the king discussing metaphysical topics, but the enlarged Pali version does not stop there,—it finally converts Milinda to Buddhism.

VI. Agama Literature in China.

It has already been hinted at how the Chinese empire began to disintegrate from the fourth century A. D. The Hiung-nus founded an empire in the north of China in early fourth century, known as the Han kingdom, because they traced their origin from a princess of the old Han dynasty. We have described how after the death of Liu-ts'ung, his two generals Liu-yao and Shi-lei divided the kingdom between themselves; the dynasties founded by them are known as Anterior Chao and Posterior Chao respectively. In course of time the Posterior Chao absorbed the Anterior Chao. We have described the condition of Buddhism in China during this dynasty. The kingdom of the Posterior Chao itself was then split up into small principalities which were at length united by Fu-k'ien of the Former Ts'in dynasty. This dynasty originated at Shen-si, but it extended its powers considerably between 350 and 394 A. D. under the leadership of Fu-k'ien (357-384), who made Chang-an his capital. In his earlier career, Fu-k'ien favoured Confucianism, but in A. D. 381 he became a Buddhist. He was evidently in close touch with the western regions, and probably through them with India, for we hear that sixty-two states of Central Asia sent him tribute. We are told also that in 381 nine-tenths of the inhabitants of North China were Buddhists, as the result of the continuous missionary activity of three centuries, conducted by the Buddhist monks of Chang-an and Loyang. It was also at this period that Buddhism was introduced into Korea (372 A. D.), and Chinese civilization penetrated into the Hermitland.[1]

Political History of North China after A. D. 316

Fu-K'ien of the Former Ts'in dynasty, A. D. 350-394

During the short period of forty-five years (350-394), when Fu-k'ien and his successors of the Former Ts'in dynasty were

1 Eliot, *op. cit.* III, pp. 250ff.

ruling, seven translators worked to render Sanskrit books into Chinese.

Dharmodhi [1] came to China during the reign of Fu-k'ien (357-384 A. D.) and translated three works in collaboration with Chu Fo-nien in A. D. 367 in the monastery of Chang-an. He translated some vinaya texts of the Sarvāstivādins, but they are all lost. Dharmapriya [2] translated in 382 A. D. a version of the Daśasāhasrikā Prajñāpāramitā known in Chinese translation as Mahāprajñāpāramitā-sūtra (Nanjio, 7). It may be mentioned here that before Dharmapriya another translation of this book had appeared in Chinese. Dharmapriya was an Indian monk, who, after coming to China, lived and preached in the northern districts, but afterwards left the North, went southwards and settled in the South, where the Eastern Tsin dynasty (A. D. 317-420) was reigning from Nanking (see above).

Dharmodhi, Dharmapriya, Kumārabodhi

Kumārabodhi [3] was a contemporary of Dharmapriya. He lived in Central Asia and was a Kuo-shih or Rājyaguru of the king of Turfan, who must have been a pious Buddhist. Kumārabodhi came to China in A. D. 382 and translated a work on the Āgamas, originally prepared by an arhat named Vasudhara. Some however are of opinion that the work was not completed by Kumārabodhi, but was finished by the learned Gautama Saṅghabhūti. [4]

But the greatest personality of this period is Dharmanandī.[5] His contribution to China is great and his name is connected with some of the most important works. He was not an Indian but a Tokharian, greatly versed in the Sanskrit āgama literature. He came to Chang-an in A. D. 384 and translated four works. It may be mentioned here that till this time no complete translation of the āgamas was available in Chinese and an official

Dharmanandī's translation of *Madhyama & Ekottara Āgama*

1 Nanjio, App. II, 52 ; Bagchi, 154 ; Chinese T'an-mo-che is transliterated as Dharmadhi ; but Dharmodhi is better, see Bagchi, *ibid.*
2 Nanjio, App. II. 42 & 55 ; Bagchi, pp. 156, 340.
3 Nanjio, App. I. 53 ; Bagchi, pp. 156-157.
4 Bagchi, p. 157.
5 Nanjio, App. II, 57 ; Bagchi, 157-160.

named Chao-cheng invited Dharmanandī to translate them. In spite of the political disturbances of the time, Chao-cheng invited Tao-an and other monks and managed to convene a religious conference at Chang-an. Dharmanandī translated the Madhyama and the Ekottara āgamas from Sanskrit with the help of Chu Fo-nien and others, a work which took them two years to finish. At this stage the capital was invaded by Yao-chang and in the confusion that followed Nandī left the city, went westward and thus left the place for ever. It was Chao-cheng, who rescued his works from destruction. But to-day we find only two of his works in the Tripiṭaka,—the Ekottara āgama (Nanjio, 543) and Aśoka-rājaputra-cakṣurbheda-nidāna-sūtra (Nanjio, 1367) or the story of the blinding of Kuṇāla, the son of Aśoka. His Madhyama āgama is lost, they say, but really it seems to have been utilised by Gautama Saṅghadeva, who revised and published it (see above).

Saṅghabhūti and Saṅghadeva

Saṅghadeva and Saṅghabhūti [1] were contemporaries of Dharmanandī. Saṅghabhūti came to Chang-an from Kashmir bringing with him several books of the Vaibhāṣika Sarvāstivādins. Among these works was a copy of Abhidharma-vibhāṣā-śāstra (Nanjio, 1279), which he translated. This work should not be confused with the great commentary on Kātyāyanīputra's Jñānaprasthāna-śāstra. The work is a digest of that large treatise, which will be described under Hiuen-tsang. Saṅghabhūti's another work of translation was the text of Ārya Vasumitra's Saṅgiti-śāstra (Nanjio, 1289 ; in 10 chap.) which he did in collaboration with Dharmanandī and Saṅghadeva. He also translated another 'Sūtra on the practice of Buddha' (Nanjio, 1352) compiled by Saṅgharakṣa [2], a monk who is said to have lived seven hundred years after the Buddha, and his date, therefore, after liberal computation, cannot be earlier than the first century A. D. He was first introduced into China by An Shi-kao in the 2nd century (Nanjio, 1326).

1 Nanjio, App. II, 54 ; Bagchi, p. 160 ; Chin. Seng-kia-po-cheng ; translated as Chung-hien, 'Company-appearing'.

2 Nanjio, App. I, 35.

Gautama Saṅghadeva seems to have been the constant friend and co-worker of Dharmanandī and Saṅghabhūti ; several translations bear the name of all the three authors. Saṅghadeva came to Chang-an in A. D. 383, whence he went to Loyang, where he translated several works mentioned above [1]. Of all his works the Madhyama-Āgama, which seems to be a revised version of Dharmanandī's work, has won him an immortal fame, because the translation is unique and complete. His other works were re-translated at a later date by worthier scholars.

Before we close this period we must not forget to mention two Chinese Buddhists, who were responsible for the maintenance of Hindu culture during these troublous times. One is Chao-cheng, a government official of Fu-K'ien, who contributed a great deal to the propagation of Buddhism. It has already been mentioned how he invited the Buddhist monks to the capital and encouraged them to translate Sanskrit works into Chinese. But for him it would have been impossible for the Indian monks to do any literary work. The other person is Tao-an, the moving spirit and guide of the age. He was born in a family of Confucianist scholars. In his childhood he received the orthodox Chinese education, but aftor the death of his parents, at the age of twelve he was converted to the Buddhist faith. He devoted his undivided attention to the study of the sacred literature and the practice of vinaya-rules and also showed unusual capacity of committing the texts to memory and grasping the meaning of same. He was greatly inspired by that mystic monk Fo-t'u-teng (Buddhadāna, see above), became his disciple and soon won an important position in the community. He inspired the Chinese Buddhists and helped the Indian monks in the work of translation as an interpreter and editor ; besides this he wrote several introductions to the important translations. Chinese critics say that Tao-an was the first to introduce a sound style of translation. None of his translations has come down to us ; but his independent commentaries, treatises on vinaya twenty-four in number, and

Two Chinese monks

Tao-an

1 Nanjio, App. II. 36 and 39 ; Bagchi, pp. 161, 335-338.

his introductions, numbering sixteen, reveal his erudition and his love for the Law of the Buddha.

On examining the sacred texts Tao-an found that there was no systematic history of the Buddhist authors and translators; nor was there any complete catalogue of the texts. He, therefore, compiled a catalogue of the Buddhist works translated into Chinese from the time of Shi-kao to that of his own. The work is known in Chinese as Tsong-li-chang-king-mu-lu, and the date of its completion has been fixed at A. D. 374 [1], in the reign of the emperor Hiao of the Eastarn Tsin dynasty. Tao-an died in 385 A. D. at the age of seventy-two. The Early Tsin dynasty, though of a short life, produced some remarkable translators under its patronage, including a talented man like Tao-an, in whom every dynasty may take pride.[2]

His catalogue of Buddhist books

This period is important in Chinese literary history, for the Sarvāstivada āgamas were completely translated into Chinese at this time. During the Early Tsin dynasty two Āgamas were rendered into Chinese; but it is better that all the four Āgamas, which were translated within half a century and which form a unit, should be treated in one place, even at the sacrifice of chronological order.

Sanskrit Āgamas in Chinese

It is noticeable that three of the four great āgamas were translated by monks who came either from Tukhāra or from Ki-pin. Guṇabhadra, the translator of the Saṁyukta āgama, alone came from Central India and the text he translated was brought from Ceylon by Fa-hien. It is also certain that though the Chinese āgamas and Pali nikāyas have many things in common, the arrangement of the subject matter is quite different [3]. The relation between the Sanskrit āgamas and the Pali nikāyas is a great problem in the history of Indian literature. The original Sanskrit āgamas are no longer in existence,[4] they

1 Pelliot, T'oung Pao, 1918-89, p. 358, f.n. 2 and 1911, p. 675; Bagchi, p. XXXV.

2 Chavannes, *BEFEO*, 1903, p. 431.

3 Eliot, *op. cit.*, III, pp. 296 ff.

4 Fragments in Sanskrit have been discovered in Central Asia.

are only preserved in the Chinese translation, which we are discussing here. These collections of sūtras are not called nikāyas but *a-han* or āgamas. There is good reason to suppose that these works represent not the Pali canon, but rather the Sanskrit collection. That one or many Sanskrit works may have existed side by side with a similar Pali work is clearly shown by the Vinaya texts, for here we have the Pali canon and Chinese translations of five Sanskrit versions, belonging to different schools, but apparently covering the same ground and partly identical.

We shall presently describe the four Sanskrit āgamas which have complete Chinese translations. But "besides these we have over 150 translations, agreeing more or less with parts of these four collections, dating from 148 to 1058 A. D. This number will be doubled, if we take into account those lost texts, which are mentioned in old catalogues, and which by their titles, seem to have been parts of these."[1]

In the first stage of the propagation of the Hinayāna texts in China we find only separate texts or sūtras translated by eminent translators. In this period An Shi-kao (148-179), Chi Chien (223-253), Dharmakṣema (266-317), Fa-chu (296-306), Dharmarakṣa (381-395) and many other minor, forgotten and unknown writers translated no less than two hundred sūtras from the āgamas, but all of them are not preserved.

Four āgamas of the Hinayāna

In the second period, the period under review, complete translation of the four āgamas were made by the Indian monks. The four āgamas are :

1. Madhyama āgama (Middle collection ; in Chinese, Chung a-han ching) translated by Dharmanandi in 384-391 (now lost) ; later by Gautama Saṅghadeva in 397-398 (Nanjio, 542).

2. Ekottara āgama (Numerical collection ; in Chinese, Tseng-yi-a-han ching) translated by Dharmanandi in 384-385 (Nanjio, 543). Another translation by Prajñāruci done in 397 is now lost.

1 Anesaki, Four Buddhist Agamas in Chinese. *Transactions of the Asiatic Society of Japan*, 1908, vol. 35, Part 3, p. 34 ; henceforward quoted as Anesaki.

3. Dīrgha āgama (Long collection; in Chinese Ch'ang a-han ching) translated by Buddhayaśas in 412-413 (Nanjio, 545).

4. Saṃyukta āgama (Classified collection; in Chinese, Tsa a-han ching) incomplete translation by an unknown writer in 350-430 (Nanjio, 546). Completely translated by Guṇabhadra in 435-443 (Nanjio, 544).

The above āgamas correspond roughly to the Pali nikāyas Majjhima, Aṅguttara, Dīgha and Saṁyutta respectively. But there is another collection in Pali viz., Khuddaka nikāya.

Khuddaka nikāya in Chinese

The Khuddaka collection as a whole is wanting in the Chinese, and probably did not form a part of the Sanskrit āgama. But in Chinese there are some texts of it incorporated or quoted in other texts of the Tripiṭaka. The various redactions of the Dhammapada,[1] the Itivuttaka,[2] various passages of the Sutta-nipāta, and portions of the Udāna are met with in various places of the Chinese Tripiṭaka; but no complete work known as Kṣudraka āgama exists. The existence of such an āgama is admitted by the Theravādins (Sthaviravādins) of the present day and in older times its existence was admitted by the Dharmagupta and the Mahāsāṅghika schools. The Sarvāstivādins, the most important branch of Hīnayāna, never mentioned the Kṣudraka āgama; they as well as the Mulasarvāstivādins definitely speak of four āgamas.

The Dharmagupta school divides the Kṣudraka āgama into the following twelve sections: 1. Jātaka, 2. Itivṛttaka, 3. Nidāna (?) 4. Vaipulya, 5. Adbhūta, 6. Avadāna, 7. Upadeśa, 8. Artha-varga, 9. Dharmapada, 10. Pārāyaṇa (Suttanipāta), 11. Kathā-vastu, 12. Sthaviragāthā.

The Mahāsāṅghikas however admit only two divisions of the Kṣudraka āgama, viz., (1) Itivṛttaka-nidāna of the Buddhas and Arhats and (2) Gāthās of Bhikṣus. We have these informations from Chinese sources[3]

1 Nanjio, 1321, 1353, 1365, 1439

2 Nanjio, 714, Itivṛttaka translated ny Hiuen tsang,

3 Anesaki, pp. 7, 10; Levi, Seize Arhats etc., *J. As.*, 1916.

The first complete translation of the Madhyama-āgama and the Ekottara āgama was made by the monk Dharmanandi of Tukhāra ; Nandi's Madhyama āgama is said to be lost, but his Ekottara survives. The latter work was corrected and definitely finished by Gautama Saṅghadeva. It seems that Saṅghadeva also corrected the Madhyama āgama of Nandi and prepared the final redaction.[1]

Madhyama āgama

The Madhyama āgama, as its title signifies, is a collection made up of the discourses of 'middle' length, delivered by the Buddha ; but it does not imply that they are all shorter than the discourses of the Dīgha nikāya. Anesaki, after carefully comparing the Chinese translation with the Pali version of the Majjhima nikāya says that the deviations are greater in this collection than in the Dīgha. It is suspected that either the Pali Majjhima has transferred some of the sūtras to Ekottara, or that the Madhyama original of the Chinese version has taken many Ekottara texts to itself.[2]

In the Madhyama āgama, there are 222 sūtras, of which 99 agree with Majjhima, 75 with Aṅguttara, 9 with Dīgha, 8 with Saṁyutta, 15 with the Khuddaka nikāya, 2 with the Vinaya ; 1 is found in the Divyāvadāna and 23 are not yet identified.[3]

In the Pali Majjhima nikāya, the number of suttas is only 152 of which only 78 are identified with corresponding sections of the Chinese Madhyama āgama ; 7 suttas of Majjhima, are met with in the Saṁyukta and Ekottara āgamas ; 6 suttas of Majjhima are met with in the Ekottara ; 14 suttas of Majjhima may be found in the Saṁyukta ; 3 suttas of Majjhima are found in different versions and 24 are not yet identified[4]

The Ekottara āgama was, as has been already said, for the

---

1 See Bagchi, p. 338
2 Anesaki, p. 40.
3 *Ibid*, p. 61
4 *Ibid*, p. 67.

first time completely translated by Dharmanandi and revised by Saṅghadeva. The Aṅguttara nikāya in Pali roughly corresponds to the Ekottara āgama. But the Chinese version differs from the Pali tradition more than any of the other three collections. "In some parts its style has the chracteristics of the Mahāyāna texts. Even where the texts agree as a whole with the Pali texts, the differences of detail are very remarkable. There are strong reasons to believe that the version was made from a text handed down by a school which had very different tradition from the Theravāda, possibly by one of the Mahāsāṅghika sections."[1]

Ekottara āgama

"The present version of the Ekottara āgama is divided into 52 sections (Vaggas), and has no designation of the numerical divisions (nipātas) such as occur in the Pali Aṅguttara." "However, the whole collection is divided into eleven nipātas, as in the Pali version. Differences between the Pāli Aṅguttara and the Chinese Ekottara are more remarkable when the texts that agree in outline in the two versions are compared in detail." Anesaki further thinks that this collection represents an intermediate stage between the Pali books and such texts as the Mahāvastu.[2]

There is another earlier but shorter version of Ekottara āgama rendered into Chinese by the Parthian monk Shi-kao, with a collection of only 44 sūtras, which is known as 'Sūtra of the seven positions and three meditations.' (Nanjio, 648)[3]

The Dīrgha āgama was the third āgama to be translated completely. It was rendered into Chinese by Buddhayaśas in 412-413 A. D., fifteen years after the translation of the Madhyama by Saṅghadeva. The Dīrgha āgama contains the longest discourses of the Buddha delivered on various occasions. Its contents, which have been outlined by Nanjio in his Catalogue, agree greatly with the Pali Dīgha nikāya. In the Chinese version there are 30 sūtras, of

Dīrgha āgama,

1 Anesaki, p. 139.
2 *Ibid.* p. 140.
3 *Ibid*, pp. 28-31.

which three (11, 12, 34) have no corresponding Pali versions. In the Pali Dīgha nikāya there are 34 sūtras, of which four,—6. Mahāli, 7. Jaliya, 10. Subha, 32. Āta-nātiya--are wanting in Chinese. The last sūtra of the Dīrgha, that of loka-dhātu, is very important for Buddhist theology. Most of the verses in the text introduced by the compiler in support of the various resorts of transmigration may be traced in the nikāyas and āgamas (ibid. p. 35). Anesaki has pointed out that the sūtra of loka-dhātu has been expanded into many sūtras at a later age (Nanjio, 549-361 & and 679). Nanjio has further analysed the chapter on loka-dhātu (Nanjio, 545. 30) in his Catalogue. It deals with the following topics : 1. Jambudvīpa, 2. Uttara-kuru, 3. The holy Cakravarti-rājā, 4. The Narakas, 5. The Nāga and birds,6. The Asuras, 7. The three misfortunes, 10. The fighting (of the devas and Asuras), 11. The three middle Kalpas, 12. The original cause of the world. A detailed explanation of these topics, however, does not fall within the scope of the present work.

Saṁyukta āgama

The Saṁyukta āgama has two Chinese versions ; one, an incomplete translation by an unknown writer about 350-430 A. D. (Nanjio, 544) and the other by Guṇabhadra referred to above.

In this Āgama, allied or kindred sayings of the Buddha are classified and grouped together, as the longer and medium discourses are put in the Dīrgha and Madhyama āgamas respectively. The earlier Chinese translation though incomplete, has a better and clearer arrangement than that of Guṇabhadra.

This Āgama is full of very short sūtras, slight and concise sketches, dealing with legends of fairies, gods, devils, with royal and priestly interviewers of the sublime teacher. We have elsewhere (Ceylon) dealt at length with the contents of the Saṁyutta nikāya.

Although the two Chinese versions differ from one another and from the Pali redaction, yet there is essential agreement between them. The eight Vargas of the Chinese Saṁyukta āgama are Skandha, Saḍāyatana, Nidāna, Śrāvaka, Mārga, Pudgala, Sagātha, Buddha or Tathāgata.[1] The Pali nikāya has two main divisions: Sagātha Vagga, in ten chapters and Nidāna Vagga in twenty-one.

---

1 Anesaki pp. 68-138; also *The Eastern Buddhist* 1924. *Books of Kindre Sayings*, translated by Mrs. Rhys Davids. Parts I, II, P, T. S, 1917-1922.

VII. The Ts'in Dynasty

Tao-an the great patron-scholar of Buddhism died in 385 ; the same year, the Tsin Emperor Fu-k'ien was murderod. Fu-k'ien was a great lover of learning and supported Buddhism staunchly. Tao-an finding the Chinese translations of Sanskrit works very defective, had spoken of a great scholar named Kumārajīva, of the neighbouring kingdom of Kucha, and had requested the emperor to fetch him to China. Fu-k'ien sent an envoy to Po Chuen, the king of Kucha for this monk ; but the Kuchean king was unwilling to part with the learned monk, who had spent about thirty years of his life as the cheif monk of the Kuchean saṅgha. The refusal of the Kuchean king was looked upon as an affront to the dignity of the emperor and Lü-kuang, the general sent as envoy, waged war, against the combined forces of the kings of Kucha, Karashar and Och-Turfan and brought the Kuchean monk prisoner to China. But before the victorious general reached Chang-an, Fu-k'ien had been murdered by Yao-ch'ang and the ambitious Lü-kuang instead of proceeding to Chang-an set up an independent kingdom at Ku-tsang (modern Wu-wei-hien) in Kansu province and kept Kumārajīva in his capital from 385 to 401 A. D.

Fu-k'ien's war with Kucha to bring monk Kumārajīva

The new dynasty set up at Chang-an in 385 after the murder of Fu-k'ien is known in history as the Latter Ts'in dynasty. When this new dynasty occupied the throne of Chang-an, there was little change in the administration or in attitude towards Buddhism.

New dynasty of Latter Ts'in, 384-417

Yao-ch'ang, the first ruler of the Latter Ts'in dynasty, ruled from 384 to 395, and his successor Yao-hing from 395 to 417. These two reigns practically cover the Ts'in dynasty. Both these emperors were earnest Buddhists and this period might be said to be one of the brightest epochs of Buddhism in China. Several well-

Ts'in emperors earnest Buddhist

known translators worked during this period ; of these, Kumārajīva of Kucha won the respect of the learned literati of China. We shall however describe the literary activity of Kumārajīva in China in the next chapter, confining ourselves here to the work done by the other translators of this age.

Chu Fo-nien[1] is the most important personality whom we meet at this epoch not merely as a translator of Sanskrit books, but also as an interpreter to a number of Indian monks who came to China.

Fo-nien, a patron and interpreter

He was a monk of Liang-cheu in the province of Kansu, and was probably an Indian by birth as the prefix *Chu* suggests. Fo-nien would mean Buddhasmṛti. He was a monk of vast erudition and wide culture, who had visited many countries and knew many languages. We have already said how Chao-cheng, the good Buddhist official, invited Saṅghabhūti and Dharmanandī to the capital to translate Buddhist Sanskrit works. One of their principal assistants was Fo-nien, who translated the Sanskrit words into Chinese, while the others explained the Sanskrit texts. This work of assistance continued for twenty years from 365 to 384. The Chinese historians say that after An Shi-kao and Che Chien, Fo-nien was the most remarkable translator. His period of activity extended over the Earlier and Latter Ts'in dynasties and in spite of his work as an interpreter he found time to translate twelve books of which eight exist to this day.

Fo-nien's translations mainly deal with the Bodhisattva-cult of the Mahāyāna. The following are the works translated by Chu Fo-nien on the Bodhisattva-cult :

1. Bodhisattvamālā sūtra (Nanjio, 445) in 12 chapters.
2. Daśabhūmi-kleśa-cchedikā sūtra—'sūtra on the cutting of the tie of passions in the ten dwellings or steps, i. e. Daśabhūmi (Nanjio, 375).
3. Bodhisattvagarbha sūtra (Nanjio, 433).
4. Ch'e-jen P'u-sa ching (lost).
5. P'u-sa P'u-ch'u ching (lost).

---

1 Nanjio, App. II, 58; Bagchi, p. 170.

6. Sūtra on the original action of the Bodhisattvamālā' (Nanjio, 1092).

His translations chiefly works on Bodhisattva

The Mahāyānists conceived that there are ten stages in the spiritual life of a Bodhisattva or an aspirant to salvation and worked out a detailed schema of the process of this spiritual evolution. As to this new cult it should be stated here that although the Bodhisattvas are endowed with many eminent moral and intellectual qualities, their most striking characteristic is compassionateness. "They represent in general, active virtue and highmindedness, in contradistinctions to the Arhats, who are inactive. One might mark the difference between the two classes of persons saying that the Bodhisattvas are compassionate, the Arhats are impassionate or passionless."[1]

Bodhisattva cult in Chinese

The earliest reference in extant Buddhist Sanskrit literature to Bodhisattva's stages or bhūmis is found in the Mahāvastu[2] ; it is also described in the Lalitavistara. In A. D. 79, Chu Fa-lan or Dharmaratna is said to have translated a version of the Daśabhūmikleśacchedikā, of which Fo-nien prepared another translation (Nanjio, 375). The earliest extant work on Bodhisattva's bhūmis or stages is the Chinese Tsien-pi-i-chieh-chu-te-ching, or the 'Sūtra on making gradually complete all the wisdom and virtue' (Nanjio, 110), translated by Chu Fa-hu or Dharmarakṣa of the W. Tsin dynasty (265-316) in 5 fasciculi. This work was however again translated from a larger recension by the great Kumārajīva, in collaboration with Buddhayaśas, both of whom we shall meet in this period (Nanjio, 105). The Daśabhūmika sūtra forms a section of the Avataṁsaka and both Buddhabhadra (418-420) and Śikṣānanda (695-699, see below) incorporated it in their series. Bodhiruci translated the text as well as Vasubandhu's commentary on it in the early sixth century (Nanjio, 1194).

1 Kern, *Manual of Buddhism*, p. 66.

2 Senart, p. 63-193, quoted by Poussin, *ERE*, article *Bodhisattva*.

Chronologically, prior to Fo-nien's translations the only work extant in Chinese was that of Fa-hu. Therefore the translations of Sanskrit works on Bodhisattva cult by Fo-nien is of highest consequence. Fo-nien was an exceptionally good Chinese writer and therefore his translation of Daśabhūmikleśacchedikā became extremely popular among the Buddhists. It is a work in 33 chapters and the subject matter treated in it are given below.[1]

The idea of Bodhisattva is the greatest innovation of the Mahāyāna Buddhism : it appealed to the Chinese as well as to the Japanese Buddhists as the highest and the most perfect ideal that a human being can set before him. We shall see more of it in our study of the Vimalakīrtinirdeśa translated by Kumārajīva, a work which inspired the Japanese people to accept Buddhism.

Besides these works another important work of Fo-nien's is the translation of the Avadāna sūtra. This work is really a commentary on the Udānavarga. In the preface to this version we are informed that Dharmatrāta, uncle of Vasumitra, was the original compiler of the Dharmapada. It is further narrated there that śramaṇa Saṅghabhūti had brought this copy of Udānavarga and its commentary from India, which was evidently translated by Fo-nien with the assistance of other monks.[2]

His translation of Avadānasūtra, a com. on the Udānavarga

The Avadāna sūtra consists of 34 chapters with a special title for each chapter. The titles of the chapters agree with those of the

1 See Rahder, *Daśabhūmika sūtram*, The Hague, 1924. The chapters are : 1. Praṇayanaṃ, 2. Adhiṣṭhāna-nirmāṇam, 3. Sūnyatā-dhyānam, 4. Rūpāyatanam, 5. Śūnyatājña, 6. Indriyamukham, 7. Prthuprajña, 8. Kumārabhūta, 9. Samāhitaṃ manas, 10. Bodhisattva mārga-vidhānaṃ. 11. Nirodhacittam. 12. Ṛddhipādāḥ, 13. Arcanā or Apacāyanā or Satkāra, 14. Vīra, Śūra, abhyupagama, 15. 'breaking the body'. a kind of Samādhi, 16. Kāyāyatnam, 17. Pratibhānam, 18. Upāyajñānam, 19. Converting the living beings, 20. Trimārga-(pari)-kīrtana, 21. Nairyānikānimitta or yānanimitta, .22. Samatākaruṇā 23. Dharmadhātu, 24. Mārga-jñānam, 25. Kāyavāṅmanas, 26. Svapnāntara-mārga vidhānam, 27. Bodhisattvābhisamaya. 28. Kie houei (prtipādana-mati). 29. Tridoṣa, 30. Nirvāṇapraśna, 31. Catvāri apramāṇāni, Karuṇā, Maitrī, Muditā, Upekṣā, 32. Brahmā's request, 33. Brahmāparindana.

2 Beal, *The Dhammapada*, translated from the Chinese pp. 27-29.

Tibetan translation of the Udānavarga[1] and in many cases with the verses themselves. This version is evidently a translation of the Sanskrit recension of the Udānavarga, while the Fa-chiu-ching done into Chinese by Vighna is doubtless the translation of a Pali version, very close to one we find in the Tripiṭaka of Ceylon. This is further corroborated by the discovery of Sanskrit fragments of Udānavarga from the Central Asian ruins which agree with this Chinese version of Fo-nien. Below we append the titles of the chapters of the Chinese Udānavarga, which will show how different it is from the Pali version or Fa-chiu-ching. The Vargas are :—

Chapters of Udānavarga

1.	Anitya. (Impermanency)	2.	Kāma (Desire)
3.	Tṛṣṇā (Lust)	4.	Apramāda (Purity)
5.	Pramāda (*not in Tib.*)	6.	Smṛti
7.	Śīla (Morality)	8.	Śikṣā (Virtuous conduct)
9.	Apavāda (Speech)	10.	Carya. (Deeds)
11.	Śraddhā (Faith)	12.	Śramaṇa
13.	Mārga (Way)	14.	Sambhoga.
15.	Dveṣa (Hatred)	16.	Bhāvanā ? (Reflection)
17.	Prakīrṇa (Miscellaneous)	18.	Apvarga (Water)
19.	Puṣpa (Flower)	20.	Aśva (Horse)
21.	Krodha (Anger)	22.	Tathāgata
23.	Śrāvaka (Hearer)	24.	Ātmā (Self)
25.	Vaipulya ? (Numbers)	26.	Bandhu (Friendship)
27.	Nirvāṇa	28.	Avalokita (Sight)
29.	Pāpa (Sin)	30.	Yuga (Day and night)
31.	Sukha (Happiness)	32.	Citta (Mind)
33.	Śramaṇa (Bhikṣu)	34.	Brāhmaṇa

It should be mentioned here that the Sanskrit Udānavarga-Dharmapada is distinctly a different work from the Pali Dhammapada. The Sanskrit work is also very ancient as is proved from the Central Asian fragment edited by Dr. Niranjan Chakravarty.

1 Translated by W. H. Rockhill 1892; the Tibetan text has been edited by H. Beck, Berlin, 1907.

It seems that several chapters of Fa-chiu-ching of Vighna were drawn from the materials of the Sanskrit Udānavarga, which must have gone to China in the early third century A. D.

The most remarkable monk of this age who came from India, was Buddhayaśas[1] the friend and guru of Kumārajīva. Buddhayaśas was born of a brahmana family of Kashmir, and when still young he felt great attraction for the teachings of the Buddha. He studied the literature of Hīnayāna as well as of Mahāyāna over and above Brahmanical works and finally became a Buddhist monk. He left Kashmir as a wandering preacher and went to Kashgar (She-le), which was a Buddhist country, and lived there greatly honoured by the king, who himself was a Buddhist. It was at this time that the young Kumārajīva was passing through Kashgar on his way back to Kucha from Kashmir. During his stay there, Kumārajīva studied for sometime under Buddhayaśas. Buddhayaśas must have remained in Kashgar for more than three decades. In 383 when Kucha was invaded by the Chinese general, the king of Kashgar went to succour that city leaving the young heir-apparent in charge of the Indian monk. But before the Kashgar army could reach Kucha, the Chinese general had gone away with Kumārajīva as prisoner, the purpose of the invasion being thus fulfilled. Ten years later (393 A. D.) Buddhayaśas went to Ku-tsang to meet his old pupil, but found that Kumārajīva had left the town for the capital Chang-an. Learning that the great Indian teacher had arrived at Ku-tsang, Kumārajīva requested the emperor to bring him to the capital. Buddhayaśas was a monk of very deep spiritual life and he refused the king's presents with the scorn befitting a spiritually advanced monk as he was; but at last he came to the capital without accepting any presents, nor expecting anything from the king. A monastery was built for this old Indian monk, from which he would preach his religion. Such was his learning that even the great Kumārajīva

Buddhayśas of Kashmir

1 Nanjio, II. 61; Bagchi, p. 200; Chin. Fo-to-ye-she; translated as Chia-ming 'intelligence-brightness,

who was more than sixty years old, when the translations under him began, would sometimes come to him, when in doubt.

The number of works translated by Buddhayaśas is not many but they are important. Fo-nien, the great scholar, whom we have already met, helped Buddhayaśas in his translations as his interpreter, while five hundred other monks assisted him in his work. Thus assisted he was able to bring out in Chinese the translation of the Dīrgha āgama. The work consisted of 23 fasc. (Nanjio, 545) divided into four vargas and having thirty sūtras. The work has been described above along with the other Sarvāstivādin āgamas in Chinese.

Translation of the Dīrgha āgama

The other work of Buddhayaśas is a translation of an important Mahāyāna sūtra called Ākāśagarbhabodhisattva sūtra (Nanjio, 68). The original is now lost; but in the eighth century Śāntideva quoted extensively from the book in his well-known work, Śikṣā-samuccaya.[1] It describes the five root sins, which a prince should avoid and other 'eight root sins' which beset young men and women, when they are inceptors and just entering on the 'Great way'. The eight sins which are described in details in the Ākāśagarbha sūtra are 1. Discouragement of Hearers; 2. Dissuading from following perfections and preaching ideals that lead to Hīnayāna; 3. Preaching Mahāyāna as substitute for rules and 'discipline'; 4. Undue disparagement of the Śrāvakayāna; 5. Self-aggrandisement; 6. Advertising one's profound knowledge; 7 and 8. Robbing the Brotherhood of its property. The means of escape from these sins is set forth in the same book, which prescribes the worship of Bodhisattva Ākāśagarbha, with some prayers and incantations.

Ākāśagarbha-bodh sattva sūtra

While the translation of the Dīrghāgama won Buddhayaśas a lasting fame in China, his Vinaya translations won him no less respect. The Chinese Buddhists for sometime past were trying to remodel the Buddhist saṅgha in the model of the Indian church and

1 Translated by Bendal and Rouse, Indian Text Series, p. 61-70

that was one of the main reasons which led Fa-hien to visit India. Buddhayaśas and Kumārajīva in the north and Fa-hien and Buddhabhadra in the south translated important Vinaya books during the first quarter of the fifth century. Buddhabhadra and Fa-hien translated Mahāsāṅghika Vinayas, Puṇyatara rendered the Sarvāstivādin Vinaya, Kumārajīva translated the Vinayas of the Mahāyāna, while Buddhayaśas translated the Vinaya works of the Dharmagupta school, in 60 fasc. (Nanjio, 1117) and the Dharmagupta Prātimokṣa (Nanjio, 1155). The Dharmagupta vinaya remained for several centuries the principal code of discipline in the saṇghas of China.

Dharmagupta Vinaya in China

It is a well-known fact that according to orthodox tradition Upāli at the first Council at Rājagṛha held immediately after the death of Lord Buddha, recited the disciplinary decisions of the Teacher and formed them into a connected whole. This is the basis of the Vinaya. But in course of time opinions on rules of conduct began to differ and cliques and schisms formed in the community of brethren. Dharmagupta, a leader of a party (circa. B. C. 240) reformed the Vinaya by a new recitation and withdrew his followers from communion with the others.

Vinaya in Buddhism

After this, the process of dissolution went on rapidly and in course of time twenty sects arose within the Saṅgha. Of these the vinayas of four sects reached China. The Vinaya of the Dharmagupta school, introduced by Buddhayaśas was the principal book of conduct in China till the 7th cent. A. D., when the Mūlasarvāstivādin Vinaya introduced by Yi-tsing became popular.

It may be mentioned here by the way that the early Han translators had spoken little of formal Vinaya rules; they had confined themselves only to the preaching of *sīla* or morality. Shi-kao, the royal monk of Parthia translated into Chinese for the first time a sūtra, said to have been spoken by the Buddha himself, on "the lightness and heaviness of the sin of transgressing the *sīla*" (Nanjio, 112). Another sūtra which illustrates the Mahāyāna conception of śīla, by observing the six pāramitas appeared in the early days of translation (Nanjio, 435). The pioneers of Buddhism in China had apparently been contented with a mere 'sowing of seeds', and they said little of discipline or Vinaya to the early converts.

It was after about two centuries and half that the Chinese Buddhists themselves wanted to know more of the Buddhist monastic life and its discipline, and Fa-hien as a student of Vinaya visited India and Ceylon in search of Vinaya texts, to which we have already referred. But Buddhayaśas' translation of the Dharmagupta Vinaya finally became the most popular in China.[1]

Another recension of the Vinaya, viz., of the Sarvāstivadin was also introduced into China during this age by Puṇyatara.[2] Puṇyatrāta and Dharmayaśas were contemporaries of Buddhayaśas and Kumārajīva both coming from Kashmir. Dharmayaśas was a very good scholar and well-read in the Vibhāṣā and his translation of *Sāriputra abhidharma śāstra* (Nanjio, 1268), which he did in 407 A. D., is a standing testimony to his labour and learning. It is said that the Ts'in king Yao-hing took great interest in this particular work. Probably after the fall of the Ts'in dynasty Dharmayaśas left the north and came to the south during the Sung dynasty. Then he proceeded westward and was no more heard of. Puṇyatrāta was also a good scholar and he worked with Kumārajīva in the translations of Sanskrit. He translated the Vinaya of the Sarvāstivādins; but his work is attributed to Kumārajīva by some authorities (Nanjio, 1160) which is however not correct.[3]

Dharmayaśas & Puṇyatrāta of Kashmir in China, Circa 400 A. D.

---

1 Wieger has given a complete translation of the Dharmagupta Prātimokṣa of Buddhayaśas, *op. cit.* pp. 489-507; also Beal, Catena, pp. 206-209. Lloyd, *The Creed of Half Japan.* pp 132-130

Recently Waldschmidt has discussed the various recensions of Prātimoksa Pali, Sanskrit, Tibetan and four schools preserved in Chinese translation in his *Bruchstucke des Bhiksunī Prātimokṣa der Sarvāstivādins* (Koniglich Preussische Turfan Expeditionen) Leipzig, 1926.

Nanjio, App. II, 62; Bagchi, 174; *Chin.* T'an-mo-ye-she; translated as Fa-cheng. 'Law-fame'.

2 Nanjio, App. II, 60; Bagchi, 176; *Chin.* Fo-jo-to-lo, translated Kung-to-hua, 'Virtue-flower'. also Puṇyatrāta.

3 Bagchi, p. 177.

VIII. The Life and Works of Kumarajiva

Few Indian names are so well-known to the Chinese Buddhists as the name of the great monk Kumārajīva [1] who lived in the time of Yao-hing, the second king of Later Ts'in dynasty (A. D. 384-417). Kumārajīva's father Kumārāyana was an Indian and his mother Jivā was the sister of the Kuchean king. Kumārajīva in his boyhood visited Kashmir and several important centres of Buddhist culture in Central Asia with his mother and returned to Kucha in A. D. 352, when he was a youngman of twenty and there he preached and propagated the Mahāyāna Buddhism for about thirty years. The fame of the Kuchean monk soon crossed the desert and mountain and reached the Chinese court of the Earlier T'sin. Tao-an, the inspirer, comrade and friend of the Buddhist monks, had spoken of Kumārajīva to Fu-k'ien, the emperor of that dynasty (357-384 A. D.). Fu-k'ien sent an envoy to the Kuchean king Po Chuen for bringing the learned monk to China. The Kuchean king refused to send the pious monk who had been living in his capital for the past thirty years. The envoy thought himself insulted and thereupon waged war on the poor Kuchean king and defeated the combined army of Kucha, Karashar and Och-Turfan. The monk was carried prisoner and treated at first very indecently by the Chinese general. But before the victorious Chinese general reached the capital, Fu-k'ien had been murdered by Yao-ch'ang in 385 A. D. The Chinese general Lu-huang thereupon set up an independent principality at Ku-tsang (modern Wu-wei-hien in Kan-su province) and kept Kumārajīva in his capital. Yao-ch'ang of the Later Ts'in dynasty sent for

Kumārāyana father of Kumārajīva

Kumārajīva, a Kuchean monk, b.332,-d.413

Lives in Ku-tasng 385-400 A. D.

1 Nanjio, App. II, 59; Bagchi, pp. 178-200; *Chin.* Kiu-mo-la-k'i-p'o; translated 'Tung-shou,' 'boy-age or longivity. For the life of Kumārajīva see Levi, *Tokharien B—la langue de koutcha, J.As. 1913*: also J. Nobel, Kumārajiva. *Sitzungberichte der Preussischen Akademie d. Wissenschaften* 1927. XX. pp. 206—228

Kumārajiva, but was refused. When Yao-chang became king in A. D. 401, he again sent for the monk, and this time the Lus had to accede to his request.

Kumārajiva came to Chang-an in A. D. 401 and the emperor who was eagerly expecting the monk at once made him the Kuo-shih or Rājya-guru. As the Rājya-guru he wielded extensive

K. lives in Chang-an 401-413 A. D.

powers and the emperor too helped him in all possible manners. Thus Kumārajiva was able to preach and propagate the teachings of the Buddha in the land of his adoption. A special hall was built by the Emperor where he preached to three thousand disciples.

Kumārajiva was a man of great erudition and culture and is considered as one of the greatest translators of Chinese Buddhist works. Though his mother tongue was neither Sanskrit nor Chinese, yet he was master of both. A Hindu monk by descent and education, he was familiar with all the twists and turns of Sanskrit and as an inhabitant of Kucha he had a good opportunity of thoroughly learning the Chinese language. Few foreigners have yet gained any distinction in writing literary Chinese, but Kumārajiva was a notable exception. On examination and comparison of the extant Chinese translations of Buddhist works and their originals, Kumārajiva found that the former were far from being either accurate or elegant. Elegance of stylo and artistic expression are generally neglected in the translations of religious books. The earlier Buddhist works in China suffered from these defects. To the Chinese, finesse

K. translates Buddhist texts

of style was always a factor of considerable importance essential to the success of propaganda depending upon literary mission. Till the time of Kumārajiva it was the non-Chinese Buddhist monks from central Asia and India who had been responsible for the translation of Sanskrit Buddhist books into Chinese. They were generally helped by the native Buddhist converts, unfamiliar with the mode of Indian thought and expression often choosing wrong synonyms for Sanskrit words. Thus the translations were generally imperfect paraphrases of Sanskrit words, sometimes becoming unintelligible even to Chinese readers. To bring them out in a more scientific and accurate form was the task undertaken by Kumārajīva at the desire of king Yao-hing. This work occupied him for the rest of his life and it was the joy and pride of his declining years. At the instance of the enthusiastic king, more than eight hundred scholars joined the staff under Kumārajīva to assist him in preparing the translations of new Sanskrit works into Chinese and revising older texts; the king himself, an ardent disciple of the new faith was sometimes present at the conference helping the labours of the scholars.

K. translates 106 works in 421 fasc. of which 56 extant

The number of works thus translated by Kumārajīva was one hundred and six in 421 fasc., of which fifty-six only are now extant the rest having perished. The Hindu monk of Kucha worked at Chang-an for twelve years before his death (A.D. 413) he had the satisfaction of seeing that the most important Mahāyāna works were rendered into Chinese.

Kumārajīva a Mahāyanist

Kumārajīva in his earlier years was however not a Mahāyānist but a staunch follower of the Sarvāstivāda school of Hīnayāna, the sect most prominent in Kucha and the adjacent oases sates. In his boyhood he was taken to Kashmir by his pious mother who wanted to give him a sound training in the Hīnayāna literature under the great teachers of Kashmir. Her wishes were fulfilled and the young boy learned thoroughly what the philosophy of that school had to teach. Thus equipped he left India for his mother's city. But on his way he stopped at Shu-le (Kashgar), where he came in contact with the royal monk Sūryasoma, a staunch Mahāyānist who was preaching in those days the Mahāyāna philosophy to the local sangha and the lay people of the city; he had taken as the basis of his lectures the well-known *tri-śāstra*, the three scriptures of the Mādhyamika school, viz., the *Mādhyamika sūtra* and the *Dvādaśanikāya* of Nāgārjuna and the *Śataśāstra* of Āryadeva. The inner meaning of Mahāyāna expounded by such a powerful monk at once illuminated the Bodhi-citta of Kumārajiva and he became a follower of the Great vehicle. This was indeed a great turning point in the life of Kumārajīva and this conversion left an indeliable mark upon the later history of Buddhism in the Far East.

In China Kumārajiva preached Mahāyāna with the earnestness and fire of an apostle and translated all the principal works of this school into a beautiful and lucid language, which not even the most fastidious judge can criticize.

K. introduces Mahāyāna Ācāryas in China

But Mahāyāna sūtras were not wholly unknown in China, before the time of Kumārajīva; but the works of Nāgārjuna and Āryadeva were not known. These two teachers greatly influenced the course of thought in the east and we shall have have occasion to refer to the subject more elaborately later on.

Origin of Mahāyāna in India.

It is an erroneous theory enjoying wide currency that it was Nāgārjuna who laid the foundation of Mahāyāna. But Mahāyāna existed long before his time. A large number of works of distinctly Mahāyānistic origin and character long since extinct are mentioned by Nāgārjuna in his writings. This makes such a theory untenable. If we do not want to go back to the remote past, when Devadatta's schism took place, to seek the origin of Mahāyāna, we hear a distinct note of Mahāyāna sounded in the first split that arose over the question of the Vajjian monks at a later age. It is not improbable that these heterodox seceders from the sangha used such texts which were condemned by the conservative element as non-canonical.

In the history of Buddhism two aspects of the teaching of the Buddha are distinctly perceived from the very early times. One we may designate as the original Buddhism, by which we mean the conservative faith represented by the Sthaviras or the elders, while the other we have named as the progressive Buddhism upheld by the liberal element of the Sangha, known as the Mahāsānghikas. By original Buddhism we again mean the doctrine preached by the Buddha himself in public, while the progressive

Buddhism stands for the doctrines brought to light and gradually developed by the close disciples of the Tathāgata on his parinirvāṇa.

Hīnyāna vs. Mahāyāna.

The first has been termed by some scholars as phenomenological perception and the latter ontological perception of the Buddha, the two aspects may also be described as exoteric and esoteric. The former he preached to the ordinary disciples in public and put stress on the śila or discipline, conduct of life or mortality, while to his inner circle consisting of the more intellectual among his disciples expounded the highest ontological or esoteric secrets. Thus the doctrine embodied in the Hīnayāna were promulgated by the Buddha himself in the early years of his ministry, while the doctrine contained in the Mahāyāna were formulated by his disciples and followers after his death. Thus Mahāyāna came te be regarded as the highest from of teaching of the Buddha and treatises or sūtras were composed by its adherents long before Nāgārjuna was born.[1]

Of the vast mass of literature known as the Mahāyāna sūtras which existed before the time of Nāgārjuna, the best known group of works was the Prajñāpāramitā, which became the canonical treatises, so to speak of the Mādhyamika school in India. We do not know definitely where, when and how the Prajñā texts originated. A tradition however ascribes the Aṣṭasāhasrikā Prajñāpāramitā to south India, whence it travelled afterwards to the north and west of India.[2] [Anesaki, *ERE*, Vol. p. 838]. It may further be pointed out that both Nāgārjuna, as well as his disciple Āryadeva came from the Southern India. It may therefore be presumed that the philosophy of Prajñā came to be expounded and expanded by those disciples of the Buddha who had migrated to the south and in the course of time a rich literature on Prajñā sprang into existence. This came to be known as the Prajñāpāramitā.

Prajñā texts of Mahāyāna.

From the south, this literature travelled north and west and

1 Kimura, Hinayana and Mahayana and Origin of Mahayana Buddhism. (Calcutta University).

2 Wu dynasty 222-280 ; 6 fasc of 13 chap

beyond India finally reaching Central Asia, it was taken by ser-Indian monks and translated into Chinese in the second century A.D. As to the exact date of the origin of the *prajñā* literature we have no reliable data, except those furnished by the Chinese sources.

The earliest Chinese translation of a prajñā text belongs to the second century A.D.; it was a recension of the Daśa-sāhasrikā prajñāpāramitā done into Chinese by Lokaksema;[1] Han dynasty: translated between 147 and 186 in 16 fasc., of 30 chap.] a second version was made of the same work by the Yueh-chi monk Chien and in the third century. The Pañcaviṁśati sāhasrikā p.p. (Nanjio, 2 appeared for the first time in Chinese in 291. It was translated by Mokṣala, a Khotanese monk. Chu Fa-hu or Dharmarakṣa another Yueh-chi of Central Asia made incomplete translation at about A.D. 300. Dharmapriya and Chu Fo-nien translated another recension of the Daśasāhasrikā in 382. (In 5 fasc. or 13 chap).

Earlier translations of prajñā texts.

On the above data we can easily hazard some observations here. The earliest translation of *prajñā* found in Chinese dates from the lattar half of the second century; the translators were inhabitants of central Asia, who got the original texts from the monks travelling from India to the west. Thus the time intervening between the composition of the text in India and the translation into Chinese may be on a modest calculation, computed to be a century, if not more. We should further bear in mind that in India books were often written for the first time on a subject which had enjoyed a popularity extending over centuries; for a pretty long time theories used to be handed down by means of *śruti* or hearing from the preceptor to the disciple and so forth. Therefore, it does not seem improbable that the prajñā theory which was in vogue amongst certain sections of the Buddhists, came to be written down long after its origin and it took some decades if not centuries for the *prajñā* to

origin of prajñā texts

1 See Nanjio, 5, 8 o.

be developed into mighty proportions of the Daśasāhasrikā p.p. and the Pañcaviṁśati-sāhasrikā p.p.

Kumārajīva's translation of prajñā works

To Kumārajīva the Chinese Buddhists owe the first good translation of a series of important prajñā books, which we shall describe in course of our study. the works are :—

1. Pañcaviṁśatisāhasrikā prajñā pāramitā in 30 fas c., of 90 chap. (Nanjio, 3).
2. Daśasāhasrikāprajñāpāramitā in 10 fasc., of 29 Chap. (Nanjio, 6).
3. Vajracchedikāprajñāpāramitā (Nanjio, 10).
4. Prajñāpāramita Hṛdayasūtra (Nanjio, 19).
5. 'Prajñāpāramitā sūtra on a benevolent king who perfects his country' (Nanjio, 17).

The term prajñā originally meant intellectual training generally. Gradually it became confined: "to the exercise of contemplation transcending all discursive and rational knowledge." Among the disciples of the Buddha, Subhūti stands foremost in practising this contemplation. "It is he to whom are ascribed the occasions of the conversations on the subject, and the various texts known as the *Prajñā-pāramitā* are handed down to us bearing his (Subhūti's) name." In these texts "all possible arguments, including a number of similes and parables etc. are used to convince man of the non-reality of what is deemed by the common mind to be the reality".[1] The gist of the whole amounts to nothing but the *śuyatā* of all phenomena.

Pancaviṃsati Sahasrikā.

The Sanskrit text of the *Pañcaviṁśati Sāhasrikā* which Kumārajīva, and before him Mokṣala and Chu Fa-hu translated, exists in the original. We must not think that the text, which has been preserved in Nepal, would agree in all details with the text, which was carried to Central Asia in the first century A. D., or with the text which Kumārajīva rendered into Chinese in the early 5th century A. D.

1 Anesaki op. cit, p. 837.

But the subject-matter cannot be very different.[1] Kumārajīva's translation of *Pañcaviṃśati sāhasrikā* was in 10 fasc. of 90 chapters, whereas Hiuen Tsang's was in 78 fasc. of 85 chapters (Nanjio 1 b); that is, his translation of the latter was bigger by 48 fasciculi. The tedious custom of embodying constant repetitions which we find so annoying in the Pali Suttas, is carried to an excess in Sanskrit Buddhist literature too. Hiuen Tsang, as we shall see, translated the voluminous *Prajñāpāramitā* works with the zeal of a convert and therefore never omitted one line of the works and translated the original with all the repetitions. But Kumārajīva was more judicious and he omitted the repetitions and superfluities and translated the *Pañcaviṃśati Sāhasrikā* in 30 fasciculi only.[2]

Kumārajīva's next translation of the Prajñā series, is that of Daśa-sāhasrikā (Nanjio, 3). This work was translated thrice before him and it is the earliest work of the *Prajña* series to appear in

Daśasāhasrikā

Chinese. In Sanskrit there is no text known by this name; and it may be that it is the *Aṣṭasāhasrikā* which is mentioned here. The *Aṣṭasāhasrikā* seems to be the basis of *Prajña* pāramitā group of literature and it is not unlikely that this version should appear first in Chinese. Kumārajīva's able translation made it very popular among the Buddhists of China.

---

1 For the details readers are referred to the original and the summary made by Dr, Rajendralal Mitra in *The Sanskrit Buddhist Literature in Nepal*, Asiatic Society of Bengal, Calcutta, 1882, p. 193). A fuller treatment of the subject will be found in the volume on Tibet, for in Tibetan we have very large number Prajñā works. see also Wallesser's German work on Prajña.

2 Kumārajīva's translation of *Pañcasāhasrikā* consists of 30 fasc., and 90 sections comprising 1468 pages of 10 columns each; each column of 20 words so that the whole work consists of 2,93,600 words. According to the same calculation Hiuen Tsang's work would consist of 7,63,400 words. "It has been calculated that there are 1,81,253 words in the *New Testament*. The translation therefore, of Kumārajīva is about half as long again as the latter, and about one-fourth the size of the whole of Bible. Hiuen Tsang's version would be four times the *New Testament*. His complete translations of P. P. consists of 600 fasciculi, "being about 80 times the size of the whole Bible," Edkins says that the Buddhist cannon in China is 700 times larger than the *Bible*. Beal, *Catena*, p. 278.

But the most popular work of the *prajñā* series, which was accepted by all the people of Central and Eastern Asia, is the Vajracchedikā-prajñā-pāramitā, now for the first time translated into Chinese by Kumārajīva (Nanjio, 13). It must have greatly influenced the Chinese mind of the day. A modern Chinese historian says that the *Diamond Cutter* has done more to popularise Buddhism with the educated classes than all other materials put together.[1] It is one of the most widely read and most highly valued metaphysical treatises in Buddhist literature and Kumārajīva's lucid translation was greatly responsible for its popularity.[2]

Vajracchedikā-its analysis

The popularity of the work in China can easily be gauged by the number of subsequent translations; these are by Paramārtha (A. D. 562), Hiuen Tsang (A. D. 648), Yi tsing (A. D. 703) and Dharmagupta (A. D. 589-618).

"At first sight it may seem as if this metaphysical treatise hardly deserved the world wide reputation which it has attained." Because to readers unaccustomed to Indian thoughts and modes of expression the whole thing would appear self-contradictory. Like all other *Prajñā* texts *Vājracchedikā* simply denies the reality of all phenomenal objects established in the ordinary mind; it might well have seemed that such a belief could not be eradicated except by determined repetition...... There are two words, in particular, which are of great importance for a right apprehension of its teaching. Dharma and Saṁjñā." In the *Vajracchedikā* these two words are not used in the ordinary sense. Dharma "means form and likewise what is possessed of form", in one word 'matter'. "What our treatise wishes to teach is that all objects, one differing from the other by their dharmas, are illusive or as we should say 'phenomenal and subjective', that they are in fact of our own making, the products of our own mind. And hence the Buddhist metaphysician tells us that all things are but names, *Saṁjñās*, and that

1 Li ung Bing *Outlines of Chinese History*, p: 177.

2 An English translation of this Chinese version was first published by Beal. *JRAS*, 1864-5; also *Catena*, pp, 276ff.

being names they are neither what they seem to be nor what they do not seem to be."

The conversation in the work is between the Buddha and Subhūti. A few paragraphs are quoted here to illustrate the nature of the treatise. Bhagavat said : If a man should say that the Law has been taught by the Tathāgata, he would slander me with untruth which he has learned. And why? Because, O Subhūti, it is said the teaching of the Law, the teaching of the Law indeed. O Subhūti there is nothing that can be perceived by the name of the teaching of the Law (para 21) In another passage Bhagavat said : 'Even the smallest thing is not known or perceived there, therefore, it is called the highest perfect knowledge." (para 22). 'In that knowledge there is no difference, it is always the same and therefore perfect.' (p. 23). He who has attained the knowledge believes neither in the idea, i. e., the name of a thing, nor in the idea of a nothing, and Buddha by using the expression. the idea or name (*Saṁjñā*) of a thing, implies thereby that it is not the idea of a thing, implies thereby that it is not the idea of a thing' (para 31). This metaphysical agnosticism is represented as perfectly familiar even to children and ignorant persons (para 30) and if it was meant to be so, the endless repetition of the same process of reasoning may find its explanation," The treatise is concluded thus :

Passages from the Vajracchedikā

As in the sky :

Stars, darkness, a lamp, a phantom, dew, a bubble,

A dream, a flash of lightning, and a cloud—thus we should look upon the world (all that was made)[1]

The gist of the *Vajracchedikā* outlined above clearly explains why it was so popular in China and in other parts of Buddhist Asia. It is one of the handiest volumes of Prajñā texts, known sometimes as the Prajñāpāramitā of three hundred Sutras (Nanjio, I. i,) and its brevity, with determined repetitions,

1 *Sacred Book of the East* XLIX, Trans. by Maxmüller and also his Introduction.

so characteristic of Buddhist works was responsible for its wide acceptance.

But in brevity no work can surpass the sūtra known as the *Prajñāpāramita-hṛdaya* introduced by Kumārajīva now in China The whole Sanskrit text as it is discovered in Japan does not exceed two printed pages and the shorter Chinese translation of Kumārajīva consists of only 262 characters. This brevity must have helped its wide circulation among the Mahāyānists all over the east. It is recited by them even now almost on all religious occasions. Kumārajīva had translated the larger versions of the Prajñā texts ; but this small work did not escape his attention ; as the whole idea of *Śūnyatā* has been expressed most clearly in a very small compass, in this work, it may be quoted here in extenso :

Hṛdaya-sūtra in 262 Chinese characters

"When the Bodhisattva Avalokiteśvara was engaged in the practice of the deep prajñāpāramitā, he perceived that the five skandhas (Rūpa, Vedanā, Saṁjñā, Saṁskāra, Vijñāna) were all empty, and he was saved form all misery and suffering. "O Śāriputra," said he, "form (Rūpa) is no other than emptiness (Śūnyatā) and emptiness is no other than form ; what is form that is emptiness, and what is emptiness that is form. The same can be said of sensation, thought, conception and consciousness, O Śāriputra, all things are characterised by emptiness : they are not born, they are not anihilated, they are tainted, they are not immaculate, they do not increase, they do not decrease, therefore in emptiness there is no form, no sensation, no thought, conception, consciousness ; no eye, ear, nose, body and mind ; no form, sound, odour, taste, touch, and objects ; no element of vision etc., till we come to no element of consciousness ; there is no ignorance, nor is there the extinction of ignorance, etc., till we come to 'there is no old-age and death' ; nor is there the extinction of old-age and death ; there is no suffering, accumulation, annihilation, path ; there is no knowledge, nor is there any obtaining because there is nothing to be obtained. The

Sūnyatā explained from the Hṛdaya sūtra.

Bodhisattva depending on the prajñāpāramitā has no obstacles, he has no fear, and going beyond all perverted and unreal views, reaches final nirvāṇa. All Buddhas of past, present and future, depending on the *prajñāpāramitā* attain to the highest perfect wisdom. Therefore, we know that the prajñāpāramitā is a great divine mantra, a mantra of great intelligence, the highest mantra, the peerless mantra, which is capable of putting aside all sufferings; it is truth and not falsehood. Therefore, I proclaim the mantra of prajñāpāramitā. The mantra to be proclaimed then is: "*Gate, Gate, pāragate, parasaṁgate, bodhi, Svāhā*" (O wisdom, gone, gone, gone to the other shore, landed at the other shore, svāhā)".[1]

Kumārajīva was however not satisfied with merely translating the prajñā texts, but introduced to the followers of Buddhism in China, the great interpreters of Mahāyāna. The Mahāyāna, it should be remembered, consists principally of two schools of thought, *viz.*, the Mādhyamika and the Yogācāra. Nāgārjuna is the traditional exponent of the Mādhyamika school, while according to another tradition the earliest teacher of Mahāyāna, was Aśvaghoṣa, the reputed founder of the Vijñānavāda theory, which came to be known as Yagācāra. The Vijñānavāda theory really developed into a system of philosophy under his brother Vasubandhu, who flourished two centuries and half after Nāgārjuna and within fifty years from the time ef Kumārajīva. It was to Kumārajīva that we owe not only the biography and works of Nāgārjuna in Chinese, but the first biography of Aśvaghoṣa, the traditional founder of Mahāyāna.

Aśvaghoṣa lived about a century before Nāgārjuna and we give here a brief outline of his life as supplied by Kumārajīva and subsequent writers. The Buddha is alleged to have declared to Ānanda the future of Buddhism in these words: "When six

1 Translated by Shaku Hannya, *The Eastern Buddhist*. 1922, Vol. II; also *SBE* Vol. XLIX, translated by Max Müller. Mr. Hannya's translation is better than that of Max Müller.

hundred years have expired, ninety different schools of the Tīrthikas will arise and proclaiming false doctrines, each will struggle against the other to destroy the law of Buddha. Then a Bhikṣu, Aśvaghoṣa by name, will in an excellent manner teach the essence of the Dharma and defeat all the followers of the Tīrthikas."[1]

Kumārjīva's Life of Aśvaghoṣa.

Aśvaghoṣa was born in an orthodox Brahmana family in Eastern India. His "intellectual acquirements were wonderfully deep" and his "penetrating insight was matchless." As was the custom of the Hindu pandits, Aśvaghoṣa made journeys to several places, outwitting Buddhist monks in philosophical discussions. At last he came to Pāṭaliputra, the famous seat of learning and the capital of the Eastern India, in order to meet the most learned among the Buddhist monks there. Pārśva, the eleventh Patriarch being informed of the paramount influence of the Brahmana tīrthika journeyed from N. India to confront and defeat this opponent of the Buddhist faith. Kumārajīva gives a detailed account of the discussion and the defeat of Aśvaghoṣa by Pārśva. After having converted this powerful Brahmana, Pārśva returned to his own country, while the disciple remained in Central India, making an extensive study of the Sūtras, in which he sought to attain a clear understanding of the doctrine, Buddhistic as well as non-Buddhistic. He swept everything before him, by his oratorial genius and he was reverentially treated by four classes of people, including the king of (Central) India who received him as a man of distinction. (Ibid p. 28). According to other accounts Aśvaghoṣa was converted by Puṇyayaśas.

At this time Eastern India was invaded by the great Kuṣāṇa King Kaniṣka who seized Pāṭaliputra. But the conqueror was bought off by the local king by the presentation of two treasures of his country; viz. a bowl of the Buddha and Aśvaghoṣa. Aśvaghoṣa was one af the four traditional luminaries of India mentioned

---

1 Mahāyāna sūtra, (Manjio, 382) rendered into Chinese by Shiah T'an-Kin, between A.D. 479-502, translated by Suzuki, *Awakening*, intro., p. 6.

by Hiuen Tsang. According to Sten Konow Kaniṣka became king about A. D. 125 ; therefore Aśvaghoṣa may he safely assigned to the end of the 2nd century A. D.

Aśvoghoṣa lived and worked in Kashmir ; we are told that he was the vice-president of the committee of 500 Arhats snd 500 Bodhisattvas organized by Kātyāyanīputra for collecting and collating the Abhidharma works of the Sarvāstivāstivādins.[1]

In the patriarchal succession of the Mahāyāna teachers Aśvaghoṣa comes next to Puṇyasaśas and in Japan he is regarded as a teacher of the Jod sect and is the first patriarch of the Avataṁsaka sect, and the twelfth of the Dhyāna (Zen) school.[2]

Nāgārjuna's Chinese biography by Kumārajīva is full of strange episodes. It does not seem to be a translation of any one Sanskrit work, but seems rather to be a compilation of various legends about him. The Chinese texts of the biography has been handed down to us most imperfectly : it did not originally belong to the Buddhist tripiṭaka and it offered in the oldest printed edition (A. D. 972) such a difficulty that it was revised throughout for the next Chinese printed edition (A. D. 1239). Therefore the present text offers tremendous difficulties to translators and editors, and Walleser advises scholars to take up Kumārajīva's biography of Nāgārjuna with great caution.[3]

Kumārajīva's Life of Nāgārjuna

Nāgārjuna was born in south India of a Brahmana family. From the earliest childhood he had heard the four Vedas recited by the Brahmanas and had himself recited those lines by heart till he mastered the sense. At the age of twenty he enjoyed an extensive reputation for his scholarship. But tired of the dull life of a scholar he threw himself into a life of careless dissipation and thoughtlessly abused his birth right. One night he and three

1 Watters, *On Yuan Chwang*, II, p. 278; *Toung Pao'* 1904, p. 278,

2 Nāgārjuna, too, is held by various sects as their patriarch. (Nanjio, *Short History of Twelve Japanese Sects*. pp. 59, 106, 115, Quoted by Watters. op. cit. II, p. 104)

3 Walleser, The life of Nāgārjuna from Tibetan and Chinese sources, *Hirth* Anniversary Volume, Asia Major, Leipzig.

of his companions entered a king's harem protected by magic ; but they were discovered and his companions were all killed before his eyes.

Soon after his escape from the palace he entered the holy order in a Buddhist temple and took the vow of leading an ausetre life. Within ninety days he mastered the three piṭakas and penetrated into their deep meaning. He learned the Mahāyāna sūtras from an old Bhikṣu named Vajrasattva, who at once rocognised that his spiritual successor had arrived and committed the secret teachings to Nāgārjuna's care. But the young monk did not succeed in appraising their worth and travelled widely in search of the still undiscovered sūtras, which might put him on the right track. In the whole of Jambudvīpa he did not find them though he searched everywhere. He came in contact with the *tīrthika*s and śramaṇas and felt so confident of his own superiority that he became haughty and proud. He was convinced that there was much filth in things wordly ; the sūtras of the Buddha though deep, were not perfect in their logic and so their logical basis must be strengthened. He who teaches must first of all develop a clear comprehension and study logic (Nyāya) ; in it there is no contradiction, in in matter (*artha*) there is no fault...He therefore gave new precepts of conduct and decided upon new garments to his disciples.

Kumārajīva's biography goes on narrating how a Nāga came to him, took him down into the ocean to a palace where in a hall he found seven baskets (piṭakas) full of sūtras. Nāgārguna studied them for three months and grasped their meaning. The good Nāga handed these sūtras to Nāgārjuna and he returned to Jambudvīpa. He however, considerably modified the teachings of the Buddha and defeated the *tīrthikas.*

Thus Nāgārjuna explained the Mahāyāna in detail and composed 'the Upadeśa of ten thousand Gāthās'. Besides, he wrote 'the splendid way of the Buddha in Five hundred gāthās', 'the great śāstra on the art of compassion of five hundred gāthās' and the Mādhyamaka śāstra. He helped the diffusion of the Mahāyāna doctrine over different parts of India. He also composed the Akutobhaya śāstra; the Mādhyamaka śāstra is contained therein. A few stories of his magic powers are also told there and the biography is finished.[1]

Kumārajīva not only compiled the biography of Nāgārjuna but also the biography of his great disciple Āryadeva. He was not however satisfied with writing out biographies but translated several of the important treatises of Nāgārjuna and Āryadeva, Nāgārjuna's philosophy of *śūnyatā* was based on the *prajñā-pāramitā* texts and he selected the Pañcaviṁśati sāhasrikā prajñāpāramitā and commented upon it. These *prajñā* texts are like the purāṇas of the Hindus, which contain every conceivable subjects and things, such as cosmology, theology, philosophy,—in brief they are little encyclopaedias of Indian culture. Nāgārjuna's commentary on the *Pañcaviṁśati sāhasrikā* is known as 'Mahāprajñāparamita śāstra (Nanjio. 1169). The original is lost, but it consisted of 100,000 granthas. The Chinese translation by by Kumārajīva although consisted of 100 fasc. of 90 Chapters, is far from being literal from the beginning to end. Kumārajīva translated most thoroughly the first chapter in 36 fasciculi and most judiciously gave an abstract of the remaining 89 chapters in 66 fasciculi; he always tried to avoide the translation of the unnecessary repititions of the originals and gave the best and the most important points of the *śūnyavāda*.

K. translates works of Nāgārjuna

Nāgārjuna's Com. on the Prajñā text

Nāgārjuna developed his theory of Śūnyavāda in several treatises, of which his *Mādhyamaka-Kārikā* is the best known. It summarises the whole theory in 404 kārikās of 27 chapters.[2]

---

1 Walleser, *op. cit.*

2 Following are the Chapters of *Mādhyamaka Kārikā.*

1 Pratya-parīkṣā (on Causality) 14 verses.
2 Gatāgata (on motion) 25 verses.
3 Cakṣurādīndriya (on the sense faculties) 8 verses.
4 Skandha (on the elements of existence) 9 verses.
5 Dhātu (on the component elements of an individual) 8 verses.
6 Rāgarakta (on passious) 10 verses.
7 Saṁskṛta (on momentaries) 34 verses.

"The first chapter is devoted to a critique of the conception of causality. It reduces our everyday conception of it and all realistic theories *ad absurdum* and thus indirectly establishes Monism (*advaita*). The rest of the work of filled with application of this result to every separate item of the Hīnayānist philosophical system."[1]

Mādhyamaka Kārikā and its ṭikā by Āryadeva

Kumārajiva translated these Kārikās of Nāgārjuna along with commentary on them by Āryadava. The Sanskrit title of the commentary is *Prāṇyamūla Śāstra-ṭikā*, (Nanjio, 1179). The original is lost and Kumārajiva's translation is the principal source of our knowledge of Āryadeva's explanation of master's Kārikās.

The fundamental doctrine of Śūnyatā is often misunderstood; therefore a few passages translated from the original Sanskrit

---

8 Karmakāraka (on Agent and action) 13 verses.
9 Pūrva (on the reality of the proceeding moment) 12 verses.
10 Agnīndhana (on the relation of fire and fuel)) 16 verses.
11 Pūrvāpara Koti (on the infinite) 8 verses.
12 Duḥkha (on the unreality of phenomenal world) 10 verses.
13 Saṁskāra (on the unreality of all the forces of life) 8 verses.
14 Saṁsarga (on the unreality of relations) 7 verses.
15 Svabhāva (on the notion of essentsal) 11 verses.
16 Bandhano-moksa (on Bondage and Deliverance) 10 verses.
17 Karmaphala (on Karma and its result) 33 verses.
18 Ātmā (on the doctrine of Soul) 12 verses.
19 Kāla (on Time) 6 verses.
20 Sāmagrī (on the nation of the totality of causes) 24 verses.
21 Saṁbhava-bibhava (on the notions of origin and end) 21 verses,
22 Tathāgata (on the reality of Buddha) 16 verses.
23 Viparyāsa-parīkṣā (on logical incongruity) 24 verses.
24 Āryasatya (on tne Four Truth's) 40 verses,
25 Nirvāṇa (on the Nirvāṇa) 29 verses)
26 Dvādaśāṅga (on the Twelve stages in the development of an individual life) 9 verses.
27 Dṛṣṭi (on false dogma) 30 verses.

Max Walleser—*Die Mittlere Lehre des Nāgārjunā* (translation from the Chinese Version of Kumārajīva)—Heidelberg, 1912.

See Mūlamadhyamaka-Kārikās (Mādhyamika sūtras) de Nāgārjuna avec la *Prasannapadā* comm. de Candrakīrti, publie par Louis de la Vallee Poussin, Billotheca Buddhica, 1903.

1 [Stcherbatsky, *Conception of Buddhist Nirvāṇa*. Leningrad, 1927, p 66]

of Nāgārjuna's *Mādhyamaka Kārikā* and Kumārajīva's Chinese translation of Āryadeva's *Ṭikā* on the same may be quoted here.

Nāgārjuna and Āryadeva explain Śūnyatā

Nāgārjuna says, "It is on account of unrestrictedness or *Śūnyatā*, that everything becomes possible, without it nothing in the world is possible" (Chap. 24 ; Kār. 14.) Āryadeva's comment on the above has been translated thus by Kumārajīvā : "It is due to absolute unrestrictedness or *atyanta-śūnyatā*, that the activity, in regular order (following the law of regularity, and of cause and effect) of all mundane and supermundane things (dharmas) is possible. If it (noumen) is otherwise, then such activity would become impossible." This is what Nāgārjuna means by *asaṁskṛtā Śūnyatā* or the principle applied to noumenal world.

He further analyses the *Saṁskṛta-śūnyatā* or the phenomenal world thus: "That which has been produced through causes and conditions (paratītya-samutpāda), we say to be 'ever-changing' (śūnyatā); it is a conventional name (Prajñapti), and may also be called 'the middle path' (Madhyama)." "There is no *dharma* which is not produced by causes and conditions. Therefore no *dharma* exists which can be called not ever-changing or *aśūnya*. (Chap. 24; Kār. 18, 19). Āryadeva thus explains the Kārikā : "I say that whatever is produced by cause and condition is Ś*ūnyatā* or ever-changing, because whatever is the outcome of the union of various causes and conditions, is limited by the law of causation. Hence those that are devoid of any particularity or *svabhāva* are *śūnyatā*."

From the translation by Kumārjīva

Further he says, "If thou thinkest that things exist on account of their self-essence or *svabhāva* (but not on account of *Śūnyatā)*, then, thou seest that they come out of causelessness" (Chap. 24 ; Kār. 16). Āryadeva thus comments on the Kārikā : "Thou sayest all things possess their self-essence or *svahhāva*. If it were so, thou then perceivest that they came out without cause and condition. Because if any phenomenon possess its own self-essence, it can neither be produced nor destroyed, such a thing is independent of cause and condition."

Nāgārjuna then says, "You annihilate cause, effect, agent, means, action, birth and death of every object." (Chap. 24, Kār. 17). "The real state of Dharma is," says Nāgārjuna," like Nirvāṇa indescribable, incomprehensible, without birth or death. It is beyond the reach of thought or language for it is absolute." (Chap 28. Kār. 7). "It was taught by the Buddha that there is ego (ātmā) as well as non-ego (anātmā), but." the new philosepher boldly declares in his new interpretation," there is neither *ātman* nor *anātman* in the real state of Dharmas." But Nāgārjuna does not say that *śūnyatā* is final, for when its work is accomplished it is our duty to rid ourselves of the conception of *Śūnyatā* itself. He says, "For the sake of removing every kind of erroneous views, the Buddhas teach *śūnyatā*. Those, however, who cling erroneously to this conception cannot be converted from their error" (Chap. 13. Kār. 8.[1] Nāgārjuna was more a dilectician than a philosopher and he carried "his negative dialectics of the Prajñā school till he reached a complete denial of any definite thought about anything." In the 22nd chapter of *Mādhyamaka śāstra* (Nanjio, 1179), Nāgārjuna "denies step by step every quality thinkable of the person of the Tathāgata. He has no physical body ; yet, apart from mind, he is an inconceivable thing. Inconceivable and unthinkable as he is, he is not a non-existence. Being (*sat*) or non-being (*asat*) is never to be predicated of him, because both are illusions. He is neither a being nor a non-being. In short, he has no substance (*ātma-bhāva*), just as every other being, both in his lifetime and after has death, has none. Any attribute, any thought of his substance, is to be denied, and thorough negations of relativities could lead to the deep insight into it in which is realized the contemplation of *prajñā*."[2] Kumārajīva's translation is called Chung-lun (Mādhyamaka śāstra) ; it was in

N, explains Prajñā

1 Sogen Yamakami, *Systems of Buddhist Thoughts*, Cal. Univ, 1912, pp. 195-200),

2 Anesaki, Docetism, *ERE.* Vol. IV, p. 830, see also the interesting article The origin of Mahāyāna Buddhism by R. C. Armstrong in *the Eastern Buddhist*, 1926, pp. 27-48. in which various opinions of modern Japanese scholars are summarised ; some of these are very radical in their views.

4 fasc. Two hundred years hence (in 632 A. D.) Prabhākaramitra translated again the text ; but this was in 15 fasciculi (Nanjio, 1185). The Chinese title of this work is *Pan-jo tan-lun* and in Sanskrit it was known as Prajñā pradīpa śāstra kārikā.

Kumārajīva not only translated the works of Nāgārjuna into Chinese but introduced his great disciple Āryadeva to the Chinese

Kumārajīva translates Āryadeva's works

Buddhists. Reference has already been made to Āryadeva's commentary on Nāgārjuna's *Mādhyamaka kārikās* rendered into Chinese by Kumārajīva. Intellectually Āryadeva was as great as his master, and contributed to the interpreting of the Mādhyamaka Philosophy. After having translated his commentary, Kumārajīva rendered into Chinese in A.D. 404 one of the principal works of Āryadeva—the "*Śataśāstra*" (Najio, 1188). This work is one of the principal treatises of the Mādhyamaka. The real philosophical foundation of Nāgārjuna's dialectics was laid by Āryadeva in his *Śataśāstra*, to which Vasubandhu and afterwards Dharmapāla (See below, Hiuen Tsang) wrote commentaries. Kumārajīva translated the Śataśāstra text of Āryadeva along with the commentary of Vasubandhu [1] who however must not be confounded with the great philosopher of that name whom we shall meet in another chapter.

Āryadeva's Śataśāstra translated

The *Śataśāstra* is written in the form of question and answer between a heretic and a believer, the conventional custom of writing books of this nature. The heretic repeatedly brings forward the arguements of Kapila and Ulūka, i.e. Nyāya and Vaiśeṣika, and tries to refute the believer who always successfully meets his opponent and defeats him finally. The treatise in its Chinese version

1 Now a series of questions arises about Buddhist chronology. Who is this Vasubandhu ? Is he the great Vasubandhu the reputed of *Abhidharmakśa* and brother of Asaṅga ? N. Peri asserts that it is the great Vasubandhu, who commented upon Āryadeva's work (*BEFFO*, XI, 1911) ; he places him circa, A.D. 350. But others reject it ; Takakusu assigns Vasubandhu to the 9th century A.D., therefore he cannot be placed before Kumārajīva. Vasubandhu himself speaks of Vṛddha-Vasubandhu and (Nanjio also suggested that this commentary might have been written by another Vasubandhu. Besides it is written simply Vasu, (Nanjio, Catalogue, p. 371' f. n,).

is divided into ten chapters ; the original does not seem to be in existence. The following are the chapters : (1) Renunciation of Sin and Merit ; (2) Refutation of Ātman ; (3) Refutation of Unity ; (4) Refutation of Diversity ; (5) Refutation of perception of senses ; (6) Refutation of the object ; (7) Refutation of the theory of the existence of effect in the cause (Pratītya-samutpāda) ; (8) Refutation of the theory according to which, in the cause there is no effect ; (9) Refutation of the eternity ; (10) Refutation of the void Śunyatā. [1]

Another powerful thinker of the age who was introduced into China by Kumārajīva was Harivarman. In the early centuries of the Christian era various religio-philosophical views were enunciated by several Ācaryas in India of whom Harivarman is one.

Harivarman's Satysiddhi *śāstra*

he is absolutely unknown in India ; because his work entitled *Satyasiddhi-śāstra* (Nanjio, 1274) is not found in the original, nor does it seem that his disciples left any literary trace in India. But in China Kumārajīva's translation became so popular with the Buddhists of that country that under the Liang dynasty (502-597) a philosophical school actually came to be established there, which took its name after the Satyasiddhi-śāstra.

In a preface to Kumārajīva's translation of Harivarman's work, San-chao, the greatest of Kumārajīva's disciples writes: "The *Satyasiddhi-śāstra* was composed by Harivarman about 890 years after Buddha's death. He was the chief disciple of Kumāralāta leader of the Hīnayānists in Kashmir." We must not take the date assigned to him by San-Chao too literally. Kumāralāta, who was the founder of the Sautrāntika school, according to the tradition preserved by Hiuen Tsang, was a contemporary of Aśvaghoṣa, Nāgārjuna and Āryadeva.[2] Thus if

---

1 G. Tucci, *Le Cento Strofe* (Śata Śāstra) texts buddhistico mahāyāna, tradotto del cinese, *Studi e Materiali di Storia della Religione*, Roma, 1925.

2 Kumāralāta " was a native of Takṣaśilā, who in early youth embraced the religious life, and became an enthusiastic student of sacred literature. He composed some tens of treatises which were widely known and read and he was the founder of the Sautrāntika school. He was brought by force from his native land to this country. In his time Aśvaghoṣa in the east, Deva in

we can take Hiuen Tsang's statement to be correct, Harivarman cannot be put later than A. D. 250. This great critical free-thinker "appeared at a time when the so-called Hīnayānists and Mahāyānists were hotly discussing the claims of their respective schools to be regarded as representatives of genuine Buddhism." He boldly said to the contending parties, "Now I am going unfold the meaning of the sacred canon in its real truth, because every Bhikṣu of every school and Buddha himself will be hearing my exposition." But it does not seem that his interpretation was up to his enthusiasm. According to his own profession he was a declared antagonist of the Sarvāstivādins and he took his stand upon the Hīnayāna in order to maintain his doctrine of absolute Śūnyatā (*Sarva-Śūnyatā-vāda*). This is the reason why Harivarman's doctrine is generally called the Sūnyavāda of the Hīnayāna, as distinguished from the Sūnyavāda of the Mahāyāna doctrine.[1] This is why the Satyasiddhi school has sometimes been included among the schools of Mahāyāna; and that seems to be the reason of Kumārajīva's translating Harivarman's work into Chinese. But epinions greatly differ as to the exact school to which Harivarman's views belonged: "Some say, he belonged to Bahuśrutīya, others, that he was a member of the Sautrāntika school, others again maintain that he was an adherent of the Dharmagupta school. There are some who go so far as to affirm that he interpreted the tenets of the Hīnayāna with the help of the Mahāyāna."[2]

Satyasiddhi School

What it preached

---

the south, Nāgārjuna in the West, and Kumāralāta in the north were called the Four Shining Suns." Watters *On Yuan Chwang*, Vol. II. p. 268: also Beal *Buddhist Records*, Vol, II, p, 302. The Chinese name *Kiu-mo-lo-lo-la* formerly transcribed as Kumālatabodha has been restored as Kumāralāta on the authority of Sanskrit but coming from central Asia, see Lüder's Brüchstücke der buddhistischer Dramen.

1 Sogen *opt cit* p. 173.

2 His philosophical views have been analysed in Sogen's work, op. cit. pp. 172-185 : the whole thing about Satyasiddhi has been drawn from that work : also see Wieger, pp. 338-440).

Kumārajīva wanted to acquaint the Chinese Buddhists thoroughly with all the philosophical theories of the Mādhyamika school and translated the most important treatises of prajña group as well as the works of the Ācaryas of Mahāyāna. The Mahāyāna which was practically introduced in China by Kumārajīva differs on some fundamental points from the Hīnayāna which had been in vogue in China till then.

What Kumārajīva taught

Kumārajīva translated selected texts from Sanskrit, which were calculated to illustrate the fundamental theories of Mahāyna. The ideal of Mahāyāna takes definite shape in the life of a Bodhisattva and some of the early translators tried to popularise this idea among the Buddhists of China. Kumārajīva's contribution in this line was very great. He translated the text and the great commentary of Nāgārjuna on the *Daśabhumi,* which forms a part of the *Avataṁsaka* (15 fas : 35 chap. Nanjio 1180). It gives an elaborate exposition of the Daśabhūmi or the ten stages of Bodhisattvahood and shows what spiritual routine a Buddhist was expected to pursue in order to obtain nirvāṇa. But before a neophyte can come to the road of Daśabhūmi, the awakening of the Bodhi-citta marks the first step towards it. Kumārajīva therefore translated a work called 'Discourse on the awakening of the Bodhicitta' *Bodhicittotpādana Śāstra* (Nanjio, 1218) alleged to have been composed by Vasubandhu. But we presume that its author was Vṛddha Vasubandhu. The Mahāyānists believe that the Bodhicitta is present in the hearts of all sentient beings, it is only dormant they say and lies crippled in the mortals. Kumārajīva's translation of the work gives us a systematic treatment of those conditions which tend to awaken the Bodhicitta from its lethargic inactivity.[1] "The Bodhicitta or intelligence-heart is awakened in us (1) by thinking of the Buddhas, (2) by reflecting on faults of material existence, (3) by observing

Bodhisattva-ideas inculcated clearly in Kumārajīva's translation.

'Bodhicittotpādana' is explained.

1 Suzuki, *opt cit* Outline of Mahāyāna p. 303.

the deplorable state in which sentient beings are living, and finally (4) by aspiring after those virtues which are acquired by a Tathāgata in the highest enlightenment."[1]

Having awakened his Bodhicitta from its unconscious slumber, a Bodhisattva will now proceed to make ten vows or *praṇidhāna.* A few of the most brilliant *praṇidhānas* quoted below will show what a high ideal of life the Mahāyānists had set up. and was propagated in China through the translation of Kumārajīva.

Selected passages from the work

(1) "Would that all the merits I have accumulated in the past as well as in the present be distributed among all sentient beings and make them all aspire after supreme knowledge, and also that this my *praṇidhāna* be constantly growing in strength and sustain me throughout my rebirths.

(2) "Would that, through the merits of my work, may, I whenever I am born, come in the presence of all Buddhas and pay homage.

(3) "Would that I be thoroughly conversant with scientific knowledge as well as the first principle of religion and gain an insight into the truth of the Good Law.

(4) "Would that all Buddhas instruct me in religious truths as best suited to my intelligence and let me finally attain the five spiritual powers of the Bodhisattva.

(5) "Would that I be able to preach untiringly the truth to all beings, and gladden them, and benefit them, and make them intelligent.[2]

The rest of the *praṇidhānas* are not quoted here. The Bodhisattva when awakened must pass through several stages of religious discipline before he attains perfection.

These stages are generally estimated by the Mahāyānists at ten. These have been most clearly expounded in a chapter called *Daśabhūmi* in the Avataṁsaka, which was rendered into Chinese

---

1 *Ibid*, p. 303.

2 Suzuki, *Ibid* p, 308).

by Kumārajīva along with a translation of the commentary on the same by Nāgārjuna. These ten stages are 1. Pramuditā, 2. Vimalā 3. Prabhakarī, 4. Ariśmatī, 5. Sudurjayā, 6. Abhimukhī, 7. Durangama, 8. Acalā, 9. Sādhumatī, 10. Dharmamegha. These are sometimes criticised as too mechanical for spiritual life, and many sects of the east "teach that is not necessary to pass through each one of these stages successively, for proper realisation may enable one to jump over or leave out several stages or even to pass at one step from the lowest to the highest degree." However these two works on Bodhisattva's Intelligence-heart (Bodhicitta) and Ten Bhūmis or stages translated by Kumārajiva helped a good deal in propagating these noble ideas among the Chinese Buddhists.

Epoch-making Vimala Kīrtinirdeśa

But the most important and almost epoch-making work on the ideal of Bodhisattva was Kumārajīva's translation of the *Vimalakīrtinirdeśa*. It was this work which was taken to Japan for preaching Buddhism. The treatise is of such a great importance that we shall discuss it in details, and a perusal of this work will be amply rewarded. San-chao, the great disciple of Kumārajīva edited the translation of his master and enriched it with a learned commentary (Nanjio, 1632). "There are also several other editions or Kumārajīva's version with commentaries, and it has long been a favourite work with Chinese students, Buddhist and non-Buddhist."[1]

A very old work

The *Vimalakīrtinirdeśa* was probably first composed in Sanskrit or in some Indian dialect much earlier than the time of Nāgārjuna (2nd century A. D.), for the sūtra is frequently quoted by Nāgārjuna in his commentary of the *Prajnāpāramitā sūtra*, preserved in Chinese through the translation of Kumārajīva, mentioned above (Nanjio 1169). The exact date of the composition of this work cannot be determined now ; but it must be a few centuries before Nāgārjuna's

1 Watters, *On Yuan Chang, II, p. 64.*

time, for it requires a considerable time before a sūtra can be quoted as an authority.

Bodhisattva sacrifices his self for others.

This old sūtra has some outstanding characteristics, which distinguish it from the older Hīnayāna texts and that must have been the reason of Kumārajīva's rendering it into Chinese. The idea of Bodhisattva is greatly developed in the Mahāyāna texts. We have already seen that according to the Mahāyānistic ideals a Bodhisattva is to sacrifice his own selfish happiness for a greater cause. He does not want to extinguish his passions which are absolutely necessary according to the ideal of the Hīnayānists ; for otherwise how could he feel any sympathy for the lower beings suffering from passions and deliver them from pain. He incarnates himself in any being even in a medical herb (Chapter VIII), in order to save all beings and lead them to the higher stage of religious life. The six pāramitās, being the preliminary means of attaining Buddhahood, are never sought by the Hinayānists, whose final goal is to become an Arhat ; but in the *Vimalakīrtinirdeśa* what are most strongly emphasised are these Pāramitās. In fact they are one of the signs distinguishing Mahāyāna from Hīnāyana.

Karuṇā or "the great mercy and compassion towards all beings" is most highly recommended in this sūtra. A śrāvaka or a Pratyekabuddha acts only for himself not for others ; his Nirvāṇa is a complete extinction which is the final goal to his life : But a Bodhisattva does not enter into Nirvāṇa for the sake of beings who suffer in the life, and whose salvation is his "sole duty."

This sūtra also lays great stress on non-attachment ; but to cling to non-attachment is still an attachment, which is condemned in this sūtra. This state is beyond either words or thought ; true non-attachment is absolute, it is not only free from all forms of attachment but free from non-attachment itself. Here is an absolute freedom of the Bodhisattva in all his life-activities, which is unknown to Hīnayānists.

"On the whole, what is most emphatically insisted upon in the sūtra is the practising of the life of a bodhisattva as against

15

that of a Śrāvaka or a Pratyekabuddha, that is to say, the Mahāyāna is strongly upheld against the Hīnayāna, the religion of laymen against the ascetic life of the monastery. Religion ought not to be made the monopoly of the priests, but the possession of all who seek it, either monks or laymen. That is why the leaders of the priesthood are treated as miserable beings destitute of supernatural powers, which they themselves admit either by compulsion or on their own account."

"It is due to this influence of the movement of the latiy that, in Japan, Shotoku Umayado (A. D. 574-633), the crown-prince... thought himself to be a Vimalakīrti and wrote a commentary on this sūtra. He was never ordained as a priest but did far more than a professional priest in propagating Buddhism in Japan.[1]

Vimalakīrti was a wealthy house-holder (gṛhī) in the great city Vaiśāli. He was a Bodhisattva of the highest order, who held lofty ideals of life. A passage from Kumārajīva's translation is quoted here, which clearly sets forth the ideal of a perfect lite which the Bodhisattva Vimalakīrti led: "though he is but a simple layman, yet observing the pure monastic discipline; though living at home, yet never desirous of anything; though possessing a wife and children, always exercising pure virtues; though surrounded by his family, holding aloof from wordly, yet adorned with spiritual splendour; though eating and drinking, yet enjoying the flavour of the rapture of meditation; theugh frequenting the gambling house, yet leading the gamblers into the right path; though coming in contact with heresy, yet never letting his true faith be impaired; though having a profound knowledge of wordly learning, yet ever finding pleasure in things of the spirit as taught by Buddha; revered by all as the first among those who were worthy of reverence; governing both the old and young as a righteous judge; though profiting by all the professions, yet far above being absorbed by them; benefitting all beings, going wheresever he pleases, protecting all beings as a judge with

Vimalakīrti, ideal of lay man

1 Quoted from *The Estern Buddhist* Vol. II, No. 3. 1923.

righteousness ; leading all with the doctrine of the Mahāyāna when in the seat of discussion ; ever teaching the young and ignorant when entering the hall of learning ; manifesting to all the error of passion when in the house of debauchery ; persuading all to seek the higher things, when at the shop of the wine-dealer ; preaching the law, when among wealthy people as the most honorable of their kind ; dissuading the rich householders from covetousness, when among them as the most honorable of their kind ; teaching Kṣatriyas patience when among them, as the most honourable of their kind ; removing arrogance when among Brahmanas as the most honorable of their kind ; teaching justice to the great ministers when among them as the most honorable of their kind ; teaching loyalty and filial pity to the princes when among them ; teaching honesty to the ladies of the court when among them ; persuading the masses to cherish the virtue of merits when among them ; instructing the highest wisdom to the Brahmana gods when among them......; showing the transient nature of the world to Śakra gods when among the guardians as the most honorable of their kind. thus by such countless means Vimalakīrti, the house-holder, rendered benefit to all beings."

"Now through those means he brought on himself sickness, and there came to inquire after him countless visitors headed by kings, great ministers, wealthy householders, lay-disciples Brahmanas, princes and other high officials. Then Vimalakīrti taking the opportunity of his sickness, preached to any one who came to him, about the transitoriness of body, impermanence of things etc. Thus Vimalakīrti rightly preached for the profit of those who came to visit him on his bed of sickness and made all these countless thousand people cherish the thought of Supreme enlightenment." The Buddha knowing of his illness asked his disciples to visit Vimalakīrti and inquire after his health. But each of them doclares that he is not worthy to approach that great man and narrates how he had been instructed by the great layman in a particular topic affecting life.

Then at last Mañjuśrī was prevailed upon to visit him. Mañjuśrī said, "O Blessed one, it is very difficult to discuss with that excellent man ; he has attained to such a profound knowledge of the true nature things, he is able to preach the essence of Law... he is perfect in wisdom and the necessary means ; yet in compliance with the order of the Buddha, I will go to inquire after his health."

The rest of the book is devoted to discussing subtle questions between Mañjuśri and Vimalakīrti, the latter showing profound power of understanding the philosophy of life.[1]

Kumārajīva's another important translation was *Saddharma-puṇḍarīka.* No book in the Sanskrit Buddhist literature gives a more accurate idea of the literature of the Mahāyāna than the *Lotus of the Good Law* ; and none gives a better impression of the changes undergone by Buddhism in certain surroundings, from its beginnings down to the earliest times of the Christian era.[2]

Saddharma puṇḍarīka in Chinese

The *Saddharma Puṇḍarīka* is a typical Mahāyāna work of the earlier days, and that is why so many monks wanted to give it to the Chinese public. "In the ancient Pali documents Śākyamuni

1 Chineses text translated into English by Hoke Idumi *The Eastern Buddhist* 1924-1925). There were seven translations of the *Vimalakīrtinirdeśa* (1) Wei-mo-ching (2 fasc.) by Yen-fo-t'ias A. D. 188 (lost), (2) Wei-mo-chich-ching (2 fasc.) by Chi Chien A. D. 222-280 (Nanjio, 147), (3) Wei-mo-la-chich-ching (3 fasc.) by Chu Shulan A. D. 265 (lost), (4) Wei-ma-chich-soishus-fa-men-ching, (3 fase.) by Dharmarakṣa A. D. 265 (lost), (5) Wei-mo-ching by Jitamita (4 fasc.) A. D. 317-420 (lost), (6) Wei-mo-chich-so-shuo-ching (3 fasc, 14 Chap) by Kumārajīva A. D. 400 (Nanjio, 146), (7) Shuo-wu-kon-chen-ching (6 fasc, 14 chapt.) by Hiuen Tsang, A. D. 664 (Nanjio, 140),

2 Poussin, The Lotus of the true law, *ERE*, Vol., 8. p. 145, The work is too well-known to students of Buddhism to be described in full. Burnouf translated it into French as early as 1852. The Sanskrit edition as well as English translation have beou published, the former appearing in the *Bibliotheca Buddhica* edited by H. Kern and B. Nanjio and the latter in the *Sacred Books of the East* done into English by H. Horn alone (Vol. XXI) Fragments of it have been discovered in Central Asia and a Manuscript is said to be procured in Tibet by the Japanese traveller Kawaguchi, and its facsimili has been published in Japan. There have been six translations of this important work in A. D. 255, 270, 286, 335, 500 and 601. The first two and the fourth were lost by 730 A. D. Dharmarakṣa's translation and its effect in Chinese Buddhism has been described above. In connection with the translation of the work we shall discuss the various texts of the works extant in those days.

is a man, a single mortal, and he moves in a historical background. In the *Saddharma Puṇḍarīka* he is a sublime being, eternal or almost eternal, who unveils in a phantasmagoric setting the 'divinity' i. e. the divine Splendour and the majestic power, which Buddhists now attribute to the Buddhas; he is a god as Hindus and Buddhists understand by the word; that is to say, he manifests himself especially by mythological performances, although he is a stranger to all notions of creation or of influence. Such a being has a history; therefore, as Kern says, this is a sort of dramatic performance, an undeveloped mystery play... It consists of a series of dialogues, brightened by the magic effects of a would be supernatural scenery."

Buddha in the text

"Although completely divine, Śākyamuni is not God in the *Lotus*. He is Buddha 'from the beginning, he is the father of the worlds, the father of the future Buddhas and saints, the universal providence. In order to save human beings and lead them to Nirvāṇa he appears in a human form which is illusory: he is born, teaches and enters Nirvāna at least as far as ordinary men can see; but in reality while illusory Śākyamunis are appearing in this world, the true Śākyamuni reigns on divine Mountain of Vultures,' surrounded by four Buddhas, and imparting to them the true teaching, the true law. It is this Śākyamuni that the *Lotus* shows." (Poussin, ibid.)

Avalokiteśvara is the principal Bodhisattva to whom devotees direct their offerings, ahd that has been amply elucidated in our study of Dharmarakṣa's translation which appeared in A. D. 286. Buddhalogy was distinctly developed as early as the first century A. D., in the *Lotus* four Buddhas are mentioned. Of these Buddhas the most important in Amitābha or Amitāyus. In the *Lotus* we read in the west, where the pure world Sukhakara is situated, there the chief Amitābha the tamer of man, has fixed his abode." (XXIV, 50; SBE XXI, p. 417.

Buddhalogy in Puṇḍarīka.

The Amitābha cult is a very old institution and it points always to a non-Indian origin; we shall discuss this subject at length in a later chapter of our treatise. The first Amitābha text known is probably *Sukhāvatī Vyūha* (in its larger recension), introduced into China by the Parthian monk Shi-Kao and his contemporary Lokakṣema in the second century A. D. Since then several translations were made. But it was Kumārajīva, who for the first time, translated a new recension into Chinese. This known as the Smaller *Sukhāvatī Vyūha*, in which Amitābha is the principal Buddha. This is one of the three principal canonical texts of the Jodo sect of Japan, the other two being the Larger recension of the *Snkhāvatī* and a dhāraṇī on Amitāyuṣ. Kumārajīva's *Sukhāvatī-Vyūha* was not only a great departure from the older Mahāyana texts, but it differed from the larger recension as well. "The Smaller Sukhāvatī-Vyūha lays great stress on the fact that people can be saved or can be born in the land of Bliss, if only they remember and repeat the name of Buddha Amitābha before their death. and distinctly denies that people are born in the paradise of Amitābha as a reward or necessary result of good works performed in the present life. This would take away one of the fundamental doctrines of Buddhism, namely the doctrine of *Karman*, or of the continuous working of our deeds whether good or bad. Instead of the old doctrine as a man soweth so he shall reap, a new and easier way of salvation is here preached, viz., as a man prayeth so he shall be saved. It is what is known to us as salvation by faith rather than by work.[1] The larger *Sukhāvatī Vyūha* (which we shall describe further down below) lays likewise great stress on prayer and faith in Amitābha, but it never neglects 'the stock of merit' (puṇya) as essential for salvation.[1] This translation of the Sukhāvatī Vyūha by Kumārajīva is considered as one of the mast important works ever translated into Chinese.

Smeller Sukhāvatī Vyūha in Chinese for the first time.

Faith in Amitābha preached.

Kumārajīva translated a large number of works from Sanskrit mostly on the Mahāyāna theology and philosophy and it will not

1 (Introduction by MaxMüller to SBE XLIX, p. viii-ix).

be possible to describe them all. He had wished to present the Chinese people with the most representative Sanskrit books and he successfully carried out his mission to a close. But before we close out the study of Kumārajīva, we would like to describe a few works, which seem to be very important. The *Sutrālaṃkāra*, alleged to have been composed by Aśvaghoṣa was rendered into Chinese by Kumārajīva. But it is now proved that this work could not have been written by Aśoaghoṣa. Various arguements against the authorship of Aśvaghoṣa are put forth. In one of the stories Kaniṣka is mentioned as a legendary person. When it is contended that Aśvaghoṣa was a contemporary of Kaniṣka. It hardly seems credible that a contemporary king would appear in a legendary character. Besides this, in Central Asia fragments of a work have been discovered called *Kalpanāmanditikā*, whose author was Kumāralāta. This *Kalpanāmanditika*, agrees with the Sūtrālamkāra, ascribed to Aśvaghoṣa and translated by Kumārajīva. The real *Sutrālaṃkāra* of Aśvaghoṣa discovered in Central Asia is said to be preserved in Berlin. Therefore the translation of the Sūtrālaṃkāra done into French by Ed. Humber, which is alleged to be the work of Aśvaghoṣa, is really not his.

Sūtrālaṃkāra: its author is not Aśvaghoṣa.

This is a collection of pious legends after the model of jātakas and avadānas narrated in prose and verse in the style of Sanskrit poetics. Many of the legends are known to us through classical sources.[1] A few stories show the spirit of Mahāyāna. It seems even from tho translation that the work, had genuine literary merits. It is of great importance for the history of Indian Literature and culture as it mentions thc epics of Rāmāyaṇa and Mahābhārata and combats the philosophical doctrines of the Sāṅkhya and Vaiśeṣika schools just as forcibly as it opposes the

Lüders, Brüchstücke der *Kalpanāmanditikā des Kumāralāta.* Also see Levi's article in J. As, Leipzig, 1926.

1 Humber Trois contes du Sūtrālaṅkāra, Conserves dans le Divyāvadāna, Befeo 1904, IV, p. 709-713.

religious views of the Brahmanas and Jainas and offers in a variety of ways to the scripts, art und painting.[1]

For the guidance of the Mahāyāna monks Kumārajīva translated the *Brahmajāla-Śūtra* (Nanjio, 1087), which has since then been recognised as the principal code of law among the Chinese Buddhist; but it is stated by San-Chao that the *Brahmajāla-Sūtra* forms the twelfth chapter of a larger work called the *Bodhisattvahṛdayasūtra* which is supposed to have been a work of 120 fasciculi and 61 chapters in the original. The rest of the work was never translated into Chinese, nor has the original work been discovered. We must warn our readers against confusing this *Brahmajāla* with the Pali work of the same name, which forms a part of the *Dīganikāya*. The Pali *Brahmajāla* agrees more or less with the *Fan-tung-ching*, the 14th chapter of the *Dīrgha Āgama* (Nanjio, 545, 554). Kumārajīva's translation is known as *Fan-wang-ching*.

Brahmajāla Sūtra the code of Mahāyāna

The text of *Brahmajāla-Sūtra* opens with a tableau in which the ancient Buddha Rocana is seen seated on a lotus with a thousand petals; each petal being a world. Rocana then gathers round him all the Bodhisattvas and discourses with them on renunciation, impermanence and such other well-known topics of Buddism. In the second act Śākyamuni appears and declares that he was in communion with the gods and with all the Buddhas. Rocana, says he, formerly dictated an abstract law, a collection of directions rather than rules. I, Śākyamuni, am about to announce concrete rules which regulate the Mahāyānist Buddhist world." Then the first ten great faults are descibed in details followed by forty-eight minor faults or omissions, which although do not extinguish the Buddhist life, will be punished either in this world or the next, if they are not expiated in time by penitence.

The wonderful literary achievements of Kumārajīva under the imperial patronage of the Tsin emperor Yao-hing, in the cause

1. Lèvi, *J. As.* 1904, pp. 77 f f. see Nariman, also Anesaki, are vol. 2, p. 159. Wieger, pp. 430-437.

of the spread of Hindu culture in China, cannot be too highly appreciated. The subtle and critical minds of Chinese literati always ignored the Buddhists, and Confucianism and Taoism were considered to be two pillars of Chinese civilization and in their national pride they tried their utmost to resist the influence of Hindu culture. But the Hindu mission was too strong to be resisted even by a people like the Chinese, Kumārajīva's translation of the Buddhist masterpieces into elegant Chinese largely contributed to the diffusion of Buddhist philosophy in China.

Estimate of his work.

Kumārajīva was fortunate in his disciples and the work which he began was continued for sometime by his worthy students. Of these San-Chao is best known. Originally he was a great lover of Lao-tsu's works and was of a mystical temperament; but a copy of *Vimalakīrtinirdśa* (the older version,) which by chance fell into his hand, immediately changed his life and calling; he left home and became a monk. He came to Chang-an in 401 A.D. and the emperor put him under Kumārajīva along with Seng-Jui and others. He all along helped Kumārajīva in the translation work; but at last he wrote a few independent treatises. Of these his commentary on the *Vimalakīrtinirdeśa* (Nanjio, 1632) in 10 chapters is well known to Chinese scholars. Another was a treatise on the precious repository (or Ratna-piṭaka-śāstra) written by him. His *Chao-lun* has two commentaries compiled by Wan-Tsai, who died in 1302, under the Yuan dynasty (A. D. 1280-1368) (Nanjio, 1627, 1628; also Bagchi p. 205). Song-Chao also wrote three prefaces, two to the two works of Kumārajīva and one to a work of Buddhayaśas (Bagchi, p. 206.) Seng-Jui,[1] another distinguished disciple of Kumārajīva, wrote prefaces to the sūtras translated by Kumārajīva and his contemporary workers (Bagchi p. 206-208.) He also compiled a catalogue of Chinese Buddhist literature called Er-Tsin-lu or the catalogue of the second Tsin Dynasity, in one

Kumārajīva's disciples.

1 See J. Nobel. *Sitzungsberichte, besoit* 22966.

chapter, very probably sometime before A. D. 413, the year of Kumārajīva's death. (Bagchi, Intro., p. xxxv-xxxvi).

During the thirty-four years of the rule of the Later Tsin dynasty, 138 distinct works were rendered into Chinese from Sanskrit, of which Kumārajīva alone was responsible for 136 works so that this period may well be termed the age of Kumārajīva.

The death of Fu-K'ien marks a new era in the history of North China; the whole country, split up into several small principalities, became a prey to the capricious rulers. In 385 A.D. the Latter Tsin dynasty was established in the same ancient town of Chang-gan, where the Earlier Ts'in ruled. But there were other cities ruled by smaller Tartar tribal chiefs, where the Buddhist church thrived under royal patronage. With Wan-Bhuan as their capital, the Western Tsins of the Chi-fu family founded a new kingdom. They ruled from 385 to 341 A. D. Chi-fu Se-fan was the first important person of the family. After Fu-k'ion's death Chi-fu Kuo-jon proclaimed himself a king and was installed at Pao-han (Modern Ho-chen in Kan-su). Under his successor Chi-fu Kien-Kui (382-412) a Śramaṇa named Shang-K'ien or Fa-K'ien, who is better known as Kien-kong, translated fifteen Sanskrit works of which ten have survived. All these translations are small sūtras : one of these is the complete translation of the story of the *Vessāntara Jātaka*.[1] There is no mention of any other translator during this period. During the three Ts'in Dynasties forty-one works in 86 fasc. (of which 22 works in 67 fasc. were in existence in A. D, 730) are said to have been translated between A. D. 350-431, by unknown translators. Of these translations only seventeen works are in existence.[2]

Western Tsin Dynasty 385-431

Shung chien 388-407

During the three Tsin dynasties 41 translations

1 Nanjio, 254 : This is a later translation of a part of fac. 2 of *Satpāramitā-sannipāta-sūtra*, Liu-tu-tsi-ching; Nanjio, 143 ; Translated by K'ang Seng-hui.

2 See *Catalogue* p. 409 ; According to Nanjio 17; Nanjio 1136 are one work *Sarvāstivāda Vinaya Vibhāsā* : c. f. Bagchi, p. 240 ; Kāśyapa-parivarta, Nanjio, 23. (43) is not mentioned have by Nanjio ; See Bagchi, p. 239).

Another dynasty that arose in northern China during the troublous fourth century was the Liang. The Tsien Liangs or the Former Liang dynasty of the Chang family had their capital at Ku-sang. They ruled from 302 to 376 A. D. The other Liang Dynasty is known in Chinese history as the Pei-Liang or the Northern Liang dynasty. The kings were of Tsu-chu family of Tarters. They had their capital originally at Chang-ye and afterwards removed to Ku-tsang (A. D. 397-439).

Liang dynasties

Buddhism greatly flourished in China under the patronage of the emperors and important state functionaries. Buddhism as a movement in a particular state or under a dynasty, always depended for its success on the sympathies of the person at the head of the government. Fortunately for Buddhism Chang T'ien-si, the prefect of Liang-chen (333-376) who was a sincere devotee did all that lay in his power to propagate his faith in his provinces. He gathered round him a group of earnest workers, of whom Sheu-luen, an Yueh-chi upāsaka was of particular importance, Sheu-luen was well-versed in the sūtra literature, specialy in the Vaipulya group, And was a staunch Mahāyānist, Another translator was Poyen, the son of the Kuchean king, who had forsaken the world to become a monk. This Kuchean royal monk had a thorough knowledge of the Chinese languages as well as of several Central Asian languages. He was well-versed in the sacred literature of the Buddhist.

The pious prefect Chang-T'ien-si and Sheu-luen

Besides there were several other Chinese śramaṇas to assist Chang T'ien-si in his pious work of translation. He was particularly anxious to give to his countrymen a clear and literal translation of original Sanskrit works, but he felt that in case of too great concentration on the beauty of the language, the sense might be lost sight of, and on the other hand, if one is too literal in adhereing to the original, the language is sacrificed. He observed in utter helplessness. "It is the saints who are capable of rendering both the sense and the beauty of the original at the same time,"

Shen-luen and his collaborators translated four works, of which only one exists. viz., the Surata paripṛcchā.[1]

The Liang emperors too can be proud of having given shelter and encouragement to about a dozen Buddhist workers. During the Liang dynasty sixty works by unknown translators are mentioned in the Chinese Catalogues.[2] Of these only seven exist.[3] Shih Tao-kung[4] a Chinese śramana translated two works at the wish of Tsin-kin Mong sken (401-458) in the town of Chang-ye. One of the books is lost and the extant work is the well-known Ratnaraśi sūtra (Nanjio, 24-44) of the Ratnakūṭa group of Mahāyāna. The original Sanskrit text of this work is lost but fragments of it have been discovered in Central Asia.

Other Translators

Shih Fa-chang (Nanjio, App. II. 65. Bagchi, p, 211). a Chinese priests of Turfan translated one work (Nanjio, 42p). Seng Chie-to[5] a monk of the western region translated a work which is lost. Tsin-k'iu Ching-Sheng[6], prince of An-yang :and a cousin of Tsin-Kin Mong-suen, the second ruler of the N. Liang dynasty, was inspired by the example of the life of Śākyamuni and left the pleasure of the world to become a monk. He was a man of vast erudition, imbued with natural piety. He went to Ku-tsang to meet Dharmakṣema (see below) and studied the *pañca-śila* under him, which he could repeat from memory. But he was not satisfied and went Khotan a place well known in those days for good scholars and rich Sanskrit libraries to continue his studies. He lived in the famous Gomati Vihāra of Khotan and studied under the Hindu monk Buddhasena. This learned monk had studied various branches of sciences and Ching-sheng studied even Hindu medicine with him and finally procured a number of manuscripts from his Guru.

---

1 (Bagchi, pp. 209ff)
2 (Bagchi, pp. 223-233).
3 (Nanjio speaks of 53 works in 75 fasc. p. 413)
4 Nanjio, App. II. 64 ; Bagchi, 2:1.
5 Nanj'o. App. II, 66 ; Bagchi, p. 212)
6 Nanjio, App. II. 68 ; Bagchi p. 221

He came back to Ku-tang and translated a work entitled 'an important explanation of the law of the meditation' in A. D. 433-439 but unfortunately the work is lost. After the destruction of the N. Liang dynesty in 439, he went southward and took refuge in the kingdom of the Ṣung, where he translated thirty-five books'[1]

Shih Che-mong[2] was a native of Sin-fong in the district of Young-cheu. He was a man of deep religious feelings and intelligence, who was always eager to visit India in order to see the holy places connected with the life of the Buddha. In A. D. 404 with fourteen friends he started from Chang-an. He passed by Tun-huang, visited Shan-shan in the south-west of Lob-nor, Kuchā and Khotan and witnessed the miracle the law had done. After a march of 2000 li the party reached the Pamirs. The ascent of the mighty mountains was so difficult that it frightened them, and nine of them returned to China. The rest marched forward; on their way their Indian companion Tao-long succumbed to the fatigues of the journey and died. Che-mong was not the man to be discouraged. even in the midst of those difficulties he with the four friends pushed on, crossed the Indus and reached Kashmir. During his sojourn in India he visited many important places, including Kapilavāstu and Kusumpura (Pāṭaliputra.) At Paṭaliputra he met a Brahman of great learning named Lo-yue (Revata.) Revata and his family were Buddhists and he was honoured by the local king; he had a stūpa of massive silver, thirty feet high. Revata was greatly surprised to learn from Che-mong that Buddhism was flourishing in China. From him he got several Sanskrit manuscripts on Buddhism, such as the Vinaya of the Mahāsāṅghikas, Nirvāṇa sutras etc. It may be mentioned here that Fa-hien had arrived at Pātaliputra only a few years back and had obtained several manuscripts from the house of this Revata.[3]

Shih-Che-mong, (404-453 A. D.)

And a party visited India

1 Nanjio App. II. 68, 83 ; Bagchi, pp. 221-o3 : also 394-398
2 Nanjio, App. II, 70 Bagchi, 224.
3 This Reveta may be the same man as the teacher of Buddhaghoṣa, the great commentator of Pali texts.

Che-mong left India in A. D. 424. On the way three of his companions died and with only one friend. out of fourteen, he returned to Liang-chu. Che-mong translated the *Nirvāṇa-Sūtra*, which he had got in Revata's house in 20 fasc., which was however lost by A. D. 730. In 437 he went to Seu-chuan, where two years latter he wrote his memoirs in 439 and he died in 452.[1]

Besides the memoirs of Che-mong and his friends, there is another record of two monks of this period who went to the west in search of Sanskrit manuscripts. Shih Fa-sheng[2] a monk of Kao-chang (Twhfan) district, went to a foreign country and returned to a China during the rule of the N. Liang dynasty. He translated 'sūtra on the Nidāna of the Caitya erected in the place where Bodhisattva threw his body to feed a hungry tiger' (Nanjio, 436).

Fa-sheng and Tao T'ai visit India

The other monk was Shih Tao-T'ai.[3] He went to the west of the Himalayas, which seems to be Kashmir, where he obtained the text of the Vibhāṣā, sūtras and śāstras. These are all evidently Sarvāstivādin treatises. The Vibhāṣā is the commentary on Kātyāyanīputra's *Jñānaprasthāna*, which he translated with Buddhavarman. His own translations are works on Abhidharma: (1) *Mahāpuruṣa-śāstra* (Nanjio, 1242) a work on Abhidharma by Bodhisattva Āryadeva, (2) *Mahāyāna Avatāraka-śāstra* (Nanjio, 1243) by the Bodhisattva Sthiramati.

Buddhavarman[4] was probably an Indian monk; but we do not know any details of his life. He translated the *Mahāvibhāṣā* in 100 chapters in collaboration with Tao-t'ai and other monks. During the political troubles of 439 A. D. forty chapters of the translation perished in fire, the remaining 60 chapters having been saved. A complete translation was made by Hiuen Tsang in 200 fasciculi, whereas Buddhavarman's consists only of 82 fasc. Out of eight

Buddhavarman, 437 A. D.

1 Chavannes Voyage de, Song-ynga dans l' udyāna et le Gandhāra: Appendix to the article BEFEO, 1903, 43; Bagchi, pp. 224 f.

2 Nanjio. App, 72; Bagchi p. 722.

3 Nanjio App. II, 71; Bagchi, 226.

4 Nanjio App. II. 69; Bachi, 223,

books of the Mahāvibhāṣā translated by Buddhavarman, we have at this day only three. (Nanjio, 1264.)

Shin Huei Kiao[1] was another writer of this period but according to Nanjio he lived during the Northern Wei dynasty. Huei-Kiao was a native of Liang-chen but he worked at Lo-yang.

Huei-Kiao Damamukha Sūtra

In the company of other seven śramaṇas he went to the west of China in search of sacred works. They stopped at Khotan where the *Pañca-vārṣika* or the quinquennial festival was in progress. Fa-hien describes a similar festival at Kashgar. This was a ceremony, which the monks from the neighbouring places attended in large numbers. In such gatherings every learned monk was expected to contribute his mite to the progress of the *Dharma-ratna*, by explainining or reciting some Sūtra and Vinaya rules. Heui Kiao and his friends, who understood Sanskrit, translates some texts recited there, into Chinese. They took note of what they heard and when they returned to Turfan, they collected it in a volume. It was at Khotan that they came across a text of the Avadāna called *Hien-yu-king* (Nānjio, 1322) or '*Damamukha-sūtra*' or 'the Sūtra of the Wise and the Fool.'[2]

The greatest translator of this period was Dharmakṣema an Indian monk whose life is so varied and interesting that a detailed study seems necessary. Dharmakṣema was a native of Central India. When he was a boy of six, his father died, but his mother wanted

Dharmakṣema

to give him a good education, and therefore put him under a teacher named Dharmayaśas. He studied the literature of the Hīnayāna and was soon able to explain its philosophy clearly. After sometime he went to a Mahāyāna teacher with whom he had long discussion on religious topics; but Kṣema was not able to defeat his adversary and in admiration

1 Nanjlo, App. II, 108 ; Bagchi. 227.

2 The Chinese translation in time came to be translated into Tibetan. The Tibetan text with the German translation was published by I, J. Schmidt—*Dsang-lun oder Der Weise und der Thor.* St. Petersburg, 1843, Also c. f. *Tibetan Tales* derived from Indian sources translated into German from Kahgyur by Schiefner done into English by W. R. S. Ralston, London.

for the teacher, he began to study the Mahāyāna literature, which he had so long neglected. For twenty years he studied the literature of the both the systems and at the end mastered two hundred thousand words of the sacred texts.

It is said that he had some trouble with the local king and left the country and went to Kashmir, which was reputed as a centre of Buddhist studies. He had with him portions of the great *Mahāparinirvāṇa Sūtrā* and several works relating to Bodhisattva mārga; but the monks of Kashmir were Sarvāstivādins and had little respect for these works of Mahāyāna. Kṣema left Kashmir crossed the mountains passed through central Asia, and settled in Ku-tsang. As that time the Hun king *Tsin-k'in* Mongtuen had occupied the territory of Liang-cheu and proclaimed himself as the king. The fame of Kṣema had reached the barbarian king, who invited him to his realm, made him his own teacher and himself became a Buddhist, He further requested him to preach the religion of Buddha in his kingdom and wanted him to translate Sacred books into Chinese. Kṣema did not at once accept that invitation, for he was conscious of his imperfect knowledge of Chinese. He devoted full three years to the study of the language, at the end of which he began the work of translation.

The first Sanskrit work that he translated into Chinese was the first ten section of the *Mahānirvāṇa Sūtra*: several persons came to assist him of whom Shame Huei song and Tasleng are best known. At their request he translated the *Mahāsannipāta Sūtra* (Nanjio 61), *Karuṇā-puṇḍrīka Sūtra* (Nanjio, 142), *Bodhisattva Caryā Nirdeśa* (Nanjio, 1586), *Upāsaka-sīla Sūtra* (Nanjio, 1089) *Suvarṇa prabhāsa sūtrā* (Nanjio, 127), and several other treatises. But the *Nirvāṇa sūtrā* translated by him was not complete because the text he used consisted of only of ten chapters, and he decided thereupon to go to the west in search of a complete copy of the text. He therefore went to Khotan where he got the second part of this work, came back to Ku-tsang and began to translate it. It took him about seven years to finish the translation (414-421), which contained three hundred thousand *gāthās*.

In the meantime troubles were brewing in the political sky of China. The barbarian king Mongsuen was hardly touched by the teaching of the Buddha and he was always waging wars with his neighbours and conquering their territories; such a war once brought great disaster on him and one of his chief lieutenants was murdered. The foolish king had thought that his appeals and prayers to the Buddha would help him in all political difficulties and in his rage proclaimed that all monks below fifty years of age should renounce that religion ; but later on he changed his mind.

Political trouble and death of Kṣema

The fame of Kṣema had long crossed the boundary of Mongsuen's kingdom and the king of Wei became anxious to meet this learned monk of India. The Wei king sent a messenger to the Tartar King ; but he was unwilling to send the monk to his rival. After sometime Kṣema wanted to proceed to the west in search of manuscripts. The king was not willing to let him go and insulted him. But Kṣema was not the man to pay any heed to the dictates of the king and he left Ku-tsang and went westward. The King suspected that Kṣema was going to the Wei king, whom he feared and hated. Thereupon he sent an assassin and got Kṣema murdered in A. D. 434. He himself soon fell sick and died the same year. The dynasty collapsed six years hence in A. D. 439.[1]

Mahāsannipāta Sūtra,

Of the twenty-five works translated by Dharmakṣema more than half are now lost and only twelve exist ; but they are supremely important for the study of Buddhism in China. The Mahāyāna sūtras according to the orthodox system of classification, consist of five large groups, of which the *Mahāsannipāta* forms the third. Dharmakṣema rendered great service to the Buddhists of China by translating completely this extensive work in 30 fasc., (Nanjio, 61).

It may be mentioned here that Lokakṣema during the Han dynasty rendered into Chinese a recension of this work in 27 chapters but it is now lost. The second Chinese version of this

1 Bagchi, pp. 212—216.

work was made by Kumārajīva but in a greatly abridged form—in three chapters only. The Mahāsannipāta does not exist in the original Sanskrit, and therefore the translation of Kṣema is of special value to the history of Indian literature.

Dharmakṣema's translation of *Karuṇāpuṇḍarīka,* (which should be distinguished from *Mahākaruṇāpuṇḍarīka* and *Saddharmapuṇḍarīka*, is of less importance. The original of the Karuṇāpuṇḍarīka is still available.[1] It gives "an account of a continent called Padmadhātu, of its king Aranemi, of his priest and 500 sons, and of its Tathāgata Ratnagarbha. It is interspersed with many anecdotes and stories concluding with directions for the dissemination of the true religion after the nirvāṇa of the Lord. The work is divided into five chapters, and its leading expounder is Śākya himself, speaking in response to queries of Maitreya and others."

Karuṇāpuṇḍarīka

Another important contribution of Kṣema to the Chinese Buddhist literature was the translation of the Suvarṇaprabhāsa-sūtra. The book has been translated into all the ancient languages of Central Asia and the original Sanskrit text has happily escaped destruction and several copies of the text are available in Europe and India. This sūtra has been studied both by Chinese and Japanese scholars; many commentaries are still extant, among which the one by Chi-yi of the Avataṃśaka school is very valuable. As it contains some passages concerning the duties of the king, it has been regarded with special attention by the imperial family of Japan; and an elaborate rite has been performed by them in connection with the recitation and exposition of the sūtra. When Prince Shotoku of Japan built the temple of Shitennji (Four-Guardian gods Temple) in Osaka in 587 A.D., in honour of the sūtra, the name was taken from the chapters in which the guardian-gods promise to protect those who recite and practise the teaching of the sūtra. When later a state temple was established by the Emperor Shomū in each of the provinces for the promotion of the

1 Rajendralal, p. 285; also Catalogue of Hodgson. (Mss. I. 21; V, 42 VI 18; VII, 34).

national welfare, a copy of the sūtra was deposited in it.[1] Studies of the sūtra have been pursued by almost all the schools of Buddhism, but chiefly by the Tendai. There are *five* Chinese translations, the first of which was made by Dharmakṣema of the Siang Dynasty." Kṣema's translation was incomplete (4 fasc. of 18 chap.) ; a more complete translation was made by Yi-tsing in 110 fasc. of 31 chapters. Yi-tsing's version agrees very closely with the Tibetan translation. However the version of Dharmakṣema became popular owing to the famous commentary of Chi-yi, mentioned above. (Nanjio. 1548 alse 1552).

There are 21 chapters in the Sanskrit text and they are : 1. Nidāna, 2. Tathāgata-āyuspramāṇa-nirdeśa. 3. Svapna. 4. Rājendra-Deśanā. 5. Kamalākara nāma Sarvatathāgata-stava. 6. Śūayatā. 7. Caturmahārāja. 8. Sarasvatīdevī. 9. Śrī-mahādevī. 10. SarvaBuddha Bodhisattvānām Sandhārani 11. Dṛḍhapṛthivī-devatā 12. Sañjaya, 13 Devendra-Samaya nāma *Rājaśāstra*. 14. Susambhava. 15. Yajñāśrayanāma Rakṣa. 16. Dasadevaputra sahasrāṇi Vyākaraṇa. 17. Vyādhi praśamana. 18. Jalavāhanasya Matsyabainaya. 19. Vyāghrī. 20. Sarvatathāgata-stava.[2]

In this work the theory of Śūnyavāda is developed in the course of describing the merits of a certain mystic formula called *Suvarṇa-prabhāsottamā*. The contents partly digress into Tantrism. The Buddha here is an eternal divine Being. A Brāhmaṇa asks for a relic of the Buddha, be it no bigger than a mustard seed (Chap. II).

But he is instructod that it is easier to have hair grown on the back of a tortoise than to find such a relic. For the Buddha is not really born, but his true corporeal form is the Dharma-kāya or Dharma-dhātu.[3]

Chinese Buddhacarita of Aśvaghosa

The other important translation of Dharmakṣema which has won for him a great fame in Buddhist Chinese literature, is the translation of Aśvaghoṣa's *Buddha-carita*. The Sanskrit original exists and it has been

1 Hokei Izumi is editing the text in *the Eastern Buddhist* 1929. Vol. V.
2 See Bendal, Catalogue of Buddhist Sanskrit Manuscripts. p. 12.
3 Rajendralal p. 241 ff ; also, Nariman, p. 82 f.

edited by Cowell,[1] and an English translation also was made by the same scholar.[2] Therefore the subject matter of the work is well-known and no summary needs be given here ; only a few notes on the text may be given.

The existing Sanskrit text of the *Buddha-carita* consists of only 17 chapters and terminates with the conversions in Benares, while the Chinese version of Dharmakṣema gives the history of the Buddha from his birth to the division of his relics after his parinirvāṇa. The Chinese translation consists of 28 chapters, that is, it has 11 chapters more and it describes the period of Buddha's life from the conversions made at Benares to his death, which we do not find in the extant original Sanskrit. The titles of the chapters and contents of this Sanskrit epic agree with those of the first seventeen chapters of the Chinese translation of Dharmakṣema (except the titles of the 11th, 16th and 17th) which omits however a few verses. The last four cantos of the existing text of the *Buddha-carita* are held as spurious and are decidedly known as the composition of Amṛtānanda, a Nepalese poet of the 8th century A. D., who himself admits that he could find no complete manuscripts of the epic. The first 25 Ślokas of the Sanskrit text also do not agree with the Chinese. Therefore it seems that Amṛtānanda got the last copy of the epic in which the first folio was missing and the last portion completely wanting. The Chinese translation made between 414-421 A. D. was done from a complete version then still available.[3]

Yi-tsing on Buddha-carita

Yi-tsing, the Chinese traveller, who visited India and the eastern islands in the seventh century speaks of the great popularity of the work. He says that the *Buddha-carita* was a voluminous poem, which recounted the life and work of the Buddha, "from

1 Anecdota Oxoniensia, Aryan Series, Part VII, Oxford, 1893.

2 *SBE XLIV* 1894; also an Italian translation by Carlo Formichi: *Asvaghosa, Poeta del Buddhismo* - Bibliothica di Cultura Moderna, G. Laterza, Bari, 1912. For a complete critical bibliography see Author's Indian Literature Abroad (China) in the *Indian Historical Quarterly*, Vol. *II, 1926, No. 1*),

3 The Chinese Version called *Fo-so-tsin-tsong-king* of the *Buddha-carita* has been translates by Beal in the *sacred Books of the East. Vol. XIX.*

the time when he was still living in the royal palace till his last hour in the park of the Śāla trees." He further says : "It is extensively read in the five parts of India and in the countries of the South sea (Sumatra, Java and the islands). Aśvaghoṣa clothed manifold notions and ideas in a few words which so delighted the heart of his reader that he never wearied of perusing the poem. Moreover, it was regarded as a virtue to read it in as much as it contained the noble doctrine in a neat compact from."[1] From what Yi-tsing says it follows that he knew the epic in the original in the form of its Chinese translations in which it consists of 23 cantos and the narrative brought down to the Nirvāṇa of the Buddha.

Dharmakṣema's translation however is greatly amplified and transposed from the original and the result can hardly be called a literal translation.

Recensions of Pariṇirvana sūtra

The Nirvāṇa class forms the fifth part of the Mahāyāna sūtras in Chinese Buddhist Tripiṭaka. Several recensions of the *Mahāpariṇirvāṇa sūtra* are found in the Chinese,[2] some large, some small, some complete, some incomplete. All these versions do not belong to Mahāyāna ; some are parts of the Dīrgha and Madhyama Āgamas and approach the Pali *Mahāpariṇirvāna Sūtra* and some belong to Mahāyāna. Fa-hien and another translator of the Eastern Tsin dynasty (A. D. 317-420) whose name is lost, translated the Hīnayāna version of the Mahāpariṇirvāṇa (Nanjio, 118, 119). Fa-hien and Buddhabhadra also made an incomplete translation of the Mahāyāna version of the same treatise in 6 fasc, of 18 chapters (Nanjio, 120). Now it is Dharmakṣema, who gave a complete translation of the *Mahāpariṇirvāṇa sūtra* in 40 fasc. divided into 13 chapters.[3] This translation of Dharmakṣema was revised at Nanking by two Chinese śramaṇas Hwui-yen and

1 I-tsing, *Records*...trans. by Takakusu, Oxford, 1896, pp. 165ff,
2 Nanjio, 113, 114, 115, 118, 119, 120, 123.
3 This work has been partially described by Beal in his *Catena*. pp. 160-188.

Hwui-kwang and another literary man named Sie Ling-yun (A. D. 424-453) in 36 fasc. and rearranged in 25 chapters. The revisors consulted also the translation made by Fa-hien and Buddhabhadra. Dharmakṣema's Mahāparinirvaṇa is sometimes called *Pei-pan*, or the Northern Book, when it is compared with its revision, the Southern Book (Nanjio, 114).

X. The Hindu Monks in South China

While Northern China was being politically torn into pieces by the Tartar hordes, who founded several small principalities in the north, Southern China, although disturbed by the struggles of its own rival princes, was somewhat free from the devastating inroads of the Tartars. It enjoyed a more settled form of government and Buddhism really flourished under the Eastern Tsin Dynasty (A. D. 317-420). The literary activity of the Buddhists during the century of rule of the Eastern Tsin has been described above (See Chap. V). A general of the Eastern Tsin named Liu-yu, who had previously gained popularity through his successful campaigns against the Tartars, founded a new dynasty at Nanking in 420, called the Liu-Sung. Becoming emperor, he took the title of Wu-ti and reigned for three years.

South China free from invasions

Eastern Tsin (317-420 A, D,) followed by Liu Sung (420-479).

Wu-ti was a patron of Confucianism ; but he was not unfavourably disposed towards Buddhism. The Sung Annals record that several embassies came to him from India and Ceylon to offer him congratulations on the flourishing condition of Buddhism in his kingdom. But other memorials are preserved in which wo read that tho Chinese officials agitated for imperial interference to prevent the multiplication of monasteries and the growing expenditure in superstitous ceremonies of the Buddhists. "This marks the beginning of the desire to curb Buddhism by restrictive legislation which the official class displayed so prominently and persistently in subsequent centuries."[1]

In 458 during the reign of Wen-ti an unhappy incident took place. A conspiracy was discovered in which a Buddhist monk was implicated, and this at once gave the officials, who were invariably antagonistic towards Buddhism, an opportunity to pass

---

1 Eliot loct, cit p. 252.

several restrictive regulations on the monasteries. The emperor Ming-ti (465-473 A. D.), who was extremely cruel as a ruler, was, however, a devout Buddhist. Such instances of an anomaly in public life and private devotion are not rare in history. Ming-ti erected a large monastery in Hu-nan, at a tremendous cost, against the opposition of his ministers.

21 Translators in 59 years at Nanking

The dynasty of the Liu-Sung with eight rulers lasted fifty-nine years and ended miserably, after a series of unwonted crimes in 479. But still, the six decades of the Sung rule were favourable to the propagation of Hindu culture and Buddhism in South China, and twenty-one translators flourished during such a short period.

Pilgrimage to India

A remarkable feature of this period is the tendency of the Chinese monks to go on pilgrimage to India. Since Fa-hien's return to South China in 414, Chinese students felt almost a romantic passion for India, the home of Buddhism. In 420, a band of twentyfive monks started for India, to visit the holy places connected with the life of the Buddha as well as the centres of Buddhist culture and learning.

The leader of this party was Fa-Yong who took the Hindu name of T'an-wu-k'ie (Dharmakara ?). He became a Buddhist while still a boy. He was inspired by the example of Fa-hien and his comrade and wanted to see India even at the sacrifice of his life.

He came out to India with twenty-four friends. In Kashmir he got a manuscript of *Avalokiteśvara-Mahāsthāna-prāpta-Vyākaraṇa Sūtrā* (cf. Nanjio 395). The party visited all the important places in North India, crossed the Ganges and went to the south from there they embarked in a ship and reached Canton.[1] The activities of the Hindu monks went on as before and they generally came to Nanking. In 423 a Hindu monk named Buddhajīva.[2] arrived at Nanking. He was a teacher of Vinaya in Kashmir, and was a Vinayadhara of the school of the Mahîśāsaka.

1 Chavannes—*BEFEO.* 1903. p.435.
2 Nanjio App. II. 73 ; Bagchi, p. 363.

The Mahīśāsaka was one of the ten branches of the early Sthaviravādins, who were still living in Ceylon in the early fifth century, when Fa-hien visited the island. We can verily presume that this school must have been well-known in the lands from Kashmir to Ceylon in the fifth century. Among the manuscripts brought by Fa-hien, were copies of the Mahīśāsaka Vinaya, Prātimokṣa and Karmavācā. Fa-hien was still alive, when Buddhajīva arrived at Nanking in 423. Now the Mahīśāsaka Buddhajīva was the proper person to translate the Mahīśāsaka works into Chinese. Therefore the whole Pañcavarga Vinaya was rendered into Chinese by Buddhajīva with the collaboration of Chu-Tao-Shang and Che-Chang in A. D. 423, in 30 fasc (Nanjio, 1122).[1] He translated the Prātimokṣa (Nanjio, 1157) and also the Karmavācā ; the latter was lost before A. D. 730.

Besides Buddhajīva two other translators deserve special treatment viz., Guṇavarman and Guṇabhadra. Guṇavarman[2] was a Kṣatriya by caste. His ancestors were hereditary rulers of Kashmir ; but his grandfather Haribhadra (Ho-lo-pa-to) was banished from the country for tyranny. His father Saṁghānanda therefore had to live in the mountains and moors. Guṇavarman since his boyhood showed signs of keen intellectual powers. He was a boy of serious temperament, who studied all the sciences and branches of the Buddhist literature and came to be known a Tripiṭakācarya. At that time the King of Kashmir died childless and the ministers wanted to elect Guṇavarman, who was probably the nearest claimant, to the throne ; but he refused to accept royal honour and power ; for his heart was hankering for things far above royalty and he left home as a monk. He must have traversed the whole of India as a Bhikṣu and in 400 reached Ceylon where he helped

Guṇavarman of Kashmir

---

1 For the contents see Beal's letter quoted by Prof. Oldenberg in his Intro. to *Vinaya Piṭaka*, Vol. I. pp. xliv-xlvi.

2 Nanjio, App. II. 75, Bagchi, 370-775 translated his life from Chinese see T'oung-pao, 1904, pp. 193-206.

the people in developing their saṅgha. From Ceylon the monk went to Cho-po or Java, where Brahmanism was flourishing. The queen-mother of Java greatly honoured the Hindu monk, who had come there with the message of the Buddha, and founded the first Buddhist monastery in the island. The fame of the Hindu monk had already spread far abroad and the Sung Emperor at Nanking, anxious to bring Guṇavarman to his capital, sent envoys with a letter to the king of Java. In the meantime, Guṇavarman, finding a favourable wind embarked on a ship owned by a Hindu merchant named Nandi and reached Canton and finally settled in a monastery at Nanking. The emperor showed him the highest regards for his learning and character.

Visited Ceylon and Java

Guṇavarman lived in China for one year only (A. D. 432); but within that short time he translated eleven Sanskrit works. He completed the translation of *Saṁyukta abhidharma hṛdaya Sūtra*, which had been begun by another Hindu monk named Iśvara[1] and done up to the tenth chapter and then abandoned. The book was in 13 chapters. But unfortunately it was lost before 730 A. D. The work was a commentary on Dharmajñāna's *Abhidharma hṛdaya* (Nanjio 1288), by Dharmatrāta. The text of Dharmajñāna had been rendered into Chinese in A. D. 391 by Saṅghavarman (Nanjio, 1287). Of Guṇavarman's other translations, *Upāli-paripṛcchā* (Nanjio, 1109) and Nāgārjuna's *Suhṛllekha* are well-known. Both are lost in the original. But the *Paripṛcchā* is quoted four times by Śāntideva in his *Śikṣāsamuccaya* (Circa. 8th century A. D.); two passages are on confession with a prayer for deliverance from sin, and another shows superiority of Mahāyāna as a vehicle to release one from sin.[2] As to the other translation *Suhṛllekha*,—alleged to have been composed by Bodhisattva Nāgārjuna and addressed to his Dānapati, a great king of the Southern India,—it will be described under Yi-tsing.

Guṇavarman in China

1 Nanjio App. II, 78.

2 Bendal and Rouse, pp. 161, 165. 173, 264.

Guṇabhadra[1] is the greatest Hindu monk of the Sung dynasty. He was a Brahmana by caste and a native of Central India.

Guṇabhadra A. D. 435-468.

He was a great authority on Mahāyāna and was nicknamed Mahāyāna. Born in a Brahmin family he had the opportunity of learning the arts and the sciences of the Hindus and had become an adept in the *pañcavidyā*, i. e. astronomy, *lipi*, mathematics, medicine and *tantra*. When he began to study Buddhist philosophy, neither his parents nor the other members of his family liked the idea of his studying it. But he was bent upon becoming a monk and no amount of active persuation on the part of his relations could keep him within the four walls of his home or within the narrow groove of Brahmanical studies. He travelled from place to place studying with good teachers. He studied completely the Hīnayāna but these could hardly satisfy his yarning heart. He became a follower of Mahāyāna, which satisfied his spiritual needs In the end he specialised in the Avataṁsaka.

He left India on his conversion to the new faith and went to Ceylon. After sometime he took ship bound for the east and with

Reaches China *Via* Ceylon

great difficulty and hardship which always attended a voyage on those days, he reached China (A. D. 426). He was well received by the Emperor Tai-tsu. The Saṅgha of the capital pressed Guṇabhadra to translate sacred texts and he rendered some important works into Chinese.

Yi-siuan, king of Nan-Ts'iao invited Guṇabhadra, who worked in the monastery of *Sin-sse*. In the meantime Yi-siuan revolted

Translated 76 Sanskrit works

against the Emperor but was defeated and beheaded; Guṇabhadra, who was in the party of Yi-siuan, was however, pardoned by the emperor and installed in his former glory. He died in 468 A. D., in his 75th year[2] Guṇabahdra had worked in China for full thirty-four years having translated 76 works, of which only 28 have come down to us.

---

1 Nanjio, App. II, 81, ; Bagchi, p. 378.

2 Bagchi, p. 378-379 ; Nanjio, App. II, 81.

It will not be possible to describe all the books rendered into Chinese by Guṇabhadra ; only the important ones are mentioned briefly. Of these the *Śrīmālā-Siṁhanāda Sūtra* (Nanjio, 58) which forms a part of the Ratnakūṭa group, and which was once more translated by Bodhiruci, is a very important text ; for it is one of the three principal texts which inspired the Japanese people to accept Buddhism. The original text is lost and only a Sanskrit passage is quoted in Śāntideva's *Śikṣāsamuccaya* (Eng. Trans. p. 44).

Śrīmālā-Siṁhanāda Sūtra

Ratna-Kāraṇḍa-Vyūha (Nanjio, 169) an important Mahāyāna sūtra, was for the second time rendered into Chinese by Guṇabhandra. It had been once before translated in 2 fasc, by Chu Fa-hu (Dharmarakṣa) in A. D. 270. In Sanskrit these two recensions of two distinct types exist in prose and in verse.[1] Of the two the prose version is indeed the later in date. Its conception is dramatic. It is related in this work how at the beginning of things appeared the Ādi-Buddha, Svayambhu and Ādinātha, who created the world by his meditation. Avalokiteśvara is derived from this spirit and he co-operated in the creation of the world fashioning from his eyes the moon and the sun, Maheśvara from his heart, and from his teeth the goddess Sarasvati.[2] This is a book which has nothing to do with the *Guṇakāraṇḍa Vyūha*, which was translated by Guṇabhadra. It gives an account of the character, teachings and miracles of Avalokiteśvara. "Avalokiteśvara refused to enter Buddhahood until all living creatures would be in possession of the Bodhi knowledge. He had a long life. He had seen three or four Buddhas pass through their mundane career during his lifetime. He had been a friend to Vipaśyī, to Śikhi, to Jina and to Śākyamuni who had held him in high esteem. His principal occupation was to provide salvation to sufferers in

Ratna-Kāraṇḍa Vyūha, Guna Kāraṇḍa Vyūha. two different works

Avalokiteśvara's ideal in Guṇakāraṇḍa

1 Satyavrata Sāmaśrami's Edition with Bengali translation ; Calcutta, 1873.
2 Rajendralala op. c. t. p. 101.

hell; but he felt equally for all. In one of his philanthropic tours he passed through Ceylon, Benares and Magadha granting salvation, and preaching the gospel of Buddha's religion even to worms and insects. Even the gods of heaven were not beyond the range of his benevolence... Reclaiming the wicked, relieving sufferers, providing food for the famine-stricken, curing the diseased, -were the daily routine of his duties. Avalokiteśvara attained to such high distinction by his noble deeds that he was called the Saṅgha-ratna, or the jewel of the Buddhist church.[1]

Translation of Laṅkāvatāra

Guṇabhadra's translation of *Guṇakāraṇḍa Vyūha* was not an entirely new work, but his *Laṅkāvatāra* (Leng-kia-a-po-to-lo-pao king) was indeed a new thing to the Chinese Buddhists. There are however, three Chinese translations of this important sūtra. The first rendered by our monk Guṇabhadra, was only in four fasc (A. D. 443); the second in ten fasc was done by Bodhiruci (513) and the third in seven fasc by Śikṣānanda of Khotan (700). The translation of Śikṣānanda is the best of the three and of Guṇabhadra is the most difficult to understand for its defective Chinese. But in form and content the translation reflects the earliest text of the sūtra, and on it were written all the commentaries.

The *Laknāvatāra Sūtra* is looked upon as one of the earliest books in which the Yogācāra philosophy is dealt with.[2] The Sanskrit text as it is now printed begins with an account of a visit to Ceylon paid by Śākya; but this chapter is not found in Guṇavarman's translation. We shall however discuss the whole question of the *Lankāvatāra* in our section on Śikṣānanda.

Guṇabhadra, as a devout Mahāyānist translated many Mahāyāna works; but the Chinese Buddhists owe a great deal to him for some

---

1 Rajendralala *op. cit.* p. 95.

2 Hodgson said that it is reckoned as one of the *Nine Dharmas* of Nepalese Buddhism and is held in high esteem but Hodgson misunderstood his interpretors and there is no such thing a nine Dharmas in Nepal.

of the important Hīnayāna works as well. The last of the four Āgamas rendered into Chinese, was the *Saṁyukta āgama* (Nanjio, 544) by Guṇabhadra. We have already described the work above under the translation of āgamas. It may be mentioned here that the text which Guṇabhadra translated was the copy brought by Fa-hien from Ceylon, three decades back. His other work on Hīnayāna philosophy was the translation of Ācārya Vasumitra's *Abhidharma Prakaraṇa pāda Śāstra* (Nanjio, 1297), the second of the six pāda-works of the Sarvāstivāda, which will however be described under the works of Hiuen Tsang.

Translates Saṁyukta Āgama

Guṇabhadra was also a translator of a version of the *Milinda-Pañho* or the question of King Minander probably an incomplete work between A. D. 435 and 455. But it was lost by A. D. 664[1]

A short but an important treatise translated by Gunabhadra, was of particular value to the Chinese Buddhists. It was called *'Atīta-pratyūtpanna hetu phala Sūtra* (Nanjio, 666), which describes the theory of chain of cause and effect in a most clear language. A passage quoted from this book will give an idea of the work.

Sūtra of Cause and Effect

"At this time, the third night of meditation, the Bodhisattva examined the nature of sentient beings and for what reason old age and death exist. Then he saw that old age and death have their origin, for apart from birth there is no old age and death. Again, the birth does not arise because of God, or itself, or without cause, but arises because of causes and conditions, for it is derived from existence or deed-process in the Kāma-dhātu, the Rūpa-dhātu or Arūpa-dhātu. Then he examined the threefold deed-process and how it arose, and saw that it was derived from four-fold attachment and how it arose, and saw that it was derived from Desire. Then he examined and how it arose, and saw that it was derived from the Feeling. Then he examined this feeling and how it arose, and saw that it was derived from Sensation. Then he examined this sensation and saw that was derived from the

1 [*BEFEO* 1924, p. 21].

six sense organs. And whence came these six sense organs? He saw that they were derived from the material and mental aspects of the personality (name and form). Then he examined name and form (Nāma and Rūpa), how it arose, and saw that it was derived from Action,. Then he examined action and how it arose, and saw that it was derived from Ignorance. Moreover, if Ignorance (Avidyā) be annihilated, then is action annihilated. If action be annihilated then is consciousness annihilated. If consciousness be annihilated, then are name and form annihilated. It name and form be annihilated then are the six sense organs annihilated. If the six sense organs are annihilated, then is feeling annihilated. If feeling be annihilated, then is desire annihilated. If Desire be annihilated then is Attachment annihilated. If attachment be annihilated, then is deed-process annihilated. If deed-process be annihilated, then is birth annihilated. Finally, if birth be annihilated, then are old age, death anguish, suffering, mental affliction annihilated.[1]

Other monks of this period

The other monks of this period were Saṅghavarman, Dharmamitra and Kālayaśas. Saṅghavrman[2] was a Hindu monk, who came to (Kien-Ye) Nanking, the capital of the Sung in A. D. 433, and translated five works, of which four remain. In 442 he went westward, but the time of his death is not known to anybody. Saṅghavarman was a pious monk and helped the saṅgha in many ways. His *Mātrikā* or notes on the Vinaya of the Sarvāstivādins (Nanjio, 1132) seems to be an important commentary. He also translated a sūtra on the fruits of Karma briefly explained by the Bodhisattva Āryaśūra (Nanjio, 1349), the well-known author of Jātakamālā. His translation of *Suhṛllekha* is also an important work.

Saṅghavarman, A. D. 442.

1. Nanjio, 664, 665, 666; see Mc Govern *Manual of Buddhist Philosophy*. pp. 170.

2 Nanjio, App. II, 80; Bagchi, p. 375; *Chin* Sang-ke-po-mo; in trans. Kumg-Kai or 'Company-armour.'

3 Nanjio, App. II, 75; Bagchi, 388. Chin. Tan-mo-mi-to: in trans. Fa-siu or 'Law-flourishing."

Dharmamitra and Kālayaśas

Dharmamitra[3] was a native of Kashmir. From his boyhood he entertained a love for Buddha's teachings and with the permission of his parents he left home to become a monk and studied under some of the best professors of the time. He left India by the N. Western land route, reached Kucha where he lived for some years ; from there he went to Tun-huang, where he built a large monastery. He moved from place to place till he came to Nanking in A.D. 424. He translated twelve works, of which six only remain. *Hastikākṣya* (Nanjio, 123) a work which Dharmamitra translated is quoted by Śāntideva in his *Śikṣa-samuccaya* ; the original is lost ; Kālyaśas[1] came from India in A. D. 424 ; he translated two works, of which one is a *Sukhāvatī Vyūha* (Nanjio, 198). There is prefixed a Chinese verse of sixty lines on Amitāyur Buddha, which is described as an imperial composition. The emperor's name is not given ; but it may be the composttion of Emperor Wen, who was a patron of Buddhism during this period.

Besides two or three Hindu monks of doubtful locality and indifferent interest, the rest of the workers were Chinese monks.

Che-yen and Pao-yun

Shih Che-yen[2] and Pao-yun[3] two monks of Liang-chou, who had accompanied Fa-hien in his tour towards the west, had stayed behind in Kashmir, without proceeding down to India. They lived in Kashmir for three years and brought some manuscripts to China. Che-yen translated fourteen works in collaboration with Pao-yen of which only four remain. It is said that Che-yen once more in his old age went to Kashmir, where he died in his 78th year. After his death, his friend Pao-yun continued the work of translation of the Sanskrit texts they had brought from India. After his return to China he became a disciple of Buddhabhadra whom he helped greatly in his days of difficulty. Pao-yun was one of the greatest

1 Nanjio, App. II 74 ; Bagchi, 391 ; Chin-Kiang-liang-ye-see ; in trans, She-Cheng. 'Time-fame'

2 Nanjio, App. II, 76 ; Bagchi, 364,

3 Nanjio, App. II, 77 : Bagchi, 367,

Sanskritists of his time and helped many Hindu monks as an interpreter. Of his four translations only one remains.

We shall not however describe the lives of all the translators of this age, whose books have not come down to us[1]. But Tsu-k'iu Ring-Cheng[2] deserves a note. We saw him working in the Northern China under the North-Liang Dynasty. After the fall of that dynasty he moved southward and settled at Nanking. He died in 464 A. D. He translated thirty-five works, of which sixteen works are extant; one is on the meditation on the Bodhisattva Maitreya's going up to be born in the Tuṣita Heaven (Nanjio, 204); another is on the secret remedy for curing the disease concerning meditation. (Nanjio, 647); another on the advancement in learning (Nanjio, 890.)

Minor translators

Shin Hwui Kien[3] whose native place is not known, translated twenty-five works, of which six are still in the Tripiṭaka[4]. Guṇasatya[5] a śramaṇa of western region arrived in China in A. D. 462, during the reign of Hio-wu-ti (454-465). He translated two books, of which both are still extant.

During the Sung rule of about sixty years twenty-one translators worked at Nanking and translated according to Kai-yuen-lu four hundred and sixty-three Sanskrit works in 713 fasc. But of this vast number only ninety-one still remain and there is no trace of three hundred and fifty-two Sanskrit books which existed in the fifth century either in the original or in translation.

463 works translated

In 479 the last ruler of the Sung dynasty Shun-ti, who held

1 Chu Fa-k'ien Nanjio II. 86; trans. 6 works, Shih Tao-yen Nanjio, II 88, trans. 2 works, Shih Yung-kung, Nanjio, II, 89; trans 3 works, Shih Fa-hai Nanjio, II, 90; trans, 2 works, Shih Sien-kung Nanjio, II 91, only one work Sanghavarman (i) Nanjio II, 92)

2 Nanjio App, II, 83 : Bagchi, 394.

3 Nanjio, App. II, 83 ; Bagchi, 399,

4 Nanjio speaks of 10 or 15 works only.

5 Bagchi, p. 398 ; Nanjio. App, II, 85 ; Gunaśila f

19

but nominal sway over the country, was forced to abdicate his throne in favour of his powerful general Su-tao-cheng. This general rose to eminence by his wars with the Wei of the North (see below) and founded the Chi dynasty. Assuming the dynastic title of Kao-ti, he reigned only four years, and was followed by six successors most of whom died in quick succession by violence.

Sung secceeded by Chi (Tsi) dynasty, A. D. 479-502

The capital of the Chi (Tsi) dynasty remained at Nanking and there was hardly any change in the attitude of the rulers towards Hindu culture and Buddhist faith. In the reign of the second emperor, one of the princes ef the house, named Tzu-liang cultivated the society of eminent monks and took part in theological discussion. From the specimen of the arguments, which have been preserved, we find that the explanation of inequalities of life as the result of *karma*, had a great attraction for the popular mind and it provoked the hostile criticism of the Confucian literati.[1]

During the short period of twenty-three years of their rule, eight translators rendered fourteen works into Chinese, of these only six are preserved. The most important translation is Sarighabhadra's *Samantapāsādika*.

Sarighabhadra[2] a monk of India came to China probably by the sea-route. He seems to have brought with him a copy of the Pali *Samantapāsādika* of Buddhaghoṣa. The Chinese title of the work is *I-Ck'i-Shan-Chien-lu-pi-po-sha :* Nanjio rendered this title as in Sanskrit as *Sudarśana-Vibhāsā Vinaya* (Nanjio 1125); but Takakusu says that there is no such work in Sanskrit of that title. According to extant tradition it is a work on the Hīnayāna. It is divided into 18 books and consists of 440 leaves, each leaf containing 400 Chinese characters. It begins with the adoration 'Namo Sabbeṣām Buddhānaṃ' and an opening verse. The first three books are devoted to the historical introduction. A short resume of the work is given

Sarighabhadra 489 A. D.

Pali Samanta Pāsādika in Chinese

1 Eliot, *op cit.* p. 253

2 *Chin.* Sêng-chich po-t'o-lo Nanjio : App. II, 95 ; Bagchi p. 408.

below : Book i-iv The history from the Buddha's death to Mahinda's death. The first section is devoted to the council of Rājagaha, which took place during the rainy season immediately after the Buddha's death at Kuśinārā. Five hundred Arhats meet under Mahākāssapa. Upāli recites the contents of the Vinaya, while Ānanda rehearses the Suttas in answer to the questions of the presiding Thera. It lasted seven months.

Next comes the Vajjiputtaya section. In this the ten points brought forward by the Vajjian Bhikkhus are given, and the Council of Vaisālī, which met a hundred years after Buddha, is shortly described. The preciding Theras of the second council were ten in number, members in all numbering seven hundred. It ended in eight months.

The third is called Aśokarāga section, which covers some three books and fifty-two folios. It describes the rise of Aśoka, his conversion to Buddhism by Ni-ch'ü-t'o (Nigrodha), his building of Saṅghārāmas and medical halls, the invitation of Moggaliputta Tissa, whose life is given at length, the examination of all Bhikkhus by Aśoka, and then the Council of Pātaliputta which lasted nine months, Tissa presiding over 1000 members. Then follow the ordinations of Mahinda and Saṁghamittā, the sending out of the missionaries, the conversion of Devānāmpriya Tissa, the planting of a branch of the Bo-tree in Ceylon, the arrival of Saṁghamittā, and lastly, the deaths of Mahinda, Ariṭṭha and others.

The whole agrees pretty well with the last portion of the third volume of the *Vinaya Piṭaka Book IV-VI.* Commentary on the introductory portion of the Vinaya i. e. the first part of the Suttavibhaṅga. The Mahāmoggallāna Khandhaka, the Sāriputta Khandhaka, and the Vānarakhandhaka etc. are explained. *Book VII-XII.* An explanation of the Pārājika rules. Book *XIII-XVIII.* The Saṁghādiśesā rules and other sections are explained. The last part (*XVIV*) gives some remarks in a very short form about the Khandhaka, Bhikkhunī Khandhaka etc, and also thirty-two questions to Upāli by Mahākassapa, and the answers as well.

Takakusu has given extracts from this work, and asserts

definitely that it was translated from Samantapāsādikā of Buddhaghoṣa in Pali. It is said that Buddhaghoṣa came to Ceylon in A. D. 430 and went to Burma about A. D. 450 with him all the works of his compilation. The manuscript of this Pali work must have been carried to China by Saṅghabhadra the translator, who probably secured a Mss. of the said work from Ceylon. According to a Chinese tradition Saṅghabhadra brought the Vinaya Vibhāsā to Canton in A. D. 489 and translated it into Chinese. He seems to have been a Hinayānist of Theravāda School.[1]

As regards the other translations of the period a brief resumé will be enough.

Eight Translators.

Dharmakṛtayaśas, a śramaṇa[2] of Central India, came to China in A. D. 481 in the time of Kao-ti (Su Tao Cheng). He translated a sūtra called *Amitārtha Sūtra* (Nanjio, 133). Mahāyāna (Nanjio, App. II, 94, Bagchi, p. 407) a śramaṇa of India, (A. D. 483-493) translated, two works, namely, (1) Sūtra of 500 jātakas, and (2) Vinaya of the Sthavira school. But both translations were lost already in A. D. 730.

Dharmamati,[3] (Chin. Ta-mo-mo-ti ; trans. Fa-i or 'law-thought') a monk of India, came to China through Khotan and translated two works, which are now lost. Guṇavṛddhi[4] was a śramaṇa of Central India, who in A. D. 493 and 495 translated three works, of which two remain. He came to China in 479.

The rest of the translators of this period were Chinese. Shih Fa-tu (Nanjio App. II, 98), Shih Fa-hua (Nanjio App, II, 100) have left no trace of their translations. Only Shih Tan-King[5] whose exact date is unknown left only two translations, viz. the *Mahāmāya sūtra* (Nanjio 382) and the *Adbhuta-dharma-*

1 J. Takakusu. Pāli elements in Chinese Buddhism. *JRAS.* 1896. p. 416-439.

2 Nanjio App. II, 93. Bagchi, p. 407 ;

3 Nanjio App. II, Bagchi, 409 ;

4 Bagchi, 410 ; Nanjio App. II, 97.

5 Nanjio App, II, 99 ; Bagchi 411.

parayāya (Nanjio 400). Adbhuta-dharma is one of the classifications of Mahāyāna sūtras.

After the collapse of the Ts'i (Chi) dynasty, Southern China passed into the hands of the Liangs. This dynasty was founded by Su-yen of the Siao family, who obtained the throne as usual in those days by forcing the weak sovereign of the Ts'i dynasty to abdicate in his favour. Su-yen killed the Ts'i emperor and took the title of Wu-ti. Wu-ti alone ruled for forty-eight years between 502 and 549 at Nanking, and during his reign the south enjoyed an interval of comparative peace and prosperity.

Liang dynasty 502-557

His reign was an important epoch in the history of Chinese Buddhism. Although successful as a warrior in the beginning of his life, Wu-ti lost all interest in war and politics on his conversion to Buddhism, and at the end died miserably at the hands of his northern rivals, the Wei. Wu-ti was originally not a follower of Buddha ; but a staunch confucianist till A. D. 510. It is said that Wu-ti was converted to Buddhism by a wandering monk named Pao-chih. The emperor became such an orthodox follower of his new religion that he not only forbade sacrifice of animals, but even the representation of living creatures in embroidery, on the ground that people might cut up such figures and thus become callous to the sanctity of life. He imitated the great Hindu-Buddhist king Aśoka and rivalled him in pious enthusiasm, if not in power and prosperity. He expounded sūtras in public and wrote a book on Buddhist ritual.[1] The emperor in his zeal thrice went into a monastery to become a monk at Nanking, and each time large sums of money had to be paid before he could return home and resume the reins of government.[2]

Wu-ti, a devout Buddhist Emperor. 502-549

Towards the close of the reign of Wu-ti, a formidable rebellion broke out, as the result of which the Liang empire was divided into Posterior Liang, and Ch'en kingdoms. The Liang Dynasty

1 Eliot, *op-cit.* p. 254.
2 Li-ung Bing, Opt, Cit. p. 120

disappeared (A. D. 557) within nine years of the death of Wu-ti (A. D. 549).

The rapid spread of Buddhism in China led to free intercourse between China and the outside world and it was in the time of Wu-ti that envoys from Korea came to China to ask for copies of Buddhist classics and specially for a copy of the Parinirvāṇa sūtra.

Relation with Funan & India

Tho Annals of the Liang further tell us that at that time China had established an intimate relation with Further India, specially with Funan[1] a great Hindu state founded in the first century A. D. In the fifth century Saivism and Buddhism flourished side by side in that country. As for Buddhism several facts show the important part it played in that state. Chinese sources mention several holy men who went from this county to China. In 538, a hair of Buddha was sent by the king of Funan and received with great ceremony in China, although strongly repudiated and criticised by the Confucianist literati.

Mandrasena of Funan A. D. 503.

Mandrasena[2] a śramaṇa of Funan came to Kien-yeh (Nanking) in A. D. 503, and translated 3 works in 11 fasciculi. Although he worked at translations, he was not well acquainted with the Chinese language and his translations are not reliable. Subhūti was another monk of Fūnan (see below). But the translations of *Saṅghabhara* of Fūnan are better known.

Saṅghabhara's Vimokṣa-mārga

Saṅghabhara[3] was a good scholar of Abhidharma and he translated eleven works between A. D. 506 and 520. Saṅghabhara translated *Saptaśatikā Prajnāpāramitā* (Nanjio, 22) a recension of *Prajñāpāramitā* of seven hundred verses, and several other Mahāyān sūtras. But the most important of his translations was the '*Vimokṣamārga Sūtra*' (Nanjio 1293).

---

1 Pelliot, to Fu-nan, *BEFEO*, 1905.

2 Nanjio, App. II, 101; Bagchi, p. 414: *Chin.* Man-to'-lo; in trans, Jo-sheng or 'weak-sound'

3 Nanjio, App. II. 102; Bagchi, 415; *Chin* Seng-kia-p'o-lo; *in-trans.* Kung-yang, 'company-nourishing.' Nanjio restored it as Saṅghapāla or Sanghavarman. But see Bagchi, *op. cit.* also Pelliot, *BEFEO*, 1903; Levi. *J. As*, 1915, p. 26.

The Chinese title of the work is *Chie-to-tao-lun* means 'The way to deliverance,' and corresponds with the Pali *Vimuttimagga*. The Chinese text agrees roughly (in some places very closely) with *Visuddhi-magga*. The terms *visuddhi* and *vimutti* denote nirvāṇa or arhatship and resemble each other in sound. Judging from the contents of the two works, the name *Vimutti-magga* must be regarded to be the original and more appropriate than Visuddhimagga. The points of agreement between the Chinese text and the Visuddhimagga had been studied in detail and thus have been accounted for by Nagai, in one way or another, on the ground of re-arrangement, interpolation or abridgement. On the whole the description of the Chinese is much simpler than that of Pali. Buddhaghoṣa the author of the *Visuddhimagga*, seems to be responsible for all such revisions.

Vimuttimagga
Visuddhimagga,
Vimokṣamamārga

Upatissa, a learned monk of Ceylon of the 1st cent. A. D. was the author of the *Vimutti-magga*. Buddhaghoṣa came to Ceylon (circa A. D. 420) and began his work of revising Pali works. Nagai says that his *Visuddhimagga* is in reality a revised version of Upatissa's *Vimutti-magga*. The *Vimutti-magga* as its contents show, is an Abhidharma exegesis, serving as a compendium of that portion of Buddhist literature. In short, the *Visuddhimagga* of Buddhaghoṣa and the *Vimutti-magga* of Upatissa are one and the same work, appearing in different attires. The earlier version is preserved in the Chinese of Saṅghabhara.[1]

Two more Hindu monks, Upaśūnya and Paramārtha, came to China during the Liang dynasty; but their principal period of activity was the time of the Chien rule and rightly it belongs to that period. During the reign of the Liang Wu-ti (A. D. 502-549), the founder of the dynasty, the first collection of Chinese Buddhist Tripiṭaka was made. We read in the Sui annals (A. D. 589-618) that the Liang Emperor Wu' paid great honour to Buddhism. He made a large

First collection of the Chinese Tripiṭaka

1 M. Nagai, The Vimutti-magga.' *Journal of the Pali Text Society*. 1917-19, pp. 60-80.

collection of the Buddhist canonical books, amounting to 5,400 volumes, in the Hua-lin garden. The Shaman Pao-Chang compiled Tāe catalogue in 54 fasc. According to *K'ai-yuan-lu* (A. D. 780), this catalogue was compiled by Pao-ch'ang under the Imperial Order. in 4 fasc, in A. D. 518 but it had been lost already in A. D. 730 ; the total of the sacred books in it is said to have been about *1432* distinct works in 3741 fasc arranged under twenty classes. This was the first collection of Buddhist sacred books made by an emperor of China.[1]

Although the catalogue of the above Imperial collection is lost, we have another catalogue in 17 fasc, of Buddhist Tripiṭaka, made by Shng Yu, about 520 A. D. (Nanjio, 1476). It mentions *2213* distinct works, whether translations or native productions, of which 276 have been identified by Nanjio with the works mentioned in the latter's catalogue.[2]

Catalogue of A. D. 520 2213 works translated.

Seng-yu (Nanjio, A. p. III, 6) was a learned monk of this period, who read and wrote much. The compilation of a catalogue in those days was not a very easy task. Seng-yu did it creditably and himself wrote 15 books. Of these *Shih-K'-iafu* or Śākya records (Nanjio, 1468) are preserved. It is the history of the Sākya family collected from various sūtras and Vinaya works of the Mahāyāna. It begins with a genealogy of the Śākya family, and ends with a record of the state of the destruction of the law of Śākyamuni. There are given separately, the lives of Śākyamuni and his parents, relations and disciples, and the records of the Vihāras and Caityas. It was a work in 10 fasc of 34 chapters. Another work, 'a collection of miscellaneous writings on propagation and illustration of the teaching of Buddha in 34 fasciculi was written by Seng-yu (Nanjio, 1479).

Seng-Yiu, A. D. 500.

Pao-Chang (Nanjio, App. III, 7) the learned monk who edited the

1. Nanjio, Introduction, p. xvii.

2. *Ibid*, Introduction, p. xii-xvii, for the date see Maspero, *BEFEO*, X, p. 113; Pelliot, *T'oung Pao*, 1911, p. 674; quoted from Bagchi, p. XLV).

Tripiṭaka under the imperial order of Wu-ti compiled a collection of extracts on different subjects from Sūtras and Vinaya works called *K'ing-lu-yi-siang* (Nanjio, 1473) in 50 fasc. under the order of the emperor.

Pao-cheng, A. D. 516-526.

The order of the subjects treated in the work follows somewhat the system of classification of *Mahāvyutpatti* or *Dharma-saṁgraha.* It was divided into 21 classes sub-divided into 40 and consisted of 639 articles. His other work was a memoir of sixty-five Chinese bhikṣuni, who lived sometime between A. D. 326 and 526 (Nanjio, 1497). Similar to this work 'Memories of eminent priests' were compiled by another Chinese monk Hwui-Chiao, (Nanjio App. III, 8) in A. D. 519. In the work of Hwui-Chiao lives of 257 men are dealt with separately, and 239 are only referred to. They were either Indian or Chinese, and not only priests but also laymen, who lived in China between A. D. 67 and 519 (Nanjio, 1490). These are classed according to their doings and sayings, under the divisions of: translation, exposition; dhyāna, exemplary diecipljne; rigidity of doctrine; comprehensive intelligence; self-sacrifice; study; attainment of happiness and miscellaneous distinctions.[1]

The *K'ai-yuan-lu* mentions 14 works in 25 fasc. by unknown translators.[2] One work by an unknown translator seems to be interesting to philologists and especially to historian of Tantrism. *T'o-lo-nitsa-tsi* is a mixed collection of *Dhāranīs*; most of these are transcribed in Chinese as well as translated. There are 185 Dhāraṇīs—mostly very short treatises.[3]

Dhāraṇī Saṁgraha, 185 Dharanis transliterated

During this period lived a celebrated Chinese layman named Fu-hi (b. 497; d. 569). He is commonly known as Fu-ta-shih or

---

1 Wyile, *Notes on Chiness Literature*, Shanghai. p. 209.

2 Nanjio mentions only 13 in the Appendix; he omits the one mentioned in the text of the catalogue No. 1475.

3 For the titles of 185 Dharanis see Courant's *Catalogue des Livres Chinois*, Bib. Nationale, Paris, 1910, Tome II, p. 564-590. Nanjio does not give the names of the Tantric texts in the collection.

the Mahāsattva or the noble-minded Fu. In China Tripiṭaka used to be deposited in a building called *Luu-tsang* (Japanese, *Rin-zo*) or 'revolving repository' because it contains a large eight-angled book-case, made to revolve round a vertical axis. Fu-hi is said to have thought that if any pious person could touch such a book-case and make it revolve once, he would have the same merit as if he had read the whole Tripiṭaka. The statue of this Chinese inventor is generally placed in the front of the 'revolving repository' and on each side of his statue, there are added those of his two sons, Pu-Kien and Pu-Chang. The father's statue represents the imperial views which he held during his life time, for he is represented as wearing the Taoist cap, the confucianist's shoes and Buddhist kāṣāya or scarf across the shoulder. There is a story that when Fu-hi in this dress saw Wu-ti (502-549), the emperor asked him whether he was a Buddhist priest, Fu then pointed to his Taoist cap; when asked again whether he was a Taoist, he pointed to his Confucianist's shoes. Being asked lastly, whether he was a Confucianist, he pointed to his Buddhist scarf.[1]

Fu-hi and the revolving repositary

1 Nanjio, *Catalogue*, Intro. p. xxvi.

XI. The Age of Paramartha

The Liang dynasty at Nanking survived nominally for nine years after the death of Wu-ti, who met an ignominious death at the hands of his rebel chief Hu-ching. Hu-ching reigned for a very short time only to die a cruel death at the hands of his rebellious citizens. Wu-ti's son Yuan-i who became emperor (552-555) was a Taoist. He was a great scholar and had accumulated 1,40,000 volumes in his private library. But he destroyed them by fire when he heard that his northern enemy the Wei were at the gate and his learning and his books were of no avail at this hour of peril. There is no doubt that a large number of Buddhist works must have perished in this way.

Successors of Wu-ti

Under the short Ch'en dynasty (A. D. 557-589), the position of Buddhism on the whole, was favourable, and the Hindu monks, who had arrived at the latter part of the Liang dynasty, continued their work of translation with much vigour and earnestness. Several Hindu monks arrived at Nanking during Wu-ti's rule, of whom the most celebrated was Paramārtha. Paramātha.[1] was a Śramaṇa of Ujjain, in Western India born in an enlightened brahamaṇa family. He was also called Kulanātha (K'iu-lo-na-t'o). Paramārtha was well-versed in literature and art. He had a passion for travel and adventure and left home in his youth, crossed the desert tracts of Rajputana and reached the plains of the northern India and probably settled in Pataliputra, the imperial seat of the Guptas.

Life of Paramārtha

In 539 appeared in Magadha a mission from China apparently in search of Buddhist manuscripts and a worthy savant. The Chinese officers composing the mission which came to India, had accompanied an envoy of Fu-nan (Cambodia), then returning home from China. The king of Magadha, probably Jīvitagupta or

---

1 In Chin., Po-lo-mo-t'o, is translated as *Chen-ti* or true-truth.

Kumāragupta[1] gladly responded to the request of the Chinese emperor Wu and decided to send Paramārtha with a large number of books belonging to the Buddhist and other sects.

Paramārtha presumably started from Tamralipti, the ancient port of Bengal, and by the sea-route reached Nanking after two years in 546, halting probably in Ceylon, Java and other Hindu colonies of the east. At Nanking the Hindu monk was most cordially received by the Chinese emperor, who offered him a beautiful residence in the Pa-yun palace and allowed him to preach the law of the Buddha from there.

Paramārtha in China

Although the king had a keen desire for encouraging the translation of sacred books into Chinese and wanted to create a new literature in imitation of the glorious epochs of the past, the political unrest of the period hampered him at every step in the realisation of his ideal. The whirl of revolution soon dislodged Paramārtha out of his quiet corner in the Pao-yun palace, and he was compelled to go about in the country with his literary treasures, till he reached the South, where he got shelter with the governor of Fu-ch'uen, an earnest devotee of the Buddhist faith. The good prefect organized a group of workers to help Paramārtha in the translation of the Sanskrit works he was carrying with him. He began to translate the *Saptadaśabhumi śāstra*, and had done only five chapters, when his whole programme was once more upset by the same political trouble that had driven him from the north. War and famine and the chaos that followed were greatly responsible for the decline of Buddhism at this time. Luckily for China, the rebel chief was murdered by Ch'en Pa-sien, who became the founder of the Ch'en dynasty and thus brought peace and order in the southern China and gave relief to the suffering millions. Paramārtha settled at Nanking where in the vihāra of Cheng-knan-ssu he with his disciples commenced to translate of the *Suvaranaprabhāsa*

Political unrest of China

1 See Smith, *Early History of India* 4 Ed. p. 331.

sūtra (Nanjio, 127, 130) and finished it in 557, the year in which the dynastic change mentioned above took place.

The next year Paramārtha returned to his mountain retreat of Cheng-kuan-ssu and visited several places. But the political unrest of the country had completely upset the peace of his mind and he contemplated to go to Burma presumably with an intention to proceed to India ; but the monks and the lay people, who loved him dearly, were unwilling to part with him and implored him to stay with them. Accordingly he settled at Nan-yue, where in collaboration with his friends revised some of the older translations.

In the reign of Wen-ti some priests and respectable citizens of Nanking came to Paramārtha to pay a tribute of honour to their old master and friend, and requested him to live there and deliver a course of lectures on the well-known Mahāyāna *Samparigraha sūtra* (Nanjio, 1183). He kept their request and lectured for several years. But his heart was yearning for his native country and he availed himself of an early opportunity when he took a small boat bound for a seaport, where he had the intention of boarding a merchant-man which proceeded towards the west. But there he was persuaded by his disciples to give up his plan again. He lived at the port for sometime but afterwards took a ship and sailed for the west. But the wind became unfavourable and he was obliged to land at a place near Canton, where he was received most cordially by the local governor, who wanted him give an exposition on the Law. There he lectured on the Mahārthadharmaparyāya śāstra, the Vijñaptimātra siddhi and other texts to the local monks. On the death of the governor his successor became his patron and wanted him to continue his work. But Paramārtha had become disgusted with the world and the ways of the people and at last attempted to commit suicide. He was however prevented from the crime and was henceforward guarded by men sent by the governor. But in spite of all the care of his disciples, Paramārtha did not recover from his malady and died at the age of 71 (A.D. 569). Thus tragically ended the life of one of the brilliant sons of India in the distant land of China. A pagoda was erected on his remains by his admirers and his disciples left the South and proceeded towards the north with the works of their master.[1]

Paramartha translates 70 works.

During the Liang Dynasty (546-557), Paramārtha translated 19 works and after the fall of that dynasty his work of translation continued as usual and the number of translations during the Ch'en (557-569) was 51; altogether 70 works were rendered into Chinese by this great Hindu monk. Of his seventy translations, only 32 are extant.

Takakusu's estimate of Paramārtha's work

"The literary activity and religious enthusiasm of the Indian guest during the declining days of the Liang Dynasty (548-557), and the early parts of the subsequent Ch'en dynasty (557-569) seems to have attracted the curious eyes of Chinese Buddhists, who thronged to listen to the new preacher in spite of all the disturbances, which they were experiencing just then. His teaching embodied a variety of subjects but throughout, as a Mahāyānist he laid earnest and persistent emphasis on the Buddhistic idealism (*vijñānavāda*) or Vasubandhu and Asaṅga. He seems to have been successful in popularising the doctrine, for on one occasion the court is said to have considered the propagation of his idealism to be dangerous to the nation. He himself was not satisfied with his work as a preacher of peace. He once said to one of his pupils: 'My original plan for which I came here will never be realized. We can entertain at present no hope of seeing the prosperity of Dharma.' But his work as a translator was simply brilliant and in every way satisfactory. We have to thank him for the preservation of several important texts, such as the fundamental works of Vijñānavādins, Vasubandhu and Asaṅga, the *Sāṅkhya-Kārikā* of Iśvarakṛṣṇa with its commentary, besides some works of Nāgārjuna, Aśvaghoṣa, Vasumitra and Guṇamati. What we value most is his biography of *Vasubandhu* which furnishes us with several otherwise unknown data, and sheds

1 Takakusu, Le Sāṅkhyakārikā, *BEFEO*, 1904, pp. 64 ff.

an unexpected light on a dark period in the history of Buddhism of the Sāṁkhya school and of Indian literature in general."[1]

One of the most important philosophical works, called *Śraddhotpāda śāstra*, which was rendered by him will engage our attention first. The alleged author of the work is the great Aśvaghoṣa. The reason why the work was at all written is clearly outlined in the introductory part of the Discourse. The author found that although the doctrines ennunciated in the work are found scattered in the Mahāyāna sūtras, yet as he discoursed that the predispositions and inclinations of the people were not the same and the conditions for obtaining enlightenments vary, therefore he now wrote the discourse.

Śraddhotpada śāstra

"There is another reason for doing so. At the time of the Tathāgata the people were unusually gifted, and the Buddha's presence, majestic both in mind and body, served to unfold the infinite significance of the Dharma with simplicity and yet in perfection. Accordingly there was no need for a philosophical discourse.

"After the Nirvāṇa of the Buddha there were men who possessed in themselves the intellectual power to understand the many-sided meanings of the sūtras only after an extensive reading of many of them. Still others lacking in intellectual powers of their own could understand the meanings of the Sūtras only through the assistance of elaborate commentaries. But there are some who lacking in intellectual powers of there own, shun the perusal of elaborate commentaries and take delight in studying and cultivating enquiries which preseut the many-sidedness and universality of the doctrine in a concise form.

"For the sake of the people of the last class I write the discourse in which the most excellent, the deepest, and the most inexhaustible

---

1 Takakusu, Paramārtha's Life of Vasubandhu and the, Date of Vasubandhu, *JRAS*, 1905, pp. 33.

doctrine of the Tathāgata will be treated in comprehensive brevity."[1]

Opinions differ as to the authorship of the work. Suzuki holds that Aśvaghoṣa, the poet of the *Buddhacarita* to be its author and asserts on the basis of the book itself that the actual founder of the Mahāyāna was Aśvaghoṣa. About this work Lèvi says that the poet of the Buddha-epic shows himself here as a profound metaphysician, as an intrepid reviver of a doctrine which was destined to regenerate Buddhism. But Prof. Takakusu dismisses the authorship of Aśvaghoṣa as altogether untenable, and lays stress on the fact that the older catalogues of the Chinese Tripiṭaka do not contain the name of Aśvaghoṣa as the author of the *Śraddhotpāda śāstra* nor it is ever found to be quoted in any work. Dr. Murakami, another distinguished Japanese scholar holds that the *Awakening of Faith* was not only not a composition of Aśvaghoṣa, but a Chinese product ; the writer he suspects, presumably tried to systematise the two Mahāyāna schools of Nāgārjuna and Asaṅga into one.[2]

Its alleged authorship of Aśvaghoṣa

The first translation of this important treatise, which profoundly influenced the course of historical development of Buddhism in the Far-East, was made by Paramārtha in A. D. 553. In A. D. 710 Śikṣānananda of Khotan translated it again. The originals of these translations were not the same, the one having been brought from Ujjaini and the other from Khotan ; and the difference is not fundamental. According to an unknown Chinese author quoted by Suzuki, the Sanskrit original brought by Śikṣānanda from Khotan was older of the two (p. 40). But of these two translations, Paramārtha's has found a more popular acceptance in China as well as in Japan, not because it is more faithful to the original, but because a learned and brilliant Buddhist scholar of China named Fa-tsang (A. D. 643-712) wrote an illuminating commentary, *Ta-sheng-chi-hsin-lun-shu* (Nanjio, 1625) which has come to be more studied than the text itself.

1 Suzuki, *The Awakening of faith*, Chicago, pp. 51-52.
2 *The Eastern Buddhist*, 1926, Vol. IV, 7.

In this great work the author expounds three most important points, viz. (1) the conception of Bhuta-tathatā, (2) the theory of the triple personality Trikāya) ; (3) the salvation by faith or the Sukhāvati doctrine.

The Sūtra lays the foundation of Vijñānavāda.

The conception of *Bhutatathatā* assumes other names such as Nirvāṇa, Bodhi, Bodhicitta, Tathāgatagarbha etc. Prof. Yamakami has clearly explained the different terms in his study (ibid, pp··· ··) "Whatever the origin of the idea of *Bhuta-tathatā* might have 'been, its absolute aspect' evidently foreshadows the *Śūnyatā* philosophy of the Madhyamaka School," as well as the *Ālaya-Vijñāna* theory, which was so highly developed by the Yogācara philosophers. So practically Aśvaghoṣa might be called precursors of both Madhyamaka and Yogācara.

"The second proposition, *viz.* the theory of triple personality, is one of the most distinctive characteristics of the Mahāyāna Buddhism promulgated by Aśvaghoṣa. The pantheistic idea of *suchness*, and the religious consciousness which always tends to demand something embodied in infinite love (Karuṇa) and infinite wisdom (Jñāna), and the scientific conception of the law of causation regulating our ethical as well as physical world, or in short the doctrine of *Karma.*—these three factors working together is the theory of triple personality."

'The doctrine of salvation by faith also appears first in the present Śāstra."[1]

The importance of this work ascribed to Aśvaghoṣa cannot be too highly emphasised. But we are grateful to Paramārtha for his having translated it and preserved it in the Chinese and thankful to Prof. Suzuki for having given an English translation of the Chinese version.[2]

1 (*Awakening*, see below, 43-44)

2 Aśvaghoṣa's Discourse on the *Awakening of Faith* in the Mahāyāna. Translated from the Chinese version by Teitaro Suzuki, Chicago, 1900).

Asaṅga and Vasubandhu founders of Vijñānavāda philosophy introduced by Paramārtha

Paramārtha introduced in China the theory of Vijñānavāda and Bhuta-tathatā conception, as propounded in the Sraddhotpāda. The real systematizers of the Mahāyāna-Vijñānavāda,—the brothers Asaṅga-Vasubandhu, were introduced in China by Paramārtha for the first time.

Paramārtha's *Life of Vasubandhu* therefore was an important contribution to the history of Buddhism. It does not seem to be a translation, but an independent work.[1] In this work Paramārtha gives incidentaly the history of Asaṅga, Vasubandhu's elder brother the first propounder of the Yogācara school of Buddhism.

Life of Asaṅga, Vasubandhu and Paramārtha

Asaṅga was born in the Kauśika family in Puruṣapura (Peshawar) in the N. W. India. He was the eldest of three brothers, of whom the youngest Viriñcivatsa was ultimately connected with him in religious and literary activities. Viriñci is not important in literature. Asaṅga was originally ordained as a monk in the Mahīśāsaka school, a branch of the most ancient form of Buddhism but he was afterwards converted to Mahāyāna and became renowned as an author of many learned works of Mahāyāna. It is said that Asaṅga received his philosophy of Yoga (Yogācāra) from Maitreya, the fifth Buddha, from the Tuṣita heaven. Maitreya is even made the author of several books, which are really Asaṅga's own writings; but to invest them with supernatural sanctity, they are ascribed to Maitreya, and fictitious stories are told about their origin. It was Hiuens Tsang who really propagated the Yogācāra philosophy in China, and Asaṇga's works will be described in connection with him. But it was Paramārtha to whom the credit of the first introduction of Asaṅga and Vasubandhu's works in China belongs.

"Vasubandhu, a contemporary of Vikramāditya (Skandagupta, A. D. 455-480, and his son Balāditya) took orders in the Sarvāsti-

1 (*T'oung Pao* p. p. 269-297, Takakasu *JRAS.* 1905, p. 30).

vāda School. having studied under Buddhamitra,[1] the whole of the Tripiṭaka of the school to which he belonged. Afterwards he studied the doctrines of the Sautrāntika (the school which accepted the Sūtra as its sole authority)[2] thinking them more reasonable, in many points, than those of his own school, and he determined to formulate an ecclectic system out of the two lines of doctrine along which his mental activity had been directed. In order to do so, it was indispensable for him first to acquire a thorough knowledge of Sautrāntika doctrines. With this object he went to Kashmir, the headquarters of the study of the doctrine, carefully disguising himself and assuming a false name, lest the scholars of that country should be jealous and refuse to instruct him. There, for many years, under the guidance of Saṅghabhadra, he studied the doctrine, against which he would frequently dispute, basing his objection on the teachings of the Sautrāntika itself. Skandila, the teacher of Saṅghabhadra, had his suspicions aroused by the extraordinary ability of the unknown student, and at last ascertained that he was none other than Vasubandhu, whereupon he advised him secretly to go to his own land, lest some factious people should kill him. Vasubandhu therefore returned to his home, where he composed a work of 600 kārikas called the *Abhidharma-Koṣa* (Nanjio 1270), a compendium of *Abhidharma-Mahābibhāṣā*, and sent it to Kashmir. The king of Kashmir, and the scholars were at first

1 Hiuen-Tsang says that he studied under Manoratha, There is no need of identifying these two persons. He could have studied under Buddhabhadra as well as Manoratha.

2 The Sautrāntikas were a branch of the Sarvāstivādins ; the other branch was the Vaibhāsikas. The Vaibhāsikas "accepted the Abhidharma books of the Sarvāstivādins (the seven Abhidharmas) as 'revealed' scripture and the commentary on them, *Vibhāsā*, as the oldest and the most authentic authoritative 'treatise' (śastra) ; on the other hand, the Sautrāntikas, who considered the seven books simply as 'treatise (Sāstra) of human inspiration and therefore liable to error, who maintained that Buddha had not composed treatises (Śāstra) dealing with Abhidharma or given indications for the composition of such treatises under his authority, but had taught Abhidharma doctrines in certain *Sūtras* and *Sūtrāntas*. According to them these *Sūtras*, the *Arthaviniścaya* etc., constitute 'the Basket of Abhidhamma,' Hence their name Sautrāntikas, the philosophers who recognize the authority of the Sutrāntas alone." (Poussin, *ERE* vol II. page 215),

delighted with it, imagining that he was expounding and propagating their doctrine, but, on the advice of Skandila, who knew that the compendium was not favourable to their sect, the author was asked to write an explanation. So he expounded the Verses in a prose commentary, with the addition of seven verses and one chapter on non-ego. These verses together with the commentary are called *Abhidharma-Koṣa-Śāstra* (Nanjio 1267, 1269). Vasubandhu afterwards travelled to Ayodhyā and was converted by his brother Asaṅga to the faith of the Mahāyāna, and composed many treatises in defence of his new creed, with commentaries on various Mahāyāna works. He died there (in Nepal according to Tibetan tradition) at eighty years of age.[1]

Vasubandhu's works in Chinese Translation

Vasubandhu, according to Nanjio,[2] is the author of 28 works of which 19 are Mahāyānistic.[3] According to Paramārtha Vasubandhu wrote commentaries on the following Mahāyāna sūtras.[4]

1. The *Avataṁsaka*—(There is no mention of it in Nanjio).

2. *Nirvāṇa-sūtra Purva-bhutotpanna-bhūtagāthā śāstra* (Nanjio 1207 ; also 1206 : translation by Dharmabodhi). This is a commentary on the *Mahā-pariṇirvāṇa Sūtra* (Nanjio 113, 114, 120).

3. *Śaddharma-puṇḍarīka Ṭīka* (Nanjio 1232) translated by Bodhiruci.

4. *Prajñā-pāramitā Vajracchedikā sūtra-śāstra* (Nanjio, 1231) ; Com. on Vajracchedikā sūtra-śāstra of Asaṅga, translated by Yi-tsing.

5. *Vimalakīrti* (Not found in Nanjio).

6. *Śrimāla-siṁhanāda* (Not found in Nanjio).

---

1 (U. Wogihara Vasubandhu *ERE* Vol. 12, p. 595-596. Takakusu, in his translation of Paramārtha's Life, names Ba-sha-su-ba-da-la as the man who went to Kipin or Kashmir to study Sarvāstivāda etc. He is not Vasubandhu, but Vasu-bhadra. But Wogihara's interpretation and construction of life-story seems sound).

2 (Nanjio App. 1, 6).

3 (*JRAS*, 1905, p. 42)

4 (*T'oung Pao*, 1904, p 296).

Paramārtha himself is responsible for the translation of eight works of Vasubandhu. These are :

1. *Abhidharma Koṣa śāstra* (Nanjio 1269).
2. *Mahāyāna Samparigraha Śāstra Vyākhyā* (Nanjio 1171)
3. 'Śāstra on the Gāthā on the state of being formerly existing and now extinct etc.' in the Nirvāṇa Sūtra (Nanjio 1207).
4. 'Śāstra on the Sūtra of (Buddha's last teaching)' (Nanjio 1209).
5. *Buddha-gotra-sūtra* (Nanjio 1220).
6. Vijñapti-mātra-Siddhi (Nanjio 1239).
7. *Madhyānta-Vibhāga-śāstra* (Nanjio 1248).
8. 'Tarka Śāstra' (Nanjio 1252).

Two more works are mentioned by Paramārtha. 'The Nature of the Ratnatraya' is unknown in the original as well as in the Chinese. The *Dharmacakra pravartana Sūtropadeśā* (Nanjio 1205) was translated by Vimokṣaprajña.

Vasubandhu's greatest work is his *Abhidharma-Koṣa Śāstra.* The book was once more translated by Hiuen Tsang and it will be fully described there. His *Vijñaptimātra Siddhi*, was twice after him translated into Chinese. *viz.*, by Bodhiruci (A. D. 508-535) and Hiuen tsang (A. D. 661). Asaṅga's *Mahāyāna Samparigraha Śāstra*, a famous book on Yogācāra was commented upon by Vasubandhu, which was translated by Paramārtha along with the text of Asaṅga's. The text with the commentaries of Wu-Sing (Agotra ?) and Vasubandhu were once more translated by Hiuen tsang (Nanjio, 171, also 1183). Vasubandhu's *Madhyānta-vibhāga-śāstra* (Nanjio, 1248) although translated by Paramārtha was once again renderod into Chinese by Hiuen tsang (Nanjio, 1244). Praramārtha does not mention this book among the works of Vasubandhu (see above), nor does he mention the 'Tarka-Śāstra' among them.

The *Tarka-Śāstra* of Vasubandhu exists only in Chinese and not even in Tibetan, where most of the Hindu Logic by Buddhist professors is preserved. This important treatise on Logic has been recently done into Sanskrit, the language from which it was translated by Prof. G. Tucci.[1]

The important works of Vasubandhu translated by Paramārtha, and retranslated by Hiuen tsang, will be described along with the latter, who was responsible for the introduction of Yogācāra in China as well as in Japan.

The works of other Mahāyāna Ācaryas were introduced in China by Paramārtha, such as Vasuvarman (Nanjio, App. 1, 44), Guṇamati (Nanjio, App. 1, 45) and Vasumitra (Nanjio, App. 1, 33).

Guṇamati Sāṁkhya teaching

We know nothing of Vasuvarman ; Guṇamati is mentioned by Hiuen tsang in his *Records.* He is said to have vanquished in discussion the great Sāṁkhya Teacher Mādhava in Magadha. Paramārtha's translation of Guṇamati's work seems to be an extract from a larger treatise with the same title. Nanjio restored the original title as '*Lakṣaṇānusāra śāstra*' (Nanjio, 1280), but the original title may have been different. This treatise cites Vibhāsā, and Sūtra-Upadeśa-śāstras, Vasubandhu, Bavarika (?) and others, and it shows an intimate acquaintance with the Sāṃkhya teachings.[2]

But Paramārtha gave the Chinese Buddhists a far better and comprehensive idea of the Sāṃkhya system than that found in Guṇamati's work above. He translated the Kārikās (Verses) and a bhāṣya of the Sāṁkhya system. The text is called *Suvarṇa Saptati-Śāstra* and contains 70 verses with a bhāṣya (Nanjio, 1300). It is stated in a note at the beginning of the translation that this work was compiled by the heretical Ṛṣi Kapila, explaining 25 tattvas or truths, and it is not the word of Buddha's. Towards the end of the work, we read that there were 60,000 verses composed by Pañcaśikha (Kāpilya), whose teacher Āsuri was the disciple of the Ṛṣi Kapila, and that afterwards a Brāhmaṇa, Iśvarakṛṣṇa selected 70 verses

The Sāṁkhya system in Chinese

1 G. Tucci. *Tarka-Śāstra*, Gaekward Oriental series, Baroda, 1926 : for the analysis of the work see Vidyabhusan's *Indian Logic* pp. 268-269, Cal. University, 1921.

2 Watters—*On Yuan Chwang*, ii. p. 108-109.

out of sixty thousand Verses (Nanjio 1300). The Chinese version contains the *Kārikās* and the bhāṣya thereto in three fasc. The Kārikās are the famous compendium of Iśvarakṛṣṇa's *Sāṅkhya-saptati*. The *Sāṅkhya-saptati*, as we find in Sanskrit, represents a collection of 72 Kārikās (verses) and is supposed to contain the essential doctrines of Sāṅkhya.

Takakusu endeavours to identify Iśvarakṛṣṇa with Vindhyavāsa, a mighty Sāṅkhya teacher and assigns him to the middle of the 5th century A. D. (*JRAS* 1925, pp. 47-52). Dr. Gopinath Kaviraj places Iśvarakṛṣṇa in a pre-Christian era.[1]

The Bhāṣya translated along with the text by Paramārtha exhibited many points of contact with the bhāṣya of Gauḍapāda. Takakusu, after a searching comparison of the bhāṣya of Gauḍapāda with the vṛtti[2] translated into Chinese, arrives at the conclusion that in citations, illustrations and even entire passages, the coincidences between the commentaries are as numerous and far-reaching as to preclude the possibility of their being explained away as accidental." Takakusu identified the author of the Kārikās with the author of the Vṛtti, and believes that by thus making Iśvarakṣṛṇa himself the author of both the Kārikās, as well as the Vṛtti, he could hardly take the edge off Gauḍapāda's oubsequent appropriation of author's work as his own.[3]

There is a tradition preserved in Chinese that Vasubandhu had a discussion with the author of Sāṁkhya ṣāstra in which he was defeated. The Sāṁkhya teacher composed the *Suvarṇa Saptati* and the king gave him a thousand golden pieces in order to commend on it.[4] This tradition, as told by Kwei-Chi, the disciple of

Suvarṇa saptati and Paramārtha saptati

1 *Jayamaṅgalā*, Introduction, p. 6, Cal. Oriental Series, No. 19.

2 Le Sāṁkhya Kārikā, *BEFEO*, 1904, pp. 1-65.

3 Prof. S. K. Belvalker, however is of opinion that Sanskrit *Māṭhara Vṛtti* is the lost original of the Sāṅkhya Vṛtti, *Bhandarkar Commemoration Volume*, pp. 171-174).

4 See life of Vasubandhu—*T'oung-Pao*, 1904, p. 285ff. Vasubandhu's teacher Buddhamitra was defeated and Vasubandhu wrote the Saptati.

Hiuen tsang, we cannot accept as historical. He only records "a traditional story concerning the controversy between the Buddhists and the Sāṁkhya philosophers, in which Vasubandhu played directly or indirectly a prominent part." Vasubandhu did take part in the discussion as all the Buddhist Ācāryas had to, to refute the Sāṁkhya and Vaiśeṣika teachers, who were the most formidable opponents of the Buddhists. It was Vindhyavāsa, a Sāṁkhya teacher, with whom Vasubandhu might have had the discussion ; this Vindhyavāsa is wrongly identified with Iśvarkṛṣṇa by Takakusu.

Vasubandhu wrote a discourse, called *Paramārtha Saptati* or seventy verses of supreme verity, to combat the work entitled *Suvarṇa Saptati*. The book is not preserved either in the original or in the Chinese translation. But the book existed in the time of Hiuen tsang and Kwei-Chi ; the latter quotes from it. Paramārtha mentions the work in his *Life* and says that after his Guru's defeat in a combat with the Sāṁkhya teacher Vindhya-vāsa "he composed a Śāstra entitled the *Paramārtha Saptati*, in which he refuted the Sāṁkhya śāstra, composed by that heretic, whose doctrine fell to pieces like the broken tiles, from the beginning to end, leaving no sentence which could hold together."[1]

It is a great pity that we have no means to know what Vasubandhu wrote to refute his powerful opponent, the Sāṁkhyas. To Paramārtha we owe the preservation of many Sanskrit works which are now completely lost to India. As a preacher of Hindu ideas in China, as a translator of Vasubandhu's philosophy in that country and as a successful interpreter of several important works of Vasubandhu and Asaṅga his services are invaluable.

Contemporaneous with Paramārtha, was the Hindu monk Upaśunya,[2] who worked under the Liang and Chen dynasties in Nanking and Eastern Wei (A. D. 534-550) in their capital at Yeh.

1 *T'oung Pao*, 1904, p. 286.

2 Chin. Yueh-p'o-sheu-na : in trans, Kao-K'ung, "high-emptiness.' Nanjio, App. II, 103, 106. 117.

Upaśunya was a son of a king of Ujjaini, who entered China by the N.-W. passage and at first lived and worked at Yeh. In 538-540 he translated three works, of which two remain. In A. D. 540 he moved southwards to the capital of the Liang dynasty at Nanking, where he translated one work. He continued his labour at Nanking during the Chen dynasty, and in A. D. 565 he translated one Sūtra called *Suvikrānta-vikramiparchhā* (Nanjio, 9), the Sanskrit text of which he obtained from a Śramaṇa of Khotan. He translated *Vimala-Kīrti-Nirdeśa* (Nanjio, 144), which should not be confounded with the work of the same name translated by Chi-Chien (Nanjio, 147), Kumārajīva (Nanjio, 146) and Hiuen tsang (Nanjio, 149), but this is the same work translated by Chu Fa-Hu (Nanjio, 145) and by Jinagupta in A. D. 591 (Nanjio, 181). Literally the title of the work is *Mahāyāna or 'Mahāvaipulya Mūrdhvarāja Sūtra'*; it is also called 'Sucintita Kumāra Sūtra.'

Contemporaries of Paramārtha

Subhuti[1] a monk of Funan came to Nanking by the sea route, translated a work which is lost.

1 (Nanjio. App. ii, 107 ; *Chin* Su-p'u-t'i ; in trans, Shan-hsien, good-appearance or 'shan-ci', 'Good-lucky' or Shan-yeh, 'Good action')

XII Hindu Culture Under the Northern Tartar

The political atmosphere of Northern China was different from what we have seen in the south. On the ruins of the Former Ts'in, sprang up many independent principalities. Fu-K'ien (357-385), who had subdued the whole of the north and extended his empire over some sixty-two states in Turkestan in the west and Corea in the East, was defeated by the king of the Eastern Chin in A. D. 384, which crushed his power and which re-affirmed the boundary between the North and the South China. Fu-K'ien was murdered in A. D. 385 and the whole empire was split up into eight separate kingdoms, some of which have already been described. One of them that rose on the fall of the Former Ts'in was the Toba Tartars ; their leader She kuei distinguished himself as a great warrior founding a new dynasty known in history as the Wei, subsequently known as Yuan (A. D. 386-532), and styled himself as Tai Wuti (A. D. 380-409).[1]

Political history of the North

The attitude of the Wei emperors towards Buddhism was altogether favourable, only occasionally patronage was replaced by persecution by some sovereign. The third emperor of the Wei, Toba Tao, canonized as Tai Wu Ti (A. D. 324-452) was one of the greatest kings of the dynasty. His reign constituted the most glorious period in the military annals of the Wei empire. Tribute poured into his court at Ping-cheng, which was then the capital of the Empire, from such distant states as Corea and Turkestan. Toba Tao was a confirmed Taoist, so was Ts'ui-hao, the minister of Education a very influential statesman[2] of the time. They conducted an anti-Buddhist campaign. Discovery of arms in a monastery of Chang-gan, added to the fury of the hostile statesman. The monks were accused of treason and debauchery and Toba Tao

Anti-Buddhist action of Toba Tao, 424-452

---

1 Parker, A Thousand years of the Tartar, p. 103,

2 (Giles, *Chinese Biographical Dictionary*, No. 1 2035)

instigated by Ts'ui-hao issued an edict ordering the destruction of Buddhist temples and sacred books, as well as the execution of all Buddhist priests. "The Crown Prince, who was a Buddhist, was able to save many lives, but no monastery or temple was left standing. The persecution, however, was of short duration. Toba Tao was assasinated in A. D. 452 and the first act of his successor Toba Chun (452-466) was to re-establish Buddhism and allow his subjects to become monks.[1]

Buddhist images in grottoes of Yuan-kang

It was at this period that Shih T'an-yao, a Chinese monk, who had great influence with the Wei Emperor (A. D. 460-465) proposed to him to make five excavations in the rocky wall of a mountain known as grottoes of Yuan-kang in the Northern Shansi. These images of Buddha were sculptured, the highest one was seventy feet high. It was in the Wei dynasty that the great Buddhist Art movement began. The grottoes in after years became famous and has drawn the attraction of the admiring world.[2]

Attitude of Wei emperors towards Buddhism

In 471 Toba Hung, who is known also as Hsien Wen ti (A. D. 466-471) had a gigantic image of Buddha, forty-three feet high constructed, which required a hundred piculs of brass and six piculs of gold. He was a pious Buddhist and abdicated his throne in A. D. 471 in order to devote himself to Buddhist studies. His successor Hsiao Wen-ti (471-499) was an ardent Confucianist and Pro-Chinese. He removed the capital from Ping-Cheng to Loyang, the centre of Chinese civilization for centuries. He changed the family name of Toba to Yuan and tried to introduce the Chinese language and dress among the Tartars. He encouraged inter-marriage and aimed at a thorough Chinisation of the Tartars. But the tide of Buddhism was too strong to be held in check. The next Emperor Hsuan Wu-ti (500-516) was a patron of Buddhism and it is said

1. Eliot, *op. cit.* p. 252.

2 Chavannes, *Mission Archæologique* 1. Partie II, p. 296 : Quoted from Bagchi, p. 242.

that during his time there were 13,000 temples in Wei kingdom. Another account says that in the reign of Hsiao Ming Ti (A. D. 546-527), there were 415 sets of Buddhist works, 30,900 temples, and more than 200,000 monks and nuns. This is doubtless an exaggeration. In the *Mirror of History* (Tung-Kien), it is told that, "Every household almost had been converted, and the member of those who had taken the vows so great that the labours of the field were frequently neglected for lack of workmen."[2]

Buddhist Population in North China

The influence of the Hindus must have been immense, as the number of Hindus residing in China at that time was more than three thousand.

At this period, the Dowager Empress Hu was the head of the Wei. She was a fervent devotee, though of very indifferent character in both public and private life; since it is said, she had no scruple in poisoning her own son to achieve her ends. Like many other women-character in history, Empress Wu is a psychological problem.

Empress Hu.

In 518 Empress Hu sent Sung-Yun and Hui-sheng[3] to Udyāna and Gāndhāra in search of Buddhist books. They procured altogether 170 volumes, all standard works, belonging to the Mahāyāna, the supply of these new manuscripts was largely utilized by the Wei translators.

Mission to India for Buddhist Books

A few weak emperors ruled rapidly in succession and in A. D. 535 N. Wei became divided into two parts, the Western and

1 See Eliot, op. cit. pp. 252ff ; Li ung. Bing op. cit. p. 113.

2 Watters quoted by Edkins. *Chinese Buddhism*, p. 111).

3 Edkins refers to an early German translation by Neumann *Chinese Buddhism*, p. 100, Beal translated it in *Buddhist Records*, Vol, I. Introduction lxxxiv-cviii ; 'The Mission of Sung-yun and Hwei-sang to obtain books in the West' (Translated from the 5th section of the History of the Temples of Loyang) Chavannes "Voyage de Song-yun dans l'Udyāna et le Gāndhāra, (518-522) *BEFEO*, 1903 pp. 379-441. The last translation is the best and most critically done

Eastern. The former existed for 17 years and latter 10, when they were succeeded respectively by North Chou and North Chi'i.

Successive political changes

North Ch'i had five rulers, whose reigns aggregated 28 years ; and it was added to N. Chou, though it had previously lost a portion of its territory to the Southern Empire, which at this time, was called Ch'en. N. China was taken in 581 by its powerful minister Yang Khien, who seven years later conquered Ch'en. Now it was that China was restored to the Chinese, and came again under the rule of one man. [1]

During 150 years, seven monks translated 69 works only

During a century and half of the Wei rule in North China only seven monks[2] (1) translated 69 works from Sanskrit of which 42 exist at the present day.

Dharmaruci & Ratnamati

Of these seven translators, four were Indians. Dharmaruci[3] was a śramaṇa of Southern India. who translated three works in 8 fasci. between 501 and 507 A. D. ; but one of them was already lost before A. D. 730. Ratnamati[4] was a śramaṇa of Central India, who came to China in A. D. 508 in the reign of Siuan-Wu-ti and worked in collaboration with Bodhiruci and Buddhaśānta ; he is said to have translated six works of which only two remain. One is the translation of Bodhisattva Vasubandhu's commentary on the great Mahāyāna work *Saddharma Puṇḍarīka,* which was also done into Chinese by Bodhiruci in the same period (Nanjio 1232, 1233). The reason for two translations of the same work by contemporaries appearing in the same dynasty is inexplicable. Ratnamati's other translation was *Mahāyānottara tantra śāstra* (Nanjio, 1236.) The authorship is unknown ; but the book

1 Li Ung Bing, *loc. cit.* 113.

2 Nanjio mentions eight, including Shih hwei Chiao (Nanjio 11, 108), whom we put under the Liang A. D. 397-439 (see above) :—Bagchi, p. 227 ; also Takakusu JRAS, 1901, p. 447.

3 Nanjio App, III ; Bagchi, p. 246.

4 Nanjio App, II, 133 ; Bagchi, 248.

contained Kārikās in 1 fasc and a commentary in II chapters of 4 fasciculi.

Buddhaśānta
520-539

Buddhaśānta[1] was the other Hindu monk who came to China about A. D. 520 and worked till A. D. 539 ; that is, his period of work falls under the Eastern Wei dynasty (A. D. 534-550). Buddhaśānta was a monk of Northern India ; in China he worked in the Pema-ssu or the White Horse Monastery at Loyang till 534 and at Yeh till 539. He translated ten works, of which only one is worth mentioning. It is Bodhisattva Asaṅga's treatise called *Mahāyāna Samparigraha-Śāstra* (Nanjio, 1184) in 2 fasc., a work which was translated in 3 fasc, by Paramārtha in South China, about thirty years after (See above ; also Nanjio 1183). In this work

Samparigraha śāstra

Asaṅga boldly declares that all Buddha-dharmas, of which Nirvāṇa or Dharmakāya forms the foundation, are characterised with the passions, errors, and sins of vulgar minds" and he describes the Buddha-dharma under seven heads, which "means anything or any Virtue, or any faculty, that belongs to Buddhahood. Non-attachment is a Buddha-dharma, love is a Buddha-dharma, Wisdom is a Buddha-dharma." The conclusion that is to be drawn from Asaṅga's definition of Buddha-dharma. may be thus summed up :" Not only is this world of constant transformation as a whole Nirvāṇa, but its apparent errors and sins and evils are also the various phases of the manifestation of Nirvaṇa.[2] Buddhaśānta's other translations are sūtra works of indifferent importance.

The most renowned of the Hindu translators of this period was Bodhiruci. He was a tripiṭaka-ācārya of North India, who arrived at Loyang in A. D. 508 and worked till A. D. 535. He is said to

Bodhiruci. A. D. 508-535

have translated thirty-nine Sanskrit works into Chinese in 127 fasc, of which thirty are in existence now. He left India in order to propagate the Buddhist faith ; crossed the Pamirs and the deserts of

1 Nanjio App, II, 115 ; Bagchi, pp. 250-252 ; *Chin.* Fo-t'o-shan-to ; in trans, Chiao-ting, 'intelligence-fixedness.

2 Suzuki. *Outline of Mahāyāna*, p. 354 ff.

central Asia and finally reached Loyang in A. D. 508, where the Emperor Siuen-wū was ruling. The Hindu monk was received by the monarch most cordially and put at the head of a community of seven hundred monks, who all knew Sanskrit. This statement that seven hundred monks knew Sanskrit does not seem improbable in the light of the fact stated above, that during the Wei dynasty no less than three thousand Hindus lived in N. China and that several thousand people had become monks. Bodhiruci began the work of translating Sanskrit works at the head of the community in a large monastery specially built for him by the Emperor in Loyang. In 534 when the capital was changed from Loyang to Yeh by the Eastern Wei sovereign, the Hindu monk also had to change his residence. In the two capitals he worked for 20 (or 26) years from 508 to 535-6 A. D.

Sanskrit culture in China

Bodhiruci translated the following important works from the Sanskrit :

1. *Vajracchedikā Prajñāpāramitā*, well-known work, which had appeared thrice was again translated by Bodhiruci. To it the great Yogācāra-teacher Asaṅga had written a Vṛtti in verse. These *Kārikās* of Asaṅga are now lost in their original ; but these were subsequently translated into Chinese by Dharmagupta of the Sui dynasty (A. D. 589-616). Asaṅga's brother Vasubandhu wrote a commentary on the *Kārikās* on Vajrachedikā of Asaṅga. It was Bodhiruci who in A. D. 509 rendered Vasubandhu's commentary into Chinese. (Nanjio 11, 1168).

Bodhiruci's translations

2. There is a sūtra in the Nirvāṇa group called *Viśeṣa cinta-brahma-paripṛcchā*. The earliest translation in 4 fasc. and 18 chapters was made by Chu Fa-tu (Dharmarakṣa) in A. D. 286 (Nanjio, 197) ; Kumārajīva made the second and revised translation in A. D. 402 (Nanjio, 190). Bodhiruci's is the third translation ; but it was a bigger text, which he translated in 6 fasc. (Nanjio, 189).

Viśeṣacinta brahma paripṛcchā

Bodhisattva Vasubandhu had written a learned commentary on this sūtra (Nanjio, 1193) in 2 fasc. which Bodhiruci translated into Chinese.

The *Viśeṣàcinta* is a very old Mahāyāna sūtra probably older than the works of Nāgārjuna. The work holds very bold and radical views about the conception of Nirvāṇa. The theory that 'Nirvāṇa and Saṁsāra are one', which is so boldly put forth in the *Madhyamaka Kārikās* of Nāgārjuna (Chapter 25 V. 19) is also put forward by the unknown author of the *Viśeṣacinta* most clearly and explicitly. Let us quote a passage from the said paripṛccha : (Chap. 11).

A few passages quoted

"Saṁsāra is Nirvāṇa, because there is, when viewed from the ultimate nature of the Dharmakāya, nothing going out of, nor coming into existence (Saṁsāra being only apparent). Nirvāṇa is saṁsāra, when it is coveted and adhered to." In another place the idea is expressed in much plainer terms : "The essence of things lies in their freedom from attachment, attribute and desires, that is in truth. In essence they are pure, and, as they are pure, we know that what is the :essence of birth and death that is the essence of Nirvāṇa, and that what is the essence of Nirvāṇa, that is the essence of birth and death (*Saṁsara*). In other words, Nirvāṇa is not to be sought outside of this world, which, though transient, is in reality no more than Nirvāṇa itself. Because it is contrary to our reason to imagine that there is Nirvāṇa and there is birth and death *(Saṁsāra)* and that the one lies outside the pale of the other, and, therefore, that we can attain Nirvāṇa only after we have annihilated or escaped the world of birth and death. If we are hampered by our confused subjectivity, this our wordly life is an activity of Nirvāṇa itself.[1]

Vasubandhu held the same view, which he expostulated in his '*Buddhagotra Śāstra*' (Nanjio 1220 : Translation by Paramārtha) and agreeing with the author of the *Viśeṣacinta* wrote a com-

1 Translated from the Chinese by Suzuki, see *Outlines*, p, 353.

mentary to it, which our monk rendered into Chinese in A. D. 531.

As *Viśeṣacinta* formed a part of the Nirvāṇa group, so *Daśabhūmika sūtra* formed a part of the large collection of sūtras known as the *Buddha-avataṁsaka mahā-vaipulya sūtra* or simply as Avataṁsaka. The earliest translation of the Daśabhūmika text was made by Chu Fa-hu (Dharmarakṣa[1]) in the third century A. D. Kumārajīva also made a fresh translation of the text in the first decade of the fifth century A. D.,[2] which remained the standard work on *Daśabhūmika.* The great Vasubandhu, after he had become a Mahāyānist, wrote a large commentary on the text of the Avataṁsaka, which explained the ten stages (bhūmi) of the Bodhisattva's spiritual life. Bodhiruci translated this commentary of Vasubandhu in 12 fasc. (Nanjio, 1194). He also translated Vasubandhu's commentary on Gayāśirṣa, a very important Mahāyana sūtra, which had been first introduced in China by Kumārajīva (Nanjio, 238). Vasubandhu's commentary was however unknown in the time of Kumārajīva. Now the commentary along with the original was rendered into Chinese by Bodhiruci (Nanjio, 1121). In Chinese Kumārajīva's version is known as 'the sūtra of Mañjuśrī on the Bodhi.' Vasubandhu's Tīkā is literally known as '*Mañjuśrībodhisattva paripṛchhābodhisūtraśāstra.*' Bodhiruci's translation is called Kia-yen-shang-ting-ching or 'Gayāparvata śirṣasūtra.' Vinitaruci, a translator of the Sui dynasty in A. D. 582 rendered it as *Gajā-śirṣa* or head of the Elephant—a clear misreading of the Sanskrit text (Nanjio, 240). Bodhiruci

Daśabhūmika Sūtra

Gayā-śirṣa, various version

---

1 See above Western Tsin Dynasty, A. D. 265-316.

2 This Chinese version was incorporated by Buddhabhadra (Nanjio, App. II 42) in his edition of the *Buddha avataṁsaka sūtra* which he published in 60 fasc. and 34 chapters (Nanjio, 87), (Eastern Tsin dynasty A. D. 317-420). Buddhabhadra was a contemporary and friend of Kumārajīva. See also Sikṣānanda's translation of *Avataṁsaka* in 80 fasc. and 39 chapters, done into Chinese between 695-699 (See below).

the second, of the T'ang dynasty in A. D. 693 rendered it as '*Mahāyāna Gayāparvataśirṣa sutra* (Nanjio, 241). There are altogether four translations of the text and one translation of the commentary of Vasubandhu in Chinese, the translator of the latter is our monk Bodhiruci. It is said that Buddha after having stayed at Uruvilva and having converted a thousand converts went to Gayā, and stopped at the Caitya of Gayāśirṣa, and there he showed them many a miracle. He also preached to them the sermon on the Fire or burning.[1] After that he preached on form (Rūpa) and its transitory nature, on Upādāna, Sañjñā, Saṁsāra etc., on the Nidānas etc., so that the king Bimbisāra and a great multitude of brahmanas and householders were converted.[2]

Complete translation of the Laṅkāvatāra.

It was Bodhiruci who made a complete Chinese translation of the *Laṅkāvatāra sūtra* (Nanjio, 176) which agrees more or less with the extant Sanskrit version. It was in 10 fasc. while the incomplete translation of Guṇabhadra of A. D. 443 was in 4 fasc. only (see above). Vasubandhu, the great Yogācāra teacher wrote a treatise basing on the *Laṅkāvatāra* called the *Vijñaptimātra siddhi* (Nanjio, 1238) which has also been mentioned under Paramārtha, who made the first translation of the treatise.

A work on four heretical schools

The *Laṅkāvatāra sūtra* mentions four heretical contemporary schools, which were antagonistic to the ideal of the Buddha. These schools are, (1) the Sāṁkhyas, who believe in oneness, (2) the Vaiśeṣikas, who believe in difference, (3) the Nigranthaputras who put their faith in both ; and (4) the Jñātiputras who believe in neither. Āryadeva, the great disciple of Nāgārjuna, wrote a treatise refuting these four heretical schools ; this Sanskrit work was rendered into Chinese by Bodhiruci (Nanjio, 1268). Bodhiruci also translated another work of Āryadeva on an allied subject. In

---

1 See *Āditya-pariyāyasūtra* ; Warren, *Buddhism in Translation* p. 351.

2 Rockhill, *Life of the Buddha* from the Tibetan Sources. p, 43.

this work Āryadeva explained the idea of salvation according to the twenty heretical schools,* also mentioned in the *Laṅkāvatāra*.

Another work on twenty heretical schools translated by Bodhiruci.

Both these works of Āryadeva are important for the clear understanding of the intellectual history of the Hindus in those days. The original Sanskrit having been lost, the only source of our information is the Chinese translation of Bodhiruci.

The Saddharmapuṇḍarīka is a well-known Mahāyāna work described above. This work is held in great honour and is considered as a canonical work by the Mahāyānists. According to the Tien-tai school, the *Saddharmapuṇḍarīka* expresses the highest and the most developed doctrines of the Tathāgata preached during the last eight years of his life.

---

* The following is the list of the twenty heretical schools :

1. The Teacher of the Śāstra of the Hīnayāna heresey.
2. That of the space (Diś).
3. That of the wind (Vāyu),
4. That of the Vedas (Vaidika).
5. That of Iśāna.
6. That of the naked Heretics, (Kṣapaṇaka)
7. That of the Vaiśeṣikas.
8. That of the Painful practice.
9. That of the women regarded as the members of a family (?)
10. That of the practising the painful practice.
11. That of the pure eyes.
12. That of the Mo-to-la (Māṭhara?)

For a separate mention of Māṭhara, along with Sāṁkhya, c. f. its mention in the Jaina texts ; *Indische Studien* xvii, 9.

13. That of the Nirgranthaputras.
14. That of the Sāṁkhyas.
15. That of the Māheśvaras.
16. That of the absence of cause (ahetuvāda).
17. That of time (Kālavāda).
18. That of drinking water,
19. That of the power of the mouth.
20. That of the Aṇḍajātaka or the original birth from egg.

(Nanjio 1269) ; G. Tucci, Un Traite d' Āryadeva a sur le "Nirvāṇa" des heretiques, *T'oung Pao*, 1927 ; also c. f. *Dialogues of the Buddha*, Vol. I, Brahmajāla sutta : Translation by W. Rhys Davids 1899, pp. 1-56.

We have seen that several Chinese translations had appeared in China of which the best one was that of Kumārajīva's.

Bodhisattva Vasubandhu the great Yogācāra teacher, could hardly neglect such an important treatise and wrote a learned commentary on it (Nanjio, 1232). The Sanskrit original is unfortunately lost, but Bodhiruci made a translation of this important treatise which is preserved in the Tripiṭaka collection.

Vasubandhu's commentary on Saddharma-puṇḍarika

Bodhiruci's other translation is the Dharmasaṅgīti (Nanjio, 426). The original text is lost, but several passages have been preserved in Sāntideva's *Śikṣāsamuccaya*, and the high ideals quoted there, should be perused most carefully. The quotations deal with the following topics : a selfless action for otbers, on meditation and mindfulness, on mind, on care in speech, on disinterested giving, on intent contemplation, on Śunya, on good resolution, on mindfulness of the Dharma etc.[1]

Dharmasaṅgīti quoted in Sikṣāsamuccaya

Bodhiruci's translation of the above treatises largely added to the literary treasures of the Chinese Buddhists and although a few of these works were done over again into Chinese by abler men like Hiuen-tsang, some of the works translated by our monk are still indispensible for the study of Indian thought both in India and abroad.

Of the other translators of Sanskrit works into Chinese, Ki-kia-ye deserves special treatment. His name seems to be Kekaya or Kikaya, a prākṛta form of Kiṁ-kārya ; some hold that he was a man of Central Asia, while other Chinese authorities claim him as a Hindu of Western India. Ki-kia-ye translated five works, some of which are very important for our purpose of the history of culture. His *Tsa-pao-tsang ching* was translated by the order of the Emperor in A. D. 472. The original of it would read '*Saṁyukta ratna-piṭaka sūtra* (Nanjio, 1329) which contained 121 tales, a few only long, but mostly short. The first story is a short version of the Rāmā-

Ki-ki-ye a Ser-indian monk,

1 Bendall and Rouse, *op. cit*, pp. 288-290.

yaṇa, which is known in Pali as *Daśaratha Jātaka* (Fausböll, No. 461). The stories in the Tsa-pao-tsang-ching are generally Jātaka or Avadāna tales.[1]

Of Ki-kia-ye's other translations, the *Bodhihrḍayavyūha sūtra* (Nanjio, 99) had once been translated by Kumārajīva under the name 'Mahāvaipulya Bodhisattvadaśabhūmisūtra' (Nanjio, 103). Ki-kia-ye was also responsible for the translation of a work of Nāgārjuna called *Upāyakauśalya-hṛdaya* (Nanjio, 1257). But the most important treatise which is alleged to him is a history of the Indian patriarchs (ācaryas) called *Fu-ta-tsang-yin-yuan chuan* or "A record on the nidāna or cause of transmitting the Dharmapiṭaka' (Nanjio, 1340). The Chinese work is not a translation of any particular book, but seems to be a compilation from different sources. As to the alleged early date and authenticity of the book, Henri Maspero doubts its genuineness and concludes after much discussion that the work was a forgery composed from older sources ; the book he says never existed in the original.[2]

His history of the Patriarchs

The history of the first twenty-three patriarchs of the Buddhist church from Mahākāśyapa to Bhikṣu Siṁha is narrated in this work ascribed to Ki-kia-ye. According to the Mahāyāna school a series of twenty-eigtht patriarchs[3] "superintended in succession the affairs of the religious community" Buddha had founded.

This treatise however describes the first twenty-three patriarchs, omitting Vasumitra, the seventh in succession, and the last four, who presumably lived after Ki-kia-ye. According to most schools there are only twenty-four patriarchs, including Vasumitra.

---

1 Some of the stories were first translated into French by Julien, *Les Avadānas*, I, pp. 68-70. The story of Rāmāyaṇa was translated by S. Lèvi, *Melanges Kern* 1903, pp. 278-281. The whole work is completely done by Ed. Chavannes, *Cinq cent cpntes* (Paris, 1911), Vol. 3. pp. 1-145. Avadāna CXI. For the discussion bet. King Nanda and Nāgasena, see *JRAS*, 1896, pp. 17-21.

2 Maspero, Sur la date et l'authenticité de Fou-fa-tsang-yin-yuan chouan *Melanges Sylvian Levi*, pp. 129-149 ; also Bagchi, p. 246.

3 Twenty-three patriarchs, including the five Chinese who succeeded Bodhidharma one after the other.

The last Patriarch Bhikṣu Siṁha, it is said, met his death in Kashmir at the hands of Mihirkula,* who died without appointing a successor.

It was during the rule of the N. Wei that the last Indian Patriarch Bodhidharma left India and came to settle in China in A. D. 520. Although Bodhidharma is not directly connected with any literary work, his influence in the history of Chinese religion is so tremendous that we cannot pass over him lightly.

Bodhidharma, the last Indian Patriarch in China A.D. 520.

Though not a translator of any Sanskrit text Bodhidharma has been famous in history as the founder of a Buddhist sect known as Dhyāna. *Ch'an-na* or Ch'an, in Chinese, and Zen in Japanese.

---

* Bhikṣu Siṁha was a contemporary of Mihirkula, who lived about 510-540 A.D. Ki-kia-ye's date is A.D. 472. This clear anachronism shows that the book was a forgery, and was never written by Ki-kia-ye. Eliot, *op. cit.* p. 307. also Watters, *On Yuan Chwang*, p. 290. The last three patriarchs, who are sometimes denied the proper honour due to them, were men of Southern India and it is quite likely that the data of the history of the Patriarchs which were collected in N. India, were insufficient.

List of the Patriarchs (Maspero, *loc. cit.*, pp. 139-142.)

1. Mahākāśyapa.
2. Ānanda.
3. Sanavāsa.
4. Upagupta. circa B.C. 250.
5. Dhṛtaka, [Dharmagupta ?
6. Mecaka.
7. Vasumitra (according to some),
7. Buddhanandi.
8. Buddhamitra.
9. Pārśva.
10. Purṇayaśas,
11. Aśvaghoṣa, circa 1st cent A.D.
12. Pi-lo (Vīra ?)*
* Kapimala Bhikṣu by Nanjio.
13. Nāgārjuna. 2nd cent. A.D.
14. Kāṇadeva or Āryadeva.
15. Rāhula.
16. Saṁghanandi.
17. Saṁghayakṣa.
18. Kumāralāta,
19. Cho-ye-to*
* Jayata by Nanjio.
20. Vasubandhu.
21. Mo-nu-lo.
22. Ho-le-ho.
23. She-tzu or Siṁha Bhiksu.
24. Basiasita ?
25. Pu-to-no-mi-to.
26. Prajñātara.
27. Bodhidharma. 1st Patriarch of China (520 A.D.)
28. Hui-k'e, 2nd (486-593.)
29. Se'ng-ts'an, 3rd (d. 606).
30. Tao-hsin, 4th (580-651).
31. Hung-jin 5th (605-675).
32. Hui-neng 6th (637-713).

(See Suzuki, *Zen Buddhism*, 1927).

According to the tradition of the Dhyāna school Bodhidharma was a son of a king of Southern India. But according to a very early contemporary Chinese record Bodhidharma was an inhabitant of Po-sseu which is identified with Persia. Thus his Indian origin is doubted.[1] Some hold the personality of Bodhidharma as a myth and they assert that the wall-contemplation of the Ch'an is borrowed from Taoism.[2]

Bodhidharma's conversations with Liang Wu-ti

According to the traditional history Bodhidharma arrived at Canton in A. D. 520 (526) and met the Emperor Wu in Nanking; the emperor who was an earnest Buddhist displayed his various work as a Buddhist propagandist to the Patriarch. The monk bluntly told the emperor that he had acquired no merit by causing temples to be built or Sanskrit books to be translated into the Chinese language. The king asked, "What is the most important of the holy doctrines?" Bodhidharma replied, "Where all is emptiness, nothing can be called holy." "Who", asked the astonished emperor, "is he who thus replies to me?" "I do not know," said Bodhidharma. The Patriarch could not come to any understanding with Wu-ti, and he left the Southern realm and went Northwards. He went to Loyang, where he spent nine years in the Shoa-lin temple gazing silently at a wall, whence he was popularly known as the wall-gazer. Various legends are connected with the life of Bodhidharma and his wonderful ascetic life had inspired many an artist to produce some of the masterpieces of Chinese painting.[3]

Buddhadharma's teaching

"The arrival of Bodhidharma in Canton in 520 was a great event for the history of Buddhist dogma, although his special doctrines did not become popular until much later. He introduced the Dhyāna school and also the institution of the Patriarchate which for a time had some importance. He wrote no books himself, but taught that true

1 Pelliot, *T'oung Pao*, 1923, p. 260.
2 c. f. Petrucci, Philosophie de la nature dans l'art d' Extreme-Orient. p. 39.
3 Suzuki, *Zen Buddhism*, 1927. pp. 165-178; Eliot *op. cit.* pp. 255.

knowledge is gained in meditation by intuition and communicated by transference of thought. The best account of his teachings is contained in the Chinese treatise (Ta-mohsue-mailun) which reports the sermon preached by him before the Emperor Wu-ti in 520. His chief thesis of this doctrine is that the only true reality is the Buddha-nature in the heart of every man. Prayer, asceticism and good works are vain. All the man need is to turn his gaze inward and see the Buddha in his own heart. This vision, which gives light and deliverance, comes in a moment. It is a simple, natural act like swallowing or dreaming which cannot be taught or learnt, for it is not something imparted, but an experience of the soul, and teaching can only prepare the way for it. Some are impeded by their *Karma*, and are physically incapable of the vision, whatever their merits or piety may be, but for those to whom it comes it is inevitable and convincing"[1]. Bodhidharma's fundamental principles were doubtless based on Nāgārjuna's Śūnyavāda, explained in mystical instead of philosophical language. Bodhidharma's teaching is called in Chinese Tsung-men or Chan-tsung ; *Chan* is the corrupted form of the Sanskrit word *Dhyāna*, and in Japanese known as *Zen*. Although its teacher never wrote any book, the followers of the silent monk made good the deficiency of their master and in later age both in China and Japan a large literature grew, which we shall describe in the course of our study.

The Northern Wei reigned at Loyang till A. D. 534 when the capital was changed to Yeh. The empire was short-lived during the Eastern Wei (534-550), and during the seventeen years of their rule, the Hindu culture flourished to a great extent in several of the monasteries of N. China.

Gautama Prajñāruci[2] a Hindu monk came to Loyang in A. D.

---

1 Eliot, *op. cit.* pp. 304f. For further details see *Wieger*, *op. cit.* Lesson 62 also Suzuki, *op. cit.*

2 Nanjio App. II, 116; Bagchi, 261; *Chin. Ku-t'an* '*Pan-jo-liu-chi*, in trans. Chi-hi, wisdom-wishing')

516 in the time of Emperor Hiao-ming of the Northern Wei. After the transfer of the capital to Yeh, Prajñāruci was installed in the monastery of Kin-hua (Suvarṇa-puṣpa) and afterwards in the Ting-chang monastery. Gautama Prajñāruci was a brahmana of Benares, (the centre of orthodox Hinduism) converted to the Buddhist faith. He must have had a thorough knowledge of the brahmanical scriptures which, added to his learning as a Buddhist doctor, became very powerful indeed. In the two monasteries at Yeh Prajñāruci translated twenty works of which thirteen exist in the modern Buddhist Tripiṭaka.

Gautama Prajñāruci, A. D. 516

Of his translations the largest was *Saddharma smṛtyupasthāna sūtra* (Nanjio, 679). It was a work in 70 fasciculi and consisted of seven chapters. These are, (1) the results of the ten kinds of good conduct (i. e., contrary to duṣkṛiti) ; (2) birth and death ; (3) the different hells ; (4) the condition of the protas or hungry demons ; (5) the birth as a beast, (6) the condition of devas, and (7) the Kāya-smṛti-upasthāna.

Saddharma smṛtyupasthāna quoted in *Sikṣāsamuccaya.*

This extensive Sanskrit treatise is lost ; but we can get some idea of the original text from *Śikṣā samuccaya*, where the ten bad paths of action and the after-consequence of them in hell is described in detail. The retribution for murder, the sin of theft, the crime of sexual passion, the result of false-speaking, of slander, of harshness, of covetousness, of malevolence etc., suffering in the held are described most vividly.[1] Another passage is referred to in the same work where we hear of banishment to the preta-world as the punishment for refusing to give some triffle spontaneously and to hell for refusing what one has promised.[2]

It is needless to describe all the sutras Prajñāruci translated.

1 Bendall and Rouse, *op. cit.*, pp. 74-81.
2 *Ibid.* p. 12.

But two works we cannot omit, being works of Nāgārjuna. His *Shun-chung-lun* or *Madhyāntānugama śāstra* (Nanjio, 1246) was commented upon by the great Yogācāra teacher Asaṅga, which treats of the doctrine enunciated in Mahāprajñāpāramitā sūtra. Asaṅga must have commented on Nāgārjuna's work from his own stand-point of Yogācāra.

Nāgārjuna's Madhyānta-anugama sūtra and Ekaśloka.

Nāgārjuna's other work translated by Prajñāruci was *Ekaśloka śāstra* (Nanjio, 1212). It consists of only one *Śloka*, with a commentary by Nāgārjuna himself. The one *Śloka* gives the whole philosophy of Mādhyamika in a nutshell. The śloka reads :

"My body (or substance) in its nature is not permanent. Thus, then, my body is not a body. My body in its nature not being a body, I therefore say that it is empty and not permanent !" Nāgārjuna in the commentary gives the reason of his composing a book in a śloka : "It is written on account of those, who in reading śāstras of great length grew weary, and also for those intelligent persons, who have studied many śāstras, and exercised their thoughts (deeply) in the sea of Buddha's law, but growing fatigued have begun to doubt about the doctrine, not by any means to be questioned or suspected, of the non-permanence of things and the nothingness of my own body. To destroy such doubts I have composed that śāstra."

After explaining the reason for writing the above work, Nāgārjuna explains his own doctrine and says, "That all kinds of acting are non-permanent, and my own body is nothing. The non-reality of my body is not separable from the non-permanence of all action, my nature and my body being nothing. Therefore there is no such thing as permanence." Then Nāgārjuna goes on explaining his own gāthā in detail.[1]

Another philosophical treatise attributed to Nāgārjuna called '*Vivādasamāna śāstra*' (Nanjio, 1251), was rendered into Chinese by Vimokṣasena, a contemporary and co-worker of Prajñāruci.

1 Edkins, *Chinese Buddhism*, pp. 305-317.

Vimokṣasena[1] was a śramaṇa of Udyāna of N. W. India and was a descendant of the Śākya family of Kapilavastu. He was well read in the sacred literature and specially in the Abhidharma of Mahāyāna. He came to China with Gautama Prajñāruci whom he respected as his *garu*, and translated five works in collaboration with him. Vimokṣasena translated the following works of Vasubandhu: (1) *Tripurṇa sūtropadeśa* 1 fasc. (Nanjio, 1196), (2) *Dharma-cakra pravartana sūtropodeśa* (Nanjio, 1205), (3) *Karma-siddha prakaraṇa śāstra* (Nanjio, 1222)[2] (4) *Ratnacuḍa sūtra caturdharmopadeśa*,(Nanjio, 1241). The last one is a treatise on a sūtra called Ratnacuḍa (Nanjio, 23.47), which forms a part of the Ratnakuṭa group and was first rendered into Chinese by Chu Fa-hu (Dharmarakṣa) of the W. Tsin Dynasty A. D. 265-316. The *Ratnacuḍa* on which Vasubandhu wrote his treatise was an important work and Śāntideva quotes no less than eight times in his *Śikṣāsamuccaya*[3] and is described as fully discussing the *Śūnyatā*.

Vimokṣasena of Udyuna.

Upaśūnya (Nanjio, App. II, 103, 106, 117), whom we have met already translated two works. Dharmabodhi[4] another monk of this period translated Vasubandhu's *commentary* on the *Mahā-parinirvāṇa sūtra*.[5]

1 Nanjio, App. II, 118 ; Bagchi, 267.

2 Once more translated by Hiuen-tsang (Nanjio, 1221).

3 Bendal and Rouse, *op. cit.*, pp. 115, 120, 217, on intent contemplation of the bo dy, p. 219, on contemplation of feeling, p:220, of thought, p 222, of the elements, p 249, on purity in action, p 284,

4 Nanjio, App. II, 119),

5 Nanjio, 1206 113, 114, 120 for the text.

XIII. Literary Activity in United China

The dynasty of the Eastern Wei passed away in A. D. 550, succeeded by the Northern T'si of the Kao family, which ruled at Yeh for twenty seven years (550-577 A. D.) only. The first Emperor of this dynasty Wen Hüen (A. D. 550-558) is considered one of the most important personages of this period in China. At that time controversy between the Buddhist monks and Chinese literati was raging very seriously throughout the land. In order to determine the relative importance of the two principal contending religions, he summoned the Buddhist and Taoist priests to a discussion. Both the religions could not be true, and one must be a superfluity. Such quarrels always required the intervention of the emperor whose judgment decided the issue in such cases. Here too, after having heard the arguements of both the parties, Wen Hüen-ti decided in favour of Buddhism and ordered the Taoist priests to become monks on pain of death. Four Taoists were executed for their faith.[1]

Emperor Wen Hüen favours Buddhism

During the reign of Wen Hüen-ti, came to China a Hindu monk of Udyāna named Narendrayaśas. Narendrayaśas, as a pious Buddhist made extensive tour in India and Ceylon and after coming back to his native place, thought of proceeding to China. With five companions, who were as adventurous in spirit as himself, Narendra started for China. The difficulties of the journey are vividly described in his Chinese biography. After crossing many mountains and deserts, they proceeded eastward and came among the Juei-Juei, who were at that time at war with the (Tu-kie) Turks. Narendrayaśas was therefore obliged to remain in the country of the Juei-Juei, who were completely defeated by the Turks between 552 and 555 A. D. During this period the Hindu

Narendrayaśas, 557-568

1 See Eliot, *op. cit.* III, 257.

monk travelled as far as the lake Ni which was situated 7000 li to the north of the country of the Turks, and may be identified with the lake Baikal in Siberia.

After the defeat of the Juei-Juei, Narendrayaśas took refuge at Yeh, the capital of the Northern Ts'i in the year 556 A. D. He came to live in the temple of Tien-ping at Yeh where he translated seven works. Narendra won the admiration and affection of all the people there for his learning and character. He was held in great esteem with other Buddhist monks till A. D. 577, when reaction against Buddhism began vigorously. Narendrayaśas and the Hindu monks were obliged to go to exile and Buddhism now entered upon a period of persecution.[1] Now while the Northern T'si were ruling at Yeh (A. D. 550-557), after a lapse of more than a century, the Yü-wan family founded a dynasty known as the N. Cheu (A. D. 557-581) at Chang-ngan. It was this power which destroyed the N. Ts'i of Yeh in A. D. 557. During the rule of the first Cheu emperor four Hindu monks came from India to Change-ngan, named Jñānabhadra, Jinayaśas., Yaśogupta and Jinagupta.

N. Cheu Dynasty 551-581

Jñānabhadra,[2] was a native of a country transliterated in Chinese as Po-t'eu-mo (Padma ?). He had studied the Buddhist Tripiṭaka and specially mastered the Vinaya. He translated a work called *Pañca-vidyā śāstra* (Wu-ming lun), in collaboration with the other three monks of the group.[3] The five sections of the book were : Śabdaśāstra, Bhaiṣajya śāstra, Śilpa śāstra, Mantra śāstra (?), Mudrā Śāstra. Unfortunately the book is lost.

Jñānabhadra, Yaśogupta, Jinayaśas, Jinagupta come to China

Jñānabhadra's friend and companion Upādhyāya Jinayaśas was a man of Magadha. After his arrival in China, he translated six Sanskrit works into Chinese during the reign of the emperor

1 Chavannes, Jinagupta, *T'oung Pao*, 1905, pp. 349-350, Footnote : translated from *Siu kao seng chuan* ; also P. N. Bose, *Indian Teachers in China*, Madras, pp. 93f.

2 Nanjio App II, 122 ; *Chin.* Jan-na-po-to-lo ; in trans. Chi-hsien, 'wisdom-wise'

3 *T'oung Pao*, loc, cit., p. 339

Wu of the Cheu dynasty (561-578), with the help of Yaśogupta and Jinagupta. Of his six translations only two exist : *Mahāmegha sūtra* (Nanjio, 187) and *Abhisamaya sūtra* (Nanjio, 195).

Yaśogupta's[1] native place is known as Yiu-p'o ; the place has not yet been identified. He translated three works of which only one remains (Nanjio, 327).

But it is Jinagupta the last of the group, who deserves special treatment. He is doubtless the greatest Hindu monk of his age. Jinagupta was a śramana of the kingdom of Gandhara and was an inhabitant of Puruṣapura (Peshawar). His family name is Kambhu, and he is a Kṣatriya by caste. His father's name was Vajrasāra.

The boy from his childhhod was religiously minded; he became a monk at the tender age of seven with the full sanction of his parents. He was fortunate in his teachers, of whom Jñānabhadra and Jinayaśas were attached to him to the last days of their life. Jinagupta left India for China in his 23rd year along with nine other monks. Six died on their way and it was only four monks, Jñānabhadra, Jinayaśa, Yaśogupta and himself who reached China in A. D. 557, after enduring untold hardship in Central Asia.

The first Cheu emperor Ming received the Hindu monks kindly: a new Vihāra was built for them and Jinagupta began to translate Sanskrit works with his friends and colleagues. But the peace-loving Hindu monks were not allowed to do their work quietly for long. A reaction set in against the Cheu dynasty during the rule of the third emperor Wu, who ruled between 561 and 577. In 574 the emperor Wu issued a decree placing a ban on Buddhism as well as on Taoism. Images and books were burnt and priests were ordered to go back to their secular life to do their duty as Chinese citizens, according to the Confucian philosophy of life. Jinagupta and others were compelled to leave China and take shelter in the

Reaction in 574 against Buddhism.

1 Nanjio, App., II, 124; *Chin.* Ye-sho-kue-to, in trans. Chang-tsang, 'Fame-concealed.

West, among the Turks. In 577 the Cheu emperor Wu Ti conquered Yeh and the N. Ts'i dynasty collapsed. Narendrayaśa and other Bnddhist monks were also driven away. In the storm of reaction it seemed for a time that Buddhism would be swept away from the country and all traces of Hindu culture would be wiped out.

Wu's reactionary attitude forced the Hindu monks to leave China. Jinagupta and his companions went westward and took shelter in the kingdom of the Turks (Tu-kie). The Kagan (Khan) T'o-po received the banished Hindus kindly. It may be mentioned here that a few years back T'o-po Kagan had brought one Huei-lin as prisoner from the kingdom of the Ts'i, who introduced Buddhism among the Turks. T'o-po Kagan became a pious Buddhist and regretted that he was not born in India. Jinagupta and his companies must bave been well-received by this Kagan. But all the Hindu monks except Jinagupta died in the land of the Turks.

Hindu monks took shelter among the Turks.

While Jinagupta was staying among the Turks, a band of Chinese itinarents came there on their way back to China from India. A few years back (in A. D. 575) a mission consisting of eleven monks had been sent by the Ts'i emperor of Yeh to bring Sanskrit books from India. When the mission returned and came to the west of China, they heard that a reaction had set in in China and that the Buddhists were being severely persecuted by the emporor of the Cheu dynasty. For the time being they gave up the idea of proceeding to thoir native land and stayed with the Turks. They soon discovered that among the Turks, there was a learned Hindu monk, who could read the Sankrit manuscripts they had brought from India. At their request Jinagupta translated the titles of these manuscripts, which were 260 in number.[1]

Manuscripts from India,

In the meantime the political atmosphere again changed in

1 Chavanues, Jinagupta, *T'oung Pao*, 1905, pp. 332-356.

favour of the Buddhists. In 581 rose at Chang-ngan a dynasty called the Sui. Its founder was Yang-chien, afterwards known as Wenti. He began his public career in the reign of Wu-ti (561-577) of the N. Cheu dynasty. After the death of the emperor Hüen in A. D. 580, Yang-chien became the Prince of Sui. The next year he became emperor, although the south under the Chan (557-589 A. D.) was not annexed until seven years later. It was in 589 that the whole of China, north and south, was brought under one emperor for the first time in the history of China. The Sui was a short lived dynasty (581 or 589-618), but it was a glorious epoch in the annals of China, and more specially for the history of Buddhism and spread of Hindu culture.

Sui Dynasty, A. D. 581-618

Buddhism received great encouragement and patronage under the new emperor. The first act of sympathy and benevolence towards the Buddhists, on assumption of the imperial title by Yang-chien was the issue of the dict of tolerance to the Buddhists. "Towards the close of his reign he prohibited the destruction or maltreatment of any of the images of the Buddhist or Taoist sects. It was the weakness of the age, says the Confucian historian, giving way to superstitions that led him to such an act as this."[1]

Buddhism greatly patronized

The ban against the Buddhists being removed, the Chinese mission that was stopping in the land of tho Turks returned to Chang-ngan. The mission brought a large number of Sanskrit manuscripts ; but the persecution of Wu-ti had left few Buddhist scholars in Cina. Therefore they looked for a competent paṇḍit who could interpret and translate these works, and their choice fell on Narendrayaśas, who was living in exile. He was summoned to the monastery of Chang-ngan in A. D. 582 and was requested to superinted the work of translation. He lived in the monastery of

Hindu monks returned from exile

1 Edkins, *op. cit.*, p. 111.

Ta-hing-chan and translated eight works in 28 fasciculi. But in 585 some trouble arose over the translations made under Narendrayaśas. A few Chinese learned monks of Ta-hing-chan found some divergences and contradictions in the translations done under him and they thought that a more qualified man should be put in charge of this responsible work and all eyes turned towards one man. It was Jinagupta, the lonely man, who had been living among the Turks for the last ten years. By a special decree by the emperor he was recalled from his exile and reinstated in the temple of Ta-hing-chan as the head of the Translation Board. Brahman (Po-lo-man) Dharmgupta and two Chinese monks Kao-t'ien-nu and Kao-ho-jen helped Jinagupta in translating the Sanskrit works. Śramanas of 'great virtue' were entrusted with the work of verifying these Chinese translations made by the first group. Two monks again revised the Chinese version and improved the style.

Translation Board and Narendrayaśas

Jinagupta recalled

Thus equipped and aided Jinagupta and his group translated 39 works in 193 fasciculi ; of which two works in 14 fasc were lost already in A. D. 730. Besides these works at the instance of the Emperor Kao-tsu, Jinagupta in collaboration with a monk of India named Jñānagata (?), a brahmana named Pi-sho-ta and three other Chinese monks translated several works on Indian philosophy and astronomy. These works, consisting of about two-hundred fasciculi, were finished in 592 A. D.

Jinagupta was made the Rājyaguru by the king of Teng, a member of the Imperial family of Sui, who used to admit him as a model of the monks. He died in his 78th year in A. D. 600. [1]

Jinagupta made a Rājyaguru.

Four other Hindu monks came to the capital of the Sui and

1. Chavannes, *loc. cit.* 1905, p. This is a translation from the Chinese *Sui-kao-seng-chuen*, Tripiṭaka, Ed. Tokyo, XXXV, 2, p. 91r-92r ; Author is Tao Siuan, 596-667 A. D.

were contemporaries of Jinagupta. One of them was Gautama Dharmajñāna [1] son of Gautama Prajñāruci, whom we have already met in the Eastern Wei dynasty. He was an Upāsaka of Vārāṇasi (Benares). After the destruction of the Northen Ts'i Dynasty by the Cheu in A. D. 577, Dharmajñāna was appointed by the latter as the governor of the Yang-sen district, probably by way of banishment from the capital. He was recalled in 582 by the first Sui emperor to the capital where he translated one work only (Nanjio, 739). Vinitaruci [2] a monk of Udyāna came to China in A. D. 582, after the ban against the Buddhists had been withdrawn by the Sui emperor. He translated two works only (Nanjio, 240,253).

Contemporaries of Jinagupta

The last monk to arrive during the Sui dynasty was Dharmagupta, a śramaṇa of Lo-lo country (Rāḍha, Bengal ?). He came to Chang-an in A. D. 590 by the Central Asian route and worked, at first in collaboration with Jinagupta, and after the latter's death, independently at the translation of Sanskrit works. One catalogue ascribes 18 works in 31 fasc., to him, while the present-day Tripiṭaka contains 10 works only [3]. Dharmagupta died in 619 A. D. i.e. a year after the fall of the Sui dynasty. Another monk of this period is Pu-ti-tang (Bodhitang ?), who is simply mentioned as a foreign śramaṇa. He translated a work 'on the consideration by divination about the results of good and bad actions' (Nanjio, 464). His exact date is unknown.

Dharmagupta A. D. 590.

During the short rule of 38 years, five Hindu translators came to China who translated no less than 60 works, of which, in spite of the ravages of time, 58 exist in the Chinese Buddhist Tripiṭaka.

In 38 years 60 works translated.

It is not possible to describe all the books translated by the Sui translators ; but two translations of Jinagupta deserve special

1 Nanio, App II. 126.

2 Nanjio App II. 127 ; *Chin.* P'i-ni-to-lu-chi ; in trans. Mieh-hsi, 'destruction-joy'.

3 Nanjio, App. II, 131 ; Chavannes, *BEFEO*, 1903, p. 439-440.

notice. They are the Abhiniṣkramaṇa sūtra, and the Saddharma-puṇḍarīka. The Chinese title of the Abhiniṣkramaṇa sūtra would mean, 'Buddha-pūrvakārya-saṃgraha sūtra (Nanjio, 680.)

The work is in 60 fasc. of 60 chapters. An English translation, in an abstract form, of this book had been published by Beal, entitled, *The Romantic History of Buddha.* At the end of this work the following titles of the Life of Buddha, as adopted by the five different schools, are mentioned.

(1) Ta-shu (Mahāvastu?) by the Mahāsāṅghikas.

(2) Ta-chuang-yen (Lalitavistara) by the Sarvāstivādins.

(3) Fo-wang-yin-yuen (Buddha's former Avadāna). by the Kāśyapiyas.

(4) Shih-kiamen-ni pan-hsin (Sakyamuni's former practice or Buddha-carita) by the Dharmaguptas.

(5) Pi-ni tsan-kan-pan (Vinaya-piṭaka-mūla) by the Mahiśāsakas.

The Saddharma-puṇḍarīka was translated by Jinagupta and Dharmagupta in A. D. 600 in 8 fasc. of 27 chapters (Nanjio. 139). Translation of this Mahāyāna sūtra appeared more than once before in Chinese and a brief résumé of the earlier Chinese translations may not be out of place. The earliest translation of the Sad. Puṇḍ was made by Chu Fa-hu (Dharmarakṣa) of the Western Tsin dynasty (A. D. 265-316) (Nanjio, 138) and we have rather exhaustively described above the part played by Dharmarakṣa in propagating the cult of Avalokiteśvara. There is another incomplete translation made by an unknown translator of the same dynasty. The title of the work is transliterated as Sa-than-fan-tho-li ching (Nanjio, 136). The next extant translation is that of Kumārajīva's, the most important and the best of all the translations (Nanjio, 134). But the translation made by Jinagupta and his friend Dharmagupta has a special interest for us for reasons given below. There is an interesting preface by a Chinese scholar, who seems actually to have taken part in the translation. (Nanjio, 134) He writes :

"The translations of Chu Fa-hu and Kumārajīva are most

probably made from two different texts. In the repository of the canon, I (the author of the preface) have seen two texts ; one is written on the palm-leaves, and the other in the letters of Kucha, Kumārajīva's maternal country. The former text exactly agrees with Chu Fa-hu's and the latter with Kumārajīva's. Fa-hu's text omits only the Gāthās of the Samantamukha Parivarta, chapter 24. But Kumārajīva omits half of the Oṣadhi-Parivarta, chapter 5, the beginning of the Pañca bhikṣuśata vyākaraṇa Parivarta, chapter 10, and the Gāthās of the Devadatta Parivarta, chapter 12, and those of Samantamukha Parivarta, chapter 25. Moreover, Kumārajīva puts the Dharmaparyāya Parivarta (the last chapter of the Sūtra) before the Bhaiṣajya-rāja Parivarta, chapter 23. Chu Fa-hu and Kumārajīva both place the Dhāraṇī Parivarta next to the Samantamukha Parivarta, chapters 24 and 25 respectively. Besides these, there are minor differences between the text and translations. The omission of the Gāthās in Kumārajīva, chapters 12 and 25, have since been filled up by some wise men, whose example I wish to follow." Jinagupta, Dharmagupta and this monk made several changes in the text, which the writer of the preface admits in details. Nanjio has, in his *Catalogue*, compared the three translations with the extant Sanskrit version of the *Saddharma Puṇḍraīka* (Nanjio, 139).[1]

This treatise is the most popular of all the Buddhist texts in Eastern Asia. It has been sometimes designated as the 'Lotus Evangel' and compared with the Gospel of Saint John by foreigners.

Tendai sect

The faith of the Chinese and Japanese Tendai sect as well as of the Nichiren sect of Japan is based on the Sad. Puṇḍ. sūtra as translated by Kumārjīva.

---

1 It may be mentioned here by the way that fragments of very old Sanskrit texts of *Puṇḍarīka* have been discovered in Central Asia and since published, Hoernle, *Manuscript Remains*, Oxford 1916. Another very early version has been discovered by the Japanese traveller Kwa-guci from Tibet. The Sanskrit text that was preserved in Nepal, has been published by H. Kern and B. Nanjio (Bibiliotheca Buddhica, St. Petersbourg).; this text however is not the oldest recension as it agrees with the Tibetan translation of the ninth century.

It should be observed that the Sad. Puṇḍ. marks an epoch in the history of Buddhism. In it Śākyamuni ceases to be an historical personage. He "is no more the itinerant preacher in flesh and blood, who for fifty years walked through the cities of N.-E. India but a being divested of all historical individuality and identified with the cosmic principle, with the truth itself. This Śākyamuni of the Sad. Puṇḍ. is no Buddha of physical body but the Buddha of original enlightenment from all eternity. He did not die in past time, nor will be born in the future. He is one and the same with those whom he enlightens. His mind contains all phenomena in time and space. His essence is oneness, and there is nothing besides him. Therefore the present world is Buddha's world, the present human body is Buddha's body, the passions are enlightenment.'"[1]

It was during this Sui dynasty that a sect called as T'ien-tai was formally formed in China which based its faith on the Saddharma Puṇḍarīka. The founder of the sect was Chi-yi, whose life and work is oultined below. His other names are Chi-che-ta-si (Jap. Chisha Daishi) or Chi-k'ai or Ch'en Chi-k'ai or Chi-k'i. The sect was called T'ien-tai, from the name of the mountain on which the monastery of Chi-yi was situated. In Japan the sect is known as Tendai.

According to the Ti'en-tai tradition, the great Mahāyāna teacher Nāgārjuna, who is placed at the head of several schools, is regarded as the ancestor of the Ti'en-tai school. But the real originator was a Chinese monk named Hui-wen (Jap. Emon) of whom we know nothing. But the spiritual and literary contributions made by Hui-ssū, the disciple of Hui-wen to the dissemination of the Ti'en-tai idea were not inconsiderable. Hui-ssū was a priest of Wa-chan in Honan and was the chief of the Madhyamaka

Hui-wen and Hui-ssu

school. In 572 he established himself with forty priests at Nan-yao, preaching to them alone on his method of attaining Nirvāna.[2] Hui-ssū's outlook on

---

1 Bruno Petzold, The Chinese Tendai Teaching, The *Eastern Buddhist* Vol. IV, 1927-28, p. 306.
2 Giles, Chin. Bio. Dict, No. 880.

Buddhism was new and provoked such antagonism that twice he was in danger of being assassinated by fanatical fellow-monks. He died in 577.

Four works are attributed to Hui-ssŭ. The first was the text of Hui-ssŭ's prayer (Nanjio, 1576), the second was a thesis on 'the doctrine of meditation and knowledge' or *Samatha, Vipasyana* as they are technically called among the Ti'en-tai (Nanjio, 1542). The third was on 'the doctrine of meditation on the absence of dispute concerning all the states of existence' (Nanjio, 1543). Besides these he explained the meaning of the chapter entitled *Sukha vihāra* of the *Saddharma puṇḍarīka* (Nanjio, 1547). The *Sukha vihāra* chapter deals with "vocation of the ministers of religion, practical rules for their conduct in and out of society. Parable of the king, who rewards his valiant warriors ; in the same way the Buddha will reward those who struggle for his sake, by bestowing upon them all kinds of favours, at last the most valuable of his boons—eternal rest[1]." Of these four works the first two can be regarded as authentic.

Hui-ssŭ's greatest disciple was Chi-yi, the Great Sage of the T'ien-tai mountains, who became the founder of the Tendai teaching.

Chi-yi founder of the Sect

Chi-yi was born in 531 A. D. in the reign of Wu-ti in Southern China in the province of Ke. As a boy he saw the downfall of the Southern empire and his mind became early impressed with the futility of earthly greatness and with the vanity of the pomp and splendour of kings. He migrated with his family to the capital of Honan.

It was at the age of eighteen that he became a śramaṇa and at twenty became bhikṣu or full priest. His genius soon became noticed by the leaders of Buddhism of that time and attracted the attention of the imperial court of Nanking. He was invited there and became the religious teacher of the crown prince. Two emperors were his patrons and friends. But the atmosphere of an emperor's court was not to his liking and he preferred to live on

1 See Kern, SBE, Vol. XXI, p, XXX.

the T'ien-tai mountains 'the platform of Heaven,' the famous seat of the white Lotus society, teaching those who came to seek spiritual knowledge detached from worldly ambitions and sensual pleasures.

The great Mahāyāna work *Saddharma puṇḍarīka* inspired Chi-yi and the beautiful spiritual concepts and ceremonials attracted him very strongly. He held that although the Bodhi-citta was present in all living beings, yet they could not of themselves realise this truism and unfold their inner self without instruction. He, therefore, held that spiritual instruction and guidance were imperative in the life of a man to remove error and illusion and establish the true ideas. The motto of the school was *Chih-Kuan*, which is a translation of the two words *Samatha* and *Vipassana* meaning calm and insight.[1]

"The T'ien-tai is distinguished by its many-sided and almost encyclopædic character. Chi-yi did not like the exclusiveness of the Dhyāna school. He approved impartially of ecstasy, literature, ceremonial and discipline ; he wished to find a place for everything and point of view from which every doctrine might be admitted to have some value."[2]

Chi-yi like most great teachers in classical times, wrote very little himself, but his lectures were faithfully recorded by his great disciple Kuan-ting.

Two group of Chi-yi's works are considered specially important, namely the so-called the *San-ta-pu* 'Three great parts', and the Wu-hsiao-pu 'five small parts.' The former group consists of three works, namely :

Literary work of Chi-yi

1. 'The profound meaning of the Saddharma puṇḍarīka' in 20 fasc. (Nanjio, 1534). It is a work which aims at explaining the essence or the true principles of the Saddharma puṇḍarīka sūtra, and is in fact a systematic description of all teachings by the Buddha, or a synthetic philosophy of all the systems of Buddhism.

1 Eliot, III, p. 310.
2 Ibid, p. 311.

2. 'The Sentences and phrases of the Saddharma puṇḍarīka,' in 20 fasc. (Nanjio, 1536). It is a textual commentary on the sūtra.

3. 'The great Meditation' in 20 fasc. (Nanjio, 1538). It contains, besides many profound theoretical discussions, the practical teaching of Tendai. It is a contemplative method on a philosophical foundation, something much deeper than has ever been offered to the world by Zen Buddhism.

To these three fundamental works on Tendai philosophy Tsan-jen wrote three commentaries (Nanjio, 1535, 1537, 1539), which are regarded as classical or canonical like the master's own writings.

Besides these 'three great parts', there are 'five small parts', which comprise :

1. 'The profound meaning of the Avalokiteśvara chapter of the Saddharma puṇḍarīka,' (Nanjio, 1555).

2. 'Explanation of the meaning of the Avalokiteśvara chapter,' being a textual commentary on the above. (Nanjio, 1557).

3. The profound meaning of the Suvarṇaprabhāsa sūtra,' (Nanjio, 1548).

4. A textual commentary on the above (Nanjio, 1552).

5. A commentary on the Amitāyurdhyāna sūtra (Nanjio, 1559) ; the authenticity of the last work is doubted by some scholars. Nanjio mentions 22 works by Chi-yi in his catalogue, which were admitted in 1024 A. D. by the imperial order in the canonical work of Buddhism.

The T'ien-tai school highly respects all sūtras of the Buddhist Tripiṭaka and rejects none. But it has a special veneration for two sūtras, the Saddharma puṇḍarīka, and the Mahāpariṇirvāṇa sūtra. Chi-yi further combined with them two other sūtras viz., Amitārtha sūtra (Nanjio, 133), and the Samantabhadra Bodhisattva Dhyāna sūtra (Nanjio, 334), which form, so to say, the prologue and the epilogue to the Saddharma puṇḍarīka.

To a T'ien-tai believer, the conviction of the unity of the whole universe and of all living beings, not a cold abstract theory, but a deep religious conviction. It pervaded the whole personality of Chi-yi and impressed it with a wonderful sweetness. Chi-yi preached to the fishes and in his piety for all living beings delivered the fishes from the avarice and cruelty of men buying up the fishing-rights from the fishermen on the sea-shore near T'ien-tai mountains, where his monastery was situated.[1]

The patronage of the emperors was manifest in various branches of Buddhist culture and the most important work was

Catalogues of Buddhist works compiled under the Sui emperor

the compilation of several catalogues of Buddhist works in Chinese. During the reign of Wen-Ti (581-605) three catalogues of Chinese Buddhist works were compiled. In A. D. 594 the Emperor asked Fa-ching, a priest who was engaged in translation and other monks of the Ta-hing-chan monastery to compile a catalogue of the Buddhist works in Chinese. The total number of books mentioned in this catalogue called *Sui-chung-ching-mu-lu*

First Catalogue

(Nanjio, 1609) is 2257[2] in 5310 fasciculi, of which the number of missing books may be about 402 in 702 fasciculi.

In 597, the second catalogue was compiled. The *Li-tai-san-pao-chi* (Nanjio, 1504), or the record of the *Triratna* under

Second Catalogue

successive dynasties, was compiled by Fa-chan-fang, a translator of Buddhist texts. The work is in 15 fasciculi and the first three fasciculi contain

---

1 Still to-day in several monastery tanks fishes live unmolested.

2 The contents of the *Sui Chung-ching-mu-lu* :

Sūtra	Mahāyāna,	784	works in	1718	fasc.
	Hīnayāna,	845	works in	1304	fasc.
Vinaya	Mahāyāna,	50	works in	82	fasc.
	Hīnayāna,	63	works in	381	fasc.
Abhidharma	Mahāyāna,	68	works in	381	fasc.
	Hīnayāna,	116	works in	482	fasc.
Later works	Extracts,	144	works in	627	fasc,
Indian & Chinese Records,		68	works in	185	fasc,
	Treatises,	119	works in	134	fasc.
		2257		5294	

Nanjio, Catalogue, Introduction, p. xviii.

a general history of Buddhism from the birth of the Buddha down to the time of the compilation of the work ; the next eleven fasciculi form a catalogue of Indian works translated into Chinese from A. D. 67 till 587. The fifteenth fasciculi is an index or a minute list of the contents of the work. This catalogue contained 1076 works in 3,325 fasciculi, of which 551 belonged to Mahāyāna, 525 to Hīnayāna. There is no book in the Miscellaneous section. Of 551 Mahāyāna works, 259 works, and of 525 Hīnayāna works 357 were by unknown translators. This catalogue was compiled by a private individual, but due to its excellence, it has largely been used by subsequent catalogues.

Third Catalogue.

The third catalogue, also called *Sui-chung-ching-mu-lu* (Nanjio, 1608), was compiled in 602 A. D. by the order of the first emperor, by Bhadanta Yen-ts'ong and other monks of the Ta-hing-shan monastery. Lay savants also co-operated in the compilation of this catalogue. The method of classification followed here was different from the one followed in the compilation of the imperial catalogue of 594 A. D.

Another Catalogue.

Nanjio speaks of another catalogue, which is recorded and described in the *Sui Annals*. "In the period Ta-yeh (605-616 A.D.) Emperor Yang ordered śramaṇa Chi-kuo to compile a catalogue of Buddhist books at the Imperial Buddhist Chapel within the gate of the palace. He then made some divisions and classifications, which are as follows :

"Sūtras, which contained what Buddha had spoken, were arranged under three divisions, (1) The Mahāyāna, (2) The Hīnayāna, (3) The mixed Sūtras. Other books that seemed to be productions of later men, who falsely ascribed their works to greater names, were classed as Doubtful Books.

"There were other works in which Bodhisattvas and others went deeply into the exploration of the meaning, and illustrated the principles of Buddha. These were called Disquisitions or Śāstras (Abhidharma.)

"Then there were Vinaya works, under each division, as before, Mahāyāna, Hīnayāna, mixed. There are also records, or accounts of the doings in the times of those who had been student of the system. Altogether there are eleven classes under which the books were arranged.[1]

The number of books mentioned here is 1962 in 6198 fasciculi But "neither the catalogue nor the compiler is mentioned in Chinese Buddhist works. The number of books is again different from that mentioned in four earlier catalogues still in existence. This may however be called the fifth collection made by an Emperor of China."

We are on the eve of the great dynasty of T'ang and before we enter into that period, let us stop for a moment and take stock of what the Chinese learnt from the Hindus. The Hindu monks did not merely carry Sanskrit books across the mountains and deserts, but they carried a culture to China ; they not only translated the Sanskrit works into the Chinese language but grafted Hindu culture in the Chinese stem.

Hindu Art in China

That China has been influenced by India in her architecture is an obvious fact ; that the Pagodas and temples are built after a Hindu pattern is admitted by the native writers. "The Pagoda is purely Indian in origin," says a modern Chinese, "we never had it before the days of Indian influence." But it is not in architecture alone that traces of Hindu influence are found. They are found in Chinese arithmetic, astronomy, astrology, literature, music, sculpture, painting, and, in fact, in almost every branch of Chinese art and science. Says a modern historian about the influence of Buddhism upon Chinese civilization : "The most important point students have to bear in mind is the extent to which Chinese civilization has been revolutionized since the coming of Buddhism. Of all the changes that have resulted

---

1 Quoted from Max Müller's *Selected Essays*, Vol. II, pp. 320-330, by Nanjio —Introduction, p. xix).

from the spread of Buddhism, those in connection with Chinese language are of the most permanent value." The *fan-tsie* system which aims at arranging the whole Chinese vocabulary phonetically under 36 initials was introduced by the Buddhist monks towards the beginning of the Sixth century A. D.

XIV. The Age of Hiuen Tsang.[1]

The T'ang dynasty marks the golden age of Chinese history. It rose after the fall of the short-lived Sui dynasty that had united China in 589. With the death of the great Sui emperor Yang-ti in 617, the dynasty came to an end and as many as seven adventurers occupied the different parts of China. But they only paved the path for the great governor of T'ai-yuan, Li-yüan who with the help of his able son Shih-Min, afterwards famous in Chinese history as T'ai-tsung, became emperor in Chang-an in 618. But his authority was disputed by eleven rivals, and it was not before ten years that Li-yüan, known as Kao-tsu in history, could re-unite the major portion of China once more under the same rule.

T'ang Dynasty, A. D. 618

The T'ang dynasty lasted (from 618 to 907 A. D.) for about three hundred years and therefore we cannot expect from our previous knowledge of history that the attitude of all the Chinese emperors towards Buddhism should be uniformly favourable. Its career and character met with various fortunes during its long lease of life. The T'angs were generally not unfavourable towards Buddhism and some of the great names of Chinese Buddhism are connected with history of the T'ang dynasty.

Various fortune of Buddhism under the T'ang

Li-yüan or Kao-tsu, the founder of the T'ang dynasty, himself was reactionary. Yang-ti, the Sui emperor, as we have already seen, had declared favourably for Buddhism, and now according to the conspectus of the new emperor Confucianism was considered as necessary to China, as wings to a bird, or water to a fish. Fu-i, the imperial historian, a staunch Confucianist and enemy of Buddhism

Reaction under Kao-Tsu's rule.

---

1 The name of the great pilgrim is differently transcribed. The reading Yuan Chuang as proposed by Rhys Davids (Walters, *Yuan Chuang*, Preface) is untenable. Two spellings are possible: Hiuan Chuang or Hiuan Tsang. The latter is widely accepted.

prevailed upon the Emperor to issue an edict against the Buddhists. Magistrates were ordered to enquire into the lives of the monks and nuns; those possessed of an impeccable character were allowed to retire into bigger monasteries, the smaller ones being closed down. Kao-tsu abdicated in 627 in favour of his son Shih-men, who is known as T'ai-tsung. [1]

Emperor T'ai-tsung, the greatest T'ang. 627-649.

T'ai-tsung was one of the greatest rulers that China ever had. His reign of 22 years (627-649) formed the golden age of the T'ang dynasty. He succeed in both the art of war and peace; but this is the subject of Chinese history. It may be mentioned briefly that T'ai-tsung made matrimonial alliance with the first great king of Tibet, Srong sam-gamo, by giving his daughter Wen-cheng to the Tibetan king. This alliance threw open Tibet to the influence of Chinese civilization. He sent an embassy to the court of Harṣavardhana [2] and made war with the usurper who succeeded Harṣa. T'ai-tsung was known to the Greek emperor and his friendship was sought for by the Sassanian king as well as by the early Caliphs. He conquered the Turks and brought Corea under him. This was the great T'ai-tsung under whom Buddhism got neither check, nor encouragement.

Prabhākaramitra Comes to China.

For several decades very few Hindu monks came to China. In 627 a Hindu monk named Prabhākara-mitra (Nanjio, App. II, 132) arrived in China. He was a monk of Nālanda, a Kṣatriya by caste. On his way to China, he lived among the Turks for some time and worked as a preacher of Hindu culture in civilizing the rude Turks.

---

1 See Eliot, III, op. cit.

2 "I may observe that the *Peh-Shi* (or 'Northern Dynasties History') speaks of a large consumption of sugar in Cambodgia as far back as the fifth century of our era. There can be no mistake about the meaning of the words *Sha-t'ang* which are still used both in China and Japan *(Sa-to)*. The 'History of the T'ang Dynasty', in its chapter on Magadha, says that in the year 627 the Chinese Emperor sent envoys thither to procure the method of boiling out sugar, and then ordered the Yang-Chou sugar-cane growers to press it out in the same way, when it appeared that both in colour and taste ours excelled that of the western Regions [of which Magadha was held to be part]." E. H. Parker, Asiatic Quarterly Review, Jan, 1904, p. 146. Quoted from H, Cordier, *Ser Marco Polo*, (1920), p 99.

"The Chinese sources have preserved an account of Prabhākaramitra and his works. His name is faithfully transcribed as Po-lo-p'o-kia-lo-mi-to. He was also simply known as Prabhāmitra. He was born in royal family of Kṣatriya descent in Central India.

His life among the Western Turks.

He left home at the age of ten years and studied under an able teacher. He at first studied the Mahāyāna-sūtras. On receiving *upasampadā* he took to the study of Vinayapiṭaka and applied himself to a strict observance of disciplinary rules. But he was by temperament meditative and liked the study of Buddhist metaphysics.

"At the end of his study he went out to travel in different parts of India. Having travelled in South India he returned to his country and went to the monastery of Nālanda (Nalan-to) in the kingdom of Magadha. There he met Śīlabhadra who was lecturing on the *Saptadaśabhūmi Śāstra* at that time. Prabhākara attended these lectures, studied and collected information on the Hīnāyāna Śāstras.

"Thus being possessed of a deep knowledge of both Hīnayāna and Mahāyāna Śāstras, he was appointed a teacher of Abhidharma at Nālanda and soon won the admiration of all his companions and disciples. He had many disciples at Nālanda and some of them, Prajñāvarman, Indravarman and others were famous for their profound erudition. Prabhākara was admired not only by the people but also by the king of the country.

"As the Buddhist disciplinary rules do not permit a Śākyaputra who have adopted the life of a monk, to live in one place for more than six months. Prabhākara thought of leaving Nālanda. He heard that nobody had as yet preached the Law of Buddha amongst the Barbarians of the north. As there were many to propagate the religion at home but none to go to foreign countries he left for the northern countries with 10 disciples, both monks and laymen. After travelling in different countries he reached the camp of Yabghu, the Khagan of the Western Turks. He taught him the Law of the Buddha.

"After a period of ten days he discovered in the barbarian sovereign a spirit of confidence and submission. Every day the Khagan sent for Prabhākara and his companions necessary food ; every morning and evening he sent them offerings with respect ; all of them received excellent treatment from the Turkish chief and found with joy in him an ever-increasing faith for Buddha and his religion.

"In A. D. 620 the king of Kao-ping came from China to the country of the barbarian herdes as ambassador. Prabhākara met him and taking this opportunity prepared himself for going to China. But the Khagan and his subjects would not let him go away. The king of Kao-ping, therefore, sent a note to the Emperor of China and the latter soon issued an official order inviting Prabhākara to come to the capital of China. He arrived at the capital with the king of Kao-ping towards the end of the same year (626 A. D.). At the request of the emperor, Prabhākara was lodged in the monastery of Hing-shen at the capital.

"The emperor was soon attracted by the great abilities and profound learning of Prabhākara and began to entertain a great respect for him. In 629 the emperor requested him to translate Buddhist text into Chinese. A committee of 19 eminent monks was appointed to help him. There were two Indian monks known as Saṅgha (Seng-ka) and Gupta (Kiu-to) on the committee and one of them served as interpreter.

The work of translation continued till the 630 A. D. These translations won him great honour from the Chinese Buddhist scholars. But the Confucian litterati soon got jealous of Prabhākara's influence. They began to poison the ear of the emperor who gradually began to show indifference towards Prabhākara. Thus a little disappointed at the end of his life Prabhākara died in the capital of China in 633 at the age of 69. His disciples erected a *Stūpa* to honour his memory."[1]

1 Dr. P. C. Bagchi, A Buddhist Monk of Nālanda among the Western Turks.—*Buddhist India* Vol. II, No 1. 1928 p. 7-9.

In China Prabhākaramitra translated three works in 35 fasc. having died in his 69th year in A. D. 633.

His literary works.

Of Prabhākara's three translations, two are retranslations of works which had already appeared in Chinese. His *Ratnatārā-Dhāraṇ-Sūtra* (Nanjio, 84) is the retranslation of the second part of the Mahāvaipulya Mahāsannipata sūtra (Nanjio, 61) done into Chinese by Dharmarakṣa of N. Liang dynasty (397-439 A. D.) His other two translations are Abhidharma works of two great ācāryas. Bodhisattva Nāgārjuna's *Mādhyamaka Kārikās* with the commentary of his great disciple Āryadeva had once been translated into Chinese by Kumārajīva (Nanjio, 1179) in 4 fasciculi. Kumārajīva always abridged his translations. Prabhākaramitra, therefore, brought out a complete translation of the same work in 8 fasciculi. The importance of the work has already been emphasized above under Kumārajīva But his greatest work is the translation of Asaṅga's Mahāyāna Sutrālaṁkāra sūtra (Nanjio, 1190). The original text of this was discovered some time back in Nepal by Sylvain Lévi who had since then published and translated it.[1]

Mādhyamaka Kārikā with Āryadeva's ṭikā translated completely.

Mahāyāna Sūtrālaṁkāra.

In the original text the name of Asaṅga does not occur and it has, therefore, raised doubts in the minds of scholars as to the claim of Asaṅga to the authorship of the sūtra. This doubt has been greatly strengthened by several facts. Firstly, the colophon of the Sanskrit text contains the name of Bodhisattva Vyavadātasamaya as the speaker (*bhāṣita*). This colophon is found in the Chinese as well as in the Tibetan versions ; therefore, the tradition of Vyavadātasamaya as the 'spokesman' of the sūtra is quite old. The name of this Bodhisattva is unknown and it is impossible to say whether this designation is applicable to Maitreya or to Asaṅga or to another person real or fictitious.

1 Mahāyāna Sūtrālaṁkāra Ed. et traduit par S. Lèvi. Tome I, Text ; Tome II. Traduction, Paris. 1911.

Prabhākaramitra in his translation assigns this sūtra to Asaṅga, whom he clearly refers as a 'Bodhisattva.' The preface to the Chinese translation by Li Pe-yo repeats and confirms this without any allusion to supernatural revelation, as found in Hiuen-tsang. According to the latter statement the sacred texts of the Yogācāra were revealed by Maitreya, the future Buddha to Asaṅga in the tuṣita heaven. The story of revelation is quite ancient; for we find that Paramārtha and the Chinese translators of the fifth century had declared the *Saptadaśabhūmi śāstra* or the *Yogācārabhūmi śāstra* as a revealed text.

Its authorship.

But Paramārtha and Hiuen-tsang belonged to the Yogācāra school and it is quite likely that they would believe in the current supernatural tales. Yi-tsing, who was not a follower of this sect, and lived only half-a-century after Hiuen-tsang, clearly stated that this work was Asaṅga's. But it is the Tibetan authors who have unanimously placed the Mahāyāna Sūtrālaṁkāra among the 'five śāstras of Maitreya.' But they maintain that the verses which are attributed to Maitreya, the prose commentary to the verses which forms a part of the work, called *Sūtrālaṁkāra-bhāṣya*, are attributed to Vasubandhu ! The name of Asaṅga is nowhere mentioned. The Tibetan translation was the work of the Hindu monk Śākyasinha and the Lotsavas dPal bregs and others, about whom nothing definite is known. Anyhow it is later than Prabhākaramitra, for, in the early seventh century there was hardly any translation or translator in Tibet. Tibetan Buddhism is based on Yogācāra ; so that it is probable that they would ascribe supernatural origin to this scripture. We would, therefore, like to trust the older and unorthodox opinion that the sūtra was the work of Asaṅga. The theory advanced by Tibetan scholars that the *Kārikas* and the *ṭīkā* were separate compositions by two different authors, is, however, contradicted by the authors of the Chinese Catalogue *Che Yuen-lu* (A. D. 1264-94) who clearly ascribes the verses and the ṭīkā to the work of Asaṅga, the Sanskrit title being transliterated

Asaṅga is the author.

as *Su-tan-lo-A-leng-kia-lo ti-kia i.e.* Sūtra-alaṁkāratikā, and it doubtless refers to the prose portion that we see in the original.

The Chinese translation of Prabhākara contains 13 sections or 24 chapters with titles prefixed to almost all of them. The Sanskrit original text and the Tibetan translation agree very closely, the number and title of the chapters exactly tallying. The Sanskrit *adhikāras* or chapters number 21. The titles of the Chinese version are given below:

I. 1. nidāna, 2. siddhi, 3. saraṇagamana, 4. gotra. II. 5. cittotpāda, 6. pratipatti. 7. tattava, 8. prabhāva. 9. paripāka. III. 10 bodhi. IV. 11 adhimukti, 12. paryeṣṭi V. 12b—VI-13 diśana, 14. pratipatti's. VII. 15 avavādānuśāsanāni, 16 upāyasahita-karma, 17. a Nāvamitra, VIII. 176.—IX. 18. pujā, 19. kalyānamitra, 20. brahmavihāra. X. 21 a. bodhipakṣa,XI. 21b.—XII. 22. guṇa, 23. caryāparatiṣṭhā. XIII. 24. buddhapujā.

The Chinese and the Sanskrit texts agree in general differing in minor details due to some unimportant changes made by scribes and editors of the Sanskrit text during these centuries. It may be mentioned here that many of the sections are reproduced *verbatim* in the Bodhisattvabhūmi, the only chapter of the Yogācārabhūmi preserved in the original Sanskrit.[1]

For nearly a quarter of a century after Prabhākaramitra no Sanskrit book was translated into Chinese till the rise of Hiuen-tsang. This great pilgrim-monk is an important figure in the Sino-Indian connection and therefore deserves a detailed study.

Hiuen-tsang's life.

Hiuen-tsang was born in A. D. 600, in the family of Chan hui, who was a Confucianist of the strict old-fashioned kind. Hiuen-tsang was the youngest of the four sons. He received his earliest education in the classics from his father and teachers along with his brothers. He was a precocious child showing cleverness and wisdom in his very early years. He was quick to receive and was imbued with a very practical intelligence. His classical training was thorough, which greatly helped him to be a good writer and stylist.

1 From the Introduction to Asaṅgaś text by Lèvi, pp. 7ff.

In the meantime, his second elder brother entered the Buddhist church, and young Hiuen-tsang followed his brother into the various monasteries and felt a great attraction for this religion which he could hardly comprehend. His mind began to change ; and he thought of becoming a monk. With this object in view he proceeded to study the sacred books of the Buddhists with all the fervour of a youthful proselyte. Finally at the age of twenty he was ordained a monk. He continued to wander about visiting all the famous monasteries of China in search of true inspiration. Under the guidance of the learned Chinese monks in those monasteries, Hiuen-tsang studied some of the great works of Buddhism and soon became famous in China as a very learned and eloquent monk. But the teaching through Chinese translation could not satisfy him, and he longed earnestly to visit the holy land of his religion, to see the sacred places connected with the life of Śākyamuni, to sit at the feet of the learned Hindu monks and clear his spiritual and philosophical doubts with their help. He had learned, moreover, to be dissatisfied with the Chinese translation of the Sanskrit books, and was desirous of procuring these books in their original language. After making enquiries and preparation, he left Chang-an, the capital of the T'angs, in the year 629, that is, two years after T'ai-tsu had come to the throne. He left secretly, without permission from the emperor, lest he should, in any way, deter him from his holy mission, and set out in his long pilgrimage of fifteen years.[1]

Hiuen-tsang leaves for India, A. D. 629

When Hiuen-tsang "expressed his desire to visit India, there seem to have been some willing to accompany him in his journey, but when he came near the desert he had only two companions, of whom one was sent back to China, as he was thought unfit for the hardships of the journey, while the other started in advance for Tun-huang and was heard of no more. Finally, when he took leave of his patron, the King of Turfan, four novices were alloted to him as his attendants. The king helped him with brotherly care and introduced him to

In Central Asia and India.

1 See Watters, *On Yuan Chuang*, 1904, Vol. I, p. 110-111.

many of the Central Asian chieftains: consequently he was welcomed everywhere and travelled with great facility. In India, too, he was patronized by King Harsha of Kanauj and had opportunities of meeting many worthies and savants of his time. At Nalanda, then the centre of Mahāyāna learning, he found an able teacher in Śilabhadra, the president of the University, and there he spent several years learning Sanskrit and chiefly Buddhist idealism. The interest of the Buddhists of his time seems too have centred in the Mahāyāna, though the Hinayāna schools were followed throughout India."[1]

Returns to China, A. D. 645.

After sixteen years of absence the pilgrim returned to China in 645 A.D., the nineteenth year of the great T'ang emperor T'ai-tsung. On the day following his arrival, the members of the various monasteries conducted Hiuen-tsang with flags and banners to the convent called Hong-fu, where he deposited the treasures he had brought from India.

Meets the Emperor.

After having deposited the treasures in the temple and visited the chief officers, Hiuen-tsang went to meet the emperor. He was received with great warmth by the emperor who listened to his accounts with keen interest. The emperor, who was a shrewd politician, tried to persuade the monk to take to secular life and serve the state with his wide experiences abroad. But the plan of the pilgrim was fixed and as soon as he could withdraw from the court he went back to the monastery to translate the Sanskrit works he had brought with him. On his petitioning the emperor appointed several distinguished lay-scholars and learned monks to assist him in the work of translating, editing and copying. In the meantime, at the request of the emperor he wrote an account of his travels, which was finished and submitted in 646, but further added to in 648 A.D. The emperor wrote a laudatory preface to this book.

His books on travel.

The record of the great pilgrim has come down to us in three forms. The first is his own work known as *Ta-t'ang-si-yu-ki* (Nanjio, 1503), in 20 fasc.,

1 Anesaki, *ERE*, Vol. 12, p. 842.

compiled by his pupil in A.D. 646. The travels cover 138 countries of which he himself visited 110 and gathered information about the rest from different sources. The character and usages of the people and the state of Buddhist learning and practices are minutely described. The book is indispensable for the study of Indian history and geography of the 7th century. In 1859 Stanislus Julien published the French translation with the title—*Memoirs sur les contrees occidentales*—Traduits du Sansckrit en chinois, en l'an 648, par Hiouen Thsang, et du chinois en Francaise etc. The only other version of *Hsi-yu-chi* is in English, translated by Samuel Beal. This was published in 1884 with the title—"*Buddhist records of the Western world*" (Trübner).

Shia-chia (Śākya) fan-chu.

The second work is a resumé of Hiuen-tsang's travels by Tao-siuan. It is called *Shih-chia fan-chu* (Nanjio, 1470), which is a record of the region of Śākyamuni. The author was a pupil of the monk and one of the assistant translators. The work was compiled in 650.

There seems to have been another work in 10 books entitled *Hsi-yu-chuan* or Record of the western region, by Yen-tsong, another pupil of the pilgrim. This record, it is said, treated more of the Indian life than the religion itself, whereas the pilgrim's *Memoirs* paid more attention to the religion than to the life. Tao-siuan says in his preface to the book mentioned above, that both these were too minute and copious for general information and that this very fact led him to a fresh compilation of his own work. No translation of it in any European language has yet appeared ; but one is urgently needed for the history of Buddhism in Eastern Asia and India.[1]

The third work is an abridged form of the *memoires* given in the *Life of Hiuen-tsang* in 10 books, compiled by Yen-tsong and Hui-li in A. D. 665. Julien made an abridged translation of this.[2]

1 Quoted with little modification from *ERE*, Article—Hiuen Tsang by Anesaki.

2 *Histoire de la Vie de Hiuen Tsang* et *des ses voyages dans l'Inde, depuis l'an 629 jusque 645 ;* published in 1853 from Paris.

Beal also made an English translation of the same—based principally on the former.[1]

Hiuen-tsang's memoir was received in China as a great book of the day. It was the record of a pilgrim, who had been to In-to (India) and spent more than fifteen years abroad studying the various peoples of India and Central Asia.

The pilgrim went to Chang-an to translate the books he had brought from India ; he was helped by twelve monks in carrying out his object. A board of nine monks was appointed to revise the composition. People who knew Sanskrit co-operated with him in the work. On presenting a series of translations to the emperor, the latter wrote a preface to them, and at the request of Hiuen-tsang he issued an edict to the effect that five new monks might be admitted to every monastery in the empire. The convents then numbered 3,716. For nineteen years the Chinese savant worked incessantly and at the close of his life he found that he had translated seventy-five Sanskrit works in 1,335 fasc. He died in his 65th year in A. D. 664.

Translated 75 works in fasc. 1335

The Chinese pilgrim had come back to his native land with a large number of books, statues, and curios collected in India which were carried on the back of twenty horses. The treasures he brought are enumerated below :—

Relics and books brought from India

1. One hundred and fifty grains of relics belonging to the body of relic.
2. A golden statue of the Buddha 3ft. 3 inches in height on a transparent pedastal.
3. A statue of the Buddha 3ft. 5 inches carved out of sandal-wood on a transparent pedastal.
4. Another figure 2ft. 9 inches.
5. A silver statue 4ft. high after the model of the Buddha preaching

1 Hiuen tsang by Shaman Hwui-li with an introduction containing an account of the works of I-tsing, Trubner.

the *Saddharma Puṇḍarīka* and other sūtras on the Gṛdhrakūṭa mountain.

6. A golden statue on a transparent pedastal.
7. Another sandal-wood figure 1ft. 3 in.

Besides these relics and statues he brought a large number of books, which numbered 657 distinct texts. The books are as follows :—

Mahāyāna sūtra	224	Treatises
Mahāyāna śāstra	192	"
Sthaviravāda sūtras, śāstras and vinaya,	14	"
Mahāsaṅghika	15	"
Mahiśāsaka	22	"
Sammitiya	15	"
Kāśyapiya	17	"
Dharmagupta	42	"
Sarvāstivādin	67	"
Hetu-vidyā	36	"
Śabda-vidyā	13	"
Total ...	657	Treatises.

Hiuen-tsang's translations mainly Abhidharma works.

Hiuen-tsang was a great Sanskritist and although a staunch Mahāyānist of the yogācāra school, his interests for Buddhist studies were varied ; and, therefore, his translated works which numbered 75, covered almost all the subjects of Buddhism out of which 40 were treatises on Abhidharma of various schools. These Abhidharma translations are his most important contributions to Chinese literature. We shall describe them a little later.

Complete set of Prajñāpāramitā in 600 fasc.

In our study of Kumārajīva, we traced the origin of the Prajñā literature and its vogue in Chinese ; but the entire set of the Prajñā literature was never translated completely before Hiuen-tsang. Hiuen-tsang had the zeal of a monk and the acuteness of a scholar and he religiously adhered to the Sanskrit texts rendering even the most irritating repetitions. His most voluminous translation was a complete version of the *Prajñāpāramilā sūtras*.

The whole set of the *Prajñapāramitā* in translation consisted of 600 fasciculi. Following are the texts of the Prajñāpāramita series :—

Titles of the treatises.

1. *Śata sāhasrikā Prajñāpāramitā* in 75 chapters (fasc. 1-400 ; Nanjio, 1.) Agrees with the Tibetan. In Sanskrit the texts exist, published by the the Asiatic Society of Bengal (in part.)

2. *Pañcaviṁśati sāhasrikā Parjñāpāramitā* in 76 chapters (fasc. 401—478). Agrees with the Tibetan. In Sanskrit the text exists. This was the text translated by Kumārajīva along with the commentary of Nāgārjuna (Nanjio, 3, and 1169).

3. *Aṣṭādaśa sāhasrikā Prajñāpāramitā* in 87 chapters (fasc. 479—537). Agrees with the Tibetan. No Sanskrit original is known to be existing.

4. *Daśa sāhasrikā Prajñāpāramitā* in 33 chapters (fasc. 538—555). Agrees with Tibetan ; but no Sanskrit text exists.

5. *Aṣṭasāhaśrikā Prajñāpāramitā* in 32 chapters (fasc. 556—585). Agrees with the Tibetan ; Sanskrit text exists : It has been edited by the Asiatic Society of Bengal. Translated into German by Max Wallesser, Heidelberg, 1914. (See Rajendralal.)

6. *Suvikrāntavikrami Paripṛcchā* (fasc. 566—573) Not found in Tibetan or Sanskrit.

7. *Saptaśatikā Prajñāpāramitā* (fasc. 574—575). Agrees with Tibetan ; also exists in Sanskrit original (see Bendal, p. 5).

8. *Pañcaśatikā Prajñāpāramitā* (?) (fasc. 576). Not found in Tibetan or Sanskrit.

9. *Vajrachedikā Prajñāpāramitā* (fasc. 577). Agrees with Tibetan, exists in Sanskrit. It has been edited by Max Müller and translated into English from the Sanskrit (*SBE*).

10. *Prajñāpāramitā Ardha-śatikā* (fasc. 578). Agrees with Tibetan.

11-15. 'Prajñāpāramitā in 1800 Ślokas' (fasc. 579-592).

16. 'Prajñāpāramitā in 1200 Ślokas' (fasc. 593-600).

This enormous work comprising 600 fasc. consists of several thousand pages of the Chinese Tripiṭaka and two prefaces were written for it by the Emperors Tai-sung (627-649) and Kao-tsung (650-683.) in both of which the labours of Hiuen-tsang are described.

Hiuen-tsang retranslated several Sanskrit texts which were already well-known to the Chinese Buddhists through the translations of Kumārajīva and other masters, such as *Prajñāpāramitā Hṛdaya sūtra* (Nanjio, 20, 19), *Vimala-kīrti-nirdeśa* (Nanjio, 149, 146-147), smaller *Sukhāvativyūha* (Nanjio, 199, 200), *Sandhinirmocana sūtra* (Nanjio, 247,246) etc. But some were done for the first time. Of these newer texts *Bhaiṣajyaguru vaidurya-prabhāsa-pūrva-nidāna* (Nanjio, 171), a treatise practically on medicine and allied subjects, was one which became very popular in China. But Hiuen-tsang has won his immortal fame in Chinese Buddhism, not so much for his translations of isolated sūtras, as for the volumes of philosophical treatises on Mahāyāna of the Sarvāstivāda school and the Yogācāra school.

Other sūtra works.

The Sarvāstivāda was one of the eighteen schools of Buddhism and was at one time the most widespread and influential. The Sarvāstivādins had a complete Tripiṭaka: their sūtras comprised the Dīrgha Āgama, the Madhyama Āgama, the Saṁyukta Āgama and the Ekottara Āgama which have already been described above. The Vinaya of this school appeared also in Chinese and exists in its entirety in Tibetan. The śāstra or Abhidharma of this school appeared in Chinese from time to time. It was Hiuen-tsang who for the first time translated the whole library of Abhidharma of the Sarvāstivādins and gave the Chinese Buddhists a complete idea of their philosophical system.

Sarvāstivāda Abhidharma completely translated

The history of the school according to southern tradition begins after the council of Pataliputra in the reign of King Aśoka (3rd century B. C.), when Moggaliputta Tissa is said to have compiled the

Kathā-vatthu (Points of Controversy) to refute the schismatic views of the time. Still it does not seem to have played any important role even then. It is said that six hundred years after the death of the Buddha, the Saṅgha was re-organised and the responsibility of this was Kātyayaniputra's, a Sarvāstivādi monk of Kashmir. It was this gifted monk, who for the first time conceived the idea of collecting and systematizing the philosophical views of Buddha in a treatise called the *Jñāna-prasthāna*. It was to this work that six authors, either contemporaries or successors, added each a supplementary treatise called pada (foot).

The six *padas* reopen the subject and try to systematize or supplement what in their eyes, was lacking to the work of their predecessors. Hiuen-tsang translated the whole set (except the last *pada*) and they will be described presently. Besides the six padas, there is a big commentarial literature, of which the *Mahāvibhāsā* is the most important work.

Jñānaprasthāna also called Aṣta-grantha.

There are two translations of the *Jñāna-prasthāna* in Chinese, one by Gautama Saṇghadeva (A. D. 383) and the other by our monk. The original text is lost. It seems to have had variant readings here and there and the translations do not present any material difference in general scope. The two bear different names, the one translated by Saṅghadeva was called *Aṣta-grantha* (Nanjio, 1273) and that by Hiuen-tsang was called *Jñāna-prasthāna* (Nanjio, 1275). At the beginning of every chapter Kātyāyaniputra raises a series of questions which are subsequently answered by him, and then deals with them one by one. The list of questions is generally omitted by Hiuen-tsang, thus making his version much shorter than that of Gautama Saṅghadeva.

The basis of the Sarvāstivāda philosophy is Kātyāyaniputra's *Jñāna-prasthāna*. Till the time of Kātyāyaṇīputra the literature of the Buddhists consisted of *Dharma* and *Vinaya*; the teachings of Śākyamuni had not yet been put on a philosophical basis. It should be borne in mind that Śākyamuni never discoursed *on* philosophy, but his teachings are highly philosophical in their nature. The basis of a religion is its philosophy, with which it combats its opponents and convinces its adherents. In order to strengthen the position of the Buddhists assailed by heretics Kātyāyanīputra wanted to edit an encyclopaedia of Buddha's philosophical thoughts, and proclaimed to all, far and near saying, "If there be any who have heard the Abhidharma propounded by the Buddha, let them communicate what they know whether it be much or little." Several contributions were received. About 500 Arhats and 500 Bodhisattvas helped Kātyāyanīputra in collecting the Master's sayings which were scattered throughout Northern India. As the chief-editor he made a selection of the philosophical ideas thus collected. When these principles did not contradict the Sūtra and Vinaya he noted them down and rejected the rest if they disagreed with these authorities. The passages selected were grouped together according to the ideas they repesented. The work is divided into eight chapters and is, therefore, called *Aṣṭa-grantha.* The work treats of matter (bhūta, bhauta). and mind (citta, caitta) with all their bearings, giving definitions and classifications when necessary. Among the subjects discussed, we find the following topics, such as Saṁyojana or the bond of human passions, Jñāna or knowledge, Indriya (organs), Samādhi (meditation), Dṛṣṭi or view.[1]

Six padas to the Jñānaprasthāna

Jñānaprasthāna is the principal work ; it is the 'body' or *kāya*, which has six feet or *pada* as supplementary volumes. Besides these, it has branches, the Vibhāṣā or commentaries and the like literature, which were rendered into Chinese by Hiuen-tsang

The first of the six *padas* is the *Saṅgīti Paryāya.* This treats of its materials according to their numerical order such as, Ekottara-dharma paryāya etc. up-to Daśa-dharma paryāya or the categories of ten. The authorship of the book is ascribed by Yaśo-

1 *ERE*, Vol. 11. Article—Sarvāstivāda.

mitra, the author of *Sphutārtha* and the Tibetan histrographer Buston, to Mahākauṣṭila and to Sāriputra by the Chinese authorities. Both these men are personal disciples of the Buddha and it does not seem probable that either of the two could be author of this work. The semi-historical portion of the book tells us that Sāriputra inspired by the Buddha, expounded this philosophy. The work was indeed compiled by a person of ability, but attributed to some contemporary of the Buddha by later generations. The author collected the more important Dharmas taught by the Buddha for suppressing the ten heterodoxical theses of the Vajjian monks.

(1) Saṅgīti Paryāya

Prakaraṇapāda is the second of the six padas of *Jñāna-prasthāna*, translated by Hiuen-tsang. More than two hundred years ago Guṇabhadra and Buddhayaśas (A. D. 435-443) translated this treatise (Nanjio, 1292). The author of this treatise is one Vasumitra,[1] who according to Hiuen-tsang composed it in a monastery at Puṣkalavatī. This treatise tries to group the subjects under a few principal heads, while the *Saṅgīti* arranges its subjects in the numerical order. There are eight chapters ; the first deals with the distinction of five subjects, such as Rūpa, Citta, Caitta-dharma, Citta-viprayukta-saṁskāra, Asaṁskṛta-dharma ; the second chapter with the distinction of ten kinds of knowledge ; the third with the distinction of Āyatana or twelve organs and objects of sense ; the fourth with the distinction of seven categories ; the fifth with the distinction of minor passions ; the sixth with the exposition of the things that can be comprehended or inferred (Anumeya ?) ; the seventh with the distinction of one thousand questions, such as Śikṣāpadas, Śrāmaṇyaphalas, ārya-vaṁsas etc. ; the eighth or the last chapter gives a resumé of the whole.

(2) Prakaraṇapāda

The *Vijñānakāya* (Nanjio, 1291) is the third of the six padas

1 For Vasumitra, see Watters, *On Yuan Chang*, Vol. I, pp. 273ff.

of the Sarvāstivāda śāstra. The title seems to mean "Body or group of (subjects connected with) consciousness." The alleged author of the treatise is Devaśarmā, who compiled this work, according to Hiuen-tsang, in Viśoka near Śrāvasti: It deals with the following subjects: Pudgala, Hetupratyaya, Ālambanapratyaya, and other miscellaneous subjects.

(3) Vijñānakāya

The *Dhātukāya* (Nanjio,1282) is the fourth of the six padas of the Sarvāstivāda Abhidharma translated by Hiuen-tsang. According to Yaśomitra and Buston, Purṇa, and according to Chinese authorities Vasumitra, was the author of the book. Kwei-chi, the great disciple of Hiuen-tsang says that there were several recensions of this work. "The larger text," he adds, "consisted of 6,000 ślokas. Afterwards, as it was found too complicated, it was abridged by a scholar in two forms, one in 900 ślokas, the other in 500 ślokas. The present translation consists 830 ślokas (and is the middle one)."

(4) Dhātukāya

The work is divided into two principal khaṇḍas: The first khaṇḍa deals with (a) ten Mahābhūmika-dharmas, such as, vedanā, sanjñā, cetanā, sparśa, etc.; (b) ten kleśa-mahā-bhūmika-dharmas such as, avidyā, pramāda, etc.; (c) ten upa-kleśa-bhūmika, such as, krodha, mātsarya, īrṣyā, etc.; (d) five moral defilements, such as, kāma-lobha, rūpa-lobha, etc.; (e) five views on dṛṣṭi, such as, satkāya, antagraha, mithyā, etc.; (f) five dharmas, such as, vitarka, vicāra, vijñāna, etc. Then, follows a series of ideas, sensations, etc. all resulting from the six sense organs. The second khaṇḍa deals with the mutual relations of 88 categories discussed under sixteen sections. It is not possible to go into further details; but the nature of the work introduced by Hiuen-tsang into China can fairly be estimated.

The fifth pada of the Sarvāstivāda Vinaya is the *Dharma-skandha* (Nanjio, 1296). Ching-mai (A. D. 664), a learned monk who helped Hiuen-tsang in translating this work writes that "Dharma-skandha is the most important of the Abhidharma works and the fountain-head of the

(5) Dharma-skandha

Sarvāstivāda system. It is a work of Mahā-maudgalāyana." Though it is now placed among the supplementary *padas*, it is not inferior in its matter and form to the principal work of the school, the *Jñāna-prasthāna*. The work is divided into twenty-one chapters, *viz.* śikṣāpada, śrotāpannas and their attainments ; attainment of purity ; result of śramaṇaship ; abhijñā-pratipāda or mental experience ; āryavaṁśa or noble race of Buddha's disciples ; right victory ; constituents of vṛddhipāda or magic power ; smṛtyupasthāna ; ārya-satya, dhyāna or meditation ; apramāṇa, arūpa ; bhāvanā-samādhi ; bodhyāṅga or branches of knowledge ; kṣudravastuka or miscellaneous matters ; indriyas ; āyatanas ; Skandhas ; nānādhātu, pratītya-samutpāda in which the twelve nidānas are explained. The contents of the book clearly manifest the highly philosophical nature of the work.

Prajñaptiśāstra, the sixth pāda, a later composition unknown to Hiuen-tsang.

Hiuen-tsang translated the above five *padas* only ; the last pada *Prajñaptiśāstra* was not translated till the 11th century by Dharmarakṣa (1004-1058). The work is considered as of doubtful character and authority and seems to be unknown in the time of Hiuen-tsang. It may be mentioned here that this is the only work, of which we find a Tibetan translation. The rest do not exist in the Tibetan.[1]

Mahāvibhāṣā

Besides these canonical works of the Sarvāstivāda Abhidharma, Hiuen-tsang translated other important works of this school, some of which in value and importance sometimes excelled the original canon. Such a work is the *Mahāvibhāṣā*, the great commentary on the *Jñānaprasthāna*. Vibhāṣā means originally 'option.' The idea seems to be that numerous opinions collected from the composers (500 Arhats) were compared with one another, and the best of them were selected as orthodox doctrines of this school. The Chinese explain it as 'comprehensive exposition,' or as 'various opinions.' Tradition says

1 The material of the Abhidharma literature is taken from an article by Takakusu, The Sarvāstivāda Abhidharma Books, *Journal of the Pali Text Society*, 1904-05, pp. 67-146.

that the Vibhāṣās are connected with the council of Kaniṣka and according to some, Aśvaghoṣa is also connected with its revision. Hiuen-tsang tells us that in the council held under Kaniṣka, the compilation of an upadeśa on the sūtras and of a Vibhāṣā on the Vinaya and Abhidharma was the chief object. One Vasumitra, who was the president of the council of Kāshmir, seem to be connected with the compilation of the Vibhāṣā.

Three Vibhāṣās or commentaries

There are three *Vibhāṣās* on the Abhidharma, the earliest of which was translated by the Kāshmir-Vaibhāṣika Saṅghadeva in A. D. 383 (Nanjio, 1299). The second translation was done by Buddhavarma and Tao-tai (A. D. 425-427). In a preface, it is said, "At a time more than six hundred years after the death of the Buddha, there were in North India 500 Arhats......who compiled the Vibhāṣā in order to suppress various opinions. A priest Tao-tai, went to the west of the Onion range, and obtained the Sanskrit text in 100,000 verses." Buddhavarma assisted by about three hundred men translated the Vibhāṣā in 110 fasc. in A. D. 427. In the meantime the Liang dynasty was destroyed and in the chaos that followed the copy of the translation was lost. The first 60 fasc. were however again produced : that is, out of eight granthas only the first four were restored ; therefore the book did not exist completely in China. Hiuen-tsang took up the work and translated it for four years from 656 to 659. It consists of eight groups, just as the *Jñāna-prasthāna*, divided into forty-three sections of 200 fasciculi ; there are 1,43,844 Chinese letters and 3,630 pages in the Tripiṭaka. The Vibhāṣā was offered in a complete form by Hiuen-tsang. The work is an encyclopaedia of Buddhist philosophy ; in it opinions of several ancient and contemporary philosophers of various schools are carefully registered and discussed. During the period of its compilation there seem to have been several philosophers, who were generally styled the Abhidharma Mahāśāstrins. There were two bodies of Śāstrins, differing in their views from each other, and these are often referred to in the text as Kāshmir-śāstrins and Gāndhāra-śāstrins, that is the scholars of

Kāshmir and the scholars of Gāndhāra. Later on, the Kāshmir-Vaibhāṣikas became famous in Northern India and outside.[1]

Vasubandhu's *Abhidharma Koṣa* in Chinese for the second time.

But the greatest of the philosophical works that was translated by Hiuen-tsang was Vasubhandhu's *Abhidharmakoṣa*, both Kārikā and commentary. The circumstances under which Vasubandhu wrote this book has been described above in connection with his life by Paramārtha. In the Kārikās Vasubandhu showed his leaning towards the Vaibhāṣikas, that is, the philosophy of the Sarvāstivāda according to the Abhidharma teaching and the Vibhāṣā-teachers ; but in his commentary Vasubandhu was more inclined towards the Sautrāntikas, that is, the philosophy of the Sarvāstivādins, as explained by in the Sūtras and criticised the Vaibhāṣikas very thoroughly.

The Kārikā and the Commentary.

Vasubandhu, though originally a Sarvāstivādin, was at heart a free-thinker, and did not, therefore, follow either his orthodox tenets or his lately adopted Sautrāntika ideas, as we have seen in his life. Scholars designated his guiding principle 'a preference of reason,' and his eccelecticism is shown in his great work, the Koṣa.[2]

What the Koṣa explained.

A very brief description of this epoch-making work of Vasubandhu, now translated by Hiuen-tsang (it was once before done into Chinese by Paramārtha—see above), may not be out of place. The *Kārikas* exist in the original Sanskrit, but not the commentary ; the latter exists in Tibetan, which has been largely used by Stcherbatsky[3] in many of his learned treatises on Buddhism and the entire Chinese translation of Hiuen-tsang has been given in French[4] by de la Vallee Poussin. The Abhidharma Koṣa is divided into nine chapters ;

1 *J.P.T.S.*, 1904-5 loc. cit.

2 Article—Vasubandhu, *ERE*, vol. 12.

3 The conception of Buddhism and the meaning of 'Dharma', RAS, 1923, pp. 76-91 ; The Soul theory of the Buddhists—*Bulletin de Il'Academie des Sciences de Russie*, 1919, pp. 823-958 : *The Conception of Nirvāṇa*, Leningraad, 1927.

4 *Abhidharmakoṣa*, in 6 Vols., E. J. Brill, Leiden.

the first eight chapters have *Kārikās*, 602 in number, which have been commented upon at considerable length in prose. The ninth chapter has no Kārikās being entirely in prose. The subjects treated in its nine chapters are as follows :—

1. *Dhātu-nirdeśa*, or a treatment of the *Dhātus* showing the nature of the substance of all things, 44 Kārikās.

2. *Indriya-nirdeśa*, contains a treatment of the *indriyas* and of the function of the Dharmas, 74 Kārikās.

These two chapters contain a general treatment of the *Sāśrava* and the *anāśrava*, that is to say, the 'defiled' or 'natural' and the 'undefiled' or 'supernatural,' the former being *Saṁsāra* and the latter *Nirvāṇa*.

3. *Loka-nirdeśa*, or a treatment of the world (Loka) considered as the outcome of the *Sāśrava*, 99 Kārikās.

4. *Karma-nirdeśa*, or a treatment of Karma, considered as the cause of Sāśrava or Saṁsāra, 132 Kārikās.

5. *Anuśaya-nirdeśa*, or a treatment of the latent evils considered as a condition (pratyaya) of the Sāśrava or Saṁsāra, 69 Kārikās.

These three chapters explain in details the causes and effects of Saṁsāra.

6. *Ārya-pudgala-nirdeśa*, or a treatment of Arhatship considered as an effect of Anāśrava or nirvāṇa, 83 Kārikās.

7. *Jñāna-nirdeśa*, or a treatment of knowledge (prajñā), considered as the cause (hetu) of anāśrava or nirvāṇa, 61 Kārikās.

8. *Samādhi-nirdeśa*, or a treatment of Dhyāna or meditation considered as a pratyaya of anāśrava or nirvāṇa, 39 Kārikās.

9. There are no Kārikās in this chapter. It contains a refutation of Ātman-theories of the Sāṇkhya, Vaiśeṣika and the Vatsiputriya school.[1]

Vasubandhu's *Abhidharmakoṣa*, when circulated among the scholars, at once raised a storm of discussion among the adherents of the Sarvāstivādins. Vasubandhu was no respector of person-

1 See Sogen Yamakami, *Buddhist Thought*, Cal. Univ., 1914, pp. 109-11.

alities and old traditions and he never scrupled to change his views when he thought he was in the right.

At that time a great Vaibhāṣika named Saṅghabhadra was living in Central India. Paramārtha, the biographer of Vasubandhu, tells us that Saṅghabhadra compiled two works and refuted the *Koṣa* in favour of the vibhāṣā which Vasubandhu had repudiated. He also is said to have challenged Vasubandhu to a personal debate, which the latter evaded on the plea of old age.

Saṅghabhadra's Koṣa-karakā or Nyāyānusāra a reply to Vasubandhu's Koṣa.

Saṅghabhadra wrote a work called the *Nyāyānusāra* or Conformity of Truth in 1,20,000 ślokas. Hiuen-tsang says that the original name of the thesis was *Koṣa-karakā* or 'Koṣa-hailstorm,' which was subsequently changed into *Nyāyānusāra* by the author, out of respect for his departed opponent. The work was manifestly written to demolish the pretention of the *Koṣa*. Saṅghabhadra's other work, *Samaya pradīpikā*, containing 10,000 ślokas, explains the doctrines of the Vibhāṣā school. The author himself writes thus about his own work : "I have already written a treatise and called it *Nyāyānusārā*. Those who are fond of philosophical speculations have to study it. With the phrases and sentences so detailed and elaborate, a research into it is a matter of difficulty. One will not be able to understand it unless one works hard. In order to make it easy to be understood by curtailing the elaborate composition, I again compiled the *Samaya-pradīpikā*. I embellished and preserved Vasubandhu's Kārikās, and regarded them as the source of reference." * * "I cut short those extensive concluding arguments which are found in the Nyāyānusāra, and set forth the right expositions against Vasubandhu's Śāstra to illustrate the true excellent doctrine to which we adhere."[1]

Samaya prādīpikā supports Vibhāṣā school.

Both these works of Saṅghabhadra were rendered into Chinese by Hiuen-tsang-*Nyāyānusāra* in eighty fasc. (Nanjio, 1265) and *Samaya-prodīpikā or Abhidharma (pitaka) prakaraṇa-śāstra* in forty fasc. (Nanjio, 1266). The above passage is from the

1 *JPTS, loc. cit.* pp. 137-138.

Chinese translation of Hiuen-tsang. There is no trace of these works in the original Sanskrit and Hiuen-tsang's translations are the only source of our knowledge.

Hiuen-tsang translated practically all the important books on the Sarvāstivāda from the Vaibhāsika as well as from the Sautrāntika points of view. None of these books is preserved in the original Sanskrit and we are indebted to Hiuen-tsang for our knowledge of those great masters of the Buddhist philosophy. The Sarvāstivāda as a school of philosophy was well-known throughout the length and breadth of India as well as in Serindia, Indonesia and China. Its Vinaya was the most widely accepted rules of conduct on the Buddhist church throughout Buddhist Asia and we shall have occasion to learn more of it in the Tibetan section. But when Hiuen-tsang translated the philosophical works of the Sarvāstivāda school, the school as a sect had practically disappeared and the Yogācāra was predominant both as a school of thought and sect. But the importance of Sarvāstivāda as a system of philosophy could in no way be denied or minimised by a careful scholar. Although an ardent follower of Yogācāra, Hiuen-tsang could not therefore neglect the philosophy of the Sarvāstivādins.

But it is to Hiuen-tsang that we owe the preservation of the valuable treatises of Yogācāra. The principal work of the school is the *Yogācārabhumi śāstra* (Nanjio, 1170). It is ascribed to the revelation of Maitreya the future Budha, to Asaṅga, who is said to have gone to the Tuṣita Heaven to receive the message. This contains descriptions of the practice of Yoga, and the seventeen stages or Bhūmis one successively attains through it. Hiuen-tsang translated the whole work in 100 fasc. The Sanskrit text is said to have consisted of 40,000 ślokas or granthas.

Hiuen-tsang translates the Yogācāra works of Asaṅga.

Asaṅga condensed the whole philosophy into a short manual called *Mahāyāna Samparigraha*, which was given in Chinese by Hiuen-tsang (Nanjio. 1247). But the book had twice before appeared in Chinese—once translated by Buddhaśānta in A. D. 531 (Nanjio,

Asaṅga's Mahāyāna Samparigraha.

1184) and again by Paramārtha in 563 A. D. (Nanjio, 1183). The commentaries to this work received no less attentian by the scholars in China.

One Bodhisattva Wu-hsin (Agotra ?), of whom we know nothing, wrote a commentary to this which was translated by Hiuen-tsang in 10 fasc. (Nanjio, 1171, 1). The other commentary on Samparigraha was by Asaṅga's brother Vasubandhu, which appeared thrice in Chinese. (18 fasc) The first was the translation made by Paramārtha ; Dharmagupta's (A. D. 590-616) was the second translation, while Hiuen-tsang's was the third (10 fasc). In the Chinese Tripiṭaka all the four translations of the commentary on Asaṅga's Samparigraha are found in one place (Nanjio, 1171).

The *Prakaraṇa-āryavācā* (Nanjio, 1177) is an exposition of the moral and practical aspects of the Yogācāra system by Asaṅga himself. Hiuen-tsang translated it in 20 fasc divided into 11 chapters. Asanga's *Abhidharma Saṅgīti Sūtra* (Nanjio, 1245) ascribed to Maitreya is really a compostion of Asaṅga, to which Vasubandhu wrote a learned commentary, which was more prized by people than the text itself. The *Kārikās* of Asaṅga were for the first time translated by Hiuen-tsang (Nanjio, 1245) along with the thesis of Vasubandhu. The thesis of Vasubandhu had already once been done into Chinese by Paramārtha, (Nanjio, 1248).

Vasubandhu's com. on Asaṅga's works also translated.

Vasubandhu as a supporter of the Yogācāra wrote learned commentaries on the principal works of the sect. But his intellectual activities were not confined to writing commentaries ; he wrote a few original treatises on Vijñānavāda, which for their learning and logic made Yogācāra into a profound philosophical system. Some of Vasubandhu's important works had already been translated by Bodhiruci and Paramārtha. The *Vijñaptimātra-siddhi* (Nanjio, 1238, 1239, 1240) or *Viṁśatikā* was translated for the third time by Hiuen-tsang. The *Triṁśatikā*, which consists of thirty verses, gives the essentials of Vijñānavada in a nutshell.

Vijñaptimātra Siddh

The thesis of the *Vijñaptimātra* can be put very briefly here, which Hiuen-tsang himself upheld and which he wanted to preach in his own land. "It teaches that phenomena, both material and non-material, originate in mind, which is divided according to its action into eight 'ideas' (Vijñānāni), *viz.* (1-5) five ideas belonging to the five sense organs, (6) idea of mind (mano-vijñāna), (7) Mind-idea or Klistamano-vijñāna, (8) Ālaya-vijñāna. The seeds or *bīja* or possibilities of all phenomena are retained in the eighth idea, whence comes the so-called object world, in consequence of which we are disturbed and rove about in painful efforts after peace. If one once fully understands that there is nothing outside our mind, then the objective world becomes non-existant to us, and those eight confused ideas are turned to our benefit and they become enlightened wisdom or *Jñāna*, by means of which we can unite the *Tathatā* or suchness, which transcends speech and thought."[1]

The subjective idealism of Asaghoṣa was placed on sound philosophical basis by Vasubandhu. It may be mentioned here that when Hiuen-tsang visited India Yogācāra was the prevalent system of philosophy followed by the Buddhists of India. It produced a series of eminent thinkers in India, and Nālandā was the principal seat of that learning. Hiuen-tsang met here some of those great masters; his teacher Śilabhadra was the disciple of Dharmapāla, an eminent Yogācāra teacher of Nālandā, who wrote a commentary on the *Śata-śāstra* of Āryadeva, one of the greatest exponents of the Mādhyamika philosophy (see above—Kumārjiva) probably to refute the doctrines of the Mādhyamikas. Hiuen-tsang, it must be observed, never translated any book on Mādhyamaka, and it seems strange that he would suddenly develop a love for Āryadeva and spread the doctrines of his opponent in belief. It seems that Dharmapāla had written this commentary on it from the Yogācāra point of view, and Hiuen-tsang translated it on that score. (Nanjio, 1189, 1190.)

Dharmapāla of Nālandā com. on Āryadeva's *Śata śāstra*, translated.

1 *ERE.* Vol. 12, Article—Vasubandhu.

It was to Hiuen-tsang that China owes directly popularization of the Yogācāra system. His fame spread far and wide and even crossed the sea and students from Japan came to him to study the system he had brought from India. In China the sect is known as Fa-hsiang (Dharma-lakṣaṇa) and in Japan as Hosso.

Hiuen-tsang founds the Yogācāra sect in China.

The history of the sects of Buddhism may be of little importance to an ordinary Chinese Buddhist, but learned and devout monks could hardly keep themselves aloof from the details of the history of the origin of Buddhism and the subsequent development of the Saṅgha. Vasumitra's *I-pu-tsung-lun-lun* gave such a history in Sanskrit. The book is lost and the title of the original seem to be '*Aṣṭādaśa-nikāya-sūtra*'. There are three Chinese translations of this work. The earliest is ascribed to Kumārajīva; but this is doubted by critical editors and according to K'ai-yuan-lu, the most authentic of the catalogues, the work was not genuine and the earliest translation was done in the Chin Dynasty, the translator's name being unknown. The second version was made by Paramārtha, and Hiuen-tsang translated it for the third time.

History of Buddhist Sects.

Vasumitra's 'Aṣṭādaśa nikāya sūtra.'

The Buddhist literature is vast and rich; but "there is however, no so well-written work on the early Buddhist schools, southern and northern, as Vasumitra's treatise. It deals first with the origin of the Buddhist schools, giving the cause and approximate date of the schisms, and then it narrates the doctrinal propositions of the schools as held in common at the time of the divisions and also the so-called differentiated views among the later sectarians."

Vasumitra's work is not a voluminous one, it ennumerates in the shortest possible form the salient doctrines of the early schools, each of which once possessed a vast literature. Owing to its extreme conciseness it is not always easy to grasp its meaning. Fortunately however, Paramārtha wrote a commentary on it. Though this commentary is now lost, yet it was utilized by Kwei-chi (A. D. 682).

who prepared his own commentary in order to obviate the defects of Paramārtha's commentary." Since then many supper-commentaries were written both in China and Japan. [1] The book consists of three sections, *viz.*, (1) Introductory Verse, (2) Divisions of the early Buddhist school and. (3) lastly, doctrines of those schools.

Another historical work of importance was rendered by Hiuen-tsang. It is a 'Record of the duration of the Dharma,' spoken by Mahā-arhan Nandimitra, *Ta A-lo-han Nan-ti-mo-to-lo so shu fa-chu-chi* (Nanjio, 1466). It is said that Nandimitra lived eight hundred years after the Parinirvāṇa of the Buddha, in the capital of King Prasenajit. He was a native of Siṁhala (Ceylon).

Nandimitra's Sixteen Arhats or guardians of the Dharma

In the text we find Nandimitra explaining to a large assembly of monks and nuns how "the Buddha when about to enter Parinirvāṇa, entrusted the supreme Law to sixteen great Arhats and their followers ordering them to protect and maintain it and to prevent its being extinguished." Arhats, as a rule, belong to Hīnayāna theology and it has been argued that the book of Nandimitra belongs to Hīnayāna also. But Lèvi and Chavannes have convincingly proved that this work is Mahāyāna Sūtra. Visser, who had discussed the subject very thoroughly, acknowledges that 'a Mahāyānist must have written the *Fa-chu-chi*, in order to attach the Arhats to his doctrine and to connect the schools by means of a cult. This Syncretism changed the character of these saints, who instead of seeking the shortest way to nirvāṇa lengthened their lives to remain in the world as the protectors of the Law and its adherents. It agrees with the tendency of the Northern School to continually enlarge its pantheon and to make all kinds of saints and deites protectors of the doctrines. Thus, although their Bodhisattvas were

1 J. Masuda, Origin and doctrines of Early Indian Buddhist Schools, *Asia Major*, Leipzig Vol. 2, Fas. 1, 1925, p. 1-75, also *Journal of Letters*, Calcutta University 1920 Vol. 1, (incomplete). There are Tibetan version of Vasumitra's work ; translated by Wassilief. Der Buddhismus, pp. 222-284. Max Wallesser is bringing out another translation of the same, This is not the place to discuss critically the historical value of the above statements, See Kimura, *Hinayāna Mahajana* etc.. Calcutta University 1927.

great and mighty guardians of the Law, they still wanted other, more terrestrial protectors, at the same time connecting the southern school with their own doctrine."[1]

The importance of the book according to Lèvi lies in this that it gives for the first time a classification of Mahāyāna canon. The canon of Mahāyāna is variously classified by different Chinese catalogues and they differ from the list of the Tibetan Kanjur.[2]

Hiuen-tsang's intellectual outlook was not confined to the study and translation of the canonical works alone, and the works of Vasumitra and Nandimitra are instances of his interest in history. Not only this. His intellectual conspectus covered the Nyāya and the Vaiśeṣika system of thought and he was responsible for the translation of a few very important treatises on these systems. These two systems played an important rolè in the controversy between the Buddhist and Hindu philosophers and were most antogonistical towards Buddhism. To fight these learned opponents Buddhist philosophers in course of time developed a system of logic of their own. The entire Buddhist logical literature is preserved in Tibetan.

Nyāya and Viaśeṣika in Chinese.

According to tradition and history Dignāga is the father of Buddhist Logic. Hiuen-tsang rendered two of Dignāga's works, *viz.* *Nyāya-dvāra Tarka śāstra* (Nanjio, 1224) and *Ālambana-Parīkṣā* or *Ālambana Pratyayadhyāna śāstra* (Nanjio, 1173),[3] the latter had once been translated by Paramārtha with a different title, which means 'Śāstra on the dust of shapeless thought (Nanjio, 1172). The *Nyāya-dvāra* of Dignāga was once again translated by Yi-tsing (see below). This work is in verse and does not seem to be preserved in Tibetan.

Dignāga's works.

1 (W. Visser, The Arhats in China and Japan, *Ost-asiatische Zeitschrift* 1922-23, pp. 67-68).

2 The Chinese treatise has been translated by Prof. Sylvian Lévi and Chavannes, Les Seize Arhat Protectuers de la Loi, *Journal Asiatique* 1916, 167 pages. Also, Watters. The Eighteen Lohans of Chinese Buddhist Temples, *JRAS*, 1898, pp. 329-347.

3 Vidyabhusan's *History of Indian Logic*, Cal. Univ. p. 101.

Śankarasvāmi's Nyāyaprevśea

But the greatest confusion has arisen about the other work on Nyāya translated by Hiuen-tsang, *viz. Nyāya-praveśa.*[1] This book has been attributed to Dignāga by all modern writers on Indian literature; this theory was started by the late Vidyabhusana, who based his information on Tibetan sources—the most unhistorical documents, and has ever since been in vogue. But this had always been denied by Chinese scholars who attributed the *Nyāya-praveśa* to one Śankarasvāmin, a disciple of Dignāga. Kwei-chi, the great disciple of Hiuen-tsang, in his commentary on the *Nyāya* definitely said that Sankarasvāmin was the author. Suguira [2] also upheld Kwei-chi's theory. Tubiauski has proved on the strength of internal as well as external evidences that the *Nyāya-praveśa* and *Nyāya-dvāra* are not only different, but so different that they could not be produced by the same author.[3]

Jñānacandra's *Daśa-padārtha Vaiśeṣika.*

Nyāya and Vaiśeṣika go hand in hand in Hindu philosophy; therefore Hiuen-tsang translated a work on the Vaiśeṣika as well. This is the only treatise in Chinese, in which the Vaiśeṣika philosophy is explained. Of course, throughout the writings of the Buddhist philosophers, the Vaiśeṣika teachers, who are the most powerful opponents of Buddhism, figure but always as a vanquished foe. Hiuen-tsang translated the Daśapadārtha Vaiśeṣika sūtra

1 The original Sanskrit text has been edited by Principal A. Dhruva of the Baneres University (G.O.S) and the Tibetan translation has been edited by Principal Vidhusekhara Bhattacharya of Visvabharati (G.O.S. 1927). Principal Bhattacharya has contributed a valuable article in the *Indian Historical Quarterly* (Calcutta) 1927, March, p, 152ff. in which he upholds the old view of Vidyabhusan and rejects the personality of Sankarasvamin. Keith discusses it in *Indian Historical Quarterly*, 1928 and holds the old theory of Dinnaga. He refutes Tubianski's views. M. Tubianski, On the authorship of Nyāyspraveśa, *Bulletin de l' Academie des Sciences de l' USSR*, 1926, pp. 975-982.

2 *Hindu Logic as preserved in China and Japan*, Chicago, 1900.

3 A large number of Commentaries and theses on Indian Logic has been written in Chinese and Japanese based principally on the two books translated by Hiuen-tsang. In the Library of the Otani University there are about 120 works in Chinese and Japanese. All this vast literature was inspired by the two works of Dignaga and Sankara-svāmin. (Japanese Catalogue of the Otani University, Kyoto, Japan p. 261ff).

of Jñānacandra or Maticandra. This book has been translated with copious notes and explanations by a great Japanese professor, H. Ui. [1] According to him, Maticandra flourished not earlier than the first half of the sixth century A. D.

It is well-known that the orthodox Vaiśeṣika accepts Six Categories only (Sat-padārtha), such as Dravya (substance), Guṇa (attribute), Karma (action), Satta or Bhava (existence), Sāmānya-viśeṣa (universality-particularity) and Lakṣaṇa (inherence). According to Hindu tradition this theory was promulgated by Ṛṣi Uluka, who was also known as Kaṇāda. Pañcaśikhi received the theory of six categories from Kaṇāda. Various Hindu legends are recorded in Chinese by Kwei-chi, the disciple of Hiuen-tsang and a great commentator. Kwei-chi says that in course of time the Vaiśeṣika was divided into eighteen schools after Pañcaśikhi.

Jñānacandra or Maticandra, whose work was introduced by Hiuen-tsang in China, was a Vaiśeṣika teacher of great ability. He seems to differ from the orthodox school and might have been one of the teachers of the said eighteen schools, if such schools mentioned by Kwei-chi ever existed. The most obvious characteristics of Maticandra's treatise are : it acknowledges ten categories, adding four more, viz. Śakti (potentiality), Aśakti (non-potentiality), Sāmānyaviśeṣa (commonness) and Abhāva or Asat (non-existence). The treatise does no mention of Iśvara, as in the Vaśeṣika sūtra ; and there is no description of the way of emanicipation (mokṣa) ; even if the second sort of merit (dharma, one of the 24 attributes) corresponds to it, it is only a definition of it. As a consequence, the author does not allude to Yoga or Yogin, or anything supernatural. The description in general is throughout concise and has no superfluity or digression. [2]

No commentaries on this treatise were composed by Chinese Buddhists ; but later Japanese writers composed as many as ten commentaries.

---

1 The Vaisesika Philosophy, Royal Asiatic Society, 1917.

2 H. Ui, *ibid*, Introduction.

We have described only a few important works translated by Hiuen-tsang as it will not be possible to deal with all. The great monk came to India when Buddhism had begun to decay and he observed the neglect by the Hindus of Buddhist works. It was at an opportune moment that he came to India and carried hundreds of manuscripts to his native land; the Sanskrit manuscripts of Buddhism, specially philosophical, have almost completely disappeared both from India and China; but they are still preserved in the Chinese language, so they are not absolutely lost and scholars who would be willing to study the Hindu mind from all its aspects might still go to those Chinese sources.

Hiuen Tsang's contribution to History of Indian Culture.

Hiuen-tsang was not only a translator, but a great teacher too. A large number of Chinese and Japanese Buddhists had their training under him, whom he inspired to devote themselves to the study of Buddhism and to the spread of the message of the Lord.

Hiuen-tsang had a number of assistants to help him in his great translation, some of whom became famous as learned compilers and independent commentators. Of these the name of Kwei-chi (Nanjio, App. III, 27) is still remembered by all scholars. His valuable writings are indispensable to the study of the Buddhist philosophical works. He is also known as a compiler of several works on Dharmagupta Vinaya (Nanjio, 116, 1128, 1154, 1156). Hwui-li, [1] another disciple, compiled the biography of the master, (Nanjio, 1494), but it was left unfinished at his death. This was continued and completed by Yen-tsung. [2] He also compiled another work in 6 fasciculi, 'asserting that Śramaṇas ought not to bow before laymen' (Nanjio, 1480).

Hiuen-tsang's disciples

Some of his contemporaries, who are not actually mentioned as assisting him in the translation, are mentioned below.

Shih Chu-tung [3] whose original surname was Chao. He was

1 Nanjio, App, III, 24.
2 Nanjio App. III, 23.
3 Nanjio, App, II, 134.

a Chinese Śramaṇa who translated four works in 5 fasc., all Dhāraṇīs,[1] between 627 and 653 A. D. Chie-fan-ta-mo (Bhagavad-dharma) ? [2] was a śramaṇa of Western India, who translated only one work on Dhāraṇī (Nanjio, 320). His date is not known, but he seems to be a monk of this period. Atigupta (?) [3] was a śramaṇa of Central India, who arrived in China in A. D

Atigupta's *Dhārani Saṁgraha*

652 and in the following two years translated a voluminous work on Dhāraṇī in 13 fasc. (Nanjio, 363). This work contains 75 dhāraṇīs. [4]

In A. D. 653 arrived in China another monk of Central India named Nandi or Punyopāya (Nanjio App II, 137). This man

Punyopaya comes to China with 1500 manuscripts.

brought with him a collection of *more than 1500 different texts* or copies of the Tripiṭaka of both the Mahāyāna and Hīnayāna schools. Nandi had made this large collection while travelling in India and Ceylon. In 656 he was sent by the Chinese Emperor Kao-tsung (A. D. 650-684), to the country of Kouen-lun i. e. Pulo Condore island in the China Sea to find some strange medicine. Having returned to China in 663 A. D., he translated three works, one of which was lost by 730 A. D.

Tu Hsin-i (Nanjio, App II, 140), a Chinese layman, and a

Tu Hsin-i.

member of the Foreign office translated a well-known Dhāraṇī called *Sarva urgati-pariśodhana-uṣṇīśa-vijaya* (Nanjio, 349). Buddhatrāta [5] a śramaṇa of Kubha, whose exact date is not known, translated one work. Buddhapāla was also a monk of Kubha ; he came to China in A. D. 676 and translated only one work.

The intellectual and spiritual level of the Chinese Buddhists had attained a very high water-mark by this time and as a sign

1 Nanjio 318, 325, 329, 494.

2 Nanjio App, II, 135.

3 Nanjio App II, 136.

4 For details see Courant, *Catalogue des Livres Chinois des Bibiliotheque Natinale*.... Geuthner, Paris, pp. 488-500 also Rajendralal, p. 80.

5 Nanjio App II, 141.

of the assimilation of Buddhist culture, new sects founded by Chinese monks, rose within the Buddhist Saṅgha. Tao-hsuen, a Buddhist monk. emphasized discipline and asceticism as the essential part of the religious life. This school bases itself on Indian authorities, but it does not appear that in thus laying stress on the Vinaya it imitated any Indian sect, although it caught the sptrit of the early Hinayāna schools. "The numerous works of the founder indicate a practical temperament inclined not to mysticism or doctrinal subtlety but to biography, literary history and Church Government." Thus he continued the series called *Kao-seng-chuan* or the Memoires of Eminent priests who lived between 67 and 519 A. D. compiled by Hwui-chiao in A. D. 519 (Nanjio, 1490 ; 14 fasc) ; he added 331 persons separately and 160 more in the course of narration (Nanjio 1493 in 40 fasc), who lived in China between A. D. 519 and 645. He wrote a history of the Śākya family (Nanjio, 1469) and a record of the country of Śākyamuni (Nanjio 1470).[1] He collected extracts, as well as documents relating to the controversies between Buddhists and Taoists.

Tao-hsuen founded the Vinaya school.

'Memoirs of Eminent Persons.'

'History of the Sākya family.'

The Dharmagupta Vinaya was the chief authority of Vinaya school and Tao-hsuen compiled a work on this four-fold Vinaya (Nanjio, 1120). It must be remembered that the Dharmagupta Vinaya was the most popular in China and it was further held that this Caturvarga Vinaya was a complete doctrine which included and transcended all the vehicles. But Tao-hsuen "insisted probably as a protest against the laxity or extravagance of many monasteries, that morality and discipline are the indispensable foundation of the religious life.'"[2]

In A. D. 664, the year Hiuen-tsang died, Tao-hsuen compiled a

1 See above—Hiuen Tsrng's book on travels.

2 Eliot, *op. cit*, p, 316.

catalogue of Chinese Tripiṭaka, which has come down to us (Nanjio, 1483). This catalogue is known as Nei-tien-lu, and is sub-divided into 10 sections. In the first section he gives a list of works, whether translations or original treatises in Chinese, with a biographical note of each author, and sums up the total number of works as 2487 in 8476 fasci. In the second section he divides the works, then in existence, about 799 in number, into three divisions. In the remaining sections Tao-hsuen makes several divisions and classifications, which are very complicated.[1]

TaoHsuen's Catalogue of Chinese Buddhist works, *Nei-tien-lu*

2487 works in 8476 fasc

A few more native writers deserve short notice. Tao-shi[2] in A. D. 656-660 compiled extracts on important doctrinal questions from various sources in 30 fasciculi (Nanjio 1474), another work in 100 fasc. was called 'Pearl-grove of the garden of Law.' This is an encycolpædia, containing extracts from the Tripiṭaka (Nanjio, 1482). Tsin-mai[3] who was a priest, compiled a work called *Ku-chin-i-ching-tu-chi* (Nanjio, 1487). It is a record of the events of ancient and modern translations of the Sūtras, which contains all the titles of translations from the venerable Kāśyapa Mātaṅga A. D. 67 to Hiuen-tsang A. D. 664 together with short biographical notes. This work is said to have been written on the figures of these translators, drawn on the wall of the 'translation hall' in Ta-ts'u-an-ssu monastery, in which Hiuen-tsang lived.

Tao-shi, 656-660

Tsin-mai

Fu-li[4] a priest wrote a polemical work in A. D. 681, in defence of Buddhism (Nanjio, 1498) against the charges by an official made in a work called *Shih-tien-chi-i* or 'a consideration of doubts in the Buddhist book.' Probably this is the last work written during the reign of Kao-tsung (650-684).

Fu-li, A. D. 681

1 Nanjio, *Catalogue*, Intro. xix; also Bagchi, xlviii.
2 Nanjio App III, 22.
3 Nanjio, App III, 25.
4 Nanjio, App III, 26.

XVI. Age of Empress Wu Tso-Tien

The Chinese empire under the first Emperors of the T'ang dynasty was the largest ever ruled by any Chinese dynasty. It extended from the Yellow Sea to the Aral Sea, and from Siberia to the Southern-most point in Farther India. The name of T'ai-tsung was not unknown to the Greek Emperor Theodosius of Constantinople, whose ambassodor reached the court of Chang-an in 640 A. D. Yazdegard, the last of the Sassanian line of Persian kings having been hunted by the Muslims from province to province, threw himself on the protection of Tai-tsung. His son died in the palace at Chang-an. Even the early Caliphs were no less eager to cultivate the friendship of the powerful Chinese emperor than their fallen foe, the last king of Persia. Missions came to Chang-an from Medina, with precious stones and horses. Japan accepted the intellectual leadership of China and Japanese monks came to study under Hiuen-tsang and other teachers ; Chinese culture, her manners and customs were adopted by Japan. On the west they came in contact with the Arabs on another plane. Between them, a monopoly of the world's commerce was successfully maintained. Fleets of Chinese junks sailed proudly into the Persian gulf, while thousands of Arab merchants settled in the southern cities of the coast. [1]

Glory of the T'angs

T'ai-tsung also established international relation with India and Tibet. Tibet had just awakened under the leadership of the great king Srong-sam-gam-po, and T'ai-tsung established a matrimonial alliance with the king by marrying his daughter with him. In India King Harṣavardhana was a contemporary ruler of T'ai-tsung. Harṣa was a mighty prince with the broad outlook of a statesman and the genuine sympathy of a devotee. He must have gained much information from Hiuen-tsang, who lived in his

China's relation with Tibet and India

1 From La Ung Bing, op. cit. p. 140-141.

capital for some time and wanted to cultivate friendship with T'ai-tsung. He therefore, sent a brahmana envoy in A. D. 641 to China, who returned in 643, accompained by a Chinese mission bearing a reply to Harṣa's despatch. The Chinese mission did not return to China till 645. The next year a second mission

Wang Hsuen-t'se in India

headed by Wang Hsuan-ts'e, who had been the second in command of the earlier embassy, came to India with an escort of thirty hosrsemen. Early in 647 or at the close of 646 Harṣa died, leaving no heir, and an usurper named Arunāsatva (?) or Arjuna (?) a minister of the late king, seized the throne.

Wang Hsuen-t'se fled to Tibet, where the great Srong-sang-gam-po was reigning; he collected an army, marched against the usurper and brought him as a prisoner to China.

Wang Hsuen-t'se once more visited the scene of his adventures, being sent by the Emperor Kao-tsung in A. D. 657 to offer robes to the holy places of the Buddhists. He entered India through Tibet and Nepal and after visiting Buddha-Gaya and other sacred places he returned home through Kapiśa or N. Afghanistan.[1]

Kao-tsung was a powerful ruler and his fame had spread throughout the civilized world, but at home he became a puppet in the hand of a harem lady named Wu-shih or better known as Wu Tso tien and delegated all his regal power to her. Wu Tso-tien was doubtless a powerful personality and no one can deny that the deeds of Wu Tso-tien entitled her to a place among the greatest

Empress Wu Tso-tien a devout Buddhist

women of the world. After the death of her husband Kao-tsung, she became the ruler of the country. During the last fifteen years of her reign, (which altogether consisted of 22 years, 682-704), the dysastic name was even changed from T'ang to Chou. Wu Tso-tien was a Buddhist, but she cannot be said to be an ornament of the

1 Levi, Les missions de Wang Hiuan-T'se dans l'Inde *J. As.*, 1900; Smith, *Early History of India*, 4th Ed., pp. 366-387. Giles, *Chinese Biog. Dict.* No. 2181.

religion she professed. She gave encouragement to Buddhist studies and offered protection to Hindu monks. She got a magnificent monastery built for the monks and some of the principal statues in the caves of Lung-men were made at her expense.[1]

It is said that the well-known Mahāyāna sūtra *Mahāmegha* was presented to her and circulated among the people with her approval. About 600 she assumed divine honours and styled herself a Maitreya or Avalokita.[2] During her regime which lasted nearly half-a-century many Hindu monks came from India and Serindia and many Chinese monks went on pilgrimage to India following the footsteps of Hiuen-tsang, described in the next chapter.

Divākara A. D. 676

Divākara,[3] a śramaṇa of Central India, came to China in A. D. 676 and translated eighteen works in 34 fasc. But in a preface to his works by the Empress Wu Tso-tien, it is said that Divākara translated only 10 works with his Chinese assistants. His translations are mainly sūtras, two being only Abhidharmas. One was the translation of the commentary on Vasubandhu's *Pañcaskandhaka-śāstra* (Nanjio, 1175) by Sthitamati[4] called Pañcaskandhaka Mahāvaipulya śāstra (Nanjio, 1175). Another abhidharma translated by Divākara was a commentary on the famous *Vajrachedikā* by Bodhisattva Kung-te-shih [Guṇada ?] (Nanjio, 1192). But of all his works, a translation of the great Buddha epic, *Lalitavistara*, was the most important which won him an everlasting name in Chinese literature. This beautiful epic has forunately come down to us in the original Sanskrit. It is a big work embodying a description of the life of the Buddha. According to some Chinese authorities, it belongs

1 Eliot, *ibid.*, III, 260 ; also Chavannes, *Mission Archeologique*, Tome 1, 2e partie.

2 Eliot, *ibid.*, p. 261.

3 Nanjio, App. II, 139.

4 Sthitamati also commented on Asanga's *Abhidharma Saṅgīti śāstra* (Nanjio, 1178, 1179) and also wrote a commentary on Nāgārjuna's *Madhyamaka śāstra* on the first 13 chapters (Nanjio, 1316).

to the Sarvāstivāda school.[1] But the work is decidedly a Mahāyāna work, of course, of the earlier type, which is a redaction of an older Hīnayāna work expanded and embellished so as to give it a Mahāyāna bias. This sūtra, it is said, was translated four times, but, Divākara's is the only complete translation, the first and the third had already been lost by 730 A. D., when the K'ai-yuen-lu was compiled. The second and the fourth translations are in existence The second or the first extant translation in 8 fasc. of 30 chapters, was done by Dharmarakṣa in A. D. 308 (Nanjio, 160). Divākara's translation is in 12 fasc. of 27 chapters and its contents have been given by Beal in his Catalogue (pp. 17-19). But the book is well-known[2] in Sanskrit and no detailed analysis is needed. To the Chinese translation of Divākara, the Empress Wu Tso-tien herself wrote a preface.

Translation of Lalitavistara

In 689 came to China a Hindu monk from Khotan named Devapriya.[3] He translated six works in 7 fasc. of which the most important seems to be the translation of Bodhisattva Sthiramati's *Dharma-dhatu-aviśeṣata-śāstra* (Nanjio, 1256, 1318). At this time, a Hindu brahmana by caste was living in China, as an envoy of some Hindu Prince. The son of this brahmana, whose Chinese name is Hwei-chi translated one work only (Nanjio, 1077)[4] in A. D. 692. The next year A. D. 693 came Ratnacinta[5] a śramana of Kashmir (Kia-shi-mi-lo) and translated seven works in 9 fasc. The same year also came to China, another great Pandit from India, named Bodhiruci, of whose work we shall know more.

Several monks visit China

Brahmana living in China

1 Wassilief, *Buddhismus*, p. 114.

2 The Sanskrit Text was first edited by Rajendralal Mitra, Bibl. Indica A. S. B. 1853—1877. An English translation of a few chapters was also done by Dr. Mitra. *Lalita-vistara* Dr. S. Lefmann... Berlin, 1874. Also Halle, 1902-1908.

3 Nanjio App. II. 143.

4 Nanjio, App. II, 144.

5 Nanjio, App. II, 148.

Almost about the same time Śikṣānanda, a native of Khotan,[1] came to China and translated some very important works brought from his native town.

Śikṣānanda's name has been transliterated into Chinese as Sheu-cha'-nan-to and is translated as Hio-hi, literally 'learning-joy.'

Sikṣānanda of Khotan A. D. 695-710

He was an inhabitant of Khotan and was a śaka (che) by race. He had great ambition in life and studied profoundly the literature of the Mahāyāna as well as the Hinayāna branches of Buddhism. This was the epoch when the Chinese empress Wu Tso-t'ien was popularising the Mahāyāna in China. It was discovered at this stage that certain sections of the Avataṁsaka sūtra were missing in the Sanskrit copy preserved in China. She came to know however that at Khotan a complete text of the sūtra existed and sent there an envoy in search of the manuscript, as well as for inviting a learned person who could translate it. As a result of the mission Śikṣānanda came to China with a complete copy of the Avataṁsaka sūtra. He was installed in the vihara of Ta-pie-chung and began to translate the Avataṁsaka in A. D. 695. The Empress used to come in person to assist him and finally wrote a preface to the translation. A śramaṇa from South India named Bodhiruci who happened to be living in China at that time and a Chinese monk named Yi-tsing[2] read out the Sanskrit text while he translated it. The work was finished in A. D. 698. In A. D. 700 he began his famous translation of the *Laṅkāvatara sūtra* which he did in collaboration with many Chinese scholars whose names are mentioned in the biography. In A. D. 704 he once returned to Khotan escorted by two Chinese. When Ho-ti ascended the throne he invited Śiksānanda to his new capital in A. D. 708 and installed him in the monastery of Ta-kien fu ; but Śiksānanda did not live long and died in 710. It is said that he translated nineteen works of which only sixteen exist.[3]

1 Nanjio', App. II, 145. 2 See below.

3 I am indebted to Dr. P. C. Bagchi for this biography to be incorporated in the 2nd vol. of his *de Canon bonddhique*.

The largest text translated by Sikṣānanda was the Avataṁsaka which appeared in its entirety for the first time in Chinese in 8 fasc., the one that existed, done by Buddhabhadra three centuries back (A. D. 398-421) consisted of 60 fasc.

The Avataṃsaka sūtra is considered by a group of people to be the ultimate "consummation of Buddhist thought, Buddhist sentiment and Buddhist experience." Suzuki most eloquently speaks of this sūtra. He says, "To my mind, no religious literature in the world can ever approach the grandeur of conception, the depths of feeling and the gigantic scale of composition as attained by this sūtra. It is the eternal foundation of life from which no religious minds can turn back athirst or only partially satisfied. It is a great pity that this magnificent literature still remains concealed in a language not so universally accessible. Not only deeply speculative minds find satisfaction here but humble spirits and heavily oppressed hearts too will have their burdens lightened. Abstract truth so concretely, so symbolically represented here, and one will finally come to the realisation of the truth that even in a particle of dust the whole universe is seen reflected—not this visible universe only but a vast system of universe, conceivable by the highest mind only."[1]

Avataṁsaka sūtra in 80 fasc.

The Avataṁsaka school claims to have been founded by Boddhisattva Aśvaghoṣa, who is looked upon as its first Patriarch, Nāgārjuna being the second. Probably this is the reason of Śikṣānanda's translating *Śraddhotpāda śāstra* for the second time which is alleged to have been written by Aśvaghoṣa, and translated once before by Paramārtha. The Chinese version of the *Avataṁsaka* and the *Śradhotpāda* by Śikṣānanda helped no doubt to strengthen the school, which had been founded during the Chan dynasty (A. D. 557-589) by Fa-shun, the first historical Patriarch of the school, more than a century before Śikṣānanda.

Sraddhotpada śāstra.

1 Suzuki, The Laṅkāvatara sūtra, *The Eastern Buddhist*, Vol. IV, 1927-28, p. 201.

Fa-shun was the contemporary of Chi-yi, the founder of the T'ien-tai. He died in 640 A. D. in his 84th year. A large ancilliary literature developed in China when the sect came to its being.

Patriarches of the Avataṁsaka school

Fa-tsung[1] the third patriarch of the Avataṁsaka school, a contemporary of Śikṣānanda and his principal assistant in the translation of the *Śraddhotpāda*, wrote several treatises on the Avataṁsaka. He wrote a work on the distinction of the meaning of Ekayāna of the Avataṁsaka sūtra and several others of similar nature. Some of his books were written at the request of the Empress Wu Tso-tien.[2]

Śiksananda's Laṅkāvatara.

Śikṣānanda's translation of the *Laṅkāvatara sūtra* (Nanjio, 177) is as brilliant as his Avataṁsaka. The Empress herself wrote a preface to this work and it became very popular. There had been three translations in Chinese and the fourth[3] one in 7 fasc., was produced in 700-704. Fa-tsang remarks thus about the last translation, in which he himself took an important part:

Sikṣananda's 704 A.D.

"As to the present one, Śikṣānanda, master of the Tripiṭaka, of Yu-tien (Khotan) is the translator, who, after finishing the translation of the Avataṁsaka ... was ordered by the Empress Tso-tien to take up once more the task of translating the Laṅkāvatara.... The translation was roughly finished.... But before he had time to revise it, he was allowed to return to his native land by the Imperial order. In 702 Mi-t'o-shan, a master of the Tripiṭaka, came from *Tu-ho-lo*, who before coming to China had spent twenty-five years in India thoroughly mastering the Tripiṭaka...By Imperial order he was requested to revise Śikṣānanda's translation, aided by such translators as Fu-li, Fa-tsang, etc : Fu-li was engaged in giving final touch to the revised Chinese version, and an Imperial preface to the sūtra was written in which its merits were extolled.

1 Nanjio, III, 30.

2 Nanjio, 1591,1592.1593,1595,1599, 1602,1625.

3 For the first three translations of the Laṅkāvatāra see *ante* under Dharmakṣema, Guṇabhadra, Bodhiruci.

"As to the four-fasciculi translation [Guṇabhadra's] the rendering is not perfect, the wording is after the western grammar, which makes even men of superior intelligence confused, not knowing how to read it, while the ignorant and unlearned are apt to give wrong interpretations.

"The ten-fasciculi one [Bodhiruci's] is somewhat fuller in paragraphs and chapters [than the preceding one], but the sacred sense is not adequately expressed…

"The Empress regretting this inadequacy ordered another translation to be made. The present one was made by comparing in detail five Sanskrit copies, and after examining the two Chinese translations [of Guṇabhadra and Bodhiruci]."

The Empress Wu Tso-tein wrote a preface to the work in which she paid the highest tribute to Śikṣānanda and his assistants.

Comparison of the Versions.

A comparison of the three extant Chinese translations with the Sanskrit text of the *Laṅkāvatara sūtra* reveals many interesting points. It at once shows that Guṇabhadra's version is very much simpler and shorter than the others. In it the first and the last two chapters are missing altogether, and there is no chapter-divisions whatever in it. Bodhiruci has 18 chapter-headings, cut into shorter sections, while Śikṣānanda's has only 10, agreeing with Sanskrit as regards chapter-divisions.

Guṇabhadra being the oldest translator, represents a more primitive *Laṅkāvatāra* than the others. Guṇabhadra, it seems, wisely omitted the first chapter and the last two chapters of dhāraṇī and gāthā. It does not seem probable that the introductory chapter in the original was added at a later age, as has been suggested by Suzuki. Guṇabhadra's text is known as *Leng-kia-po-to-lo pao ching* or Laṅkāvatāra ratna sūtra. The title of the work proves beyond doubt that the story of Buddha's descent on Laṅkā (Ceylon)-peak was already a part of the treatise, which Guṇabhadra, however, omitted while translating. The ninth and tenth chapters are also omitted in Guṇabhadra's translation. Bodhiruci and Śikṣānanda's translations contain, in the ninth the dhāraṇis and in the tenth the gāthās. In the Sanskrit there are 884 verses taking up about one-fourth of the entire text. Of these over 200 are found in the main text itself, about 650 gāthās are newly-added ones. Śikṣānanda, however, excluded these repetitions from its gāthā chapter. There are 890 quatrains in Bodhiruci and 656 in Śikṣānanda. These verses of the *Sagāthakam* chapter express the thoughts of the text most definitely and they do not seem to be any part of the original work, so that they can easily be made into a separate work.[1]

The first chapter.

The first chapter, which is not found in Guṇabhadra's text gives the outlines of the whole sūtra in the form of a dialogue between the Buddha and Rāvana, Lord of the Rākṣasas in the Isle of Laṅkā. When the Buddha, coming out of the Nāga's palace, views the castle of Laṅka, he smiles and remarks that this was the place where all the Buddhas of the past had preached regarding the excellent understanding of Enlightenment realised in their inner consciousness, which is beyond the analysis of logic, and is not the state of mind attainable by the Tīrthikas, Śrāvakas and Prateyeka-Buddhas. The Buddha then adds that for this reason the same dharma will be propounded for Rāvana. In response to this, the latter, making all kinds of costly offerings to the Buddha, sings in the praise of his insight and virtues, "O Lord, instruct me in thy system of doctrine which is based on the self-nature of mind, instruct me in the doctrine of non-ego, free from prejudices and difilements, the doctrine that is revealed in thy inmost consciousness." In the conclusion of the first chapter, the Buddha reaffirms his doctrine of inner realisation.

But from the second chapter Rāvana disappears and the rest of the work is in the form of dialogues between the Buddha and the Bodhisattva Mahāmati.

The *Laṅkāvatāra sūtra* is generally held as one of the chief works on Vijñānavāda as it principally explains the Five Dharmas, the three characteristics of Reality (*svabhāva*), the eight kinds of consciousness (*vijñāna*), and the two forms of Non-ego

1 See Suzuki, *The Eastern Buddhist*, 1929, March, vol. V. No 1.

(*nairātmya*). In brief it teaches absolute idealism and refers to the Ālayavijñāna as the storage of all *karmic* seeds and is therefore looked upon as the principal yogācāra work. The subject-matter of the work is not systematically developed as in most Mahāyāna sūtras, but is developed by a series of notes of various lengths. The philosophical and religious ideas contained in these sutras are very difficult to comprehend, due to terseness of expression and the abstruse nature of the subject ; but the details of such speculations do not fall within the scope of the present work.[1]

The Laṅkāvatāra sūtra is closely connected with the Ch'an (Zen) Buddhism in China. According, to Tao-hsüuan's *Biographies of the High Priests,* it was Bodhidharma, who brought a copy of the *Laṅkāvatāra sūtra* and handed over the same to his disciple Hui-k'e. He rejected all the Buddhist Scripture, but is said to have told his disciple the following words :

"As I observe, there are no other sūtras in China but these, you take them for your guidance, and you will naturally save the world." This supposed connection between Bodhidharma and the sūtra has been greatly exaggerated by Zen disciples. But there has been emphatic protest against such phantastic theories and even a Zen master (985-1061) of the Sung dynasty, said boldly, "No, that is a mere invention of a busybody."

Tao-hsüan, the official biographer of the High priests traces the line of transmission from the beginning from master to disciple and show that the Laṅkāvatāra played an important part in the history of Zen. This sūtra attracted the attention of the intellectual Chinese Buddhists and Fa-tsang wrote a sort of general introduction to the study of the Laṅkāvatāra which is considered to be

1 For the detailed study see Suzuki. *Zen Buddhism*, pp. 74-82. 1927, also. Suzuki, various articles in *The Eastern Buddhist*, 1927-28-29.

The Laṅkāvatāra Sūtra Ed. by Bunyiu Nanjio, Bibliotheca Otaniensis, Kyoto, the Otani University Press, 1923, also Published by the Buddhist Text Society, Calcutta : the latter is very incorrect. There are 10 chapters *viz,* 1. Rāvanādhyeṣaṇā. 2 Saṭ-triṁśat-sāhasra-sarva-dharma-samuccaya. 3 Anityatā. 4 Abhisamaya. 5 Tathāgata-nityānitya-prasaṅga. 6 Kṣanika. 7 Nairmāṇika. 8 Māṁsa-bhakṣaṇa. 9 Dhāraṇī. 10 Sagāthakaṁ.

the most valuable literature ever written in connection with the sūtra. A few commentaries have been written on Fa-tsang's work by Japanese scholars. During the Ming dynasty the Laṅkāvatāra seems to have been studied much and there are altogether 15 commentaries on the sūtra from Chinese scholars, which are included in the supplementary part of the Tripitaka.

XVII. Bodhiruci and the Amita Cult

The reign of Empress Wu Tso-tien has become famous in Chinese history for the galaxy of writers it produced on Buddhism. The literary activities of Śikṣānanda the most well-known of the translators of this age, have been described above, while those of Yi-tsing, another great worker in the cause of the spread of Buddhism will be done in the next chapter. In this chapter, we shall however, confine ourselves in describing the literary work of another great translator, Bodhiruci, whose name has come down to us as a great interpreter of a number of important texts.

The other writers of this period were not so brilliant as these translators. Li-wu-T'ao[1] was a brahmana of the country of Lan-po (Lamgham) of North India, who translated only one dhāraṇī: Mitrasena[2] a śramaṇa of Tukhara. was responsible for only one dhāraṇī. Ratnamati[3] a śramaṇa of Kashmir, translated seven works on dhāraṇī in 9 fasc., and died in China at his hundredth year in 721. Pramati[4] a śramaṇa of Central India together with Meghaśikha a Chinese monk translated a sutra in 705.

Bodhiruci's original name was Dharmaruci; but it was changed by the Empress Wu Tso-tien. Dharmaruci was a brahmana by caste of the Kaśyapa family, who emigrated to China in the last decade of the 7th century. Between 693 and 713 Bodhiruci translated 55 works in 111 fasc. of which 41 are found in the present-day edition of the Tripiṭaka. It is said that he died in 727 at his 156th year of age.[5]

Dharmaruci *alias* Bodhiruci 693-713

Bodhiruci's greatest work is the compilation of the *Ratnakuṭa*

---

[1] Nanjio, App. II, 146.
[2] Nanjio, App. II, 147.
[3] Nanjio, App. II, 148
[4] Nanjio, App. II, 151.
Nanjio, App. II. 150.

group of Mahāyana sūtras. The Ratnakuṭa consists of 49 sūtras,[1] which Bodhiruci edited in Chinese for the first time. Of these sūtras, Bodhiruci himself was responsible for the translation of 25 works, while of the rest, some were translations made by previous writers and a few by his contemporaries. The entire work consisting of 120 fasc. was finished in 713. It may be mentioned here that in the Tibetan Kanjur the entire Ratnakuṭa of 45 sūtras, (in Chinese a few have double translation) was translated from the Chinese. In the Chinese edition, there are two prefaces one by Emperor Jui Tsung (A. D. 684 only, then 710-712 A. D.), who gives a life of the Hindu savant. The second preface was written by Su-no, a contemporary of Bodhiruci. The sūtra of the Ratnakuṭa varga are really separate works without any apparent tie of of union among them. Some of these sūtras are the translations of Bodhiruci himself, while others were done by different scholars.

His translation of Ratnanakuṭa in 120 fasc.

Ratnakuṭa consists of 45 separate sutras

The most widely read book of the series is the Sukhāvatī vyūha which we shall describe in details. Some sūtras of this group group have already been described above, such as *Ugra-paripṛcchā Rāṣtrapāla paripṛccā Pitā-pūtra samāgama* etc.

[1] The follwoing sutras of the Ratnakuṭa are quoted in the *Śikṣā-samuccaya* compiled by Śāntideva, the pages refer to the English Translation.

(9) Daśadharmaka p. 5, 8. 114.

(12) Bodhisattva Pitaka. 187. 188.

(15) Mañjuśrī buddhaka-kṣetra guṇa-vyūha, quoted as °alaṁkāra sūtra see p. 14, 15, 54, 171.

(16) Pitā-putra samāgama p. 177, 226.

(18) Rāṣtrapāla paripṛcchā, p. 55, 152, 190, 197, 197, 285.

(19) Ugra-paripṛcchā, p. 11, 21, 39, 89, 83, 113, 130, 133, 141, 144, 149, 176, 187, 188, 190, 191, 194, 245, 248, 263, 283.

(25) Ādyāśaya Sañcodana. p. 17, 100. 105-114, 316.

(28) Vīradatta paripṛcchā, p. 37, 217.

(29) Udayana Vatsarāja paripṛcchā p. 85.

(37) Siṁha paripṛcchā p. 5, 53 ; (43) Kāṣvapa parivarta p. 52.

(44) Ratnarāśi-sūtra p. 56. 127, 129, 134, 135, 194, 273.

(45) Akṣayamati sūtra quoted. as a paripṛcchā, p. 12, 24, 36, 37, 115, 118 : 185 ; 204, 214, 221, 248. 254 : 260, 261, 264, 283.

(47) Ratna-cuda paripṛcchā quoted as sūtra, p. 115 ; 120, 217, 222 249,289.

(48) Srīmālādevī simhanāda p. 44.

Kāśyapa parivarta, another sūtra of the Ratnakuṭa group

The *Kāśyapa Parivarta*[1] an important sūtra, which forms the 43rd chapter of the Ratnakuṭa group, is described here. The oldest translation *Fo-i-jih-mo-ni-pao-ching* (Nanjio, 57) in 127 chapter in one fasc, is ascribed to Lokakṣema (Nanjio II. 3) of the 2nd century A. D. The second was made in the Tsin dynasty (265-420 A. D.) in 143 chapters (Nanjio 58), the translator's name being lost. But Forke, the German Sinalogue, definitely asserts that the translation was made during the Chin Dynasty (350-431). The third version is the one done by Bodhiruci and is incorporated in the Ratnakuṭa group. But this version is practically the second version, which Bodhiruci utilized (Nanjio 23. 43). The fourth translation in 165 or 161 chapters of 5 fasc. was made in the Sung dynasty (960-1127 A. D.) by Shih-hu (Dānapāla 980-1000 A. D., Nanjio, 805).

One fact is obvious to readers, that Indian literary works, as a whole, have always a tendency to grow during the course of centuries. Like most Buddhist sūtras, the *Kāśyapa Parivarta* concerns itself to a considerable extent with ethics and with philosophy. Great stress is laid on veracity and we read in chapter 8, that a Bodhisattva should renounce his fortune, an entire kingdom, or even his life, rather then suppress a true speech. Special rewards are in some cases promised to these who follow certain moral precepts. Among the philosophical sections of the parivarta, the exposition reminds one of the philosophy of Nāgārjuna and Āryadeva. Some passages ascribed to these philosophers seem indeed, as if they were based on the *Kasyapa Parivarta*, which is indeed an earlier work.

"The denunciation of the selfish śrāvakas, who are described as in every respect inferior to the Bodhisattvas, also fills a considerable number of our chapters. In chap. 105-107, for instance

---

[1] *Kāśyapa Parivarta*, which has been recently published in the original Sanskrit, with the Tibetan translation, and four Chinese translations by Baron A. von Stael-Holstein, the Russian Professor of Sanskrit in the Peking University, Commercial Press, Shanghai, 1926.

the śrāvakas are reproached with looking in the wrong direction for the causes of their spiritual misery. They should look inward for those causes, not outward. The śrāvakas are in these chapters compared with a dog, who, after having been hurt by a clod of earth as responsible for its pain, and attacks the clod, instead of attacking the man."[1]

Sukhāvatī Vyūha and the sect of Jodo.

The Sukhāvatī vyūha of the Ratnakuṭa group has been responsible for a great movement in the Eastern Asia. In Japan there is a Buddhist sect called *Jodo* or Pureland; the books on which the members of this sect chiefly base their faith are two *Sukkāvatī vyūhas*, the large and small, and the *Amitāyur-dhyāna-sūtra*. The translations of the *Larger Sukhāvatī vyūha* by Saṅghavarman (A. D. 252; Nanjio, 27), of the *Smaller Sukhāvatī* by Kumārajīva (A. D. 405; Nanjio, 200), and of the *Amitāyur-dhyāna sūtra* by Kālayaśas (A. D. 424, Nanjio 198), are called the '*Three Sūtras*' of the Jodo sect. Of these the larger Sūkhāvatī appears *twelve* times in Chinese translation, and attracted the attention of several Chinese and Japanese commentators. In the Chinese Catalogues of Buddhist Tripiṭaka we find the list of these twelve translations of the Larger sūtra or the Ta-ching; Bodhiruci's translation, which is incorporated in the Ratnakuṭa group, is the eleventh in the list.[2]

---

[1] *Op. cit*, Intro. by Stael-holstein.

[2] The following is the list of the twelve translations of the Larger Sūkhāvatī vyūha :—

(1) '*Amitāyur sūtra*' Wu-liang-sheng-king, 2 fasc, by An Shih Kao A. D. 148-170 (Han dynasty)—Lost.

(2) '*Amita-śuddha-samyaksambodha-sūtra*' Wu-liang-ts'in-tsing-p'in-tang-chiao-king, 3 or 4 fasc. by Leu-chia-chang (Lokakṣema A. D. 147-186 (Han dynasty). First of the five existing translations (Nanjio 25)

Twelve translations of the larger Sukhāvatī Vyūha; five extant.

(3) '*Amita-sūtra*', Ō-mi-t'o-king 2 fasc. by Chu-Chien, A. D. 223-253 (Wu dynasty). Second of the five existing translation (Nanjio 26).

(4) '*Amitāyur sūtra*' Wu-liang-shen-king, 2 fasc. by K'ang Sang-k'ai (Saṅghavarman) A. D. 252 (Wei dynasty). Third of the five existing translations (Nanjio 27).

(5) '*Amita-śuddha samyaksambodhi-sutra*', Wu-liang-ts'in-tsing-p'in-tang-chiao-king, 2 fasc. by Po-yen, A. D. 257 (Wei Dynasty)—Lost,

Of these translations only five exist; besides these there is another work entitled 'Mahā-Amitāyus-sūtra' (Ta-ö-mi-to-king), compiled by a Chinese minister Wang Jih-hsin, A. D. 1160-1162 (Southern Sung Dynasty) and consists of extracts from the proceding extant versions, except from that of Bodhiruci's.[1]

The *five* extant Chinese translations seem to have been translated from *three* different texts or copies of the text, differing from each other considerably. Of the five versions Saṅghavarman's (A. D. 252) is considered the test and is held as the sacred text of the Jodo. It may be mentioned here that the *Larger Sukhāvatī* had been introduced in China by An Shi-kao in the latter half of the second century A. D., which is however lost. The earliest extant version is the one done by Lokakeṣma (A. D. 147-186), a contemporary of Shih-kao and like him a Serindian. But the smaller Sukhāvatī was introduced for the *first time by Kumārajīva* in the early fifth century. We shall however take this opportunity to make a wider survey of the Sukhāvatī cult and a comparative study of the two texts of the Sukhāvatī vyūha.

Introduction of Sukhāvatī in China.

In the larger Sukhāvatī vyūha the historical Śākyamuni is the

---

(6) '*Amitāys-sūtra*', Wu-liang-shen-king, 2 fasc. by Chu Fa-hu (Dharmarakṣa), A. D. 266-313 (Western Tsin Dynasty)—Lost.

(7) '*Nava Amitāyus sūtra*' Sin-wu liang-shen-king, 2 fasc by Buddhabhadra, A. D. 398-421 (Eastern Tsin dynasty)—Lost.

(8) '*Amitāyur-arhat samyaksambodhi sūtra*',—1 fasc. by Chu Fa-li, A. D. 419 (Eastern Tsin Dynasty)—Lost.

(9) '*Nava Amitāyus sutra*', Sin-Wei-liang-shen-king, 2 fasc. by Pao-yen A. D. 524-453 (Earlier Sung Dynasty)—Lost.

10). '*Nava Amitāyus sutra*', Sin-wu-liang-shen-king, 2 fasc. by Dharmamitra (Earlier Sung Dynasty)—Lost.

(11) '*Amitāyus-Tathāgata-pūrṣad*' Wu-liang-shen-ju-lai-hui, 'the sutra spoken by the Buddha on the Tathāgata Amitāyus, at an assembly' 2 fasc. by Bodhiruci, A. D. 693-713 (T'ang Dynasty). Fourth of the five existing translations. (Nanjio 235).

(12) '*Mahāyāna Amitāyur-vyūha sūtra*', Ta-sheng-wu-liang-shen-chwang-yen-king, 3 fasc. by Fa-hsien. A. D. 982-1001 (Later Sung Dynasty). Fifth of the five existing translations. (Nanjio 863).

[1] Maxmüller,—*Buddhist texts from Japan*. Introduction, p. iv-vi. Anecdota Oxoniensia. Aryan Series Vol. I, part II, Oxford. Clarendon Press, 1883.

teacher. The work begins with a diologue between the Buddha and his disciple Ānanda. Bhagavan Buddha was staying at Rājgṛha on the Gṛdhrakūṭa mountain and Ānanda observed the glorious countenance of Bhagavat and asked whether this was due to his Bodhi-knowledge or to his remembrance of former Buddhas. Bhagavan praised Ānanda for thus questioning him and related to him how there was a line of 81 Tathāgatas or Buddhas beginning with Dīpaṅkara and ending with Lokeśvararāja. During the period of the last Tathāgata, a bhikṣu called Dharmākara sang gāthās in praise of Lokeśvara and expressed his wish to become a Buddha. When asking for instruction, and particularly for information as to the right qualities of a Buddha country, Lokeśvara at first told him that he should find them out for himself. But when Dharmākara declared his inability to do so. Lokeśvara consented to explain these qualities After he had listened to Lokeśvara Dharmākara wished to combine all the good qualities of the 84 Buddhakṣetras and concentrate them upon his own, and, after an absence of five Kalpas, he returned to the Buddha with his own pranidhānas or prayers for the good qualities of his own Buddha-kṣetra. Then Dharmākara tells Lokeśvararāja in a long prayer of 46 stanzas what he wishes and wills his own Buddha-kṣetra to be. This prayer forms really the basis of the Sukhāvatī conception and are very famous and often referred to by Northern Buddhists. It is in fact, under the form of the prayer, a kind of prophcy of, what according to Dharmākara's ideas, Sukhāvatī or the land of Bliss ought to be. Dharmākara wishes that "his name should be known in all existing regions; that whoever should make use of his name should at once be placed under his jurisdiction entirely and exclusively; that he could by a ray emitted from his heart illuminate every being he wished, at no matter what distance; that every dying person, however great a sinner he was, who repenting wished sincerely to be reborn in his kingdom, would immidiately be reborn in his kingdom, would immediately be reborn here after

Larger Sukhāvatī Vyūha

Summery of the text

his death, to be instructed there, improved and placed on the road to salvation."

"In his time Dharmākara became the Buddha Amitābha *i. e.*, infinite life or light and that, which he desired was realised. The land of Amitabha[1] the Sukhāvatī or Pureland, is situated to the west of our world, beyond the thousands of nearer lands of Buddhas; spring is there perpetual. All those who inhabit it are of male sex, and of the same adult age. The bodies are not material but etheral. Clothes present themselves by simply wishing for them, and food in the same way. However, the duration of the sojourn with Amida, is only transitory, not eternal. The Pureland is not a paradise, but a place of purification, of illumination, of orientation toward definite salvation."

Two Bodhisattvas are mentioned having left this Buddha-kṣetra to be born is Sukhāvatī *viz.*, Avalokiteśvara and Mahāsthānaprāpta. Then follows a new description of the excellences of Sukhāvatī in which the blessings prayed for in the former pranidhānas are represented as realised, and the inhabitants of Sukhāvatī described as in full enjoyment of all blessings.

"Ananda then expressed a wish to see Amitābha and the Bodhisattvas face to face, and at the same moment Amitābha sent a ray of light illuminating the whole world. They could see the people of Sukhāvatī and the people of Sukhāvatī could see Śākyamuni and all the inabitants of the Sahālokadhatu.

Then a dialogue follows hetween Bhagavat and Ajita, Bhagavat asking Ajita whether, after seeing the people of Sukhāvatī, he thinks that there is any difference between the *Paranirmita-vaśavaratin* gods and the human beings in Sukhāvatī. Ajita says that he sees none. Next comes a question why some of the people are born there miraculously out of lotus flowers, while others are born after dwelling for some time within the lotus. The reason is that the former have had firm faith in Amitābha, the latter had entertained some doubts. Lastly Ajita asks whether people of this and other worlds are born in the Sukhāvatī, and Bhagavat gives a long

1 Chin. A-mi-to. Jap. Amida.

enumeration of those who either from this or from other Budha-kṣetras have risen to Sukhāvatī. The whole ends with the usual panegyric of the Sukhāvatī-vyūha sūtra, and an account of the rewards for learning, writing, repeating and teaching it.[1]

The two Sukhāvatis differ from each other on smaller points. The smaller *Sukhāvatī-vyūha* lays great stress on the fact that people can be saved or can be born in the Sukhāvatī, if only they remember and repeat the name of the Amitāva as a reward or necessary result of good works performed in the present life. The larger Sukhāvatī lays likewise great stress on prayer and faith in Amitābha, but it never neglects 'the stock of merit, as essential for salvation."[2]

The third Amita book is the Amitayur-dhyāna sūtra, translated by Kālayaśas in A. D. 429. In this sūtra, Queen Vaidehi, wife of Bimbisāra of Magadha weary of this wicked world, is comforted by Śākyamuni who teaches her how to be born in the Pureland and instructs her in the three kinds of goodness. These are (i) wordly goodness; such as filiul piety, loyalty, respect for parents, etc.; (ii) morality of that internal and unworldly kind which is the first foundation of the religious life and (iii) the goodness of practice, which includes the practical application to life to the four great truths and six pāramitās or cardinal virtues. A good seed produces good fruit in abundance. If we sow the seed of the three goodnesses we shall reap, as a fruit, the manifold bliss of the Pureland. Towards the end of the sūtra, Buddha says. "Let not one's voice cease, but ten times complete the thought and repeat the words Namo Amitābhāya Buddhāya or adoration to Amitābha Buddha. This practice is the most excellent of all."[3]

The two Sukhāvatī vyūhas and the Amitāyur-dhyāna sūtra form the basis of the Jodo sect once prevalent both in China and Japan, now a powerful sect in Japan. According to Chinese tradition of

1 See Bendal, Cambridge Catalogue, pp. 74-76 : also *S. B. E. op. cit.*
2 Maxmüllar, *S. B. E.* XLIX, Introduction, viii, ix.
3 SBE. vol. XLIX, Part II, pp. 161-169.

the Jodo school, Śākyamuni Buddha had prophesied before the people assembled on the mountain peak in Lankā (Ceylon) that there should appear in South India a great teacher named Nāgārjuna, who should destroy the conflicting views of Entity and non-Entity and teach the Mahāyāna. Nāgārjuna taught that there are two ways of life, the one a road of difficulty and pain, "like a toilsome journey by land," and the other, one of ease and pleasure, like "an easy voyage in a fair ship over smooth waters." It is ascribed to Nāgārjuna that he declared, "Only let him ever call upon the name of the Tathāgata, and gratefully commemorate the great all-embracing vow." It is for this reason that Nāgārjuna is considered as the Founder of the Sukhāvatī sect and is known as the first Patriarch.

Jodo sect and the Sukhāvatī vyūha

Vasubandhu, according to the same tradition, is the second Patriarch, who, they say, eloquently preached that salvation lies in the faith on Amitābha. The larger Sukhāvatī vyūha popularised the cult of Amita in China. Some of the well-known Chinese Buddhists of the age, such as Tao-an and Hui-yuan greatly moved by the spiritual message of Amita, began to preach the doctrine of love in China. The larger Sukhāvatī, it may be reminded, had been introduced in China in A.D. 251 by Sanghavarman; but the smaller one was only made known to the Chinese a century and a half after, by Kumārajīva circa 404. Inspite of Hui-yuan's responsibility for the introduction of Amita's cult, he is not reckoned among the patriarchs. But it was he who for the first time gathered into a distinct body, a band of monks and laymen for invoking Amita's forgiveness, called the Society of White Lotus in A.D. 386. Hui-yuan died A.D. 416

For about a century and a half we do not hear anything of the Amita cult. In the early 6th century A.D. Tan-luan, a confirmed Taoist became a Buddhist under the influence of Bodhiruci of the Sui dynasty (A.D. 508-558), who was working at Layong. Tao-luan received the teaching of the Pureland and burning the ascetic books put his faith in the

Tan-luan an Amidist

paradise of bliss. He followed the teachings of Vasubandhu, which he had learned from Bodhiruci, and clearly taught that Amita's great vow was the effective cause of birth in paradise. It was at this time that Bodhiruci translated Vasubandhu's commentary on the Aparimitāyu sūtra (Nanjio, 1204).

Bodhiruci's disciple Tan-luan (Jap. Donran) displayed an extraordinary zeal for the propagation of Amita cult. Tan-luan died in A.D. 600 and was succeeded by Tao-ch'ao (Jap. Doshaku) several years after him, as the head of the sect. In Tao-chao's hand the Amita doctrine greatly developed. He taught that Amita must be considered to be a personal Being and not a mere abstract ideal, that the innumerable practices for perfecting righteousness by one's own efforts are of no value, and the invocation of the Name which comprises all virtues, he praised as beneficial. He further showed that in all ages it is the principle of mercy that alone rules and draws men. Though a man had done evil all his life, yet, if he were once brought near to the great vow, he would reach the land of bliss and enjoy the fruits of salvation. This is the reason why Tao-ch'ao put great stress on the Larger Sukhāvatī vyūha, and which he handed over to his disciple, the great Shan-tao (Jap. Zendo). Shan-tao was the first that understood the true will of Buddha Sākyamuni in his age, and that had pity alike for those who practised meditation or moral good, as for those who lived in wickedness. Shan-tao further "taught that the effect of salvation is given by the Holy light and the sacred name of Amida, and expounded the great ocean of wisdom contained in the fundamental vow. The believer, having rightly received the adamantine heart of firm faith, and having answered to the calling of the Tathāgata with a joyful heart, like Vaidehi, Queen of Bimbisāra, to whom Śakyamuni first gave the teachings about Amida in the Aparimitāyu sūtra, receives the threefold assurance and immediately enters into the happiness of the Eternal Life."

Tao-ch'ao develops Amita cult

It is said that this Chinese monk converted the whole Chang-an and even the Emperor Kao-tsung became an Amidist. Many marvellous exploits are spoken of him.

The cult of Amita is a mystery in Buddhist literature and religion. In India we hear nothing of it; neither Fa-hien nor Hiuen-tsang spoke of its existence in India. Buddha's religion of rationalism is opposed to the *Bhakti* cult of Amita. His paradise is always referred to as existing in the west. It is suspected that very early influence of Gnostic Nestorian Christians among Central Asian Buddhist created this faith. It is suggested that Shan-tao received assistance from some Christian in his commentaries.[1]

In course of time a considerable Buddhist literature grew in China; a large cemmentarial literature was also written. The Jodo literature differed from that of all the other sects of China in its tone of simplicity, of sincerity, of charity, of favour; it comprises of the kinds of writings, such as, didactic works, dithyrambs or prayers, acts, exhortations to the laity and biographical notices. Tan-luan's *Liao-lun an-lo ching-t'u-i* and Tao-ch'an's *An-lo-chi* are didactic treatises of best sort. Tan-laun's *Tsan A-mi-t'o-fo-chih* contain some of the most beautiful prayers to Amita Buddha. Each strophe begins with the invocation, "Salutation to thee, from full heart, and in all confidence, O Amitabha," and ends thus, "We desire that we, and all beings, may be reborn in thy kingdom of peace and happiness."[2]

It is not possible to recount here all the numerous works that were written by the Chinese Buddhists inspired by the Sukhāvati vyuhas. In Japan a vast literature grew inspired by the same spirit of *Bhakti*. The influence of these tiny books was enormous and it still wields a great hold on the mind of the people.

Its importance in Eastern Asia

1 Lloyd, *Shinron and his work*, pp. 50-54; also The Creed of Half Japan, p. 219.

2 Wieger, *loc. cit.* p. 591*ff.*

XVIII. Yi-Tsing and the Chinese Monks in India

During the first three centuries of the Buddhist Prapaganda in China, the Chinese Buddhists never came in direct contact with India. All their knowledge about Buddhism was derived either from the Buddhists of Central Asia or from a few Hindu monks who came from North-Western provinces of India. No Chinese came to India before Fa-hien; he was the first Chinese who brought knowledge about India direct from India. The monk has left us a book on traval which gives an accurate though inadequate information about Indian and Central Asian Buddhism. The path of the pioneer was followed by several batches of pilgrims, but few of them have left any record of their experience abroad; nor any biographer has written a detailed account of their achievements. The most well-known of the Chinese travellers, who linked China spiritually with India was Hiuen-tsang, whose book of travels and biography by his disciples are available to the English and French speaking peoples. His work known as the 'Record of the Western Countries,' when published, created great sensation in China and subsequently inspired many a pious monk to visit the holy land of Śākyamuni. These monks came to India with the humility of a learner: with them the study of Sanskrit and Buddhism was not for an academic distinction, but for the solution of the problems of misery that beset mankind. With this object in view these monks from Eastern and Central Asia left their homes for the unknown lands of India, with an attitude of mind quite different from that of the militant crusaders of the middle ages, who also wanted to see the land of their saviour. Thus the relation established between India and China, lasted through several centuries and even now the sacred name of the Amita Buddha or the Buddha of the unbounded mercy, is still ringing in the ears of millions of devotees.

With Fa-hien begins China's direct contact with India

Hiuen-tsang's contribution to Sino-Indian Fellowship

Prajñadeva of Nalanda's letter to Hiuen-tsang

The relation established with India during Hiuen-tsang's stay in the monasteries continued to be intimate and cordial even after his departure from India. A very interesting document is preserved in Chinese in the form of correspondence between Sthavira Prajñadeva of Nalanda and Hiuen-tsang. The letter of Prajñadeva was conveyed by a monk of Budha-Gaya who went to China several years after the return of Hiuen-tsang. The letter, which was presumably written in Sanskrit, is now preserved in Chinese translation in the Annals of the T'ang dynasty. It reads thus :

"The one whom the assembly of men of great science (Mahāyānsaṅgha) in the temple of Mahābodhi, beside the Vajrāsana of the marvellous and the blessed Bhagavan, the Sthavira Prajñadeva (Chin. Hoei-t'ien) sends this letter to Ācārya Mokṣadeva (the Sanskrit name given to Hiuen-tsang by the monks of Nalanda) to the Kingdom of China, who knows thoroughly and grasps the sūtras, the vinaya and the śāstras. He wishes most respectfully that he may have ever little illness and little pain. I, Bhikṣu Prajñadeva, have now composed 'A panegyric of the Mahāparinirvāna of the Buddha' and 'A treatise on the knowledge of the comparative value of the sūtras and śāstras' etc. I have made them over to Bhikṣu, Fa-Chiang, who will take them to you. Amongst us, the Ācārya with vast knowledge, venerable and bhadanta Jñānaprabha (Shi-kuang), the celebrated disciple of Śīlabhadra of Nalanda, joins me in enquiring of your news. The upāsakas, every day go on in offereing you their bows and salutation. Now, we all together, send you a pair of white clothes to show you that in our hearts we have not forgotten you. The way (to China) is long ; therefore do not take into account the smallness of the present and we wish that you accept it. Now, as regards the copies of sūtras and śāstras you want, we can send them to you, if you send us the list. Now, Mokṣācārya, this is what we wish you to know."

This letter was given to Hiuen-tsang by Fa-cheng, who lived in China for some years and then returned to India. It was through him that Hiuen-tsang sent a reply to the venerable Jñānaprabha. The letter must have been written in Sanskrit by Hiuen-tsang and it is preserved in Chinese translation. It reads thus :

Hiuen-tsang's answer to Prajñādeva's letter

"Some years past, an envoy returned and I learned that the grant master Śīlabhadra has ceased to live. On hearing this news I was overwhelmed with a grief for which I could find no consolation. Alas ! the boat on this ocean of suffering has gone down ! the eye of men and the devas dim put out. Can any one express the sorrow that his disappearance has caused us ? Formerly, the *Prajnā* (Great Intelligence) hid its shine, Kāsyapa went on glorifying its great work; when Saṇavāsa left the world Upagupta disclosed his good rules and now that a leader of the Law has returned to the true place (Nirvāna), the masters of the Law should perform their task in their turn. My only desire is that pure explanation and subtle discussions should expand in floods vast like those of the four seas and that the Blessed Science and its beautiful majesty should be enternal like the five mountains.

"Of the sūtras and śāstras which I brought, I have already translated the Yogācārabhūmi śāstra kārikā and other works ; altogether about thirty books have been translated.

"At the present time, the son of Heaven (the Chinese Emperor) of T'ang dynasty, by his personal saintliness and by his ten thousand happinesses should rule the country and give peace to the peaple ; with the love of a cakrarāja may he spread far away the transformation which a dharmarāja spreads. For, with regard to the sūtras and śāstras which have been produced we have obtained the favour of a preface by the divine brush [imperial preface] ; the officials concerned have received the order for distributing the texts in the kingdom ; even the neighbouring countries shall receive copies as a result of the order. Although we are at the end of the last period of images,[1] the bright glory of law of Dharma is very sweet and very perfect. It is not different from what the

1 There was a tradition about the disappearance of two images near the Buddha-Gaya, when Buddhism would come to an end.

transformation was at Śrāvasti and the garden of Jetavana. This is what I humbly desire you to know.

"While being wrecked in the Indus (Sin-tu) I lost a bundle of sacred books[1]; now I write here the list (of books) at the end of this letter. If you have occasion I beg you to send them. Herewith a few small things that I send you as offering, wishing you should kindly accept them."

After Hiuen-tsang's return the spirit of travelling abroad was greatly stimulated among the Buddhist youth of China and for several years the reigns of the T'ang rulers were specially propitious for such adventures. The last of the monk travellers of this period was Yi-tsing, whose name is well-known to us from the translation of his *Record* into English by Takakusu. For our purpose the importance lies in the fact that he was responsible for the translations of a number of Sanskrit works; but his biography of eminent monks is of no less consequence. We shall therefore give a brief outline of the life of Yi-tsing and then proceed to describe the lives of the monks who came before him.

Yi-tsing's Record and Biography.

Yi-tsing was born in 635 in modern Cho-shan (in Chi-li), during the reign of the T'ang Emperor T'aitsung (627-649). The boy had the usual Chinese education; but since his twelfth year he began to study the sacred books of Buddhism. He took pravarjyā, when he was fourteen years of age. It was, he tells us, in his eighteenth year (652), that he formed the intention of travelling to India, which was not, however, fulfilled till his thirty-seventh year (671). During some nineteen years of the interval he seems to have applied all his youthful vigour to the study of Buddhism, so as 'not to render his life useless by indulging himself in secular literature.'

Yi-tsing's travel, A. D. 671-695.

Yi-tsing was a great admirer of Fa-hien and Hiuen-tsang. While he was staying at Chang-an, he may have witnessed the 'noble enthusiasm of Hiuen-tsang' and after his death the great funeral

[1] This incident is given in his biography. H. T. lost several books and various flower-seeds of India which he had gathered. See Beal. p. 191.

ceremony carried out under the direction of the Emperor, made a lasting impression on his mind and he was more than ever fired with the desire of visiting the Buddhist countries.

Yi-tsang, was one of the many pilgrims who left China for India. He took the southern sea-route and left Canton in 671 A. D. He came to (Sumatra) Śrīvijaya, that island empire of the Hindus, where he lived for a few months and learned Sanskrit. Then he sailed for India and reached Tāmralipti the port of Bengal in 673. In India he visited the Nalānda monastery, Gaya and the various other important places, studied Buddhist vinaya thoroughly and left India from the port of Tāmralipti in 685. He came back to Śrīvijaya in 689 spending several years in Ceylon and worked there till 695, when he returned home. Śrīvijaya was a great centre of Hindu culture, and Yi-tsing selected the place as most advantageous for his literary activities as he could easily secure the help of Sanskrit paṇdits. He sent his translations of various sūtras and śāstras in 10 volumes, including the *Nan-hai-chi-kuei-nai-fa-ch'uan* (The Record and the memoires of the contemporary monks) through a Chinese monk who was returning home in 693.[1]

His life in the East.

His biography[2] tells us that Yi-tsing was twenty-five years abroad (671-695) and travelled in more than one hundred thirty countries ; he came back to China in 695 in the time of Empress Wu Tso-t'ien, bringing with him some 400 different texts of Buddhist books, the ślokas numbering 500,000 and a real plan of the Vajrāsana (the seat of Buddha-Gaya) of the Buddha.

Yi-tsing translated 56 works in 230 fasciculi ; he began by collaborating with Śikṣānanda of Khotan in the work of translation but later on they worked independently. He died in A.D. 713 in in his 79th year. His life and works are greatly commended by the Emperor Chung-tsung his contemporary T'ang ruler in the preface to the Tripiṭaka catalogue.

---

1 *Record*, General Introduction, p. xxxvi.
2 Chavannes, *Memoires* p. 193ff.

Yi-tsing furnishes us with a clear conspectus of the Buddhist sects as they existed in India in the latter half of the seventh century. We have already spoken of the eighteen sects, which divided the Buddhist church in his early stage. But all these different sects in course of time ceased to keep up their distinctive character and some of them even lost their individual existence. Yi-tsing, however, divides these sects into four principal groups or nikāyas.

Description of the Buddhist sects of India.

(1) The *Mahāsāṅghika nikāya*, comprised seven sub-divisions ; but was apparently the least influential school. The three piṭakas, belonging to it contain 100,000 ślokas each or three lakh stanzas altogether, which if translated into Chinese, would amount to a thousand Chinese fasciculi.

(2) The *Sthavira nikāya* sub-divided into three. They had a Tripiṭaka, same as the above. This is the school to which Pali canons belong. It was predominant in South India, Ceylon, and was also found in the Eastern Bengal.

(3) The *Mūla-sarvāstivāda nikāya* with four sub-divisions. They had a Tripiṭaka as extensive as the above schools. Almost all belonged to this school in N. India and it was flourishing in Magadha.

(4) The *Sammitiya nikāya* with four sub-divisions flourished in Lāṭa, and Sindhu. The three piṭakas of this school contain 200,000 ślokas, the Vinaya alone having 30,000 ślokas. All these opinions were followed in Magadha, because the holy places of Magadha and the University of Nalanda attracted all shades of opinion, and Bengal seems to have been singularly catholic.[1]

The chief aim of Yi-tsing's visit to India and the southern islands was to study the discipline or vinaya of the Baddhists. He writes, "On account of some misinterpretations handed down, the disciplinary rules have suffered and errors constantly repeated, have become customs which are contrary to the original principles. Therefore, according to the noble teaching and the principal customs

His object to study Vinaya

[1] Eliot, *opt cit*, II, p. 192 ; *Records*, Intro. xxiii, xxiv 4-5.

actually carried on in India, I have carefully written the following articles which are forty in number, and have divided them into four books. This is called *Nan-hai-chi-kuci-nai-fa-chuan* i.e., the Record of the Sacred Law sent home from the southern sea." (Records, p. 18). The contents of the *Record* will at once shew the nature of observations made by Yi-tsing during his travels.

Record of the Sacred Law.

Yi-tsing's greatest contribution to Chinese Buddhist literature is his translation of the vinaya of the Mūlasarvāstivādins. The vinaya of this school is a vast collection, which covers about eight volumes of the Chinese tripitaka. The Chinese translation was done under the superintendence of Yi-tsing. The translation was begun in 703 and finished in A. D. 710 and at the time of completion 54 persons were engaged in the work.

Mūlasarvāstivāda Vinaya.

The whole vinaya literature translated by Yi-tsing consists of seventeen[1] treatises of various sizes; of these six are not mentioned in the catalogue of Nanjio. Besides these, Yi-tsing translated two works; *viz.*, Mūlasarvāstivāda Vinaya saṁgraha of Jinamitra, a work in 14 chapters (Nanjio, 1127) and the M.-S. Nikāya Vinayagāthā of Vaiśākhya in 3 chapters (Nanjio, 1143). The last work in verse is a summary of the Vinaya, which was translated by Yi-tsing in India while staying in the monastery of Nalanda. Yi-tsing also wrote two original tracts on the vinaya of the Mūlasaravāstivāda school which are also found in the Chinese tripiṭaka. (Nanjio, 1508, 1506).[2]

The vinaya[3] of the Mūlasarvādins has also been accepted as the canon by the Tibetans. It is known as Dulva in the Kanjur collection of the Tibetan tripiṭaka and comprise 13 volumes of Xylographic print. The Tibetan is divided in seven parts:

---

[1] *Ibid*, p. 19-20.

[2] S. Levi, Les element de formation du Divyāvadana. *Toung Pao.* 1907, pp. 110-112.

[3] Wassilieff, Le Bouddhism d'apres Vinayas, *Revue de l'historie des religion* 1896, pp. 318-325; translated from the Russiam by Syivain Levi.

(1) Vinaya vastu, (2) Prātimokṣa (3) Vinaya vibhāga, (4) Bhikṣunī Prātimokṣa, (5) Bhikṣuni vinaya vibhāgha, (6) Vinayavastu, (7) Vinaya uttra grantha.

The Chinese vinaya and the Tibetan dulva however differ in their arrangement. The Mūlasarvāsṭivāda vinaya was translated into Chinese in the first decade of the eighth century, while the Tibetan dulva was translated during the ninth century. It appears from this that from the seventh century the Mūlasarvāstivāda vinaya began to gain popularity in Northern India. Yi-tsing distinctly speaks of the popularity of this school and describes in his *Records* the vinaya rules prevalent in the islands of the South Sea. He further held the Mūlasarvāstivāda nikāya as one of the four principal sects of Buddhism, the other three were the Sthavira, Mahāsāṅghika and the Sammitiya schools. The Mūlasarvāstivāda according to him was divided into four branches: (1) the Sarvāstivādins, (2) the Dharmaguptas, (3) the Mahiśāsakas, (4) the Kāśyapiyas. In Chinese vinayas of the following sects are preserved:

(1) Sarvāstivāda vinaya done into Chinese in A. D. 404 by Puṇyatara (and Kumārajīva).

(2) Dharmagupta vinaya translated A. D. 405 by Buddhayaśas.

(3) Mahāsāṇighika ninaya in A. D. 416 translated by Buddhabhadra and Fa-hien.

(4) Mahiśāsak a vinaya translated in A. D. 424 by Buddhajıva.

(5) Mahāyāna Sthavira vinaya in 483-493 (lost) and a part of tho Samantapāsādika by Saṅghabhadra in 489.

(6) Mūlasarvāstivāda[1] in A. D. 703-710 by Yi-tsing.

---

[1] The following is the complete list Yi-tsing's translations of the vinayas.

1 Vinaya—50 fasc. [Ch. Tripitaka xvi, part, 8 and 9] (Nanjio, 1118)
2 Bhiksuni vinaya 20 fasc. [XVI. 10] (Nanjio, 1124)
3 Saṁyukta vastu (?), 40 fasc. [XVII, 1 & 2] (Nanjio 1121)
4 Saṅghabhedaka vastu 20 fasc. [XVII, 3] (Nanjio, 1123)
5 Bhaiṣajya-vastu (?) 18 fasc. [XVII, 4 ; pp. 1—79]
6 Pravarjyā (Upasampada) vastu (?) 4 fasc. [XVII. 4 : pp. 80-97]
7 Varṣa-vāsa-vastu (?) 1 fasc. [XVII. 4 ; pp. 98-101]
8 Pravarana-vastu (?) 1 fasc. [XVII, 4; pp. 101-104]
9 Carma-vastu (?) 1 fasc. [XVII. 4 ; pp. 104-111]

The above dates show that the principal vinayas were introduced in China between A. D. 404 and 425, that is, within the first two decades of the fifth century. But the Mūlasarvāstivāda vinaya was introduced in China full three hundred years after the appearance of the vinaya of the above school. During these three hundred years, the vinaya of the Dharmagupta sect was most popular in the Buddhist saṅgha. The late introduction of the Mūlasarvāstivāda vinaya by Yi-tsing in China, does not however preclude its claim to antiquity. It may be mentioned here that the Divyāvadāna, a Sanskrit work of Buddhist stories[1] is practically based on the Mūlasarvāstivāda vinaya.[2] Out of 38 sections consisting of about 655 printed pages of the *Diyyāvadāna*, only six sections of about 100 pages have no corresponding Chinese varsion ; most of the sections about 21 have corresponding Chinese in the vinaya of the Mūlasarvāstivādis.[3]

This school probably orginated at Mathura and developed a literature long before at the third century A. D. The Aśokāvadāna is considered to be also a vinaya of this school, which was translated in the third Century A. D.[4]

We owe our knowledge of our vinaya of the M.-S. School to Yi-tsing who in his *Records* gives a detailed study of the vinaya or disciplines in the Buddhist kingdom of his times. Further in his *Records* Yi-tsing mentions the names of the famous Hindu thinkers of India, first, 'of an early age,' second 'of the middle age,'

---

10 Kaṭhina (civara) vastu (?) 1 fasc. [XVII. 4 ; pp. 112-113] The whole texts of Vinaya of the Mūlasarvāstivāda represented by Yi-tsing, amounted to about 170 fasciculi (*Records*, Intro. p. xxxviii)

11 Nidana. 5 fasc. [XVII. 5 ; pp. 1-20] (Nanjio 1137)

12 Mātṛkā, 5 fasc. [XVII. 5 ; pp. 20-38] (Nanjio 1134)

13 Eka-śata Karma, 10 fasc. [XVII. 5 ; pp. 38-77] (Nanjio, 1131)

14 Vinaya Sūtra or Prātimokṣa, 1 fasc [XVII. 5 ; pp. 77-84] (Nanjio, 1110)

15 Bhikṣuni Prātimokṣa sūtra 1 fasc. [XVII. 5] (Nanjio, 1149)

16 Vinayanidāna mātrkā gāthā 15 leaves [XVII. 5 pp. 93-96] (Nanjio, 1140)

17 Saṁyukta vastu gāthā 10 leaves [XVIII. 5 ; pp. 97-99] (Nanjio, 1141)

[1] Cowell and Neil. *The Divyāvadāna*, 1886, in Roman Script.

[2] Levi, *loc.-cit.*

[3] Levi, *loc.-cit.* p. 110.

[4] Przyluski···*Legende de Asoka*, op. *cit.*

and thirdly 'of late years' and of his age. The age preceding Yi-tsing was a glorious era for Indian philosophy. Yi-tsing mentions by name the following magnate of the age.[1] Dignāga,[2] the great logician stands at the top of the 'recent year' teachers followed by a galaxy of the brilliant writers; (2) Dharmapāla, the teacher of Sīlabhadra of Nalanda, many of whose commentaries were rendered by Hiuen-tsang in Chinese; (3) Dharmakīrti, the most famous commentator on logic made great improvement in the dialectics; (4) Śīlbhadra, pupil of Dharmapāla, President of Nalanda and Guru of Hiuen-tsing; (5) Sthiramati, a pupil of Vasubandhu and commentator; (6) Guṇamati, devoted himself to the schools of Dhyā; (7) Siṁhacandra; (8) Prajñāgupta, fully expounded the Saddharma by refuting all antagonistic views; (9) Guṇaprabha, popularised for a second time the study of vinaya; (10) Jinaprabha, was the teacher of the Chinese monk Hiuen-chao, who was in Nalanda in A. D. 649.[3] Of these names the most well-known is that of Dignāga. Eight books are mentioned against this great logician of middle ages.[4] We have seen above that Hiuen-tsang translated two works of Dignāga, *viz.*, *Nyāyadvāra Tarka śāstra*, (Nanjio, 1224) and *Ālambana Parīkṣā*, (Nanjio, 1173) and also *Nyāya Praveśa*, a work attributed to Śaṇkarasvāmin by Chinese authorities and to Dignāga by Tibetans. Yi-tsing translated several works of Dignāga;[5] he retranslated Nyayadvāra (Nanjio, 1223) which had been done by Hiuen-tsang and translated Dharmapala's (Nalanda) of commentary on the Alambana Parīkṣā (Nanjio, 1174).

Famous Hindu thinkers of India

Dignāga, the Logician

---

[1] *Record*, p. 181.

[2] Jina is a mistransliteration by Takakusm, Watters, on Yuan Chwang.

[3] Chavannes, *Memoire sur less Religieux Eminents*, p. 17.

[4] *Records*. p. 186-187

[5] A chart of Dignaga's works shown;

From Yi-tsing's *Records*	*Nanjio*	Tibetan *Tunjur*
1. "Sāstra on the meditation on the three works."		Trikāla-parikṣā

Yi-tsing translated two works of Asanga with the commentaries by Vasuhandhu (Nanjio, 1208 and 1231 ; 1230) ; but two of his other translations deserve special treatment. One is a hymn by Mātṛceṭa and the other a letter by Nāgārjuna. Mātṛceṭa used to be confused with Aśvaghoṣa ; but now the two personalities are clearly distinguished. Mātṛceṭa's Sanskrit poems are lost in the original ; only some fragments have been discovered in Central Asia, where readers will find more details.

His translation of Mātṛceṭa's hymns.

We learn from Yi-tsing that once Mātṛceṭa was quite popular in India among the Buddhists. Yi-tsing says that "in India numerous hymns of praise to be sung at worship have been care-

---

2.	Sarva-lakṣana dhyāna-śāstra Kārikā.	Sarvalakṣana dhyāna-śāstra (N. 1229). Trans. by Yi-tsing.	
3.	Sastra on the meditation on the object.	Alambana-pratyaya dhyāna sāstra (N. 1173) by Hiuen-tsang.	Alambana Parīkṣa
4.	'Sāstra on the Gate of Cause	Hetudvāra śāstra (Hetucakra damaru acc. to Tubianski) Nyāya praveśa acc, to V. Bhatta charya, Kieth and others. (Nanjio, 1216)	Hetucakra damaru or (I)Nyāya-pravesa alleged to Sankarasvāmin by Chinese (2) Second translation from the Chinese.
5.	Sastra on the Gate of the Resembling cause	'Hetvābhāsa dvāra Śastra' (Reconstructed)	
6.	Nyadvāra (Tarka) Sāstra.	(1) Nyāyadvāra Tarka Śāstra by Hiuentsnag (N. 1224)) (2) by Yi-tsing (N. 1223).	
7.	Prajñapti hetu samgraha (?) Śāstra,	Prajñapti hetu Samgraha (?) Sāstra by Yi-tsing (N. 1223)	
8.	Śastra on the grouped inferences	Chang-Chung-lun by Yi-tsing (N. 1256)	Pramāñ samuccaya. * For Tibetan see Vidyabusan's *Medeival India Logic*, pp. 89-101

fully handed down." Mātṛceṭa's was one of those admirable stotras. "Mātṛceṭa by his great literary talent and virtues excelled all learned men of his age...He composed first a hymn consisting of 400 ślokas, and afterwards another of 150. He treats generally of the six pāramitās and expounds all excellent qualities of the Buddha...All who compose hymns imitate his style...Throughout India everyone who becomes a monk is taught Mātṛceṭa's two hymns, as soon as he repeats the fifteen śīlas. This course is adopted by both the Mahāyāna and Hīnayāna schools." Yi-tsing further enumerates six reasons of its being so popular with the monks in India. "Firstly, these hymns enable us to know the Buddha's great and profound virtues. Secondly, they show us how to compose verses. Thirdly, they ensure the purity of language. Fourthly, the chest is expanded in singing them. Fifthly, by reciting them nervousness in an assembly is overcome. Sixthly, by their use, life is prolonged, free from disease." (*Record*, p. 157-158), Yi-tsing therefore translated this work into Chinese (Nanjio, 1456).

Nagarjuna's Suhṛllekha

His other work is the translation of *Suhṛllekha* of Nāgārjuna. It was not a new work in Chinese. It had appeared twice before him in the Chinese language, once done by Guṇavarman in A.D. 431 (Nanjio, 1464) and again by Saṅghavarman in 534 A. D. (Nanjio, 1471). But Yi-tsing's translation greatly popularized it in China. He writes "Bodhisattva Nāgārjuna wrote an epistle in verse which is called *Suhṛllekha,* meaning, 'Letter to an intimate friend'; it was dedicated to his old Dānapati, named Jetaka Śatavāhana, a king in South India. The beauty of the writing is striking, and his exhortations as to the right way are earnest. His kindness excels that of kinship, and the purport of the epistle is indeed manifold."

"We should," he writes, "respect and believe the Triratna and support our fathers and mothers. We should keep the śīla, and avoid sinful deeds. We should not associate with men until we know their character. We must regard wealth and beauty as the foulest of things. We should regulate well home affairs and always remember that the world is impermanent." He treats fully of the conditions of *prefas* and of the Tiryak-yoni, likewise of the gods, men and the hell-spirits. Even though fire should be burning above our head, he further writes, we ought to waste no time in putting our Mokṣa, reflecting on the truths of twelve nidānas.

"He advises us to practise the three-fold wisdom (three prajñās), that we may clearly understand the 'noble eight-fold path' and teaches us the 'four truth' (catvāra ārya satya) to realise the two-fold attainment of perfection. Like Avalokiteśvara, we should not make any distinction between friends and enemies. We shall then live hereafter in the Sukhāvatī for ever, through the power of the Buddha Amitāyus, whereby one can exercise the superior power of salvation over the world."[1]

But the history of the Sino-Indian contact cannot be told without a reference to the lives of the eminent monks who visited India and her colonies during the short period intervening the time of Hiuen-tsang and Yi-tsing, a period of less than half a century. Yi-tsing's *Si-yu-chi-fa-kao-seng-chuan* (Nanjio 1491), contains the biographies of 60 such monks, who went out of China in search of Law. Chavannes in the Introduction to the *Memoire*[2] calls attention to the remarkable fact that in a single generation sixty persons were found willing to undertake such a perilous journey. Moreover, he shows good reasons to believe that there were many more pilgrims of whose wanderings no record has been preserved and that the actual number of those pious palmers must have amonnted to several hundreds.[3]

Yi-tsing's 'Eminent Monks.

Sixty monks came to India in half a century

[1] *Record,* p. 161-162 ; the king referred to here seems to be an Andhra king, who bore the title of Satavahana. For the entire translation see H. Wenzel, *bes ses-pai-phrir-yig* 'Friendly Epistle' from the Tibetan version, *J.P.T.S.* 1886

[2] *Memoire compose a l'Epoque de la Grande Dynastie T'ang sur les Religieux Eminents qui allerent chercher la loi dans le pays d'occident par I-tsing*—Traduit en Francais par Edouard Chavannes. Henceforward referred *Memoire.* Leroux. Paris, 1894, 218 pages.

[3] *Ibid.*, Indroduction, pp. xx-xxi.

Yi-tsing in his preface to his memoir has aluded to the journeys of Fa-hien and Hiuen-tsang, who proceeded to the Western countries to procure Buddhist books and pay reverence to sacred relics. He briefly describes the hardships and dangers of the route, and the difficulty of finding shelter and entertainment in the different countries as there were no temples set apart for Chinese priests. He then goes on to ennumerate the names of the pilgrims referred to in his Memoires.[1]

We shall however describe very briefly the more important travellers, who came to India, either as pure pilgrims or as collectors of Sanskrit manuscripts.

Hiuen-chao, a native of Sien-chang in the district of T'ai, come from a distinguished Chinese family. He forsook the world and took the Hindu name of Prakāśamati (Pan-kia-shi-mo-ti), a custom usually followed by non-Hindu monks. He got himself ready for visiting the sacred places of India, and for the purpose of studying the scripture, came about A. D. 638 to Chang-an where he began to learn Sanskrit in a monastery. With the mendicant's staff in hand, Hiuen-chao proceeded westward, passed through Su-li (Sogdiana) traversed Turkistan, crossed Tibet and came to Jālandhara (She-lan-t'uo) having narrowly escaped death at the hands of brigands.

Hinen-chao called Prakāśamati

He lived in Jālandhara and passed four years there. He was honoured by the local king who detained him and made all arrangements for him. Hiuen-chao studied sutra and vinaya and gained proficiency in Sanskrit literature. Having acquired some knowledge, he proceeded towards the south, and came to Mahābodhi, where he lived for four years. There he meditated upon the marvellous work of the Lord Buddha and applied himself

[1] S. Beal, Indian Travels of Chinese Buddhists *Ind. And.* 1881, pp. 109ff 192ff, 246ff. *The Life of Hiuen-tsang* by Shaman Hwei-li with an introduction containing an account of the works of I-tsing by Samuel Beal...with a preface by L. Cranmer-Byng, Trübner, Pop, Ed., 1914.

heart and soul to comprehend the meaning of the Abhidharma.

Studied at Nalanda

From there the Chinese monk went to Nalanda, where he lived for three years. There he studied the *Madhyamaka śāstra* of Nāgārjuna and the *Śata-śāstra* of Āryadeva under Jinaprabha, who is mentioned by Yi-tsing in his *Record* (p. 181) and the yogācāra with Ratnasiṁha. (*Ibid.*, p. 184).

Then Hiuen-chao went up to the country to the north of the river Gangā (Ganges) and was welcomed in the Sinja vihāra by the king Jambu where he passed three more years. In the meantime, Wang-Hiuen-ts'e, the ambassador, who had lived in the court of Harṣavardhana and had returned to China, spoke highly of the virtue of this Chinese monk in his official report. Hiuen-chao was ordered from home to return to China and accordingly he went back by the route through Nepal and Tibet with some Sanskrit books.

At Loyang Hiuen-chao was greatly honored for his knowledge and he commenced to expound the essential portion of the Buddhist Law. With a group of Chinese monks he began to translate the *Sarvāstivāda Vinaya saṁgraha* (Sa-pus-to-pu-lu-shi)[1] But he could not finish the work as he was ordered by the emperor to go to India to bring the Brahmana Lokāyata (Lu-kia-i-to) who knew the art of longivity and who seem to be a man of Orissa.[2] Hiuen-chao set out again, passed by the way of the piled-up rocks (asmakūta) along the steep and craggy road that leads across rope-bridges into Tibet. Having escaped with life from a band of Hiung-nu robbers he arrived at the border of North India. There he met the imperial Chinese envoy, who was taking back the Lokāyata to China. Hiuen-chao visited several countries and at last came to Nalanda, where he met Yi-tsing. After this he wanted to go back to China by the N. W. route ; but that was blocked by the Tajiks (Arabs, Mussalmans ?), then he tried

---

[1] Translated afterwards by Yi-tsing in A. D. 700, Nanjio, 1127.

[2] *Memoire*, p. 21.

the Tibetan route, which he found equally closed to traffic. Therefore he returned to Magadha, where he died aged 60 odd years.

Tao-hi was a monk of Li-ch'eng, in the district of Ts'i. He took the Hindu name of Śrīdeva (she-li-t'i-p'uo). He came to India by the northern route through Tibet and after visiting several kingdoms came to Mahābodhi, paid respect to the sacred trees and spent several years there. He also lived in Nalanda where he studied Vinaya and Sanskrit language. He had talent for literature. In Mahābodhi he engraved one tablet in Chinese, and at Nalanda he copied more than four hundred chapters of Buddhist texts, old and new, which he meant to take to China. He was a contemporary of Yi-tsing, but he did not meet him. Tao-hi died at the age of fifty.

Tao-hi called Śrīdeva

Studied at Nalanda.

She-pien was a man of the same district as Tao-hi. This monk was well-versed in Sanskrit and the *Vidyāmantra*, by which probably Tantra is meant. In company of Hiuen Chao he came to the Western India and arrived Amarakuva, (?) whose king greatly honoured him. He met his countrymen Tao-hi in the royal temple there. This monk died at thirty-five, without performing any great act.[1] She-pien was accompanied by a man of the capital, Chang-Ngan known by his common name Wong-po and by the church name Matisiṁha (Mo-ti-seng-ho). Arriving at the middle country, he dwelt in the temple of Sin-che, but could not progress in the learning of Sanskrit. He returned homewards by way of Nepal and died on the way at the age of forty.[2]

Wong-po or Matisiṁha.

Tao-fang, Tao-sheng and Shang-min were all men of the district Ping. Tao-fang came to India by the route through Nepal, stayed at Mahābodhi for several years; while Yi-tsing visited India Tao-fang was still living

Tao-fang.

1 Memoire as well Beal No. 3.
2 Memoire, No. 15, Beal No. 13.

in Nepal (Nāpa-luo).[1] Tao-sheng took the Sanskrit name Candradeva. In 649 he came to India by the Tibetan road, studied at a place twelve stages to the eastward of Nalanda, the Hīnayāna scriptures for many years. Returning to China through Nepal he died.[2] Chang-min came by sea route, which will bo described below.

Tao-sheng or Candradeva.

Hiuen-hoei was a native of the capital who came to India by the N.-W. route, entered Kashmir and took charge of the elephants of the king. Afterwards he visited several places and went back to Nepal where he died.[3]

Hiuen hoei.

A Chinese monk, whose native name is not given, accompanied the envoy that came to India (probably under Wang Hiuen-tse) by the N.-W. route to Fo-k'o-luo (Puṣkalavati and not Balkh) and lodged in the Nava-vihāra. In this monastery the principles of Hīnayāna were taught. Having becoming a priest, he took the name of Citravarman. He learned a little Sanskrit and returned home by the Northern route.

Yi-tsing also speaks of two men, sons of the wet-nurse of the princes of Tibet (probably the Chinese Princess Wu-cheng who was married to Srong-bstan-gam-po of Tibet) who spoke Sanskrit well and understood Sanskrit books. Lung, a Chinese monk, whose place of origin Yi-tsing is unable to tell, came by the Northern route wishing to visit the sacred place. Lung was fortunate in having been able to secure a Sanskrit copy of the *Saddharma-puṇḍarīka* in Mid-India and went to Gāndhāra, where he died.

Of Sin-chiu, whose Sanskrit name is Śraddhāvarman (not Charitravarman of Beal, No. 25) Yi-tsing does not give the place of origin. He came te India by the N.-W. route and lived in the Sin-che monastery in the country of An-mu-lu-po (Amarāvati). In an upper room of the temple he constructed a sick chamber for the

Sin-Chin or Sraddhā-varman.

[1] Memoire, 11 ; Beal 10.
[2] Memoire 12 ; Beal 11.
[3] Memoire 16 ; Beal 14.

sick brothers. He died there at the age of thirty-five (Yi-tsing 30 ; Beal 25).

Chi-hing or Prajñādeva.

Chi-hing, of Ngai-chan, whose Sanskrit name is Prajñādeva (Pan-jo-ti-p'uo) came to India, and lived in the famous monastery of Sin-ch'e, where so many foreign monks lived (Yi-tsing 31, Beal 26). Many a Chinese monk came in search of Sanskrit MSS. but died without fulfilling their purpose.

Several Korean monks in India

Yi-tsing mentions several Corean monks who came to India in this time. Āryavarman was a Corean, who left Chang-an in A. D. 638 and set out with a view to recover the true teaching and to adore the sacred relics. He lived in the monastery of Nalanda copying out many sūtras, where he finally died aged seventy odd years.[1]

Studied at Nalanda

Hwei-yeh [2] another Corean set out for India in A. D. 638, arrived at Nalanda and there studied sacred books. Yi-tsing, while living at Nalanda one day came across the library of the monk, which consisted of Chinese books and Sanskrit copies made by him. The priests said that the monk had died the same year, at about sixty years of age.

Hiuen-'tai or Sarvajnadeva, a Korean.

Hiuen-t'ai, another Corean monk, called by the Sanskrit name of Sarvajñadeva, came by the Tibetan road to India (650-655 A.D.). He came as a pilgrim and visited several holy places. Hiuen-ko, a Corean who came to India with Hiuen-chao (No. 1) only to die at Mahabodhi. Two other priests of Corea started from Chang-Ngan by the southern sea-route and came to Śrīvijaya (Sumatra) and died in the country of Pu-lu-ssa to the west of Śrīvijaya.[3]

Hwei-lun was a native of Corea, who adopted the Hindu

---

[1] Memoire 4, Beal 4.

[2] Hwie-nieh of Beal

[3] Memoire, 8 & 9 ; Beal 8.

name of Prajñavarma (Pan-jo-po-mo). He came from Corea by sea to the modern Fu-kien and Koang-tong and thence by land and water went to Chang-an. There he received an imperial order to proceed to the West in company of Hiuen-chao (see above) as his servant. After reaching India he visited all the sacred places and at last came to stay at the monastery of Sin-chè in the country of Amaravati where he lived for ten years.

Hwei-lun or Prajñavarma

Hwei-lun proceeded eastward and came to the monastery called Gandhara-chaṇḍa which had been built by the people of Tu-ho-lo or Tokharisthan, for the convenience of their monks. It was a rich monastery. Hwei-lun lived there and acquired good knowledge of the Sanskrit language and studied the Abhidharma works. When Yi-tsing visited India Hwei-lun was still living here ; he was then about forty years old.

While at Nalanda Yi-tsing met a man of Tu-ho-lo or Tukhāra. It was Buddhadharma (Fo-t'o-ta-mo) a priest of that country, where Buddhism was still flourishing. He was a man of great size and strength but of gentle disposition. He wandered through the provinces of China and went to the West and came to India, when Yi-tsing saw him.

A man of Tu-ho-lo

He speaks of another monk of Central Asia. Saṅghavarman (Seng-kia-po-mo) was a man of K'ang, which is the Chinese name of Sogdiana (*i. e.* Samarkhand). In his youth he crossed the sand desert and went to China. In 656-660 he was ordered by the Emperor to accompany the ambassador who was proceeding towards India. Saṅghavarma visited the Mahābodhi temple and the Vajrasana, where he burnt lamps for seven days and seven nights continuously. In the garden of the Mahābodhi, this monk engraved the image of Bodhisattva Avalokiteśvara on a Aśoka tree. He was held in great esteem by his contemporaries, with whom he however returned to China. But the very soon he received imperial order to go to the district of Kiao (Cochin-China) to administer relief to the people who were

Saṅghavarman of Central Asia

suffering from famine and pestilence. This Bodhisattva daily distributed food and wept for the orphans and was called by the people 'the weeping Bodhisattva.' He died shortly afterwards from infection caught there at about sixty. (Memoire 33 ; Beal 28).

Insulindia, Centre of Sanskrit Culture

During the T'ang dynasty the sea-route from China to India was greatly used by traders and pilgrims. The peninsula of Further India and the islands of the Indian Ocean had been Hinduised and some of the places had international reputation as a centre of Hindu culture, such as, the kingdom of Śrivijaya of Sumātra, the Ka-linga province of Java, Funan or ancient Annam. Everywhere Sanskrit was studied and Chinese pilgrims found scholars to help and shelter to rest. Yi-tsing himself came by this route and mentions a large number of monks who came to India by the same route.

Chang-min

Chang-min[1] was a monk of the district of Ping, who took this sea-route ; two of his country-men had come by the land-route and we have met them before. He was very pious and longed to be reborn in the Western Paradise of Amitābha. While in Loyang he had vowed to write out the sacred book of Prajñāpāramitā in 10,000 chapters. He travelled throughout China preaching the doctrine ; at last coming to the coast, he embarked a ship for Ho-ling which is a part of Java,[2] whence he proceeded by sea to Malaya (Mo-lue-yu) and thence wishing to go to India he took another merchant-ship. The ship foundered in a storm ; the Chinese monk and his companion monk sat quietly in the ship while others struggled to reach a boat.[3] Yi-tsing, who took the sea-route from China and lived for many years in Indonesia speaks of a large number of such monks, who came as far as Cochin-China and Ceylon and could not fulfil their desired pilgrimage.

---

1 Not Sheng-ti as in Beal, No. 12.

2 Pelliot, *BEFEO*. iv.

3 Yi-tsing 13 ; Beal 12.

Several monks of the district of Yih are mentioned by Yi-tsing who came by this southern sea-route. Ming-yuen was a doctor of Dharma, whose Sanskrit name was Cintādeva. He came to Tonkin by sea and then to Ho-ling or Java, whence he came to Ceylon. Ceylon was famous for Buddhist relics and specially as tradition has it, that a tooth of Buddha was deposited in the Danta-pura monastery. This monk in his enthusiasm for religion and greed for relics tried to steal the famous tooth-relic, but the poor monk was detected and disgraced.

Ming-guen or Cintadeva.

I-long was a priest of the Ch'ang-tu of the district of Se-chuan. He was well-versed in the Vinayapitaka and in the interpretation of the Yoga. He set forth from Chang-an with a priest of his own district named Shih-an and his younger brother I-hiuen. They travelled through the Southern provinces, came to the port of Wu-lei, embarked a merchantman and came to Fu-nan and then to Long-kia, which is old Dvārāvati, a Hindu colony in the east. Shih-an died here and I-long with his other companion went to Ceylon and made searches for the different Vinaya texts. He worshipped the tooth-relic and returned through W. India.[1]

I-long and Chang-an

Hui-ning[2] was a monk of the district of Yih. He left China by sea in the year 665 A.D. and passed three years in the island of Java (in the country of Holing or Kalinga). Here in this place lived a Hindu monk named Jñānabhadra with whom Hui-ning translated a part of the Mahāparinirvāṇa Sūtra (Nanjio, 115). This Jñānabhadra we met under the translators of the early T'ang dynasty (Nanjio, App. II, 133). Hui-ning, however, left for India, but Yi-tsing was unable to trace him there.

Hui-ning, A.D. 665.

---

[1] Chavannes, 22, 23, 24; Beal 19.
[2] Chavannes 25; Beal 20.

Yun-k'i[1] was a priest of Kiao. He travelled with T'an-juen (see below) and must have come to Kalinga (Java) where he met Jñānabhadra. Yun-k'i spent ten years of his life in the islands of the Southern sea and became well-versed in the language of Kun-lun and partly acquianted himself with Sanskrit. Kun-lun is identified with Pulo-condore and the language referred is the Malaya. Yun-k'i afterwards retired to a lay life and resided at Śrīvijaya in Sumatra. Yi-tsing found him there while he compiled the *Memoire.*

Yun-k'i.

Mokṣadeva[2] (Mo-ch'a-t'i-po,) a monk of Cochin-China came to India, by the southern route; he visited Mahābodhi, where he died at the age of twenty-four.

Mokṣadeva.

Kwei-ching, also a native of Cochin-China, came by the southern route with his master Ming-yuen, who was disgraced in Ceylon. He came to India and saw there Hiuen-chao (No. 1). He visited several holy places and died young, aged thirty years only. Another monk from Cochin-China was Hui-yen.[3] He went to Ceylon.

Kwei-chung.

Mahāyānapradīpa (Mo-ho-ye-na po-ti-i-po; *Chin.* Ta-tseng-teng) does not seem to be a proper name; it means the Lamp of Mahāyāna. Pradīpa went with his parents to the country of Dvārāvati (Siam). He returned to the Chinese capital with the imperial ambassador Yen-siu and lived there for several years studying the sacred books. Afterwards he went by the southern sea route to Ceylon, gathering on way images of the Buddha and copies of Sūtras, and Śāstras. In Ceylon he worshipped the tooth-relic of Buddha. Then he proceeded through South India and reached Eastern India (Bengal) embarking at Tāmralipti. Tāmralipti was not only a seaport, but a great centre of culture too. Fa-hsien lived here for some years. Pradīpa

Mahāyānapradīpa.

1 Chavannes 26; Beal 21, Wan-ki.
2 Chavannes 27; Beal 22; Mochadeva.
3 Memoire 29; Beal 24.

lived for twelve years and became master of the Sanskrit language. There he expounded the *Nidāna-sāstra* (*c. f.* Nanjio, 1227) and other sacred books. He then proceeded to Nalanda, Mahābodhi; then to Vaisali and the Kusi country, and finally died at Kushinagar, in the Parinirvāna temple at about sixty.[1]

Pei-an and She-an.

Two priests, named Pei-an and Shih-an, both from the district of Kao-ch'ang, were coming to India. But unfortunately they died on the voyage. Their Chinese books which they were bringing with them, such as Assanga's *Yoga-sāstra* (Yogācara-bhumi) (Nanjio 1170) and other Sutras and Abhidharma works were brought to Srīvijaya, where Yi-tsing probably saw them.[2]

T'an-juen.

T'an-juen[3] a man of Loyang, travelling through the southern parts of China, came to Cochin-China, thence went by ship to Pupen, north of Kalinga in the island of Java, where the ardent monk died at the young age of thirty.

I-hui.

I-hui[4] was another monk from Loyang, eminent for his scholarship. He heard the explanation of *Mahāyāna-samparigraha* of Asanga[5] *Abhidharmakosa sāstra* and other books. But he was not satisfied with the translation and sometimes the contradictions troubled him much. He, therefore, wanted to come to India and set out for the purpose. But at Lang-kia-chu (Dvāravati) the devoout monk died at the age of thirty only.

Tao-lin or Śilaprabha.

Tao-lin, a Chinese priest of the district of King, had taken the Hindu name of Śilaprabha (She-lu-po-p'o). In a ship he passed tho Copper-pillars, which was built by a Chinese general in A. D. 42, and arrived at the country of Lang-kia or Dvārāvati. Thence he

---

[1] Chavannes 32; Beal 27.

[2] *Memoire* 34, 35; Beal 29.

[3] Chavannes 36; Beal 31, has *Wan-yun* incorrectly.

[4] Chavannes 37; Beal 31.

[5] Nanjio, 1183, 1184 and 1247.

went to Kalinga (Java) and came to Tāmralipti in Bengal, where he studied Sanskrit for three years. Here he studied the Vinaya of the school of Sarvāstivāda, Yoga and probably Tantra. After visiting the Vajrāsana and worshipping Mahābodhi he passed to Nalanda (Na-lan-t'u), where he studied and examined the sutras and the sastra of the Mahāyāna and penetrated into the Abhidharma-kośa. After a year or two he visited different holy places, went to the Western India and passed a year in Ladak. Here Tao-lin received a new the magic prayers, that is, Dhāraṇis.

Speaks of Vidyādhara pitaka, a work on magic and Alchemy

The magic prayers received are known in Sanskrit (P'i-t'i-t'u-lu pi-te-kia), *the Vidyādhara pitaka.* The Sanskrit text of this magical work is said to have consisted of 100,000 ślokas, which if translated into Chinese would represent 300 chapters. It is said that the great portion of this work was lost and a little was intact. Ārya Nāgārjuna (A-lo-ye No-kia-li-chu-na) specially studied the important parts of the work. One of the disciples of Nāgārjuna named Nanda, a man of great intelligence, penetrated into the spirit of those rules. He spent twelve years in Western India, studying this. Dignāga[1] the great logician studied it. Till then this text had not been studied by any person from China and that is the reason why Tao-lin made researches into the subject. Yi-tsing while at Nalanda, also studied the essentials of the doctrine ; but nowhere does he give the details of it and we cannot know what the *Vidyādhara pitaka* was. It seems that it was a book on magic and alchemy, the latter being connected with the life of Nāgārjuna.

Tao-lin lived in North India some time, went on pilgrimage to Kashmir, then to Udyāna from where he passed through Kapisa ; after this what happened to Tao-lin Yi-tsing cannot say.[2]

Ta-kuang and Hui-ming were priests from the same district

---

[1] Chen-na, not Jinr, *Memoire* p. 103 ; but Dignāga.

[2] Chavannes 42 ; Beal 34.

Tao-kuang & Hui-ming

as Tao-lin. The one died at Harikela (Arakan ? Ho-li-ki-lo) in the Eastern India and the other could go only as far as Champa (Champo)[1] owing to the ship being stopped by contrary wind.

Hiuen-k'oie

Hiuen-k'oei[2] was a priest of the district of Kiang-ning, who came of a good family which was known for its literary talents as well as for military virtue. He died very young before he could finish his project.[3]

Ling-yun and Seng-Shé

Ling-yun and Seng-shé, two monks passing through Annam came to India. Ling-yun erected under the Bodhi-tree a figure of Maitreya Buddha of exquisite workmanship. Seng-shé arrived at Samatata (Eastern Bengal) ; the King Harṣabhaṭa (Ho-lo-she-po-cha) greatly revered the Triratna and was a Upāsaka, who sincerely believed in the Buddhist religion. Buddhism was prospering there, when Seng-shé came.

Hiuen-yen

A disciple of Seng-shé, Hiuen-yeu came with him and remained in Ceylon.[4] She-hung was a nephew of the ambassador Wang Hiuen-tsé, who came to the court of Harṣavardhana. He came by the southern sea-route and passed through all the important places mentioned so many times before. At Mahābodhi he passed two years studying Sanskrit, Abhidharma kośa, Logic and Medicine. At Nalanda he consulted the Mahāyana sūtras. He also studied Hīnayāna in the temple of Sin-ché in North India. He visited the holy places and was in Kashmir, when Yi-tsing wrote his biography (Chavannes, 51).

She-hung studied at Mahabodhi and Nalanda.

---

[1] Chavannes 43, 45 ; Beal 35. 36.

[2] Chavannes 46 ; Beol 37, has Hiuen-ta.

[3] *Memoire* page 111.

Beal makes awful mistakes here. He jumbles the life of Hiuen-koei with that of Yi-tsin, who narrates his own biography just after Hiuen-k'oei's. It is very amusing to find that the life of Yi-tsing is told as the life of Hiuen-koei, (*Ibid.*, p. 114-125 ; see also I-tsing's *Record* by Takakusu, Introduction, pp. ii-xxxxvi.

[4] Chavannes 49, 50 ; Beal 39, 40.

In campany with She-hung travelled another monk named Wu-hing. He arrived at Śrīvijaya and then went in the royal ship for fifteen days to Malaya and in another fifteen days to Kie-ch'a which is identified with Atchen, the north-west part of Sumatra, which was in the seventh century also a great centre of Hindu culture. There he waited during the winter and going west for thirty days, the ship he embarked reached Nāgapatana (Negapatam in the Coromondol coast), whence after two days' voyage he came to Ceylon. Here he adored the tooth-relic and then again he took another vessel, which went north-east for a month and reached (Ho-li-ki-lo) Arakan (?), the eastern frontier of Jambudvīpa where he lived a year. After this Wu-hing and She-hung travelled together. They went to Mahābodhi and then to Nalanda. Wu-hing took lesson of the Yoga (Yogācārabhumi) and heard the explanation of the Kośa and exercised contemplation. From here he went to Tilāḍhaka temple where he studied the Nyāya (Logic) according to Dignāga. He also translated a few works into Chinese.[1]

Wu-hing

Studied at Nalanda

Several other monks started by the sea-route for India; but failing they reached the Insulindia. Fa-chen, Ch'eng-wu and Ch'eng-ju came as far as Sumatra. Ta-tsin came as far as Malaya (Chavannes 53-56). Bhiksu Cheng-ku, who took the Hindu name of Sālagupta, was a keen and intelligent monk, whom Yi-tsing met at Śrīvijaya (Chavannes, 57). Cheng-ku's disciple Hoei-yeh who took the Hindu name of Saṅghadeva was with him in the same town. (Chavannes, 58). Bhiksu Tao-hong (Buddhadeva) and Bhikṣu Fa-lang or Dharmadeva were the other monks whom Yi-tsing met (Chavannes, 59, 60).

Some came as fas as Srivijaya.

The short biographical notes of these monks who came out of China to visit India clearly show the intimate intellectual relation that was established between these two countries since the visit of Hiuen-tsang.

---

[1] Chavannes 55; Beal 42.

XIX. Tantrism in China

The great empress Wu Tso-tien weakened by age and illness, was forced in A. D. 704 to abdicate in favour of her son Chung-tsung, whom she had put in prison in the glorious days of her power.

Regime of Wu Tso-tien ends in 704.

Chung-tsung unlike her mother was a week sovereign and fell a victim to the harem-intrigue (709). After a general insurrection, headed by the son of Jui-tsung, brother of Chung-tsung the intriguing women of the palace and their accomplice were put to death and Jui-tsung was placed on the throne of China; but after an uneventful reign of four years, he abdicated in favour of his son Hiuan-tsung.

Hiuan-tsung "reigned for 45 years (713-755) which was the longest reign of the T'ang dynasty. It was also a most celebrated one, both on account of the splendours with which it began and the disasters that brought it to a close." After the abdication of Wu Tso-tien, there does not seem to have any change in the religious outlook of the soveriegns, and two Buddhist monks were appointed to high offices. Orders were issued that Buddhist and Taoist temples should be built in every district. But Hiuan-tsung's reign began with a temporary reaction, when he forbad the building of monasteries, making of images of Buddha and the Bodhisattvas, and declared the copying sūtras a crime. Twelve thousand monks were ordered to return to the world.[1] Inspite of this set-back a few Hindu monks came to China and left a permanent impress in the intellectual history of China and Japan.

Attitude towards Buddhism unchanged.

In A. D. 716 arrived in Chang-an, the capital of the empire, a Hindu monk named Śubhakarasiṁha, an inhabitant of Central India. It is said that Śubhakarasiṁha was a descendant of Amṛtodana, an uncle of Śākyamuni, and lived in the monastery of

Śubhakarasinha, A. D. 716

[1] Eliot, *Ibid.* III, p. 261.

Nalanda. He came to China when about eighty years old bringing with him many Sanskrit works out of which five were translated by him. He died in his ninty-ninth year in A. D. 935.[1]

Pioneer of Tantrism in China

Śubhakara might well be called a pioneer for introducing Tāntrik literature in China. Having come to the court of China, he "won over the celebrated Chang-sui, better known as I-hsing, to whom he taught the Indian sciences, I-hsing (672-717 A. D.) helping him in return by translations."[2]

Śubhakara believed that the Buddhist monks in China were wasting their time in fruitless philosophical speculations and the Chinese people were not capable of abstract thinking. Therefore, leaving on one side all theories. whether these were Hīnayānist or Mahāyānist, accepting all the Buddhas, the Bodhisattvas, the Hindu gods and the Chinse Shen, rejecting all dogma, all tradition, all explanations Śubhakara invented for the poor suffering people, a pantheon of deities, taught them to invoke gods by *mantras*. He therefore transliterated the Sanskrit *mantras*, unintelligible to the Chinese, into Chinese idiograms, and the ignorant people believed all the more in the virtue and efficacy of the *mantras*. In the writings of the sect, the litanies of the Buddhas and Bodhisattvas to be invoked, contained more than a thousand names, all pure fiction. The principal deities Vairocana and Vajrapāni, are the universal protectors and saviours. Śubhakara said that people should know that all the corners of the world are filled with counterforces or forces working against our *siddhi*, which they conceived as evil-working goblins ; that above this world there are powerful beings, able to protect those who invoke them ; that the devotee has only to choose well, and to recite the proper formula.[3]

---

1 Nanjio, App II, 154.

2 Giles, *Biog. Dict.* No. 902. I-hsing's (I-hang) reformed calendar was adopted in 721. He was the author of a large work on ritual and of some mathematical treatises.

3 Wieger, *loc. cit.* p. 536.

Although Śubhakara is acknowledged as the pioneer of Tāntrism in China, some hold that it was Po Śrīmitra of Kucha, who came to China in 307-312 A. D., was the first monk to translate Tantrik texts. According to Tibetan chronicle *Dub-thah-selkyi-melon*[1] Śrīmitra "diffused the knowledge of Tāntrism by translating the Mahāmāyurī and other Dhāraṇīs into the Chinese language. Although contemporaneously with him many other eminent Indian Tantrikas came to China, yet very few books on Tantra were translated for the public. The sage Kumaraśrī (Po Śrīmitra) also did not communicate his Tāntrik lore to the general public, but to only one or two of his confidential disciples, so that Tāntrism made little progress in China." If this statement is correct, then the history of Tantrism in India would go back to the second century A. D. and the chapter of the history of Indian Religion should be rewritten.

Tantrism introduded by Po Srimitra of Kucha in 307 A.D.

During the period of four hundred years that intervened between Po Śrīmitra and Śubhakara, a number of Dhāraṇīs and texts of allied nature had appeared in Chinese and we have had occasion to refer to them in our study before.

In India at this time composition of Tāntrik literature formed a special feature of Buddhism with certain sections of the people. Śāntarakṣita, Padmasambhava, Kamalaśila and a host of other Indian writers flourished in this epoch and went to Tibet. Similarly a few Hindu monks went to China to preach the Tantra cult, of whom Śubhakara was the pioneer. But the real founders were Vajrabodhi and his disciple Amoghavajra. They arrived in China in A. D. 719.

Vajrabodhi was born in Mo-lo-ye (Malaya in S. India) in 660 A. D. (circa). He was a brahmana by caste and was a preceptor of the king of Kien-che (Kāñcī). He went to Nalanda with his teacher for studying Hīnayāna. In his evening of life, at the age

Vajrabodhi, founder of Tantrism in China

[1] Translated by Sarat Chandra Das *JASB*, 1882. p. 93 ; but the Tibetan authority always should be handled with care and discretion.

of fifty-eight, Vajrabodhi with his favourite disciple Amoghavajra went to China in A. D. 719. He died in A. D. 732 at the 71st year.[1]

Between A. D. 723 and 732 Vajrabodhi translated into Chinese eleven Tantrik works. His works reveal his intimacy with Vajrayānic scripture and even his name Vajrabodhi seems to be an adopted one. This old Tantrik monk well-knew the responsibility of possessing esoteric knowledge and was very cautious in imparting its secret to the Chinese Buddhist lest it would be misunderstood. He therefore instructed only two Chinese monks in this mystery, but gave a thorough education to his disciple Amoghavajra, who had been with him since his boyhood.

Amoghavajra established Tantrism

Amoghavajra was a śramaṇa of Northern India and brahmana by caste. In A. D. 719 he arrived in China, a young neophyte of twenty-one years, following his guru Vajrabodhi who was then about 58 years old. After the death of the Guru, Amogha gave an impetus to the study of Tāntrism. "The demand for Tantras became such, that Amogha was officially despatched (741-746) by the imperial government to India and specially to Ceylon to bring back from there the greatest possible number." (Weiger, p. 536). After his return from the Indian tour, he was honoured with the title of Chu-tsang, *i. e.* 'Repository of Wsdom' by the emperor Hiuan-tsung. Amogha, however, wished to return to his own native land ; at first he was allowed to go ; but at the last moment the emperor withheld the permission and Amogha had to come back to the capital in 746. Various honorofic titles were conferred on him by the emperor Tai-sung (763-779) to make good his suffering in thus being prevented from going home. Amogha has left a note about his own self, which is quoted below.

His life.

"From my boyhood I served my late teacher (Vajrabodhi) for fourteen years (719-732), and received his instruction in the doctrine of Yoga. Then I went to the five parts of India and collected several sūtras and

[1] Nanjio, App. II. 153.

śāstras, more than 500 different texts, which had hitherto not yet been brought to China. In A. D. 746 I came back to the capital. From the same year to the present time (A. D. 771) I translated 77 works in more than 120 fasciculi." Amogha translated altogether 108 works and died in 774 in his seventieth year. (Nanjio, Ap. II. 155). He is said to have performed many miraculous work for the good of the emperor, who, being pleased with the results, granted him a piece of land supporting three thousand tenants. Hui-lang, a Chinese disciple was installed in Amogha's place as a Vajrācārya. Vajrabodhi was the first, Amogha the second and Hui-lang the third patriarch of the Shingon (Mantra) sect.

Amoghavajra by his character and conviction made Tāntrism the fashionable sect of the time. But it should be noted that in the numerous works attributed to Amogha, one finds none of the immodest things, which sometimes characterizes some of the Tantra works of India and Tibet. What Amogha preached may be gauged from the short quotations from Tantrik works, which are rare and concise.

His Teaching.

"Man is not, like the banana, a fruit without a kernel. His body contains an immortal soul, which the Chinese Tāntrists say, has the face of a child. After death, the soul descends to the hells to be judged there. Pardon of sins, preservation from punishments, so often promised to the devotees, are explained by the Tāntrists, not as a derogation from justice, but as the effect of an appeal made in favour of the guilty soul, by some transcendent protector. That appeal obtains for the soul a new life, a kind of respite during which it can ransom itself by doing good work, instead of expiation by the torments of hell. The sect believes that the infernal judges prefer the ransom as more fruitful than the expiation, and always willingly grant the appeal of any who solicits that favour. Any one, who having been a devout Tantrist, has asked before his death to be reborn in the domain of such or such a Buddha, is supposed to have claimed it himself, and it is granted to him according to his request. As to those who have done nothing to save themselves, sinners and unbelievers, their relatives and friends, or the bonzes, may interject an appeal in their favour, even after their death....... The devotion of the Tantrists to the salvation of the dead is very great."[1] Various *mantras*, which were translated and transliterated by the Tantrik monks, are known to ward off the evils done by various demons, of which they count 60,049. There are spirits of mountains, woods, steppes, sands, fields, cemetries, fire, water, air, trees, roads, etc. The whole universe is thus spiritualized ; every thing has a meaning, a soul of its own.

Kobo-daishi, a Japanese monk, learns Tantrism.

In spite of the great honour showered and titles conferred on Amoghavajra, the great teacher, in spite of the royal help Tantrism received, the doctrine never became acceptable to the Chinese. But in Japan it took root. Kobo Daishi, who came to China for Buddhist studies, learned the secret of *mantra* and founded a sect in Japan known as Shingon.

Philosophy of Tantra or Mantrayāna (Shingon)

Shingon sect is described as cosmo-theism. It "found expression in an extremely comprehensive and striking combination of spiritual ideals and material embodiment, of speculative thought and mystic ritual, and in a union of the Buddhist, Hindu, Persian, Chinese and Japanese panthoons into one cycle centred in Buddha..... It may be designated as a synthetic or symbolic Buddhism. It views the universe as a cosmo-theism, or more emphatically, it difines the total cosmos as Divinity, whereof particular features may, for certain purposes, be assembled under the forms of separate deities ; and its art was an attempt to represent these innumerable deities, saints, demons, angels and other ultra-human beings embodying the inexhaustible beauties, powers, activities and mysteries, by means of pictures, statues, symbols and rites."[2]

---

[1] Wieger, *op. cit.* pp. 537-38.

[2] Anesaki, *Buddhist Art*, chapter III.

Mudrās and Mantras

In Mantra and Tantrayānas, the *mudrā* or posture of the body, arms and fingers count a good deal and volumes have been written on the subject. Further, there have been attempts to unify all possible varieties of saints, deities, spirits and demons with the central world-soul, Buddha, or a plane surface arranging the figures side by side according to classes within squares and circles called *maṇḍalas*. *Maṇḍalas* represent graphically the cosmo-theistic world-view in its entirety. A large number of works are found in Chinese and Tibetan on the *maṇḍalas* and the pictorial art of Japan and Tibet specially greatly helped in visualizing the grouping. Bold painters of China, Japan and Tibet conceived impossible representations of these symbols and Vairocana, the cosmic-Buddha of Mantrayāna, has been the subject of art from the brush of masters. The Acala Vairocana or Immovable Deity known in Japan as Fedo has been painted by many painters.[1]

Many *mudrās* are represented in the Chinese Tripitaka, numerous *mantras* written in the Gupta script are found copied there with equivalent Chinese ideograms for transliterating Sanskrit sounds. Below we quote three *mantras* used in the invocation of Acala Vairocana or Fudo :

Invocation of Acala-Vairocana in Gupta Script in the Tripiṭaka

1. Namah Samanta-Vajrānāṁ (Adoration to the All-vajra-hum).

2. Namah Samanta-vajrānāṁ Caṇḍa Mahāroṣana sphoṭāyo huṁ trāṭa hāṁ māṇi (Great Wrathful one, Destroy, Hum, Trāt, Hām, mani).

3. Namah Sarva-tathāgatebhyo viśvamukhebhyah Sarvatha trat Caṇḍa mahāroṣaṇa Khaṁ, Khādi, Khādi, Sarva-vighnaṁ huṁ trat hāṁ māni (Adoration everywhere to all the Tathāgatas, to the Allfaced ones in all place ! Trat. O the Terrible one ! O the wrathful one, Kham, Destroy, Destroy every obstruction).[2]

---

[1] *Eastern Buddhist*, Otani, 1922, Vol II, p. 129 *ff*.
[2] *Ibid*., p. 153.

XX. THE LAST PHASE UNDER THE T'ANG

The emperor Hsüan Tsung in the latter part of his reign had become a puppet in the hands of the harem ladies and had lost all the brilliances he had shown in his youth. But inspite of the degeneracy he still kept up his intellectual interest. His reign was really the golden age of Chinese poetry and painting. Many of the poets were Buddhists and some of the artists glowed with the inspiration of the Tien-tai teaching. The most important work in the course of Buddhist culture, is the seventh collection of the Tripiṭaka, made under his auspices.

Golden Age of Art and Poetry

This catalogue is generally called *Kai-yuen-lu* (Nanjio, 1485), and is considered one of the best catalogues of the Buddhist works. It was compiled by the priest Che Sheng in 730 A. D. and gives a complete list of all the translations of Buddhist works during the past six hundred years (664 years), from the year A. D. 67 up to the date of the publication, 730 A. D., embracing the labour of 176 individuals ; the whole amounted to about *2,278 separate works*, many of which, however, were at that time already lost. This catalogue has often been referred to in our study.

K'ai-yuen-lu catalogue of Buddhist Tripiṭaka A. D. 730

Che Sheng divided his work into two parts, the first of which gives the translations in the order of their completion, according to the successive dynasties, under each of which several translators are given chronologically with the works they had executed, and a statement of those which were still extant, and those lost, with a biographical notice of each translator following the catalogue of his works. At the end of the first part is a list of forty-one Catalogues[1] which had been previously issued.

The second part contains the same works under a different

---

[1] See Bagchi, *Le Canon Bouddhique*, Introduction, chapter, II, Les Sources, pp. XXXII-LI.

classification, divided into seven sections, stating those of which both the translation and original are extant, incomplete portions of works, epitomes, defficiencies supplied, retranslations, and heterodox innovations. The last two sections contain a classification according to the great division of Mahāyana and Hinayana, sub-divided under three heads of sūtra, Vinaya and Abhidharma. The latter part includes also a list of works historical, geographical, and biographical in two divisions, the first being translations from the Sanskrit and the second native Chinese productions. The work is conceived on a comprehensive plan and contains much valuable information.

There is a summary of the above catalogue by the same author with the title of *Kai-yuen-shih-chiao-lu-liao-chu* (Nanjio, 1486), giving the name of each work, and the author with the index character under which is to be found in the great imperial collection. This may be called the seventh collection made by the order of a Chinese Emperor.[1]

Emperor Hsüan Tsung's envoys in India

Hsüan Tsung with all his faults loved culture and letters, and pageantry which made his court brilliant. The splendours of the court faded and his reign ended tragically in disaster and rebellion. But even on the eve of his downfall, his intellectual interest had not forsaken him. In A. D. 751 the Emperor sent a mission to the king of Kipin. The staff included a man named Wu-kung. The Chinese ambassador returned after fulfilling his political mission; but Wu-kung was ill at that time and was therefore left behind in a monastery of Gandhara (K'ien-to-lo). Wu-kung made a vow of devoting his life in the service of Buddha when he would recover. He recovered and the Ācārya conferred on him the Sanskrit name of (Ta-mo-t'o-lu) Dharmadhatu. He became a monk at his 27th year in 757, that is, six years after he came to India. He spent four years in learning the Sanskrit language. He was very diligent

Wu-kung, a Chinese in India, A. D. 751

[1] A. Wylie, *Notes on Chinese Literature*, Shanghai, 1902, p. 208.

in his studies and visited all the holy places, residing three years in the Nalanda monastery. Then he returned to Udyāna and expressed his intention of returning home. But the Adhyakṣa refused him permission to leave the country on the ground that he was not satisfied with China, which he had visited in 750 A. D. When he saw Wu-kung (Dharmadhatu) was pining for his country and family, then the Adhyakṣa granted him permission. He further gave him a copy of the Sanskrit text of *Shi-ti-ching* (Dasabhumi śāstra) and *Hui-hsiang-luen-ching* (Bhavasaṁkrānti sūtra) which formed together one volume.

Wu-kung visited several countries and passed through all the important towns of Central Asia and came to Kucha, the native city of Kumārajīva, where he wanted to translate the Sanskrit text into Chinese with the help of the monks. Thence he went to Pei-ting (Wu-rumchi), where Śiladharma, a monk of Khotan, translated the Sanskrit texts, the śramana Shan-sin verified the text, and Wu-kung verified the Sanskrit and the translation.

Wu-kung, on his way to China, took the northern route through the land of the Uigurs (Turks), to avoid the trouble of the Gobi desert. The Turkish king was not a follower of Buddha and Wu-kung left the Sanskrit texts in the Pei-ting monastery and went home with the Chinese translations.

Wu-kung returns after 40 years, A. D. 790

The Chinese traveller reached Chang-an in A. D. 790 and presented the relic and the book to the emperor and received royal honours. In his whole travel, he had passed forty years (751-790) and came back home an old man of sixty.[1]

Chavannes and Lèvi, who have translated the Chinese biography of Wu-kung, thus summarizes the life and work of the Chinese itinerant :

---

[1] The texts translated by Wu-kung are not mentioned in Nanjio's catalogue. But in the Tokyo edition and Corean edition (XXII, 25) the translation on *Daśabhumi Sūtra* is preceded by a long introduction which means, "Memoir on a new translation of *Daśabhumi Sūtra*, etc. executed in the *Cheng-yuen* period (789-804) of the great T'ang dynasty." This memoir was written by Yuen-chao, a friend of Wu-kung, who had related his life to him.

"The monk Wu-kung, who in the Saṅgha, at first bore the name of Fu-kue or Dharmadhatu, was born in A. D. 730, started in 751 for the Western countries and returned after an absence of forty years in 790. In the interval he visited Central Asia, and India as a zealous pilgrim rather than as an intelligent observer. Not a good scholar himself, he was obliged to apply to others for interpreting the sūtras, which he brought, as well as for writing his reminiscences. His long travels have been not a little instructive. He has seen much, but he has not retained much. Though his notes are meagre and dry, yet they do not fail to interest us. They give us a glimpse into the state of Central Asia in a troubled and obscure period. They illumine the unexpected prosperity and vigour of Buddhism in those regions on the eve of the day when the faith disappears. They reveal an all Turkish supremacy, which can hardly be suspected, even over the border of India and Afghanisthan. If Wu-kung remains far behind Hiuen-tsang and even Fa-hsien, his biography at least forms a precious complement and a natural sequel to the gallery of eminent monks who went in search of the Dharma in the western country in the time of the great T'ang dynasty."[1]

Wu-kung left China in 751 when the great T'ang emperor Hsuan Tsung (713-756) was on the throne. During his absence from China the emperor Su Tsung (756-763) and T'ai Tsung (763-780) reigned and he returned in the reign of emperor Te-Tsung (780-805) in A. D. 790. During the reigns of these emperors few Indian came to China; the only monk that came was Prajña of Kapisa who came to China in A. D. 785 and lived till A. D. 810, that is, he lived and worked in China during the reigns of emperors Te Tsung (780-805), Shun Tsung (805-806) and Hsien Tsung (806-821).

Prajna come to China, 785 A.D.

Prajña translated only four works. But they were all large

[1] Levi and Chavannes, *J.As*, 1895 (Sept.-Oct.) translated from the French by P. N. Bose. Itinerary of Wu-kong (751-790). *Calcutta Review*, 1922, pp. 188-193, pp. 486-498.

texts. He translated a chapter of the practice and prayer of the Bodhisattva Samantabhadra in the Mahāvaipulva Buddhāvataṁsaka sutra (Nanjio, 89). This is a latter and fuller translation in 40 fasciculi of a text similar to that of the last chapter of the *Avataṁsaka* translated by Buddhabhadra (circa 400 A. D.) and Śikṣānanda 700 A. D. (Nanjio, 87-88). At the end of the book there is a letter addressed to the Chinese emperor by the King of Wu-cha of South India, who presented to the former his own copy of the Sanskrit text of this chapter in A. D. 795 and Prajña with other monks translated the book in A. D. 796-798. The three translations of the Avataṁsaka are generally distinguished by the number of fasciculi, as sixty, eighty and forty Hue-yen-ching (Nanjio, 89.)

Translation of the Avatamsaka in 'forty'

Prajña translated the Mahāyāna Mūlajāta Hṛdayabhumi Dhyāna sūtra in 8 fasciculi of 13 chapters. (Nanjio, 955). There is a preface added by the emperor Hsien Tsung (806-820) of the T'ang Dynasty. Some very beautiful and edifying hymns to Mahāyāna are found in the text, which are quoted below for their beauty.[1]

Mūlajāta Hṛdayabhūmi sūtra

"Those who repent as prescribed by the Dharma,
Altogether their earthly sins uproot,
As fire on doomsday the world will consume,
With its mountain-peaks and infinite seas."
"Repentance burns up of earthly desires the fuel ;
Repentance to heaven the sinners is leading ;
Repentance the bliss of the four dhyanas imparteth ;
Repentance brings showers of jewels and gems ;
Repentance a holy life renders firm as a diamond ;
Repentance transports to the palace of bliss ever-lasting ;
Repentance from the triple world's prison releases ;
Repentance makes blossom the bloom of the Buddha."

Prajña's other two translations are 'Deśānta-pālapati-dharani-

[1] Suzuki, *Outlines of Mahayana Buddhism*, p. 375, 381, 395.

sūtra' (Nanjio, 978) and 'Mahāyāna buddhi ('reason') ṣatpāramitā sūtra' (Nanjio, 1004), 10 fasc. each. According to the catalogue *Chi-tsing* (A. D. 1654), the first sūtra is a later translation of the chapter two of the Mahāvaipulya Mahāsannipāta sūtra (Nanjio, 61.)

There is, however, a tradition about the translation of the Satpāramtiā sūtra. There were living in China at that time Nestorian Christians who were respected for their piety and devotion by the people in general. Among them was a learned man named King-ching or Adam, who erected the Singanfu monument. Prajña translated the sūtra mentioned above in collaborotion with this Nestorian priest and offered it to the emperor Te Tsung. The emperor, however, refused to receive it, saying that King-ching (Adam) should devote himself to preaching the doctrines of *Meshiho* (Messiah), leaving the Buddhists to propagate the teachings of Śākyamuni. The book therefore appears in Prajña's name.[1]

Ajitsena

The last Hindu translator of the T'ang dynasty is Ajitasena.[2] He was a śramana of Northern India, whose exact date is not known. It is not mentioned under which dynasty he lived. But in the *Chi-tsing* he is put in the T'ang Dynasty. He translated three sūtras. (Nanjio, 966, 967, 1048).

What China owes to India

Now at the close of the great T'ang dynasty let us make a resumé of the work done by the Buddhist workers in China. From 618, the year in which the T'ang dynasty arose, to 719, the year in which Amoghavajra the last great Hindu monk came to China—a period of a hundred years is the brightest period of Sino-Indian contact. During this period more than sixty monks went to India and her

---

[1] G. Sakurai in the *Hansei Zasohi*, Vol. XIII, p. 12, refrrred to by Lloyd in his *Creed of Half-Japan*, p. 203.

[2] Nanjio has confused here. He made two persons of Wu-neng-sheng and O-chi-ta-sien. (Nanjio, App II. 157, 158). Wu-neg-shang meant 'Ajita,' unconquered; while O-chi-ta is Ajita and Sien is Sena; they are one and the same person.

colonies and about twenty-five workers worked in translation. After Amoghavajra (719) only two monks came to China; the last century was practically barren. So during the eighth century, about four hundred works were translated in Chinese from Sanskrit, of which 380 remain to this date.

Hindn Astronomy in China

In departments other than Buddhist literature, the influence of the Hindus was also felt. In 721 I-hsing (mentioned above under Śubhakara), a Chinese monk and astronomer, who came under the influence of Śubhakara was employed by the emperor to improve the Chinese calendar. I-hsing's method of calculation was based upon that of one Gautama Siddha, a Hindu monk. About the same time, arithmetical knowledge made rapid progress in China, and it is probable that the Chinese received much help from such brahmanical book on arithmatic as had been translated by the Hindu priests. These books are now hopelessly lost, although their names remain recorded in the catalogue of the Sui dynasty without any remark concerning them.[1]

Buddhist Ceremonies

Several ceremonies of Buddhist origin were at this time grafted into the Chinese life by the enthusiastic monarchs. Emperor Su Tsung in 760 appointed a ceremony for his birthday in accordance with the Buddhist religion. Buddhas and Bodhisattvas were personated by palace ladies and others, while the courtiers performed the usual ceremony before their sovereign. His son Tai Tsung was more devoted than his father. The sūtra of the Benevolent King (Jen-wang-ching) was brought to court in a state carriage with the same parade of attendants and finery as was usual in the case of a Chinese emperor setting out from the palace. When his territory was invaded Ta Tsung set his monks to chanting prayers; and it was by him that the Hindu Pandit Amoghavajra was honoured with the title of Duke. In 819 the emperor Hsien Tsung sent commissioners to escort a relic of Buddha from Feng-hsiang to the capital. This was the occasion that brought a strong protest

[1] Li-ung Bing, *op. cit.*, pp. 156-157.

from Han-yu[1] and his "*Memorial on Buddha's Bone*" has immortalized the name of the author.[2]

Subsequent history of Buddhism in China

Reaction however set in, when in 845 A. D., 4,600 monasteries and 40,000 smaller buildings were destroyed and more than 2,60,000 monks and nuns were compelled by imperial order to return to lay life. The disgust of the imperial authority can be well appreciated when we take into consideration the fact that a population of able-bodied men and women of more than quarter of a million were living an idle life, forsaking their primary duty towards their parents, their society and their state. But the effect of the reaction was but temporary; Wu Tsung, the author of the persecution died almost immediately thereafter, and his policy was reversed by his successor Hsüan Tsung, who in his latter life fell under the influence of the Taoists like his father, and died of the elixir of life ministered by the priests of Taoism. His successor I-Tsung (860-874) was an ostentatious and dissipated Buddhist. He showed more reverence to the relic of Buddha than his predecessor had shown inspite of the remonstrances of his ministers, which proved of no avail.[3] During the last decadent days of the T'ang dynasty, when emperors were nominally sovereigns, there is little of importance to recount about the spread of Buddhism with the help of the emperors. But from amongst the learned section of the Buddhist community, the Chinese Buddhist literature was greatly enriched with commentarial and ancillary literature by the monks of the Avataṁsaka, Dyāna, Tien-tai and other schools.

---

1 Giles, Chinese Biog. Dicty, No. 632; Han-yu born 768 died 824.

2 Eliot, *loc. cit.* III. p. 266-267; also Wieger', *Texts Historiques*, Hsien Hsien (China), Vol. III. p. 1726 ff; also Giles, *Chinese Literature*, pp. 200ff.

3 Eliot, III, p. 268.

XXI. The Last Hindu Monks

Epoch of 'Five Dynasties.'

The T'ang dynasty collapsed after a long and chequered career of about three hundred years in the year 907, followed by a troubled period known as the Epoch of Five Dynasties. It derived its name from the fact that in the small space of fifty years, five ephemeral dynasties followed one another in quick succession. Most of the emperors of these dynasties were indifferent to Buddhist culture, and one of them, an emperor of the Later Chou dynasty (951-960), suppressed monasteries and coined bronze images into currency. But in the South China where the authority of the so-called emperors of north had not reached, Buddhism flourished in the province of Fu-kien under the princes of Min and the dynasty which called itself Southern T'ang.[1]

Sung dynasty, 960.

In 960 the Sung dynasty was founded by Chao K'uang-yin, who adopted the dynastic title of T'ai Tsu (960-976). The Sung emperors had to struggle hard against many Chinese princes as well as the Khitan, a Tartar people of North. Inspite of the political unrest, the cultural aspect of the people did not suffer much, and some of the best artists, such as Li Lung-mien, was inspired by Buddhism. It was the contemplative or Dhyāna school of Bodhidharma which had the greatest influence on art and literature of China in this period.

Block-painting system in China.

It was at this period that the block-printing system was popularized in China, and largely used in printing and popularising the national literature. Chao K'uang-yin, the first Sung emperor, who was not very friendly to Buddhist principles, could not object to the printing of the Chinese Tripiṭaka. In 972 the first printed edition of the Tripiṭaka was published with an imperial preface. This may be called the eighth collection made by order of an emperor, though no catalogue or index seems to have been compiled on the

Printing of the first Tripitaka A.D. 972.

[1] Eliot III ; p. 267.

occasion. The blocks of wood on which characters were cut for this edition were said to have been 1,30,000 in number. After this between 972 and 1368, under the Sung and Yuen dynasties, as many as twenty different editions were printed, but accounts of these, except a few, are not available.[1]

275 works translated under the Sung dynasty

The first edition of the Tripiṭaka did not, however, close the work of translation, for 275 works were rendered into Chinese during the rule of the Sung. Spiritual contact with India continued under Sung; henceforward more Chinese śramaṇas went to India than before; but the number of Hindu monks coming to China decreased. On the whole, there was an appreciable decrease in the volume of religious literature after A. D. 900. This decrease in output of literary production or translation is natural; for by this time most of the important and even a large numer of unimportant and useless works had been rendered into Chinese.

Decrease of output

The later part of the T'ang rule and the rule of the Five Dynasties, mark a total absence of Buddhist translation. But the Buddha's teachings preached by the Hindu monks, had been able to inspire the intellectual and spiritual section of the Chinese Buddhist to take lively interest in the study of Buddhism itself; they were no longer tied to translations; numerous treatises were written on the translated texts and independent theses were composed by the learned monks of China.

During the rule of more than a century and half of the Sung dynasty (A. D. 960-1127) ten translators translated 275 Sanskrit works into Chinese. Of these, three Hindu translators are most important, Dharmadeva, Dānapāla and Tien-si-tsai who were greatly honoured by the Sung emperor T'ai Tsu.

---

[1] Nanjio, Intro. p. xxviii f. n.

Dharmadeva came to China in A. D. 973; he was a monk of the Nalanda university. There are two periods of his life in China. From 973 to 981, he was known as Fa-tien, when he translated 46 Sanskrit works; in 982 he received from the emperor T'ai-Tsu (976-997) the honorofic title of Chuang Chiao-ta-shih, and changed his former name to Fa-hsien. From that time (982) to the year of his death in 1001 A. D. he translated 72 more works; altogether the number of his translations is 118. (Nanjio, App II, 150). Of his numerous works about 32 are retranslations of sūtras previously done, some of which had twice, thrice and even four times been translated before his day. Of the rest which he translated for the first time, a large number was Dhāraṇī, some of very insignificant value. There are also a few transliterated verses and Dhāraṇīs. Books of definite Tantrik type were largely translated, which betrays that the spirit of Amoghavajra was not yet dead in Chinese Buddhism. A few of Dharmadeva's transliterated poems and Dhāraṇīs may be may be mentioned. These have special value with philologist, who want to study Chinese phonetics. Some of the texts are:

Dharmadeva, A. D. 973-1001

Transliterated Sanskrit Verses and Mantas in Chinese script

(1) *Aṣṭamahāśrī-caitya saṁskṛta stotra* or laudatory verse in Sanskrit on the eight great auspicious caityas composed by King Śilāditya (Nanjio 1071). The Sanskrit original has been restored by Sylvain Lévi.[1] There is also a Tibetan translation of the stotra.

(2) *Trikāya saṁskṛta stotra* or laudatory verse in Sanskrit on the Three-bodies of Buddha—Dharmakāya, Sambhogakāya, Nirmanakāya. (Nanjio, 1072).

(3) *Mañjuśrī nāmāṣṭaka saṁskṛta stotra.* There are 19 verses transliterated into Chinese, while a few others are translated (Nanjio, 1673).

---

[1] Actes du Xime Congres internationale des orientalistes: 1894, p. 189.

(4) *Mañjuśrī Bodpisattva śri-gāthā* (Nanjio, 1074, 1387).

(5) *Ārya-Vajrapāni-Bodhisattva-nāmāṣṭaka Saṁskṛta stotra* (Nanjio, 1075).

(6) *Sapta-jina stava* (Nanjio, 1065).

(7) *Gaṇḍistotra* (Nanjio, 1081).

Aśvaghoṣa's Gaṇḍi-stotra restored into the original.

The last stotra *Gaṇḍi-stotra* is attributed to Aśvaghoṣa. This stotra has been restored into Sanskrit by Baron A. von Stael-Holstein from the transliterated Chinese of Dharmadeva with the help of Tibetan translation. Transliteration into Chinese ideograms of Sanskritic sounds is an extremely difficult task ; still more difficult is the task of restoring those Chinese ideograms into Sanskrit originals, after centuries when the phonetic-value of Chinese words have undergone definite changes, and when sound-values change from district to district. Only very expert sinologues acquainted with the old pronounciation and well-versed in Sanskrit can achieve success in this hard work. By way of illustration we shall quote one verse from the *Gaṇḍi stotra*.[1]

Difficulty in the restoration work.

Chin. pu lu chah po po kan ngo pan ngo so
Sans bh ru kse pa pa ri ga bhaṅ go s-
Chin. mo lo she lo so lo so tah po chah mo
Sans. ma ra śa ra sa la sa t pa kṣ ma
Chin. to lo chah po tai
Sans. tā rā kṣi pā tai ....

It reads :

1. Bhrūkṣepāpāṅga bhaṅga smarasāra salasatpakṣma tārākṣi pātaih

2. Prauḍhānangāngānānam lalitabhujalatālāsalīlāpadaṅgaiḥ

3. Saurīḍaih sasmitoktaih Kalamṛdu-madhurāmodaramyair-vacobhi.

4. Bhrāntaṁ ceto na citraiḥ smarabala balajayino yasayatasmai namost'u

[1] Kien-chui-Fan-Tsan etc. Bibiliotheca Boudhica XV, 1913 ; with a Russian Introduction, Index.

Dharmadeva rendered another work into Chinese, which is ascribed to Aśvaghoṣa, who is the alleged author of the preceeding work. This is *Vajrasuci*. In the Chinese catalogues this book is ascribed to Boddhisattva Dharmayaśas (Nanjio, 1303). But other traditions attach it to Aśvaghoṣa.[1] This book was known in Nepal as a Buddhist work of Aśvagoṣa and was first translated by B. H. Hodgson.[2] Vajrasuci is also considered as an Upanishad,[3] and Weber says that the work which is called *Āpta-Vajrasuci*, and *Tripurī* are Śaṅkara's compositions. The works are written from vedantic standpoint[4].

Aśvaghosa's *Vajrsuci* refutes Caste-system.

The Vajrasucī is a refutation of the brahmanical caste system and such an invective against caste had never been written before. But its utility in Chinese is nil as there is no caste problem in their society and it was only translated because its authorship was ascribed to Aśvaghoṣa.

In the year 980 two Hindu monks came to China T'ien-si-tsai, a monk of Jalandhara or Kashmir, whose name has not been restored and Dānapala (Shih-hu) a monk of Udyāna. Both were learned monks and they worked in collaboration with Dharmadeva. For their learning and zeal for Dharma, in 982 the emperor T'ai Tsung decorated the three Hindu monks with imperial titles and formed a Translation Board with them. Each of the monks was asked to translate one work into Chinese. There were also other Chinese monks well-versed in Sanskrit, who were engaged to supervise the translations; others were appointed to make the Chinese style idiomatic and perfect. The emperor T'ai Tsung, the author of this action, although not a Buddhist himself, always favoured Buddhism,

Tien-si-tsai (name unrestored) A. D. 980-1000

---

[1] *ERE* Vol. 2, p. 159, Article Aśvaghosa by Anesaki.

[2] *Transactions of the Royal Asiatic Society, 1830, pp. 160-169.*

[3] *One hundred and eight Upanishads*, Nirnayasagara Press, Bombay, 1917, No. 38, p. 222).

[4] Weber, *History of Indian Literature*, Eng. Trans. pp 861-162, see also his *Die Vajrasuci des Asvaghosa*, 1860.

which is evident from the honour and attention he showed to these monks. Further he erected in the capital, at enormous cost, a stupa 360 feet high to contain relics of Buddha.

T'ien-si-tsai came to China in 980 and died in 1000 A. D. Besides his work as monk, he translated 18 Sanskrit works. Of his translations a few are important texts and deserve special treatment.

Translates *Mañjuśrī Mūlatantra*

The *Mañjuśrī-mūla Tantra* (Naujio, 1056) is one of the most important Tantra works rendered into Chinese by T'ien-si-tsai. The Tibetan version of it exists and recently the Sanskrit original has been published.[1]

A brief statement regarding Mañjusri's relation with China may be casually made. According to Chinese tradition the present home of Mañjuśrī is in China. He is represented in the Nepalese Mss. as a god worshipped in China, and who according to Nepalese tradition came from China to Nepal.[2] It seems that Mañjuśrī cult, like that of Amitabha, was of Central Asian origin, as much as T'ien tai, and Chan (Zen) are products of Sino-Indian contact. "The subjects dealt with in the text are mantric texts of Kumāra-Mañjuśrī Boddhisattva Mahāsattva, which bestow, on all humanity long life, health, wealth, happiness and other desired objects ; the way and means of attaining the mantric powers ; the science of Astrology, omens and other similar matter. The sermons given are found in the form of conversation between Bhagavat Śakyamuni and Kumāra Mañjuśrī and Pārasad Maṇḍala.[3]

The Sanskrit text is very corrupt and sometimes difficult to comprehend. Therefore a comparative study of the Sanskrit text the faithful Tibetan translation and the intelligent Chinese rendering of T'ien-si-tsai, will be of great value to the proper understanding of the meaning.

---

[1] *Ārya Manjuśrī-kalpalatā*, Edited by T. Ganapati Sastri, Trivandrum Sanskrit Series No. 70, 76, 84.

[2] *ERE* Vol, 8, p. 416.

[3] Preface to Sanskrit Text, *ibid* : also see Wieger, *loc. cit.*, p. 370.

Translation of the entire Uddanavasya

Tien-si-tsai's other important translation is the *Dharmapada-udānavarga* (Nanjio, 1434). This was the last of the four versions of the *Dharmapada*, three already existing.

The four translations of the Dhammapadaa

The earliest translation of the *Dharmapada* is said to have been done by An Shih-kao (148 A. D) ; but it does not exist.[1] The earliest of the extant translations is that done by Vighna (A. D. 224). The title of the work is Fa-chiu-ching or Dhammapada-sutta. In preface the Chinese editor states that śramaṇas in after ages copied from the canonical scriptures various gāthās, some four lines and some six, and attached to each set of verses a title according to the subject they explained. This work of extracting and collecting is ascribed to Ārya Dharmatrāta, probably the author of *Saṁyukta Abhidharma śastra* and other works (Nanjio. App. I. 31), and uncle of Vasumitra. We are further told that the original consisted of 500 verses ; but in China thirteen new chapters were added making up the whole to 760 verses in 39 chapters.[2]

The third Chinese *Dharmapada* is quite different from the above two. While the first and second was presumabaly based on the Pali *Dhammapada*, the third was doubtless based on the Sanskrit recension. It has already been described above. It consists of 33 chapters, each verse followed by a large explanatory note. Really it is a book on Avadāna. It was translated by Fo-nien in A. D. 410. The text is said te have been brought from Kashmir.

The fourth translation by our monk consists of 33 chapters and has verses only, which amount to about a thousand. It agrees more with the Tibetan Udānavarga translated in the 9th century by Vidyāprābhākara. The Sanskrit *Dharmapada* is lost in India ; but fragments of it have been discovered in Central Asia.[3]

---

[1] Bagchi *loc. cit.* p. 22ff.

[2] See above page 33.

[3] Parts of the sūtra have been published in several journals. But the entire text is said to be preserved in Berlin. For the Sanskrit text See Author's Central Asia.

Dānapala (Shih-hu), a contemporary of Dharmadeva and T'ien-si-tsai, came to China in A.D. 980 and was honoured by the emperor in 982 with the other two monks. He translated altogether **111** works, most of which are *Dhāraṇīs*. These dhāraṇīs had become popular with a certain section of Buddhist population of China and it seems there was a demand for such staff.

Dānapala, A. D. 980.

Among Dānapāla's translation are a few works of Nāgārjuna. It seems very strange that Nāgārjuna[1] should appear after several centuries in Chinese. Dānapāla translated the following works :

Nagarjuna's Few works translated.

(1) *Lakṣana vimukti-bodhi-hṛdaya-śāstra* (Nanjio, 1304).
(2) *Gāthā ṣāṣṭi-yathārtha śāstra* (Nanjio, 1307).
(3) *Mahāyāna bhava-bheda śāstra* (Nanjio, 1305).
(4) *Mahāyāna gāthā-viṁśati śāstra* (Nanjio, 1308).
(5) *Buddha-mātrikā prajñāpāramitā mahārtha sangīti śāstra* (Nanjio, 1309).
(6) *Mahā-pranidhānotpāda gāthā* (Nanjio, 1316).

Dānapala translated a large number of sūtras which had already appeared in Chinese ; but his translations were invariably from a larger recension of the text. Texts had a tendency to swell in bulk ; for each generation of pandits added something of their own in the older body of the text. The *Kāśyapa parivarta* (Nanjio, 805), the *Ratnamegha sūtra* which he did with Fa-hu (Nanjio, 964), the *Raṣṭrapāla paripṛcchā* (Nanjio, 873) were all translations of larger recensions. Besides these he translated a few sūtras from the *Saṁyukta*, *Madhyama* and other Āgamas. It is inexplicable why Dānapala translated the sūtras from the Āgamas, when the whole of these Āgamas were already existing in Chinese.

During the reign of the third Sung emperor Chen Tsung

T'ien-si-tsai had translated Nāgarjuna's *Bodhi-carya sutra* (N. 1354).

[1] This Sūtra, says Lévi, greatly corresponds with Śāntideva's *Bodhi-caryā vatāra BEFEO*, 1902, p. 203-205; see below.

(997-1022) came to China Fa-hu (Dharmaraksa ?) a śramaṇa of Central India in the year 1004 A.D. and worked at translation till A.D. 1058, when he died in his ninety-sixth year. Emperor Jen Tsung (A.D. 1022-1063) honoured the Hindu monk with a special title (Nanjio, App. II, 162).

Other translators.

In 1009 a translation board was formed by the imperial order with (Fa-hu) Dharmarakṣa, Wei-tsing and others as members. Some of Fa-hu's translations are important texts. His *Bodhisattva pitaka* is a large work in 40 fasc. (Nanjio, 23,12). Śāntideva quotes from this work in his *Śikṣa samuccaya*. His translation of the *Tathāgata Acintyaguhya-nirdeśa* (Nanjio, 1043) covered 20 fasc., while the earlier version (Nanjio 23,4) by Dharmaraksa of the W. Tsin dynasty (A.D. 265-316) consisted of only 7 fasc. The *He-vajra Tantra* (Nanjio, 1060) is a famous Tantra work translated by Fa-hu in 5 fasc. of 20 chapters. The Sanskrit original exists.[1]

An Imperial translation board. A.D. 1009. Dharmaraksa and others,

His another important translation was an Abhidharma work which is unknown in the older Tripiṭaka collection. It was admitted into the canon during the Sung dynasty. The *Mahāyāna Saṅgīti Bodhisattva-vidya-śāstra* was translated by Fa-hu in collaboration with Sūryayaśas in 25 fasc. of 18 chapters (Nanjio, 1298). The author of this work has been mentioned as Bodhisattva Dharmayasas or Dharmakīrti. Its identity was long concealed and it was discovered by Dr. Wogihara of Japan to be a translation of Santideva's *Bodhicaryāvatāra*. The Chinese translation is in 18 chapters while the original Sanskrit is in 19 chapters.[2]

Bodhicuryā vatāra of Sānideva in Chinese

Fa-hu is also well-known as the translator of the last pāda

[1] For the Sanskrit text, see Catalogue of the *Hodgson Manuscripts* III, 45, 46.

[2] Bendal's Introduction, p. xxix to *Śikṣa samuccaya*, Biblotheca Buddhica.

of the Sarvastivāda Abhidharma. Prajñaptipāda śāstra (Nanjio, 1317). We have seen that all the pādas and the bulk of the Abhidharma works of this school had been translated by Hiuen-tsang but he does not seem to have known the existence of this work, otherwise he would have translated it. According to Chinese authorities, however, this work is the last pāda; but there is no indication that this work belongs to the Sarvāstivada school. In Chinese text there is no mention of the author; but Yasomitra and the Tibetan scholar Buston mention Maudgalāyana as its author. It may be interesting to note that in Tibetan no Sarvastivada Abhidharma exists except the *Prajñaptipāda śāstra*.[1]

Prajñaptivāda śāstra the last pada of the Sarvāstivāda Abhidharma.

Of the contemporaries of Fa-hu, Wei-tsing and Sūryayaśas should be mentioned. Wei-tsing (Nanjio, App. II, 163) translated the first 13 chapters of the commentary of of Sthitamati on Nāgarjuna's *Mūla-madhyamaka kārikā*. (Nanjio, 1316). Sthitamati's commentary was known in Chinese before this time. Kumārajiva translated the commentary of Aryadeva some six hundred years before.

Wei-tsing and Sūryayaśas.

The other co-worker Sūryayaśas rendered into Chinese two works alleged to have been composed by Aśvaghoṣa One is '*Guru-sevā-dharma-pañcasadgāthā*' or Fifty verses on the law or rules for serving a teacher (Nanjio, 1080) and the other *Dasa-duṣta-karma-mārga sūtra* (Nanjio, 1379). We do not know whether this Aśvaghoṣa is the same poet-philosopher whom we met in the early days of Mahāyāna.

Chi Chi-siang (Jñānasri), a Hindu śramana arrived in China in A. D. 1053; two works are ascribed to him. (Nanjio, App. II, 164). Another śramaṇa named Suvarṇa-dhāraṇī, came in 1153 A. D. and translated two books (Nanjio, App. II, 164). Maitreyabhadra (Tzu-hsian) a śramaṇa of Central India, who is said to have

[1] Takakusu in *Journal of the Pali Text Society* 1904-1905 p. 77, F. N.; also 116-116.

been a Kuo-shih or Rājya-guru of the Liao dynasty (907-1125) came to China. Five works are ascribed to him.

The last work of the Sung dynasty is the translation of *Jātakamālā*, made by śramana Shao-te, Hwui-sung and others in 16 fasciculi. The first four fasciculi contain fourteen Jātakas after Aryaśūra's text, while the latter 12 fasciculi form a commentary by Tsi-pien Sheng-t'ien or Muni Jinadeva (?), being divided into 34 sections. But this translation is not good and has therefore not found favour with the Chinese people.[1]

Aryaśūra's *Jātakamālā* in Chinese.

In the Sanskrit *Jātakamālā* there are 34 'Jātakas', but the Chinese translation contains only 14 stories. All the stories are not Jatakas, but are simple stories from real life, devoid of any Jātaka element. What is the reason of this discrepancy ? In comparing Chinese Sanskrit and Pali texts we always find that the Chinese, translators invariably abridged the texts more or less and ommitted the details ; but they hardly failed to give an exact transcription of the essential points. In case of the translation of the Jātakamālā it seems that the Sanskrit text had not attained its present definite shape when it reached China, or it may be that the original text in its complete form had not reached the translators or it may be that the translators did their work with negligence and in part. Following are the 14 stories found in the Chinese *Jātakamālā*.

(1) Bodhisattva nourishes the tigress by sacrificing his own body. (2) The King Sibi saves the life of the dove (3) The Bodhisattva errs in demanding alms (4) Miraculous transformation (5) The Bodhisattva escapes the effect of poison (6) The King of the Hares nourishes a brahmana by the sacrifice of his life. (7) The King of the Dragons destroys enmity by his compassionate heart. (8) Consequences of an alms of little importance (10) Tathāgata is omniscient and does not enjoy the property of

[1] The Sanskrit text is preserved and has been edited by H. Kern, *Jātakamālā*. Harvard Oriental Series ; trans. by Speyer ; a detailed analysis of the work is not needed.

others. (11) The Buddha pours water on the head of a sick bhiksu and cures him (12) The effect (puṇya) of a prayer addressed to tri-ratna (three jewels) (13) Eminent gifts which were given to those who build stupas (14) Effect of the accession into the monkish life.

In Tibetan there are 101 stories of which the first 34 agree with the Sanskrit version of Aryaśura.[1]

The output of translations during Sung dynasty was indeed very meagre ; but it was amply compensated by original writing on Buddhism by Chinese monks. Native scholarship shone brilliantly under the earlier Sung rulers who were great patrons of art and promoters of literature. Jen Tsung (1022-1063) the fourth emperor, whose time was specially famous for great literary men, encouraged learning and appointed fifty Chinese youth to study Sanskrit, but showed no particular favour to Buddhism[2].

Sanskrit study under the Sung emperors.

Wang An-shih, the great reformer of China "wrote a book full of Buddhist and Taoist fancies, and though there is nothing specifically Buddhist in his political and economic theories, it is clear from the denunciations against him that his system of education introduced Buddhist and Taoist subjects into the public examinations."[3]

From this period onwards troubles arose in the frontiers and Hsi-hsia (Tanguts), a hardy race of people dwelling in the N.-W. of China and the Kitan Tartars were becoming arrogant and troublesome. Hui Tsung (1101-1126) the last Sung emperor was actually carried a prisoner by the Tartars. During his reign there was persecution of the Buddhists and Buddha and the Arhats were enrolled in the Taoist pantheon by the imperial decree.

Political disin-tegration.

[1] A. O. Ivanovski, Sur une traduction Chinoise du recueil bouddhique "Jātakamālā", Memories de la section orientale de la Société imperiale russe d'archeologie (Petersburg, 1893) Translated from Russian into French by M. Duchene, *Reveue de l' histoire des Religions*, 1903, Vol. 48, pp, 298-335.

[2] Eliot III, p. 270.

[3] Eliot III, p. 270 refers to Biot's *L'instruction publique en China*, p. 354.

No more Hindus in China.

For fear of the Tartars the capital at Chang-an was shifted south of the Yang-tse river and Han-kow became the seat of government. The Sungs continued to rule in South China till A. D. 1286. During the century and half of their rule in the south, no Hindu came to China, but native writers increased in member.

Chinese writers on sectarian doctrines.

The literary activity of the T'ien-tai and the Avataṁsaka (Hua-yen) schools has already been narrated above. The other important school of thought was the Dhyāna or Chan. The school was started in the sixth century by Bodhidharma, as a reaction against all sorts of intellectual scholasticism and it repudiated the study of scripture. But several volumes were written on silence and with years a large literature grew. Two hundred and thirty works belonging to the sect were published in the Manchu dynasty.[1]

But not more than two dozens of their works which were mainly written during the Sung dynasty are found in the Tripitaka.

Yuen Shen.

Yuen Sheu[2] a priest of the Chan school, whose exact date is not known, wrote three treatises, of which his *Tsung-chin-lun* a work in 100 fasc records as Mirror of the Dhyāna school. (Nanjio, 1489).

Tao-yuen's biography of Eminent Buddhists.

Tao-yuen[3] wrote a large work in 30 fasc in A. D. 1006 on the history of the Hindu and and Chinese patriarchs of the Dhyāna school. In the first 26 fasc 1712 persons are mentioned; and in the remaining part accounts of 22 eminent priests and their verses and composition are collected (Nanjio, 1524).

Chi-sung's literary works.

Chi-sung[4] is one of the writers of the sect; he was famous for his literary talents. He wrote four works. One was a 'treatise on

[1] Wieger, *Bouddhisme Chinois* p. 108; Also M. Courant, *Catalogue des livres Chinois* II, pp. 646-689.

[2] Nanjio App. III, 45.

[3] Nanjio, App. III. 49.

[4] Nanjio. Ap. III, 54.

the right school of transmitting Law,' in which the author asserts that Bodhidharma was a patriarch of the orthodox school, which was repudiated by certain persons (Nanjio, 1528). The other was a history of the patriarchs and eminent priests of the Dhyāna school (Nanjio, 1529). The third treatise was a collection of miscellaneous compositions. (Nanjio, 1530). These three works of Chi-sung drew the attention of literati of his ago. The emperor Jen Tsung (1023-1063) was the first to discover the greatness of Chi-sung. It is said that when the emperor read the following sentence of Chi-sung 'I do my best for the sake of the Law, but not for my own sake'—he at once ordered the works of Chi-sung to be admitted into the can on, and gave him the honourable title Ming-chiao ta-shih or the great teacher who illustrates the teaching (of Buddha). This event took place in A. D. 1062. (Nanjio, 1530).

His works admitted into the Tripitaka by Imperial order.

The master of Dhyāna school seldom wrote themselves their mystical epigrams. It was always done by their disciples. A Dhyāna teacher named Yuen-yu-fo-kuo's teachings were recorded by Shao-lung and others. (17 fasc. Nanjio, 1531). Another teacher was Ta-hui-pu'-chiao. He had a large following and his disciples wrote down his sayings. Yuen-wan, a disciple, compiled his teacher'e saying in 1165-1173 A. D. Hwui-jen, Tao-sien and Hwang-wan-chang also collected the epigrams (Nanjio, 1532). Tso-tsang-chu (Nanjio, App. III, 73) another writer of the Dhyāna school, collected the sayings of 43 eminent Dhyāna teachers in a work of 48 fasc (Nanjio, 1659). This work, was compiled in the South China and was unknown in the Northern collection of the Tripiṭaka. Another large work, that is found in the Tripiṭaka is the complete collection of verses of the Dhāyna teachers in 40 fasc. It was at first collected by Fa-ying about 1174-1189, which consisted of 325 articles, 2100 verses by 122 teachers. More than a century hence the work was

Other Dhyana teachers and their sayings.

continued by Pu-hwui (1295-1318) which consists of 493 articles, 3050 verses by 426 teachers (Nanjio, 1680). These details are given here only to show how far the Dhyāna school was successful in the period under our survey. *Fan-ming-i-tsi* (Nanjio, 1641), a work in 20 fasc, is a explaining dictionary of the Buddhist technical terms composed by Fa-yun in 1151 A. D. This work is indispensible for Buddhist study.

XXI. The Closing Scene

T'ai-Tsu was the first emperor of the Sung dynasty. He became emperor in 960 and ruled till 976 A. D. During his rule between 964 and 976 three hundred Chinese sramanas went out to India to visit the holy places of Buddhism. The enthusiasm, that we saw during the T'ang period, immediately after Hiuen-Tsang's return from India is manifested again in the lives of these Chinese monks. But at this period there is no able biographer like Yi-tsing, who could record the incidents in the lives of these holy pilgrims. The biographies of these monks are recorded in two works. One is *Fo-tsu-t'ung-chi* (Nanjio, 1661), a history of Chinese Buddhism or 'Records of the lineage of Buddha and Patriarchs' in 54 fasc compiled by Chu-pwan[1] a T'ien-tai priest of the 13th century (1269-1271 A. D).[2] The other source is the *Sung-shi* or the Annals of the Sung dynasty, written by the State historian T'o-t'o, the Mongol.[3]

Between 964 and 976, three hundred Chinese came to India

Biographies of monks

In A. D. 965 when the Sung emperor T'ai Tsu was reigning, śramaṇa Tao-yuen returned from his Indian tour. He had left China in 947 during the Han dynasty. He had passed abroad eighteen years between his departure and return ; he had stopped twelve years on his way and six years in India. He procured a relic

Tao-yuen returns in 965

---

[1] Nanjio. App. III, 68.

[2] See Wylie, *Notes on Chinese Literature*, p. 209-210.

[3] The later source was reproduced by Ma Twan-lin in his immortal work *Wen-hsien-t'ung-kao* (See Wylie, p. 69). The chapter dealing with the International relation between China and India was translated by Stanislus Julien in his *Melanges de geographie asiatique* pp. 169-178. The whole source is again tapped and retranslated by the great French Sinologue ED. Chavannes, Les Inscriptions Chinois de Bodh-Gaya App. II. *Revue d l'historie des religions*, 27e Annee, Tome XXXIV, 1. Jul. Aout. 1896 pp. 43-58 ; also for its translation see *Shyama*, 1922, No. 3 & 4, Chinese and Indian travellers by P.N. Bose,

of Buddha, vases in crystal and of stone and forty pages of Sanskrit texts written on palm leaves. He took these offerings to the emperor T'ai-Tsu, who inquired of him on the manners, mountains, rivers and itineraries of countries through which he had passed. On his way home, he had passed through Khotan, and described everything to the emperor.

Ki-ye's account of India

Śramana Ki-ye was one of the pilgrims of this period who wrote a short account of his journey.[1]

The itinerary of Ki-ye and the description of India by Tao-yuen probably induced emperor T'ai-Tsu to pass an imperial order to the effect that monks would be sent out to India in search of Dharma. At that time one hundred and fifty-seven men, among whom was the sramaṇa Hing-chin, responded to the call. They desired to go to the Western countries for searching Buddhist books. For all the countries through which they had to pass, such as, Karashar, Kucha, Khotan, Pou-lou-sha or Peshwar, Kia-che-mi-lo or Kashmir, etc., the emperor granted them *lettres patentes* asking the respective states to furnish the pilgrims with guides. We have this much record from the Chinese history; but we do not know what happened to them.

Hundred and fifty seven Chinese monks came to India for obtaining MSS.

But it is not the Chinese who continued to come to India during the Sung period, we find Hindu monks still struggling through the inhospitable Central Asia, run over by the Mohammedans, either to preach the Saddharma, or to escape the reaction in the native country or to find favours in the Chinese court for their religious beliefs. After a lapse of nearly two hundred years—the last monk Prajña

No Hindu monk went to China for two centuries.

[1] The account has been translated into English by G. Schlegel. Itinerary to the Western Countries of Wang-nieh in A. D. 964. *Memories du comite sinico-japonais, XXI, 1893, pp. 35-64.*

Ed. Huber, L' Itineraire du pelerin Ki-ye dans l'Inde, *BEFE-O*, 1902, p. 256-58. Chavannes, Notes sinologues; L'Iteneraire de Ki-ye. *BEFE-O*, 1904, p. 75—81.

having come in 785—during which period no Hindu seems to have gone to China, in the year 972, there arrived at the royal court three sramanas from Western India, K'o-tche, Fa-K'ien, and Tchen-li. Another sramana came from Sāketa (Sou-ko-t'o) in India; he offered relics and flowers of Mañjuśrī. Another batch of fourteen Hindu sramanas from India also came in this year.

Sramanas for West India A. D. 972.

Next year, in 973, came to China (Fa-t'ien) Dharmadeva one of the greatest translators of this age, whom we have already met. Two years later, Śaṅkhasvara, son of the king of Eastern India, came to render homage and pay tribute to the emperor. In 977 Ki-siang, a sramaṇa of Western India, brought some palm leaf Sanskrit manuscripts. Next year, returned from India, Ki-ts'ong, a monk of the temple of K'ai-pao, with his companions. He offered Sanskrit books, a relic of a stupa to Buddha, leaves of Boddhi-tree and broom of peacock-feathers. Another sramana from Central India brought some relics and curios for the emperor.

Dharmadeva A.D. 973, Śaṅkhasvara, 975.

More monks with Sanskrit MSS. arrive.

Some years back (in 971), a young prince named Mañjuśrī had come to China. He was the son of the king of Western India. "According to the laws of India, when the king of a state died, the heir-apparent succeeded him; all the other sons left the world and entered religion. They no longer reside in the country of their birth." Mañjuśrī, therefore, left India and "went to China with the Chinese monks." Emperor T'ai Tsu (960-975) asked him to live in the temple of Hsiang-kuo. He observed the Vinaya rules rigorously. He became the favourite of the people of the capital and riches and gifts flowed to him. All the monks became jealous of him. But as he did not understand the Chinese language, they fabricated a supposed request by which he asked to return to his country. That request was complied with; when the imperial decree was made known Mañjuśrī was filled with stupor and indignation. The monks

Manjusri, 971.

advised him that for the sake of decree he must go. He remained still for a few months and then went away (978 A. D.). He said that he would go towards the Southern Sea to return to India on a merchant boat. It was never known where he had gone to.

Tien-si-tsai came to China, A. D. 980

In A. D. 980, the great Hindu monk Tien-si-tsai, a Tripiṭakācārya and native of Kashmir and Shi-hou (Dānapala), another master of Tripiṭaka and native of Udyāna came to China. These great masters are translators of a large number of Sanskrit works, and will be mentioned again.

Kuang-yuen returns from India

Two years hence, the Chinese monk Kuang-yuen, a native of Ch'eng-tou (province of Se-choan) returned from his travels in India. He came to the palace of T'ai-Tsung (976-997), the second Sung emperor, and offered to him an impression of the cranium of Buddha, some palm manuscripts and a few leaves of the holy Bodhitree. He had also brought with him a letter from Mo-si-nang (Mahāsena), an Indian king. The emperor asked Dānapala to translate the letter. The letter reads thus:

Brings a letter from Mahāsena a Hindu king

"Humbly I have heard it said that in the kingdom of Che-na (China), there was a Son of God; perfectly wise and perfectly saintly, his fortune and his power are supreme. I am ashamed of my little chance which deprives me the chance of going to you to pay you homage. Kung-yuen by the imperial grace has obtained a Kāṣāya-cloth to offer to Śākya Tathāgata of the Vajrāsana (Buddha-Gayā). He came and suspended the cloth and after having made the offering, he has humbly wished that the emperor of China should have prosperity and intelligence, longivity and long authority; he has further desired that all sentient beings be transported beyond all the places where they

Purport of the letter.

are submerged. With respect I send through Kuang-yuen a relic of Śākya for your acceptance.[1] (XI).

The year following the arrival of Kuang-yuen, there returned to China another Chinese monk named Fa-yu, who presented to the emperor a relic of the skull-bone of the Buddha, and palm-leaf manuscripts in Sanskrit. Before he started he had got a precious ornamented *dais* of dragons, and a Kāṣāya, which he proposed to offer to Vajrāsana (Buddha-Gaya) when he got to Central India. He received from the emperor *patent-letteres* for various kingdoms through which he passed. On his way back he met a Hindu monk at San-fo-tsi (in the W. Sumatra) named Vimalaśrī, who expressed his desire to go to China for translating books and obtained permit from the emperor. (VIII).

A.D. 982. Fa-yu visite India, brings palm leaf Mss. and other curios.

During the period of 982-987 several foreigners came. T'se-houn, a Chinese monk returned from Western countries ; he came with a Turkish monk, Mi-tan-lo (Mitra), and brought letters from the king of N. India ; it seems that they had visited Buddha-Gaya and Nalanda (XIV). The Sung annals also speak of the arrival of a brahman (P-lo-man) named Yong-che and a Persian named Aliyan to the capital. The text connected with these two persons has been completely translated by Julien.

Tse-houn returns with a letter from a king of India.

A Brahman and a Persian arrive.

In 989 or 990, a Hindu śramaṇa of the Nalanda monastery came to the royal court and offered relics of Buddha and Sanskrit manuscripts. A Chinese monk named Chung-ta, also came back with relics and books after having passed ten years abroad (XVI). The same year also came a monk from Campa, the great Hindu colony of Further India, with several items of curios and offered them to the emperor.

989 A.D., a monk of Nalanda comes with Mss.

A monk from Campa

[1] There are a few points of difference between different texts ; these are discussed by Julien and Chavannes,

In 992 Ki-siang a monk of India, who is known as new Ki-siang, presented to the emperor a pretentious translation which he called the sūtra of collection of magic powers of Mahayana; but the great Hindu monk and translator Dharmadeva (Fa-tien) denounced that work as not based on any Sanskrit original and the emperor had it burnt. (VII).

Ki-siang, a Hindu monk translates a spurious work, condemned by Dharmadeva.

Kālaśānti (?) a śramaṇa of Central India (995), Rāhula, a śramaṇa of W. India (997), Ni-wei-ni, a śramaṇa of Central India, Fo-hou of W. India (998), all arrived with relics, books and other curios in the court. (XVIII, XIX, XX).

Kalasanti, Rahula, other Hindu monk arrived A.D. 995.

In 997 the second Sung emperor T'ai-Tsung was succeeded by Chen-Tsung, who reigned for a quarter of a century (997-1022 A.D.). The most important of these Hindu monks who came to China in his reign (A.D. 1004) was Tripitakācārya Fa-hu, of whom we shall speak more in details (Nanjio, App. II 162). In the same year came sramana Śīlabhadra of N. India, who also brought some Sanskrit manuscripts like his other coreligionists. (XXI). In the next year a monk of Kashmir and another from W. India came both bringing Sanskrit manuscripts (XXII).

A.D. 1004, Acarya Fa-hu, a great translator comes.

Silabhadra and other monk.

Five years latter (A.D. 1009), we find again two monks coming to China. Chong-te, a śramaṇa of W. India came to the royal court bringing a few relics, some Sanskrit texts and an impression of Vajrasana. Kio-kie, a śramaṇa of Central India came to the court. He also brought some relics, an impression of the Vajrāsana and a few leaves of the sacred tree. When Kio-kie, returned to India, he received by an imperial decree a Kāṣaya-cloth to be offered to the Vajrāsana of Mahābodhi. The monk also received silver, tea and fruits for his route. (XXIII). In the succeeding years (1011-15) several sramanas came, all bringing Sanskrit texts

Chong-te, a monk of W. India.

Kio-kie, a Hindu monk returns from China to offer Kasaya cloth to Bodhi tree.

and relics. In 1015 the kingdom of Sou-lien in the Southern sea, sent an ambassador to China for offering tribute and sacred books of India. (XXVI). In 1016 several monks arrived. T'ien-kio, a śramaṇa of Udyāna, Miao-te of Ceylon, several śramaṇas from Kaccha (?) in W. India, one from Central India, another from Varendra (Fo-lin-tai) or eastern India ; all arrived with books (XXVII). This is the last year in which any Hindu came to China during the reign of Chen-Tsung.

A. R. 1016, several monks arrive.

Chen-Tsung was succeeded in 1022 by Jen-Tsung who had a longer career than his predecessor (1022-1063) ; but during his long reign of nearly forty years only five monks came struggling to China, each carrying a bundle of Sanskrit books, which they either wanted to propagate in China or save from the reaction, which had set in in India. The last year in which a Hindu monk came from India was 1053. Che-ki siang, a śramaṇa of W. India with his companions came in that year bringing probably the last Sanskrit book to China.[1]

Emperor Jen-Tsung 1022-1063

Five monks came with Sanskrit books

1053, is probably the last year when a group of Hindu monks arrived in China.

We have described above the international relation between India and China for a period of a hundred years beginning with the first Sung emperor in 960 and ending with the fourth Sung emperor in 1063. During this forgotten century of Indian history, when our historians are busy describing a border raid by the Muslims Turks, more than three hundred Chinese monks wended their way to India, for a kingdom more lasting than those coveted by their healthier contemporaries. India was still sending her monks abroad in China and Tibet in North and to Ceylon, Burma and Southern Seas to preach the Gospel of Maitreyī and Karuṇā.

Spiritual, International relation, A.D. 660-1063.

[1] I have not always translated the French text ; sometimes I have summarized several versions and sections in one paragraph and have omitted unnecessary details and disputes regarding the text.

CHAPTER XXII.

YUAN-MANCHU PERIOD.

By the end of the twelvth century a new nomadic power was organized and consolidated in Central Asia. "A Turkish people from the country to the north of China rose suddenly to prominence in the worldy affairs and achieved such series of conquests as has no parallel in history. These are Mongols."[1] They were a horde of nomadic horsemen , their central camp was Karakorum in Mongolia.

Rise of the Mongols

At this time China was divided into three empires, that of Kin Tartars in the north with Peking as their capital, that of Sung in the south with its capital at Nan-king, and Hsi-hsia in the centre. The military campaigns of Chenghiz Khan the great leader of the Mongols brought a new element in the politics of Asia. The different Mongolian tribes were united in 1206 A. D. under their leader who then carried his victorious arms almost to every part of Asia. in the west up to Bulgaria, Serbia, Hungary and Russia, in the east up to the Pacific, and to the south it touched the borderland of China, Tibot and India.

Chenghiz Khan 1206 A. D.

On the death of Chenghiz, his son and successor Ogotai succeeded in conquering the N. China from the Kitans. Ogotai died in 1241 and Mankou Khan was elected the Great Khan ; and it was during his reign that his younger brother Khublai Khan extended the Mongol supremacy over Southern China as far as Yun-nan in 1253 A. D. The ascendency of the Great Mongol chief Khublai to power in 1259 marks a new era in the history of Buddhism, a short period of glorious activities just before the commencement of the declining days.

Khublai Khan 1259.

---

[1] Wells—*A short History of the World, p. 169.*

Mankou Khan was a tolerant emperor. In 1251 he conferred on Li Tche-tchiang, the title of the head of Taoism, and on Hai-yun that of Buddhism. In the following year he honoured a certain Na-mo, as Kuo-shih or rājyaguru of some 'western' country and entrusted to him the work of general administration of Buddhism in the empire.

Fight between the Taoists and the Buddhists.

We have already seen that Chinese Buddhism was on its wane, the quality of work had degenerated and the interest of the Sung emperors had flagged. The Taoists were growing powerful; under the last Northern Sung emperor Hui-Tsung (1101-1126) Taoism was reorganized and by the imperial decree the Buddha and his Arhats were enrolled in the Taoist pantheon; temples and monasteries were allowed to exist only on condition of describing themselves as Taoist. This particular act of persecution did not last long; but since then the whole attitude of the people and their rulers underwent great change. The Taoist had begun to misapproprite the properties of the Buddhist saṅghas and regular plagirarism went on with Buddhist pantheon and books.

Mankou Khan convenes a religious meeting.

The Buddhists in their helpless state sought redress from the Mongol chiefs. Mankou Khan convened a great meeting at Karakorum in 1254, in which Christians, Mohammedans and Buddhists took part. In this meeting the Buddhists did not fare well and again in 1255 another meeting was held in the Khan's palace. Mankou Khan himself, with some of his officials attended the discussion. Fu-yu represented the Buddhists. In this meeting the Taoists were defeated and they were ordered by an imperial decree to return the Buddhist establishments occupied by them. But the Taoists were too powerful to listen to an imperial decree from Karakorum.

The next year (1256) another assembly was called by the Khan. Learned Buddhist monks came there in numbers to take part in the discussion ; but the Taoists did not attend. The Mongol Khan took it to be an admission of the incapability of the the Taoists and he recognized the superiority of the Buddhists in these terms : "Just as the fingers come out of the palm of the hand, the Buddhist doctrine is likewise the palm, the other religions are like the fingers."

Buddhists are declared superior to the Taoists.

No action was however taken against the Taoists by Mankou Khan, and he delegated his younger brother Khublai to deal with the matter.

In 1258 Khublai Khan convened a great religious assembly at Shang-ton (N-W. of Dolon-nor), which was attended by about 300 Buddhists monks and 200 Taoists ; two hundred Confucianists served as arbiters. Amongst the Buddhists there was Na-mo, the kuo-shih of Western countries, and abbot of Shao-lin temple, the famous Tibetan monk Phags-pa (1239-1280), the nephew of the great Sāskya Paṇdit, of whom we shall know more in our Tibetan studies. Phags-pa, though he was only nineteen years of age played a decisive role in the discussion. It is said that a Buddhist monk came from Yun-nan to attend this congress of religions. In the discussion which took place, the Buddhists came out victorious through the eloquent exposition of young Phags-pa. The Taoists were defeated and seventeen of their leaders had to shave their heads and become Buddhist monks according to the contract entered beforehand. The Buddhists got back 237 monasteries which they had lost. Khublai recognized the superiority of Buddhism and ordered the Taoists texts desparaging Buddhism to be burnt.

Khublai convenes another meeting and Buddhism delared superior

When Khublai Khan became emperor of China, he appointed Phags-pa as the rājyaguru in 1260, and recognized him as the head of the Buddhist church. Khublai established a special relation between Tibet and China through the Lamaist hierarchy and from this time

Phags-pa Rajya-guru.

Tibetan lamas began to take lead in the Buddhist activities in China and Mongolia. Phags-pa's attempt to reform the script of the Mongolians and his other contribution to Mongolian civilization has been discussed elsewhere (Central Asia). He attempted the work of organising the work of translating Buddhist texts into Chinese and translated himself a Hīnayana Vinaya—called the Mūlasarvāstivāda Karmavāca (Nanjio, 1137). This scholar died very young, at the age of 42 only, in 1280 having been greatly honoured by the Mongol emperor, who gave him the title of the great and precious Law.[1]

His work for Mongolians.

The Mongol emperors were extremely superstitious and showed their sincere devotion to the Buddhist religious literature. Khublai Khan saw that the monasteries in Peking were all supplied with books and ordered the priests to recite them on stated days. It was at this epoch that a new collection of Tripitaka was published under his imperial order (1280-81). This catalogue was compiled by Ching-chi-siang, together with some Hindu, Tibetan and Chinese priests and officials. This catalogue is generally called Chu-yuen-lu (Nanjio, 1612). These are translations made by 194 persons under twenty-two dynasties in the period of 1219 years from 67 A. D. to 1285. Besides these there are 95 Indian and 118 Chinese miscellaneous works. The compilers of the Chi-yuen-lu[2] compared the Chinese translations with the Tibetan translations of the Kanjur and Tanjur, and added the Sanskrit title in translation, and gave a note after each Chinese title, stating whether both

Collection of Tripitaka 1280-81.

[1] Quoted and adapted from Dr. P. C. Bagchi's India and China—Greater India Society, Bulletin, No. 2,

[2] Divisions and Classifications:

1.	Sutra	Mahayana	897	in	2980	fasc.
		Hinayana	291	in	710	fasc.
2.	Vinaya	Mahayana	21	in	56	fasc.
		Hinayana	69	in	504	fasc.
3.	Abhidharma	Mahayana	117	in	628	fasc.
		Hinayana	38	in	708	fasc.
	Total		1440	in	5586	fasc.

translations were in agreement or whether the book was wanting in the Tibetan version. This comparison, however, seems to have been made only through a catalogue of the Tibetan translations, and not actually with the translations themselves. Nevertheless, it is curious to see that there have been so many Chinese translations, which are similar to, though they do not agree exactly with the Tibetan translations.[1]

Another catalogue

Another catalogue compiled originally by Wang-ku of the Sung dynasty (960-1280) was continued by Kwan-chu-pa in A.D. 1368. This catalogue entirely depends upon the previous one and adds a short account of the contents of each book.[2]

Latter Mongol emperors

The attitude of the Yuen or Mongol dynasty (1280-1368) was considerably favourable to Buddhism. Enormous sums were expended on subventions to monasteries, printing book and performing public ceremonies. Reference has already been to the literary interest shown by Khublai Khan. The second Mongol emperor Jen-Tsung (1311-1320) showed equal interest for literary work. He ordered further translations to be made into Mongol and later had the whole Tripitaka copied in letter of gold.[3]

Sha-lo-pa, disciple of Phags-pa.

In 1314 Sha-lo-pa, a disciple of Phags-pa translated a work of his master into Chinese, *Cheng-su-chu-lun* (Nanjio, 1320). It was compiled by Phags-pa for the sake of Chan-chin, the crown-prince of Khublai. This is a useful and interesting manual of Buddhist terminology, consisting of extracts from several sutras

---

1 Nanjio. Intro. p. xxii ; also for the contents see Julien, *Journal Asiatique*, 1849 pp. 353-446.

2 The catalogue was first sent by M. P. Habauc of Russia to S. Julien of Paris in 1844. After a careful study, Julien published a Concordance Sinico Sanskrit in the *Journal Asitique*. 1849, pp. 351-446. Buniyo Nanjio, while compiling his great catalogue made use of this valuable catalogue in which many Sanskrit names have been restored, J. P. T. S, 1905, p. 81.

3 The activities of the Mongol emperors for strengthening their literature have been described fully elsewhere.

and sastras. A few translations were made in this period by persons of whom we know little.

Historical books and books on miscellaneous topics were largely added by native writers at this epoch. Of such work I should mention only one. It is Nien-cheng's great work on the *History of Buddhism*, called Fo-tsu-li-tao-tung-tsai (Nanjio, 1637), which begins with the so-called first ruler of China Phan-ku, down to A.D. 1333 or 1344, when the compilation was completed. It relates several events concerning not only Buddhism, but also Confucianism and Taoism.

Nien-cheng's History of Buddhism.

We have come to the close of the literary activity in the form of translating Sanskrit books into Chinese. The Yuen dynasty probably saw the last translation done from Sanskrit. The Buddhism of the Yuan dynasty specially of the capital was greatly affected by Lamaism. The last emperor Shun-ti is said to have witnessed indecent plays and dances in the company of Lamas and created a scandal which contributed to the downfall of the dynasty. The Mongols were driven by the native Chinese dynasty known as Ming. The Ming dynasty reigned from 1368 to 1644.

Buddhism of Yuan period affected by Lamaism.

Few Ming emperors showed personal interest in religion and their favour was always guided by some political motive. Tai-tsu the first Ming emperor, in 1377, by an imperial decree, ordered that all monks should study *Laṅkāvatara sūtra*, *Prajñāpāramitā Hṛdaya sūtra*, and *Vajrachedikā*. He also called together the priests of the Dhyāna school to write commentaries and thereupon Tsung-lo and Ju-chi wrote three brief commentaries on the above three works (Nanjio, 1613, 1614, 1615).

Ming Emperor Tai-tsu encourages study of Buddhist texts.a

The third emperor Ch'eng-tsu, when a boy was educated by a Buddhist Priest and the emperor imbibed Buddhist and literary tendencies. He wrote ten laudatory compositions in prose and verse between 1410 and 1415, which were incorporated in the Tripiṭaka (Nanjio, 1616). He compiled another book in nine fasciculi, known as '*Memors of spiritual priests*' in which 209 priests both native and foreign are mentioned, from Kāśyapa Mātaṅga 67 A. D. to P'u-an of the Southern Sung dynasty (1127-1280), who are in narration preceded by some priests of the Yuan dynasty (1280-1368). The emperor selected those priests, whose actions seemed very wonderful and almost supernatural, as they are described in older memoires. (Nanjio, 1620). On the whole Buddhism flourished under the Mings and got the imperial support from time to time with intervals of persecution. The reign of Wu-tsung (1506-1521) was extremely favourable to Buddhism. The emperor himself was a learned Buddhist scholar who knew Sanskrit as well as Mongol and Arabic. The study of Sanskrit had been throughout encouraged in China and books on grammer and lexicon were written in Chinese. During the Ming rule, Sanskrit study decayed in China ; still Yun-lo founded in 1407 a school of languages for training interpreters at which Sanskrit was taught among other tongues.[1]

Emperor Ch'eng-tsu composes verses on Buddha

Also 'Memories of the spiritual priests.'

Ming Emperor Wu-tsung favoured Buddhism and knew Sanskrit.

A. D. 1407, Sanskrit still for training interpreters.

During the Ming dynasty the thirteenth catalogue of the Chinese Tripitaka was published in 1368-1396 in 3 fasciculi ; this was the catalogue of the southern collection of edition of the Chinese Buddhist canon, published in Nanking, under the reign of the first Ming emperor T'ai-tsu (1368-1396). It was re-issued by the third emperor of the same dynasty with more books (Nos. 1622-1662 of Nanjio's Catalogue) added to it and finally published by Mi-tsang a Chinese monk at the beginning of the seventeenth century. This was the basis of B. Nanjio's Catalogue.

Catalogue of Chinese Tripitaka.

1 Eliot III, p. 278.

The Chinese Tripiṭaka was preserved in manuscripts for more than nine hundred years from 67 A. D. to 972 A. D., when it was printed for the first time. After that year at various times Tripiṭaka was reprinted and it is not less than twenty times that it was issued during the Sung and Yuan dynasties (960-1368); but during the trouble occuring towards the end of the Yuan period, all of them perished, and those only taken to Japan were preserved. Under the Manchu rule which began in 1644 and ended 1910, the Chinese Tripiṭaka was published by the emperors Shih-Tsung and Kao-Tsung, who ruled between 1703 and 1795. In modern times, a reprint of the Chinese Tripiṭaka has been published by Mrs. Hardoon in 1913 at Shang-hai. The editions published in Japan, which are the standard and best editions of the Tripitaka, are described in our section of Japan.

Subsequent editions of Tripiṭaka in China.

Of all the collections of the Tripiṭaka the Ming Catalogue has been made famous by the English translation done by the great Japanese scholar, Buniyo Nanjio. His *Catalogue of the Chinese Translation of the Buddhist Tripitaka*[1] first gave a comprehensive idea of the rich Buddhist literature of the Eastern Asia. His catalogue enumerates 1662 works classified into four divisions.

Contents of the Ming Tripitaka translated by Nanjio.

1. Sūtra Piṭaka (Ching-tsang).
2. Vinaya Piṭaka (Lu-tsang).
3. Abhidharma Piṭaka (Lun-tsang).
4. Miscellaneous works (Tsa-tsang).

The first three contains translations and the fourth original Chinese works. The first division called Ching or Sūtras amounts to nearly two-thirds of the whole, for it comprises no less than 1081 works and is subdivided as

(a) Mahāyāna sūtras 541 Books.
(b) Hīnayāna sūtras 240 Books.

[1] Oxford, Clarendon Press, 1883.

(c) Mahāyāna and Hīnayāna sūtras, (admitted into canon during the Sung and Yuan dynasties) 300 Books.

The *Mahāyāna Sūtras* comprise of works most esteemed by Chinese Buddhists. It is divided into seven classes (1) Prajñāpāramitā class 22 works, (2) Ratnakuṭa class 38 works, (3) Mahā-sannipāta class 26 works, (4) Avatamsaka class 26 works, (5) Nirvāṇa class 13 works, (6) Sūtras of Duplicate translations excluded from the preceeding five classes 250 works, (7) Sūtras of Single translation, excluded from the five classes 166 works.

The Vinaya Pitaka is sub-divided into Mahāyāna and Hīnayāna texts. The Mahāyāna Vinaya consists of only 25 works. The Hīnayāna sections comprises of five well-defined recensions of the code, besides extracts. compendiums etc. These are 60 in number, (1) Vinaya of the Sarvāstivādins. (2) The Vinaya of Mūla-sarvāstivadins of Yi -tsing, (3) Vinaya of the Dharmagupta schools, (4) Vinaya of the Mahīśāsakas, (5) Mahāsaṇghika Vinaya.

The Abhidharma Piṭaka is also divided into Mahāyāna and Hīnayāna. They are philosophical works of Aśvaghosa, Nāgārjuna, Asaṇga, Vasubandhu, Āryadeva and other Mahāyāna masters. They represent two principal schools of thoughts, Yogācāra and Madhyamika. There are 94 works in this division. The Hīnayāna Abhidharma chiefly represents the Sarvāstivāda school and contains 37 works. It shows no correspondence with the Pali Piṭaka. Besides these there are about two dozen works on Abhidharma of the Mahāyāna and Hinayāna, successively admitted into the canon during the Sung and Yuan dynasties.

The miscellaneous portion contains books of the sages and wise men of India 147 in number, and works written by Chinese writers on Buddhist subjects 195 in number. Some of the works of the latter section was admitted into the canon during the Ming dynasty.[1]

[1] Nanjio, Intro., p, ix, x.

The Chinese Tripitaka is a literary and bibliographical collection rather than ecclesiastical canon. It contains translations of Indian works on Buddhism and such books as possess a certain age and authority. It contains history, biography, travel books, lexicons and books on various subjects and therefore it can well be said to be an encyclopaedia of Buddhist knowledge of China and India.

ALPHABETICAL LIST

OF

SANSKRIT WORKS

Translated

into

Chinese

(with the names of translators)

	Translation	*Nanjio*	*Page*
Akṣayamati paripricchā	Bodhiruci	(23.45)	250
Akṣaramatimirdeśa	Chu Fa-hu (Dharmarakṣa)	(74)	39
	Chi-yen & Pao-un	(77)	
Akṣobhyasya-Tathāgatasya vyuha	(1) Lokaksema	(68)	17
	(2) Bodhiruci	(336)	250
Aṅgulimālīya sutra	Gunabhadra	(434)	139
Acintyaprabhāsa (bodhisattva) nirdeṣa	Kumarajiva	(396)	188
Acintya-buddha-viśaya nirdeṣa	Bodhiruci	(23.35)	250
Ajātaśatru-kaukritya vinodana	(1) Lokakṣema	(174)	17
	(2) Chu Fa-hu (Dharmarakṣa)	(182)	39
	(3) Abridged	(183)	
'Atīta pratyutpanna hetu-phala sūtra.'	Gunabhadra	(666)	142
Adbhutadharma-paryāyā	(1) Anon-Han Dynasty	(260)	
	(2) Hiuen tsang	(261)	211
	(3) ? T'ang-ching	(400)	
Anakçara granthaka rocana garbha sūtra	Divākara	(221)	242
Anantamukha-viniśodhana-nirdeṣa	Bodhiruci	(222-223)	250
Anākāra-cintā-rajas (?) sastra	[Dignāga] Paramartha (1172)	(232)	233
Anantamukha-sādhaka dharani (?)	(1) Chi-Chien	(353)	28
	(2) Kung-te-chih & Hsuen chang	(354)	
	(3) Saṅgha-bhara	(355)	150
	(4) Buddhabhadra	(356)	61
	(5) Buddhaśānta	(357)	174
	(6) Gunabhadra	(358)	142
	(7) Jinagupta	(359)	193
	(8) Chi-yen	(360)	144
Anavatapta Nāgarjuna paripricchā sūtra	Chu Fa-hu (Dharmakakṣa)	(437)	39
Antarābhava sūtra	Fo-nien (Buddhasmṛti)	(463)	80
Aparimitayu-sutra	Sanghavarman	(27)	143

	Translation	*Nanjio*	*Page*
Aparimitayus-sutra-sāstra	[Vasubandhu]		
	Bodhiruci (1)	(1204)	250
Aparivartya-sutra (see Avaivartya sutra)			
	(1) Chu Fa-hu (Dharmarakṣa)	(150)	39
	(2) Anon. Liang Dynansty.	(151)	
	(3) Chi-yen & Pao-yun	(158)	144
Abhidharma koṣakarika	[Vasubandhu]		
	Hiuen tsang	(1270)	225
Abhidharma-koṣa-sāstra	[Vasubandhu]		
	(1) Hiuen tsang	(1267)	224
	(2) Paramartha	(1269)	163
Abhidharma-Jñānaprasthāna-śastra	[Kātyayaniputra]		
	(1) Gautamasanghadeva	(1273)	70
	(2) Hiuen tsang	(1275)	219
Abhidharma Prakaranapāda	[Vasumitra]		
	(1) Hiuen tsang	(1277)	221
	(2) Gunabhadra and Bodhiyasas	(1292)	139
Abhidharma Prakarana-śāsana śāstra	[Sanghabhadra]		
	Hiuen tsang	(1266)	228
Abhidharma Mahāvibhāśā śāstra	[Ed. by Kātyāyaniputra]		
	(1) Buddhavarman (incomp)	(1263)	126
	(2) Hiuen tsang	(1264)	223
Abhidharma Vijnāna-kāyapāda śāstra	[ArhatDeva-sarman]		
	Hiuen-tsang	(1281)	8222
Abhidharma Sangttiparyāyapāda	[Sariputra]		
	Hiuen tsang	(1276)	221
Abhidharma Skandapāda	[Mahamaudglyana]		
	Hiuentsang	(1296)	222
Abhidharma Hridayasāstra	[Dharmajñān]		
	Gautama saṅghadeva and Hwui-yen	(1288)	54
Abhidharmāmrita(rasa) śāstra	[Ghoṣa]	(1278)	
	Anon. Wei Dynasty	(509)	
Abhiniśkramaṇa sutra (?)	(1) Nieh Tao-chan	(680)	46
	(2) Jinagupta		193
Amitābha-vyuha			
Amitayus-sutra	An Shih-Kao	(Lost)	25
'Amita śuddha-samyak-sambuddha-sutra			
	Lokakṣema		23
'Amita sutra'	Chi-Chien	(26)	28
'Amitayus sutra'	Sanghavarman	(27)	22
'Amita suddha samyak sambuddha sutra'		(Lost)	
	Po Yen		23
'Amitayus sutra' (Lost)	Chu Fa-hu (Dharmarakṣa)		39
'Amitayus (Nava) sutra'	(1) Buddhabhadra (Lost)		
	(2) Pao-yun (Lost)		
	(3) Dharmamitra. (Lost)		144

	Translation	Nanjio	Page
Amitayur-arhat-samyak sambuddha sutra' (Lost)	Chu Ta-li		
'Amitayus-Tathagata-parshad'	Bodhiruci	(235)	250
'Amitayur vyuha sūtra (Mahāyāna)	Fa-hsien	(863)	305
'Amitayur Dhyānasūtra	Kālayasas	(198)	254
Amitartha sūtra	Dharmakṛtayaśas	(133)	148
Amonhapāśa kalparaja	Bodhiruci	(317)	250
Amoghapāśa dhāraṇī	(1) Jinagupta	(312)	193
"	(2) Li Wu-Thao	(314)	
Amoghopaśa Hṛdaya śāstra	(3) Bodhiruci	(315)	25
"	(4) Hiuen-tsang	(316)	211
"	(5) Ratnacinta	(313)	
Artha-viniścaya-dharmaparyāya	suvarnadharani (?)	(1015)	
Alpākṣara Prajñāparamitā	T'ien-si-tsai	(797)	307
(Pūrṇamukha) Avadānaśataka	Chi-Chien	(1324)	29
Avadāna sūtra Dharmatrāta	Chu Fo-nien	(1321)	82
Avalokiteśvara bodhisattva Samantamukha parīvarta of the Saddharma Puṇḍarika	Kumarajiva	(137)	
'Avalokiteśvara-b-Mahāsthānaprāpta-b- vyākaraṇa sūtra	Than-wu-chie (Dharmakāra)	(395)	136
Avalakiteśvara-mātā dharani	Fa-hsien	(910)	305
'Avidyārakṣa-sūtra'	Anon. Ts'in Dynasty	(1369)	
Avalokiteśvara Ekadaśa mukha dhāraṇi	(1) Yaśogupta	(327)	189
	(2) Hiuen-tsang	(328)	211
Avaivartya (?) sūtra	(1) Chu Fa-hu (Dharmarakṣa)	(150)	39
	(2) Anon. N. Liang	(157)	
	(3) Chu-yen and Pao-yan.	(158)	
Aśokadattā Vyakaraṇa	Buddhaśānta	(23132)	174
	Chu Fa-hu (Dharmaraksa)	(42)	39
'Aśoka (rāja) Avadāna sūtra'	Anon. E. Tsin	(1344)	43
'Aśoka rāja sūtra'	Saṅghapāla	(1343)	44
'Aśoka-rāja Jibanī'	An Fa-chin	(1459)	43
Aṣta Buddhaka	(1) Chi-chien	(299)	28
"	(2) Chu Fa-hu (Dharmarakṣa)	(300)	39
"	(3) Saṅghabhara	(301)	150
"	(4) Jinagupta	(302)	193
Aṣta Buddha sūtra	Gautama Prajñāruci	(400)	185
Aṣta maṇḍalaka sūtra	(1) Fa-hsien	(880)	305
	(2) Amoghavajra	(981)	291
Aṣta-sahasrika-Prajnaparamita	Hiuentsang	(1 e)	95,217
Aṣṭaguru-sutra'	Chi-chien	(710)	28
Aṣṭa-mahā-śri caitya samskrita stotra'	Fa-hsien	(1071)	305

	Translation	*Nanjio*	*Page*
'Aṣṭādaśa-nikāya sūtra' [Vasumitra]			231
	Hiuen tsang	(1284)	
Aṣṭādaśa-sāhasrikā p. p. (i.e.)			
	Hiuen tsang	(1 c)	231
Aṣṭādaśa ākāśa-śāstra	[Nāgārjuna]		
	Paramārtha	(1187)	154
Akāśa garbha-bodhisatha-dhārani-sūtra			
	Dharmamitra	(69—70)	
" " sūtra	Buddhayaśas	(68)	86
" sūtra	Jina gupta.	(67)	
Adyāśaya sancodana	(1) Jinagupta	(37)	
"	(2) Bodhiruci	(23.25)	255
'Ārya Nāgārjuna b.-suhrillekha	(1) Sanghavarman	(1440)	-
"	(2) Yi-tsing	(1441)	
"	(3) Guṇavarman	(1464)	
'Ārya-tārā b. Saṅskrita stotra'	Shih-hu (Dānapāla)	(1079)	
'Ārya Vajrapāni b. nāmaṣtaśataka samskrita stotra'			
	Fa-hsien	(1075)	
'Ārya-Avalokiteśvara b. guṇa stotra'			
	Shih-hu (Dānapalā)	(1076)	
Ārya-Avalokiteśvara b.-Samskrita Stotra			
	Fa-tien (Dharmadeva)	(1078)	
'Āryatrāta Buddhamatrika vimśati pujā stotra-sūtra'			
	An Tsang	(1068)	
Alambana Parikśa (pratyaya-dhyāna śāstra) [Dignaga]			
	Hiuen tsang	(1173)	233,271
'Āgamokta-dvādaśa-nidāna-sūtra'			
	An Hiūen	(1339)	18
Ugra-pariprecha			23,252
	(1) Sanghavarnian	(2319)	
	(2) An Hsuen	(33)	
	(3) Chu Ta hu (Dharmaraks	(34)	
Udanavarga	[Dharmatrata] (Dharmasamgraha mahartha gathā sūtra) Tien-si-tsai	(1439)	82
"	(Avadāna) Fo-nien	(1321)	309
'Udayana Vatsarāja Paripriccha'			
	(1) Bodhiruci	(23.29)	350
	(2) Fa-chu	(38)	
	(3) Fa-thien (Dharmadeva ?)	(788)	
Upāya Kauśalya-hridaya śāstra [Nāgārjunā]			
	Ki-Kie-ye and Than-yao	(1257)	181
Ullambana sūtra'	Chu-Fa-hu (Dharmaraksa	(303)	42
Usnisa-Cakravarti (Etantra xākṣara Prasāsta Buddha-Uṣnīsā-States)			
	Amoghavajra	(1023)	

	Translator	Nanjio	Page
Ekottara-āgama [cf. Aṅguttara nīkāyā]			
	Dharmanandī	(543)	53.55,73,76
	Gautama Prajñārūci		
Ekaśloka sāstra [Nāgārjunā]	Gautama Prajñāruci	(1912)	186
'Ekākṣara-Uṣnisa-cakrarāja sutra'	Amoghavajra	(1024)	
Kaṇakavarna pūrvayoga	Gautama Prajñaruci	(390)	
Karaṇḍavyuha sūtra	T'ien-si-tsai	(782)	
Karuna-puṇḍarika sūtra	Dharmarakṣa	(142)	130
Karmavibhāga Dharmagrantha(?)	An Shih-kao	(685)	
Karma-siddha-prakaraṇa śutra	[Vasubandhu]		
	Hiuen tsang	(1221)	187
	Vimokṣaprajña	(1222)	
Karmāvaraṇa pratisaraṇa (praticchedana) (see Triskandhaka)			
	Jinagupta and Dharmagupta	(1090)	
Karmāvaraṇa visuddhi mahāyana sutra			
	Anon. Ts'in Dynasty	(1094)	
Kāśyapa-parivarta	Anon	(23.43)	253
	Lokakṣema	(57)	
	Anon. Ts'in Dynasty	(58)	
	Shih-hu (Dānapāla)	(805)	310
Koṣa-Karaka (see Nyāyānusara)			227
Kusalamula-samparigraha sutra	Kumarajīva	(425)	
Kusumasañcaya-sutra	Chi-chia-ye and Than-Tao	(402)	
Kauśika-prajñāpāramita	Ship-hu (Dānapāla)	(865)	
Kṣamavati-vyākaraṇa sutra	Bodhiruci (N. Wei)	(461)	
Kṣamākāra-bodhisattva sutra	Chi-Chien	(378)	
Kṣudraka Agama	(Dharmagupta School)		74
Gaṅgottara upāsikā paripriccha	Bodhiruci	(23.31)	250
Gayāsīrṣa	Kumārajīva	(238)	
	Bodhiruci (N. Wei)	(239)	
	Vinitaruci	(240)	
	Bodhiruci (T'ang)	(241)	250
Gayāśīrṣa-tikā [Vasubandhu]	Bodhiruci (N. Wei)	(1191)	
Garuḍa-garbha-rāja (or tantra)	Amoghavajra	1054)	
Garbha sutra	Bodhiruci	(23.13)	250
	Yi-tsing	(23.14)	
	Chu Fa-hu (Dharmarakṣa)	(32)	
	Fo-nien	(433)	
Guṇaratna-Saṅkusumita-paripricchā			
	Bodhiruci (T'ang)	(23.34)	
Guhya-garbharāja	Shih-hu (Dānapāla)	(1026)	
Guhya-samaya-garbha-rāja	Shih-hu (Dānapāla)	(1029)	
Grahamatrikā-dhāranī	Fa-t'ien (Dharmadeva)	(3 11)	
Ghanavyuha	Divākara	(444)	
	Fa-hu (Dharmarakṣa)	(971)	
Ghanti sūtra	Fa-t'ien (Dharmaeva)	(1081)	

	Translator	*Nanjio*	*Page*
Cakṣur-viṣodhana vidyā	Than-wu-san (Dharmarakṣa)	(483)	
Cakṣur-viṣodhana vidyā-dhārani	Amoghavajra	(982)	
Caturdāraka Samādhi sutra	Chu Fa-hu (Dharmarakṣa)	(116)	
	Jivagupta	(121)	
Catuṣka-nirhara sutra	Divakara	(266)	
	Sikṣānanda	(520)	
Catussatya sutra	An Shih-kao	(598)	
Catussatya śāstra [Vasubandhu]	Paramartha	(1261)	
Candragarbha sutra	Narendrayaśas	(63)	
Candraprabha Kumāra sutra	Chu Fa-hu (Dharmarakṣa)	(230)	
	Guṇabhadra	(231)	
Candraprabha-bodhisattva avadāna sūtra	Fa-t'ien (Dharmadeva)	(852)	
Candrottarā-darikā-vyākaraṇa-sūtra	Jinagupta	(441)	
Cintāmaṇināma sarvaghātamṛtyu vāraṇita (or vāraṇa) dhāraṇi	Shih-hu (Dānapāla)	(802)	
Candidevi-dhāraṇi	Divākara	(344)	
	Vajrabodhi	(345)	
	Amoghavajra	(346)	
Caitya-pradakṣiṇa-gāthā	Sikṣānanda	(458)	
Jāṅguli-vidyā	Amoghavajra,	(961)	
Jambhala-galendra-yathālabdha kalpa	Fa-t'ien (Dharmadeva)	(1045)	
Jātaka-nidāna	Chu Fa-hu (Dharmarakṣa)	(669)	
Jātaka-mālā [Arya-sūtra]	Shao-te, Hwui-sun and others	(1312)	
Jñanottara-b. paripriccha	Nandi	(23-38)	
	Chu Fa-hu (Dharmaraksa)	(52)	
	Shih-hu (Dānapala)	(926)	
Jñanolkā-dhāraṇi-sarvadurgati-pariśodhani	Devaprajña	(496)	
	Shih-hu (Dānapāla)	(835)	
Jvalapraśamani-dhāraṇi	Amoghavajra	(984)	
Tathāgatagarbha sutra	Buddhabhadra	(384)	
	Anon	(443)	
Tathāgata guṇa-jñāna-acitya-viṣaya-avatāranirdeśa	Jinagupta	(91)	
	Sikṣānanda	(93)	
Tathāgata-jñānamudra	Anon.	(255)	
	Chi-Chien	(256)	
„ „ samādhi sutra	„		
„ „ sutra	Jñānaśrī(?)	(1014)	
Tathāgata-pratibimba-pratisthanusaṁsā	Devaprajña	(288)	
	Anon.	(289) (296)	
T—Mahākāruṇika-nirdeśa	Chu Fa-hu (Dharmarakṣa)	(79)	

	Translator	*Nanjio*	*Page*
T—acintya gūhya-nirdeśa	Chu Fa-hu (Dharmarakṣa ?)	(233)	
	Fa-hu (Dharmarakṣa ?)	(1043)	
Tarka śāstra [Vasubandhu]	Paramārtha	(1252)	
Triśambara (or bala) nirdesa	Bodhiruci	(231)	250
	Dharmarakṣa (Liang Dynasty)	(24)	
Triskandhaka	Jinagupta & Dharmagupta	(1090)	
	Saṅghapāla	(1103)	
	An Shih-kao	(1106)	
'Damamukha sutra'		(1322)	127
Daśacakra-kṣitigarbha	Hiuant-sang	(164)	
	Anon	(165)	
Daśdig-andhakāra-vidhvainsana sūtra			
	Chu Fa-hu (Dharmarakṣa)	(515)	
Daśadharmaka	Buddhaśānta	(13.9)	
	Saṅghapāla	(29)	
Daśabhūmika śāstra [Vasubandhu]	Bodhiruci (N. Wei)	(1194)	
Daśabhūmika sūtra	Chu Fa-hu (Dharmaraksa)	(110)	
	Kumārajiva-Buddhayaśas	(105)	41,297,177
'Daśabhūmi kleśa chedika'	Fo-nien.	(376)	80
'Daśaduṣta karma mārgasāstra' [Aśvaghoṣa]			312
	Suryayaśas (?)	(1379)	
Daśa-sāhasrikā-prajñāpāramitā			
	Hiuen-tsang	(1d)	
	Lokaksema	(5)	17
	Kumārajiva	(6)	95
	Dharmapriya and Fo-nien	(7)	
	Chi-chien	(8)	
	Shi-hu (Dānapāla)	(927)	
'Daśa-padārtha vaiśesika' [Jñānacandra]	Hiuen-tsang	(1295)	234
Dīrghanakha-parivrājaka	Paripricchā Yi-tsing	(634)	30,74,76
Dīrghā Āgama	Buddhayaśas and Fo-nien.	(545)	85
Devata sūtra (?)	Hiuen-tsang	(753)	
'Dudriṣti sutra	Anon. Early Sung.	(584)	
Dvādaśanikāya śāṣtra [Nāgārjuna]	Kumārajiva	(1186)	
Dvadaśa-buddhaka dhāraṇī	Jinagupta	(336)	
	Yi-tsing	(335)	
'Dvacatvāriṁsa sūtra'	Kaśyapa Mātanga	(678)	7
Dharmagupta bhīkṣukarman	Hiuen-tsang	(1128)	
Dharmagupta bhikṣunikarman	Guṇavarman	(1129)	
Dharmagupta vinaya	Buddhayaśas and Fo-nien	(1117)	269
Dharma-cakra-pravartana sutra	An Shih-kao	(657)	
	Yi-tsing.	(658)	
Dharmatrata-dhyāna-sutra	Buddhabhadra	(1341)	
Dharmadhatu-prakrity-asambheda nirdeśa			
	Mandra	(23.8)	
Dharmadhatu-hṛdaya samvata-nirdeśa, (same as above)			

	Translator	*Nanjio*	*Page*
Dharmapada (text)	Vighna	(1365)	
„ Avadāna sūtra (com.)	Fa-chu and Fa-li	(1353)	
„ Avadāna (com)	Fo-nien	(134)	
„ (Udānavarga text)	T'ien-sitsai	(1439)	
Dharma-śarira sūtra	Fa-hsien	(921)	
Dharma-vinaśa-sūtra	Anon.	(470)	
Dharma saṅgīti sūtra	Bodhīruci	(426)	
'Dharma-haṅgraha'	Shi-hu (Dānapāla)		
Dhātukāyapāda (Abhidharma) [Vasumitra]	Hiuen-tsang	(1282)	
Dhāraṇi-saṁgraha	Atigupta		
Dhvajāgra-keyura-dhārani	Dānapala	(795)	
Nanda-pravaryya-sūtra	Fa-chu	(660)	
Niyatāniyatagati mudrāvatāra	Gautama Prajñāruci	(132)	
	Yi-tsing	(131)	
Nīlakantha-[Sahasrākṣa-sahasravāhu avalokiteśvara vṛddhādhāraṇī kaya sutra	Bodhiruci	(319)	
	Chi-t'ung	(318)	
'Nidānacayā sutra.'	K'ang Mong Siang	(733)	20
Nyāyadvāra tarka-śāstra [Nāgārjuna]	Hiuen-tsang	(1224)	
	Yi-tsing	(1223)	
Nyāya-praveśa Tarka-śāstra [Saṅkarasvāmin]	Hiuen-tsang	(1216)	
Nyāyānusāra-śāstra [Saṅgnabhadra]	Hiuen-tsang	(1265)	
Pañcaviṁśatisāhasrika Prajñāpāramita	Hiuen-tsang	(1b)	
	Moksala and Chu Shu-lan		
	Or Suklaratna	(2)	
	Kumārajiva	(3)	94
	Chu Fa-hu (Dharmaraksa)	(4)	
'Pañcasatikā' p.p.	Siang-kung	(16)	
	Hiuen-tsang	(1h)	
Pañcaskandhaka śāstra [Vasubandhu]	Hiuen-tsang	(1176)	
Pañcaskandhaka vaipulya śāstra [Sthitamati's-com.]	Divakara	(1175)	
Padmacintāmaṇi dhāraṇi sutra	Siksānanda	(321)	
	Ratnacinta	(322)	
	Yi-tsing	(323)	
	Bodhiruci	(324)	
	Dānapāla	(829)	
Paramārtha-dharmavijaya sūtra	Gautama Prajñāruci	(210)	
	Jinagupta	(211)	
Paramārtha saṁvṛti satyanirdeśa	Chu Fa-hu (Dharmaraksa)	(1084)	
	Fa-hai	(1089)	
	Kumārajīva	(1101)	
Parṇa-savari-dhāraṇī.	Amoghavajra	(975)	
Pitaputra-Samāgama	Narendrayaśas	(23.16)	
Punyabala avadāna.	Dānapala	(953)	

	Translator	*Nanjio*	*Page*
Puṣpa kūṭa.	Chi Chien	(337)	
	Anon. E. Tsin	(338,339)	
,, ,, Dharaṇi.	dānapāla	(857)	
Pūrṇa paripriccha	Kumarajīva	(23.17)	
Prajñaptipāda śāstra [Mahamaudgalyāyana]			
	Fa-hu (Dharmarakṣa)	(1317)	
Prajñāpāramitā ardhaśatika	Hiuen-tsang	(1)	
	Bodhiruci	(18)	250
	Dānapāla	(897)	
	Vajrabodhi	(1033)	
	Amoghavajra	(1034)	
Prajñāpāramitā-sañcayagāthā	Fa-hsien	(864)	
Prajñapāramitā hṛdaya sūtra	Kumārajīva	(19)	98
	Hiuen-tsang	(19)	
	Dānapāla	(935)	
Prajña-pradīpa śāstra tikā [Nāgārjuna & Aryadeva]			
	Prabhākaramitra	(1185)	
Prātimokṣa sūtra	Kumārajīva	(1160)	
	Yi-tsing	(1110)	
Pratimokṣa vinaya (of the Kāśyapīya nikya)			
	Gautama Prajñarcci	(1108)	
Pratitya samudpāda śāstra [Suddhamati]			
	Bodhiruci (N. Wei)	(1211)	
Pratitya samudpāda sūtra	Chi-chien	(278)	
	Hiuen-tsang	(279)	
Pratyutpanna-buddhā-sammukhāvasthita samādhi sūtrā			
	Lokakṣema	(23)	
	Fa-chung	(421)	
Pratyeka-buddha nidānaśāstra.	Anon.	(1262)	
Pradīpa-dāniya sūtra	Narendrayaśas	(428)	
Prabhā-sādhanā	Bodhiruci	(2311)	
Praśānta-viniścaya-pratihārya samadhi sūtra	Hiuen-tsang	(522)	
Pranyamūla śāstra-tikā (see Madhyamaka śastra)	[Nāgārjuna and Āryadeva]		
do	tikā [Sthitamati]		
	Wei-tsing	(1316)	
Buddhacarita-kāvya [Aśvaghosa]	Dharmakṣema	(1351)	131
Buddhacarita	(see above Abhiniskramana sūtra)		
Buddhapitaka nigraha sūtra	Kumārajiva	(1095)	
Buddhabhasita-samantajvalamālā-viśuddha-sphuṭikṛta-cintamaṇi-mudrā-hṛdaya-aparājita dhāraṇi pratisara mahāvidyā rāja.			
	Amoghavajra	(1042)	
Buddhabhūmī	Hiuen-tsang	(502)	
Buddhabhumi sūtra [Bandhuprabha]			
	Hiuen-tsang	(1195)	
Buddhasaṅgiti sūtra	Chu Fa-hu (Dharmaraksa)	(401)	

	Translator	*Nanjio*	*Page*
Buddha hṛdaya-dhārani	Hiuen-tsang	(439)	
	Fa-t'ien—(Dharmadeva)	(825)	
Buddha-avataṁsaka sūtra	Buddhabhadra etc	(87)	
	Siksānanda	(88)	
	Prajña	(89)	
'Bodhicittotpādana śāstra' [Vasubandhu ?]	Kumarajīva	(1218)	110
Bodhivakāo (vṛksa) nirdeśa sūtra	T'ien si-tsai	(791)	
Bodhisattva-earyā-nirdeśa	Gunavarman	(1085)	
	Dharmarakśa	(1085)	
'Bodhimaṇda vyūha dhāraṇi sutra'	Amoghavajra	(1025)	
'Bodhimaṇda bhāṣita Ekākṣara-uṣṇīśa-cakrarajā sutra			
	Amoghavajra		
Bodhisattva piṭaka.	Hiuen-tsang	(23.11)	
	Fa-hu (Dharmaraksa)	(1005)	
Bodhisattva piṭaka-avatamsaka	Mañjuśri-mūlagarbha-tantra		
	T'ien-si-tsai	(1056)	
Bodhisattva-buddhānusmrti-samādhi			
	Kung-te-chih and Hsuen-chaṇg	(71)	
Brahmajala śūtra	Chi-chien	(554)	
	Kumārajīva	(1087)	120
Bhadrakalpikā sūtra	Chu Fa-hu (Dkarmarakṣa)	(403)	
Bhadrakā-ratri	Yi-tsing	(500)	
Bhadracāri-pranidhāna	Amoghavajra	(1142)	
Bhadrapāla śreṣṭhī paripricehā	Jinagupta	(23.3 a)	
	Divākara	(53)	
Bhadrapàla sūtra	Lokaksema	(76)	
Bhadra-māyākāra parıpṛcchā	Bodhiruci	(23.21)	
	Chu Fa-hu (Dharmaraksa)	(35)	
Bhavasamkrānti sūtra	Buddhaśanta (284)	(7)	
	Bodhirucī	(285)	N. wei
	Yi-tsing	(526)	
Bhikṣuṇī pratimokṣa-sūtra	Yi-tsing	(1148)	
	Fa-yin	(1161)	
Bhūtadāmara mahātantrarāja	Fa-tien (Dharmadeva)	(1031)	
Bheṣajya-guru purvapranidhāna	Dharmagupta	(170)	
Bheṣajyaguru-vaidurya prabhāsa pūrvapraṇidhāṇa	Hiuen-tsang	(171)	
Bhaiṣajyarāja bhaiṣajya-samudgati sūtra	Kālayaśas	(305)	
'Mañjuśrī satya nāma sūtra'	Prajña	(1030)	
Mañjuṣri paripṛcchā	Divākara	(264)	
Mañjuśri buddha-kṣetra-guṇavyūha	Sikṣānanda	(23.15)	
	Mandra	(23.46)	
	Chu Fa-hu (Dharmarakṣa)	(31)	
Mañjuśrī-vikṛḍita sūtra	Chu Fa-hu (Dhamarakṣa)	(184)	
	Narendrayaśas	(185)	

	Translator	Nanjio	Page
Mahāyāna samparigraha śāstra [Asaṅga]			
	Paramārtha	(1183)	
	Buddhaśānta	(1189)	
	Hiueu-tsang	(1247)	
Mahayāna-abhidharma (saṁyukta) Sangīti śāstra [Sthitamati]			
	Hiuen-tsang	(1177)	
Mahāyāna abhisamaya sūtra	Jinayaśas	(195)	
	Divakara	(196)	
Mahāyanottara tantra śāstra	Ratnamati	(1236)	
Maharatnakuta sūtra	Bodhiruci	(23)	
Mahā-vajra meru śekhara-kūtāgāra dhāraṇī	Dānapala	(842)	
Mahā vaipulya mahāsannipāta utadrapala-sūtra			
	Jinagupta	(75)	
	Dharmarakṣa (N-Liang)	(61)	
Mahā vairocana-abhisambodhi	Subhakrisṇa and Yi-hsin	(530)	
Mahāśarya sūtra (Mahāsri) sūtra	Amoghavajra	(958)	
Mahāsangha bhiksu vinaya	Fa-hien and Buddhabhadra	(1150)	
'Mahāsanni-pātā sūtra'	Dharmaksema	(61)	129
Mahā saṅgha vinaya	Buddhabhandra and Fahien	(1119)	
Mahā-sahasra-pramardana sutra	T'ien-si-tsai	(784)	
Mahiśāsaka-karman	Ai-t'ung	(1153)	
Mahi śāsaka vinaya	Buddhajiva and Chu Tao-Shang	(1122)	
Mātaṅgi sūtra	An Shih-ka.	(643)	
	Anon. Tsin Dynasty	(644)	
	Chi-Chien and Chu Lūh-Yen	(545)	30
	Chu Fa-hu	(696)	31
Māyājāla mahātantra mahāyāna gambhīranāya-gūhya-paraśi-sutra			
	Fa-hsien	(1022)	
Māyopamā-smadhi	Chu Fa-hu	(47)	
'Milinda-praśna'	Anon. Tsin Dy.	(1358)	
Mūlasarvastivāda nikāya-bhiksuṇī vinaya.			
	Yi-tsing	(1124)	
Mūla sarvāstivāda nidāna	Yi-tsing	(1133)	
„ bhiksuṇī vinaya.	Yi-tsing	(1149)	
„ mātrikā	Yi-tsing	(1132)	
„ vinaya	Yi-tsing	(1118)	
„ vinaya-gathā	Yi-tsing	(1143)	
„ vinaya-nidāna-mātūkā-gāthā			
	Yi-tsing	(1140)	
„ vinaya-sūtra	Yi-tsing	(1110)	
„ ekaśata karman	Yi-tsing	(1131)	
Mekhalā-dhārani	Dānapāla	(940)	
Maitri pratijñā-dhārañi	Fa-hsien	(890)	
Maiteya paripṛcchā	Bodhiruci	(23.42)	
	Chu Fa-hu	(55)	
„ „ dharmāsṭa.	Bodhiruci (N. Wei)	(23.41)	

	Translation	Nanjio	Page
Maitreya Vyākaraṇa	Kumārajīva	(205)	
	Anon. Ts'in Dy.	(206)	
	Yi-tsing	(207)	
Yogācārabhūmi Sāstra [Maitreya]	Hiuen tsang	(1170)	
„ „ „ Kārikā [Jinaputra]	Hiuen tsang	(1201)	
Ratnakāraṇḍavyūha.	Chu Fa-hu	(168)	
	Guṇabhadra	(169)	
Ratnakūṭa,	Jinagupta	(51)	
	An. Shih-kao	(251)	
Ratnakūṭa śāstra,	Bodhiruci (W.-wei)	(1234)	
Ratnacūḍa paripṛcchā	Chu Fa-hu	23-40)	
Ratnajāli paripṛcchā	Chu Fa-hu	(385)	
Ratnamegha Dhāraṇī	Amoghavajra	(962)	
Ratnamegha sūtra	Dānapāla, Fa-hu, Wei-tsing	(964)	
	Bodhiruci	(152)	
	Mandra and Saṅghapāla	(153)	
Ratnarāśi	Shih tao kung	(23-44)	
Raśmi-nirhāra-saṅgirathi	Bodhiruci	(23-11)	
Rājavavādaka	Tsu Chu Ching-shang	(248)	
	Hiuen tsang	(249)	
	Yi-tsing	(250)	
Rājavavādak sūtra	Dānapāla	(988)	
Rāṣṭrapāla paripṛcchā	Jinagupta	(23·18)	
	Dānapāla	(873)	
Laṅkāvatāra sūtra	Guṇabhadra	(175)	
	Bodhiruci (W.-Wei)	(176)	
	Śikṣānanda	(177)	
Lalitavistara	Divākara	(159)	
	Chu Fa-hu	(160)	
Lokānuvartana sūtra	Lokakṣema	(386)	
Vajrakumāra tantra	Amoghavajra	(1064)	
Vajragarbha-ratnarāja sūtra	Dharmadeva (Fa-t'ien	(869)	
Vajrachedikā prajñāpāramitā	Hiuen tsang	(1j)	
	Kumārajīva	(10)	96
	Bodhiruci (W.-Wei)	(11)	
	Paramārtha	(12)	
	Yi-tsing	(14)	
„ „ śāstra [Asaṅga]	Dharmagupta	(1167)	
„ „ śāstra [Vasubandhu]	Bodhiruci (W.-Wei)	(1168)	
„ „ vyākhyā [Asaṅga and Vasubandhu]	Yi-tsing	(1231)	
Vajrabhairava-tantra krodhatattvarāja	Fa-hsien	(1062)	

	Translation	*Nanjio*	*Page*
Vajramaṇḍa dhāraṇī	Jinagupta	(372)	
	Buddhaśānta	(373)	
Vajraśuci (Dharmayaśas)	Dharmadeva	(1303)	
Vatsa-sūtra	Chi-chu'en	(233)	
	Chu Fa-hu	(234)	
Varmvyūha nirdeśa	Boddhiruci	(23.7)	
Vasudhara Dhāraṇī	Anon. Ts'in Dy.	(472)	
	Dharmadeva (Fa-t'ien)	(787)	
	Dānapāla	(809)	
Vijñaptimātra siddhi (Maitreya)	Hiuen tsang	(1197)	
„ (Vasubandhu)	Boddhiruci (W.-Wei)	(1238)	
„ „	Paramārtha	(1239)	
„ „	Hiuen tsang	(1240)	
„ „ (tikā Dharmapāla)	Yi-tsing	(1210)	
Vinaya nidāna-sūtra	Chu Fo-nien	(1130)	
Vinaya mātrikā	Saṅghavarman	(1132)	
Vinaya viniścaya upāli paripṛcchā	Bodhiruci	(23.24)	
	Anon. Ts'in Dy.	(36)	
Viniṣodhana nirdeśa	Chu Fa-hu	(23.4)	
Vibhāṣā vinaya	Saṅghabhadra	(1279)	
Vimalakrīti nirdeśa	Upasūnya	(144)	
	Chu Fa-hu	(145)	
	Kumārajīva	(146)	
	Chi Chien	(147)	
	Hiuen tsang	(149)	
	Jinagupta	(181)	
Vimaladattā paripṛcchā	Nieh Tao-chan	(23.33)	
	Chu Fa-hu	(41)	
	Gautama Prajñāruci	(45)	
Viśesacinta-brāhmaṇa paripṛcchā	Bodhiruci (W.-Wei)	(189)	
	Kumārajīva	(190)	
	Chu Fa-hu	(191)	
„ „ sūtra-tika [Vasubandhu]	Bodhiruci (W.-Wei)	(1193)	
Viradattāparipṛcchā	Bodhiruci	(23.28)	
Vyāsa paripṛccha	Bodhiruci	(23.49)	
	Gautama Prajñāruci	(60)	
Vyūha paripṛcchā (see Srimaladevi)			
Sataśāstra [Aryadeva and Vasubandhu]			
	Kumārajīva	(1188)	107
Satāśāstra vaipulya [Aryadeva]	Hiuen tsang	(1189)	
Sātaśāhasrika Prajñāpāramitā	Hiuen tsang	(1a)	
Sāriputra paripṛcchā sūtra	Anon. E. Tsin	(1152)	
Śāriputra abhidharma śāstra	Dharmagupta and Dharmayaśas	(1268)	

	Translation	*Nanjio*	*Page*
Sālisambhava sūtra	Anon. E. Tsin	(280)	
	Chi chien	(281)	
	Fa t'ien (Dharmadeva)	(818)	
	Dānapāla	(867)	
	Amoghavajra	(963)	
Sūraṅgama samadhi	Kumārajīva	(399)	
Sraddha baladhānāvatāra mudrā sūtra			
	Bodhiruci (W-Wei)	(90)	
'Śraddhotpāda śāstra [Asvaghoṣa]			
	Paramārtha		
	Siksānanda		
Śrīkaṇṭha sūtra	Shang-chien	(398)	
Srīgupta sūtra	Narendrayaśas	(232)	
Srīgūhya-samāja tantrarāja	Dānapāla	(1027)	
Śrīmatī brāhmaṇa paripṛcchā	Chu Fa-hu	(342)	
	Bodhiruci	(343)	
Srīmālā-devī Simhanāda (see Vyūa. paripṛcchā)			
	Bodhiruci	(23-48)	
	Guṇabhadra	(59)	
Srī-sarvabhūta dāmara-tantra	Dharmadeva	(1031)	
Saḍaksara vidyā mātra	Anon. E. Tsin Dy.	(390)	
	Anon. Liang Dy.	(391)	
	Bodhiruci	(331)	
Sanmukha Dhāraṇī	Hiuen tsang	(493)	
Saṭpāramita sannipāta'	K'ang Seng huei	(143)	35
Saṁyukta āgama	Guṇabhadra	(544)	
	Anon. (small portion only)	(547)	
Saṁyukta-abhidharma hṛdaya śāstra			
	[Dharmatrāta] Saṅghavarman	(1287)	
Saktavarga āgama sūtra (?)	Anon. E. Tsin Dy.	(546)	
Saṅghabhedakavastu	Yi-tsing	(1123)	
Saṅghāṭi sūtra dharmaparyaya	Upaśūnya	(449)	
Satyasiddhi śāsta [Harivarman]	Kumārajīva	(1274)	108
Saddharma Puṇḍarīka	Kumārajiva	(134)	116
	Anon. W-Tsin	(136)	
	Chu Fa-hu	(138)	
	Jinagupta and Dharmayaśas	(139)	
„ „ „	śāstra-tīkā [Vasubandhu]		
	Bodhiruci (W-Wei)	(1232)	
	Ratnamati	(1233)	
Saddharma samādhi sūtra	Chi-yeṇ	(135)	
Saddharma-smṛtyupasthāna sūtra			
	Gautama Prajñāruci	(679)	
	Dharmadeva (Fa-t'ien)	(804)	

	Translation	*Nanjio*	*Page*
Sandhi-nirmocana sūtra	Guṇabhadra	(154)	
	Hiuen tsang	(247)	
	Bodhiruci (W-Wei)	(246)	
Sapta-tathāgata-pūrva praṇidhāna viśesa-vistāra	Yi tsing	(172)	
Saptati (see Sāṅkhyakārīkā)			
Saptadaśa-bhūmika śāstra-yogācārya	(see Yogācāryabhūmi)		
Saptabuddhaka (Fa-t'ien)	Dharmadeva	(860)	
Saptabuddhaka sūtra	Jinagupta	(367)	
	Anon. Liang Dyn.	(368)	
	(Fa-t'ien) Dharmadeva	(793)	
Saptaśatikā prajñāpāramitā	Hiuen tsang	(1. g)	
	Mandra	(21 and 23.46)	
	Saṅghapāla	(22)	
Samantabhadra Dhāraṇī	Anon. Liang Dyn.	(475)	
	Chi-t'ung	(494)	
Samantamukha parivarta	Bodhiruci	(23.10)	
	Chu Fa-hu	(30)	
Samantamukha praveśa-raśmi-vimaloṣṇīṣa-prabhā-sarvatathāgata-hṛdaya-samavirocana dhāraṇī	Dānapāla	(790)	
Sarvatathāgata-viṣayāvatāra	Anon. T'sin	(85)	
Sarvatathāgata. adhiṣṭhāna-sattvāvalokana-buddhakṣetra- nirdeśana-vyūha [Yi-tsing]		(504)	
Sarva-tathāgata adhisthāna-hṛdaya-gūhyadhātu-karaṇḍamudrā dhāraṇī	Amoghavajra	(957)	
Sarvadurgati-pariṣodhana uṣṇīṣa vijaya-dhāraṇī	Buddhapāla	(348)	
	Tu Hsing-i	(399)	
	Yi-tsing	(350)	
	Divākara	(351-352)	
	(Fa-t'ien) Dharmadeva	(796-871)	
Sarvadharma guṇa vyūharāja	Yi-tsing	(498)	
Sarvadharma-pravṛtti-nirdeśa sūtra	Jinagupta	(163)	
	Kumārajīva	(164)	
	Shao-te	(1012)	
Sarvanasya (?) putranaḍagupilāya (?) kalpa-rāja	Fa-hsien	(1038)	
Sarva-puṇya-samuccya-samādhi-sūtra	Chu Fa-hu	(128)	
	Kumārajīva	(129)	
Sarva-buddha-viṣayāvatāra	Saṅghapāla	(56)	
	Dharmaruci	(245)	

	Translation	Nanjio	Page
Sarva-buddha-viṣayāvatāra-jñāna-lokālaṇkāra-sūtra			
	(Fa-hu) Dharmarkṣa (?)	(1013)	
Sarva-buddhāṅgavatī dhāraṇī	Devaprajña	(495)	
Sarva-roga-praśamaṇi dhāraṇī	Amoghavajra	(983)	
Sarva abhaya pradāna dhāraṇī			
	Dānapāla	(998)	
Sarvāstivāda vinaya	Kumārajīva	(1115)	
„ „ vibhāsā	Anon. Ts'in Dyn.	(1135-1136)	
„ „ Saṁgraha	[Jinamitra]		
	Yi-tsing	(1127)	
Sāgara-nāgarāja	Chu Fa-hu	(456)	
„ „ paripṛcchā	Yi-tsing	(457)	
„ sūtra	Dānapāla	(840)	
Sāgaramati paripṛcchā	Wei-tsing and Fa-h	(976)	
Sānkhya kārika,	Paramārtha	(1300)	
Siṁha-nādikā sūtra	Buddhaśānta	(262)	
	Divākara	(263)	
Siṁha-paripṛcchā (see Subāhu)			
Sitātapatra-dhārṇī	Amoghavajra	(1016)	
Sukhavati vyūha			
	(see above Amitayu)		118
Subāhu paripṛcchā	Kumārajīva	(23.26)	
	Bodhiruci	(23.31)	
	Chu Fa-hu	(49)	
	Anon. W. Tsin	(50)	
Sumati-dārikā paripṛcchā	Bodhiruci	(23.30)	
	Chu Fa-hu	(39)	
	Kumarajīva	(40)	
Sumeru-garbha,	Narendrayaśas	(66)	
Surata paripṛcchā	Bodhiruci	(23.27)	
	Po-Yen	(43)	
	Chi.-Shih-lun	(44)	
Suvarṇa-prabhāsa sūtra	Dharmarakṣa	(127)	
	Po-Kuei and Jinagupta	(130)	
„ „ uttamarajasutra	Yi tsing	(126)	
Suvikrāntivikarmi-paripṛcchā			
	Hiuen tsang	(1.f)	
	Upaśūnya	(9)	
Susthitamati paripṛcchā	Dharmagupta	(23.36)	
	Chu Fa-hu	(47)	
	Vimokṣa prajñā and Prajñāruci	(48)	
Susiddhikāra-mahātantra- Sūddhanopāsikā pātra?			
	Subhakarasiṁha	(533)	
Sūtrālaṁkāra tikā [Asaṅga]	Prabhākaramitra	(1190)	

	Translation	Nanjio	Page
Sūtrālaṁkāra śāstra [Aśvaghosa ?]	Kumārajīva	(1182)	119
Sūryagarbha sūtra	Narendrayaśas	(62)	
	Translation	*Nanjio*	*Page*
Stri-vivarta vyākaraṇa-sūtra	Chu Fa-hu	(214)	
	Dharmayaśas	(215)	
	Dharmarakṣa	(236)	
	Dharmamitra	(237)	
Svapna-nirdeśa (see Viniṣodhana)			144
Hastikkṣyā	Dharmamitra	(193)	
	Chu Fa-hu	(194)	
Hevajra tantra	(Fa-hu) Dharmarakṣa	(1060)	

LIST OE THE TRANSLATORS OF THE CHINESE TRIPITAKA*

I. Latter Han Dynasty A.D. 25-200 (Capital Loyang)

Translator			Page
1. Kaśyapa Mātaṅga (A.D. 65)	(1)	1	8
2. Dharmaratna (Chu Fa-lan) (A.D. 65-70)	(5)	0	11
3. Lokakṣema (Leu-kia-khan) (A.D. 147-186)	(23)	12	17
4. An Shi-kao (A.D. 148-170)	(176)	55	14
5. Chu Fo-cho (A.D. 172-183)	(2)	0	18
6. An Huen (A.D. 181)	(2)	2	18
7. Chi Yao (A.D. 185)	(11)	5	19
8. K'ang Kiu (A.D. 187)	(1)	0	
9. Yen Fo-t'ian (A.D. 188)	(7)	1	19
10. K'ang Mong-siang (A.D. 194)	(6)	2	19
11. Chu Ta-li (A.D. 197)	(1)	1	19
12. Dharmaphala (T'an Kuo) (A.D. 207)	(1)	1	19
Anonymous translation	(307)	16	20

II. The Wei Dynasty, A.D. 220-265 (Loyang)

Translator			Page
1. Dharmakāla (A.D. 250)	(1)	0	22
2. Saṅghavarman (K'ang Sang-K'ai) (A.D. 252)	(3)	3	22
3. Dharmasatya ? (T'an-wu-ti,) (A.D. 254)	(1)	1	23
4. Poyen (A.D. 257)	(6)	1	23
5. Dharmabhadra the Parthian (An Fa-hien)	(2)	0	24

III. The Wu Dynasty A.D. 222-280 (Nanking)

Translator			Page
1. Chi Chien (A.D. 223-253)	(127)	49	28
2. Vighna (A.D. 224)	(1)	1	33
3. Chu Lin-yen (A.D. 230)	(4)	3	34
4. K'ang Seng-hui (A.D. 241-280)	(14)	2	34
5. Chi Kiang-Liang tsie	(1)	0	
Anonymous translators of Wei and Wu Dynasties	(110)	3	38

IV. The Western Tsin Dynasty (Loyang) A.D. 265-316

Translator			Page
1. Dharmarakṣa (Chu Fa-hu) (A.D. 284-313)	(211)	92	39
2. Kālaruci (A.D. 281)	(1)	0	
3. An Fa-k'in (A.D. 281-306)	(5)	2	43
4. Chu She-hing (A.D. 260-270) [Not found in Nanjio]			46
5. Mokṣala (A.D. 291)	(1)	1	46, 47
6. Chu Shu-lan (A.D. 291)	(2)	0	46, 47
7. Nie Cheng-yuan (A.D. 290-306)	(3)	2	48
8. Nie Tao-Chen (A.D. 286-312)	(54)	4	46, 43
9. Po Fa-tsu (A.D. 290-306)	(23)	5	46, 48
10. Shih Fa-li (A.D. 290-306)	(4)	3	45
11. Wei She-tu (Not found in Nanjio)	(1)	0	46
12. Chi Min-tu („ „ A.D. 290-306)	(2)	0	46
13. Shih Fa-Chiu (A.D. 307)	(133)	23	46
14. Chi Fa-tu (A.D. 301)	(4)	2	
15. Nārāyaṇa (Jo-lo-yen)	(1)	1	46
16. Fo-t'u-teng			50
Anonymous translators	(63)		

The Eastern Tsin Dynasty (Nanking) A.D. 317-420

Translator			Page
1. Po Srimitra (A.D. 307-342)	(3)	3	52
2. Chi Tao-chan (A.D. 335)	(2)	0	
3. Chu T'an-wu-lan (Dharmaratna) 381-395	(111)	29	53
4. Gautama Saṅghadeva (A.D. 391-8)	(5)	3	54
5. Kālodaka (A.D. 392)	(1)	1	64
6. K'ang Tao-ho (A.D. 396)	(1)	0	56
7. Buddhabhadra (398-421)	(15)	7	64
8. Dharmapriya (A.D. 400)	(1)	0	64,69
9. Vimalaksa (A.D. 406)	(2)	1	
10. K'ang Fa-suen (A.D. 326-342)	(1)	0	64
11 Fa-hien (A.D. 399-414)	(4)	4	59,61
12 Jitamitra (397-418)	(25)	2	64
13 Nandi (A.D. 419)	(3)	1	64
14 Chu Fa-li (Dharmabala) (A.D.419 ?)	(1)	0	64
15 Shih Sung-kung (A.D. 420 ?)	(3)	0	64
16 Shih T'ui-kung (A.D. 420 ?)	(1)	0	64
17 Shih Fa-yung (A.D. 420 ?)	(1)	0	64
Unknown translators	(93)	35	64

The Former Ts'in Dynasty A.D. 350-394 (Chang-an)

Translator			Page
1 Dharmadhi (A.D. 367)	(3)	0	69
2 Kumarābodhi (A.D. 382)	(1)	1	69
3 Saṅghabhuti (A.D. 381)	(3)	3	70
Dharmapriya (see above)	(1)	1	69
4 Dharmanandi (384-391)	(5)	2	54,69,
Gautama Saṅghadeva (above)	(3)	1	70
5 Tao-an	(40)	40	71

The Latter Ts'in Dynasty A.D. 384-417 (Changan)

Translator			Page
1 Chu Fo-nien (A.D. 374)	(12)	7	80
2 Dharmayasas (A.D. 407)	(3)	2	87
3 Puṇyatara (Fo-jo-to-lo) (A.D. 404)	(1)	1	87
4 Kumārajiva (A.D. 401—412)	(106)	50	88
5 Buddhayasas (A.D. 403)	(4)	4	84
6 Seng-chao (A.D. 414)	(7)	3	121
7 Seng-jui	(10)	10	121
8 Tao-heng	(2)	0	

* The figure within bracket indicates the number of works translated. The other figure is the number of works extant.

Page

United China

The Sui Dynasty A.D. 581-(589) 618 (Changan.)

The Ta'ng Dynasty A.D. 618-907 (Changan)

Page

The Latter Tsin Dynasty. A.D. 936-947

The Later (Northern) Sung dynasty A.D. 960-1127, K'ai-fung (Honan)

The Southern Sung Dynasty A.D. 1127-1280

			Page
9. Shan-yueh (T'ientai)	1230	1	
10. Chi p'an (T'ien-tai)	1267-71	1	
11. Tao-chan		1	
12. Wang-ku		1	
13. Chie huan (T'ientai)		1	
14. Miao hsi and Chu-an		1	
15. Tso-tsang-chu		1	

N.B. No Hindu monk came from India

The Yuen Dynasty, A.D. 1280-1368 (Yen-ching)

1. Pagspa, the Tibetan,	A.D. 1271-80	1	327
2. Sha-lo-pa	d. 1314	1	327
3. Tsi-nah-ming-to-li-lien-to-lo-mo-ming, an India Sramana		1	
4. Shih Chi-huei of Turfan		1	
5. An-tsang-a Chinese		1	
6. Ching-chi-siang	1285-87	1	
7. Siang-mai (Dhyāna)	1291	1	
8. P'u-huei	1295-1318	1	
9. Kuang Chu-pa	1300	2	
10. Wan-ts'ai	1302	2	
11. Ts'ing-meu	1320	1	
12. Ts'u-tsi	1321-23	1	
13. Yuan-chiao (Avatamsaka)	1322	1	
14. Nien-chang	1333	1	
15. Mong-jun (T'ien-tai)	1342	1	
16. Wei-tso (Tien-tai)	1342	1	
17. Huai-tso (Ti'en tai)		2	
18. P'u-jui (Avatamsaka)		1	
19. Te-huei and 20. Ta-su		1	
21. Liu-mi		1	
22. P'u-chao a Corean ; (Dhyāna)		1	
23. Chi no		1	
24. Chi-cho (Dhyāna)		1	
25. Chu-ting (Dhyāna)		1	

The Ming Dynasty A.D. 1368-1644

1. Tsung-lo and 2. Ju-chi	A.D. 1378	1
3. Chang-tsu (Emperor)	1403-1424	2
4. Yuen-tsing	1431	1
5. Ju-pa	1488-1505	2
6. Yi-ju		1
7. Tsu-chang		1
8. Tsing-shan		1
9. P'u-t'ai	A.D. 1622	1